AF669549

Introduction to Linux : Installation and Programming

This book is an outcome of the First FOSS Teachers Training Program (TTP-I) conducted by NRCFOSS during 6th June to 18th June 2005 at the AU-KBC Research Center, MIT Campus, Anna University, Chennai. Much of the material presented here are based on the lecture notes of this TTP, and includes contributions from the following persons :

Mr. Abhas Abhinav
Deeproot Linux, Bangalore.

Mr. S. Anand
AU-KBC, Anna University, Chennai.

Mr. Bharathi Subramanian
MIDAS Communications, Chennai.

Mr. Mahesh Shinde
C-DAC, Pune.

Prof. S.V. Ramanan
AU-KBC, Anna University, Chennai.

Mr. M.K. Saravanan
ST Microelectronics & NUS, Singapore.

Prof. G. Sivakumar
C S E Dept., IIT, Mumbai.

Prof. N.B. Venkateswarlu
GVP College of Engg, Visakhapatnam.

Mr. Zia Saquib
C-DAC ACTS, Pune.

Introduction to Linux : Installation and Programming

Edited by :

N. B. Venkateswarlu, Ph.D

GVP College of Engineering
Madhurawada, Visakhapatnam – 530041

National Resource Centre for Free/Open Source Software (NRCFOSS), Chennai
(www.nrcfoss.org.in)
publication series

BS Publications
A unit of **BSP Books Pvt., Ltd.**

4-4-309/316, Giriraj Lane, Sultan Bazar,
Hyderabad - 500 095
Phone : 040 - 23445605, 23445688

Published by

4-4-309/316, Giriraj Lane, Sultan Bazar,
Hyderabad - 500 095
Phone : 040 - 23445605, 23445688
e-mail : info@bspbooks.net

ISBN : 978-93-52300-17-4 (HB)

Dedicated to

Them who encourage Freedom and Openness

Foreword

It gives me great pleasure to be associated with the publication of this book by the National Resource Centre for Free/Open Source Software (NRCFOSS) functioning in our University. There are many aspects of the creation of this book that are worth noting in this context. It has been conceived and produced by a group of over 10 experts in this field from all over India who contributed to teaching this material to 100 teachers of 50 Engineering Colleges in Tamilnadu in June'05. In this sense this is a truly collaborative effort by the FOSS enthusiasts from academia, R&D and industry, and is in consonance with the collaborative spirit that characterizes the FOSS movement itself.

I am certain that this would serve as an excellent text book for introducing FOSS courses in the Engineering Education Programs in India as well as elsewhere. The Anna University has already prescribed this as the text book for the FOSS Electives that are being offered as a part of the Anna University Curriculum for the Engineering Institutions in Tamilnadu. I understand that the teachers involved in the NRCFOSS Program who would be offering this course to the students are being supplied with over 500 slides based on the contents of this book which can be used in the class rooms. It is also heartening to know that the book itself would be available on the web for free viewing and can be accessed by all interested persons. I am confident that widespread availability of such material would go a long way in encouraging and promoting the large scale use of FOSS, which is one of the main goals of setting up the NRCFOSS in our University by the Department of Information Technology, Ministry of Communication and Information Technology, Govt. of India. My congratulations to the editor of this book and the entire NRCFOSS Team for this effort, and I look forward to seeing many more such publications from them.

I take this opportunity to record our appreciation of the close collaboration we are having with the Centre for Development of Advance Computing (C-DAC), Govt. of India, through which the NRC FOSS has been set up. I also warmly acknowledge the generous support given by the Dept. of Information Technology, Government of India that has made this possible. I am very happy that Anna University has been selected to play this pioneering role in the promotion of FOSS and its applications in India.

Prof. D. Viswanathan

Vice Chancellor
Anna University,
Chennai.

Preface

Since early 1970, Unix operating system has gone through many a metamorphosis. As of now, a number of Unix variants are in vogue. While some of them are commercial, others are available freely. In recent years, Linux, a public domain, freely available Unix variant has attracted the attention of the software community. So far, Unix was believed to be the bread and butter of Computer Science interns. However, because of this freely available Unix variant, many people are becoming Unix/Linux enthusiasts, especially in India.

Hundreds of books had been written in the past, exploring various facets of Unix such as user commands, shell programming, system administration, network management, Unix internals, device drivers, and kernel development. In this book, we attempt to bring into focus, the Linux features and other topics in the open source arena so as to enable the user to start working under the Free/Open Source regime. This book assumes that the reader has hands on exposure to an operating system such as Windows (as a user) and C programming.

This book attempts to expose the reader to both Linux installations and programming, and should be useful to a novice Linux enthusiast. In a step by step fashion, it describes how to install Linux, make and swap partitions, and configure network, proxy server as well as web server. In addition, network installation along with SLIP, PPP connections are explained. Detailed explanations are given how to run web servers, email servers and print servers on a machine. Besides elementary Linux/Unix commands, emphasize is also on shell and awk programming which are vital for system administration.

Those who are new to networks, are advised to go through the separate chapter on this topic before actually trying to install the network. A chapter on System Logging is included to provide necessary details for the administrators who monitor the activities/processes in their system.

Chapter on X windows deals with the architecture of X windows system. How GUI is developed under Linux is explained with Qt and Gtk libraries using live examples. Python language is explained with concept-oriented examples, with emphasis on Web enabled applications.

- Editor

Acknowledgments

There are many people to whom we are profoundly indebted while bringing out this book – foremost of them being those thousands of Linux enthusiasts from the FOSS community who actively participate in mailing lists and contribute to the growth of Linux. I am equally thankful to my co-faculty members at the First Teachers Training Program held in June 2005 at AU-KBC Centre for their permission to use their material for this book.

By its very nature, a book like this would draw heavily from a large number of sources, and it is our pleasure to acknowledge this debt—the table given in the next few pages is a list of such sources which we would like to acknowledge here. If there are any omissions in this table, the same is entirely unintentional and may please be brought to our attention.

I would like to express my sincere thanks to the Vice Chancellor of Anna University for agreeing to write a foreword to this book, as well as for agreeing to make this a text book for the FOSS Elective Course being introduced in the Anna University.

Consistent interest, help and encouragement received from Prof C.N. Krishnan, Prof S.V. Ramanan, Dr. S. Srinivasan, Mr. Hariram Aathreya, Mr. Senthil Anand and other members associated with NRCFOSS at the AU-KBC Centre is also warmly acknowledged.

It is also my pleasure and privilege to acknowledge and appreciate the constant encouragement and support that I have received from the Principal, the Secretary, the staff and students of the GVP Engg College, Visakhapatnam, as well as the colleagues, friends and administrators of JNTU and the Andhra University College of Engineering. Also, my thanks are due to RIT (Berhampur), GIET(Gunupur), SSIET(Nuzvid), Vishnu Engg College (Bhimavaram).

I would like to express my thanks to Mr. Nikhil Shah and Mr. K.S. Raju, of BS Publications, Hyderabad for bringing out this book within the committed time frame.

Finally, I owe special thanks to my wife Dr. Sarada and daughter Appu, for bearing with me during the preparation of this manuscript and for sacrificing their marvelous Sunday evenings as well.

- Editor

Acknowledgement of sources from where materials have been taken and used in this book

Whole or Parts of Section ...	Is taken from ...
1.1	http://jan.netcomp.monash.edu.au/ssw/intro/generic.html
1.2	http://jan.netcomp.monash.edu.au/OS/l1_2.html
1.3	http://jan.netcomp.monash.edu.au/OS/l1_2.html http://infocom.cqu.edu.au/Archives/Units/1998/Autumn 85321_Systems_Administration/Old_Stuff/1996_Website/85321/85321_1996/docs/study-guide/chap3/chapter3.html
2.3	http://jan.netcomp.monash.edu.au/OS/l1_2.html
3.1	http://www.telenovela-world.com/~spade/linux/LDP/abs/html/textproc.html, http://infocom.cqu.edu.au/Archives/Units/1998/Autumn 85321_Systems_Administration/Old_Stuff/1996_Website/85321/study-guide/chap3/chapter3.html
4.1	http://www.kevinboone.com/boot.html
5.1	http://www.telenovela-world.com/~spade/linux/LDP/abs/html/why-shell.html
6.1	http://www.aboutdebian.com/install3.htm
6.2	http://www.aboutdebian.com/install3.htm
6.3	http://www.aboutdebian.com/install3.htm
7.1	http://stanton-finley.net/fedora_core_4_installation_notes_nocss.html
7.2	http://stanton-finley.net/fedora_core_4_installation_notes_nocss.html
8.1	http://www.kplug.org/apache_tutorial
8.2	http://www.kplug.org/apache_tutorial
10.1	http://www.sendmail.org/email-explained.html, http://www.rettesoft.hu/download/kerio/MailServer_5.5/MailServer_5.5_manual/kms55-en-v1.pdf
11.1	http://www.cups.org/doc-1.1/overview.html
11.2	http://www.cups.org/doc-1.1/sam.html
11.3	http://www.cups.org/doc-1.1/sam.html
12.1	http://www.netfilter.org/projects/iptables
12.2	http://www.informatik.uni-hamburg.de/SVS/teaching/ws2004-05/netzsicherheit/Exercises_Part4_b.htm
12.3	http://www.squid-cache.org
12.4	http://www.blue.net.au/support/linux/setup_squid_proxy.html

Contd....

Whole or Parts of Section ...	Is taken from ...
13.1	http://infocom.cqu.edu.au/Archives/Units/1998/Autumn/85321_Systems_Administration/Old_Stuff/1996_Website/85321/study-guide/textbook/chap6.html
13.2	http://infocom.cqu.edu.au/Archives/Units/1998/Autumn/85321_Systems_Administration/Old_Stuff/1996_Website/85321/study-guide/textbook/chap6.html
13.5	http://infocom.cqu.edu.au/Archives/Units/1998/Autumn/85321_Systems_Administration/Old_Stuff/1996_Website/85321/study-guide/textbook/chap6.html
13.6	http://infocom.cqu.edu.au/Archives/Units/1998/Autumn/85321_Systems_Administration/Old_Stuff/1996_Website/85321/study-guide/textbook/chap6.html
14.2	http://infocom.cqu.edu.au/Units/aut2000/85321/Resources/Study_Guide/Chapter_10
14.3	http://infocom.cqu.edu.au/Units/aut2000/85321/Resources/Study_Guide/Chapter_10
15.1	http://infocom.cqu.edu.au/Units/aut2000/85321/Resources/Study_Guide/Chapter_12
15.2	http://www-128.ibm.com/developerworks/library/pa-migrate2
16.1	http://infocom.cqu.edu.au/Units/aut2000/85321/Resources/Study_Guide/Chapter_14
16.2	http://infocom.cqu.edu.au/Units/aut2000/85321/Resources/Study_Guide/Chapter_14
16.3	http://infocom.cqu.edu.au/Units/aut2000/85321/Resources/Study_Guide/Chapter_14
16.5	http://infocom.cqu.edu.au/Units/aut2000/85321/Resources/Study_Guide/Chapter_14
17.1	http://infocom.cqu.edu.au/Units/aut2000/85321/Resources/Study_Guide/Chapter_15
17.2	http://infocom.cqu.edu.au/Units/aut2000/85321/Resources/Study_Guide/Chapter_15
17.3	http://infocom.cqu.edu.au/Units/aut2000/85321/Resources/Study_Guide/Chapter_15
17.4	http://infocom.cqu.edu.au/Units/aut99/85321/Resources/Print_Resources/Textbook/chap16
17.5	http://infocom.cqu.edu.au/Units/aut99/85321/Resources/Print_Resources/Textbook/chap16
18.1	http://users.actcom.co.il/~choo/lupg/tutorials/c-on-unix/c-on-unix.html
18.2	http://users.actcom.co.il/~choo/lupg/tutorials/c-on-unix/c-on-unix.html
18.4	http://users.actcom.co.il/~choo/lupg/tutorials/c-on-unix/c-on-unix.html
18.5	http://linuxgazette.net/issue84/hawk.html
18.6	http://users.actcom.co.il/~choo/lupg/tutorials/c-on-unix/c-on-unix.html
18.7	http://users.actcom.co.il/~choo/lupg/tutorials/c-on-unix/c-on-unix.html
19.2	http://www.gnome.org/~newren/tutorials/developing-with-gnome/html/ch03.html
20.2	http://www.enterprisenetworksandservers.com/monthly/art.php/1685
20.3	http://konst.org.ua/articles/en/linuxcom.gnutools.html
21.1	man pages
22.2	http://dinosaur.compilertools.net/flex
23.1	http://www.network-theory.co.uk/docs/pytut/tut_6.html
24.1	http://www.iu.hio.no/~mark/unix/unix.html
25.1	http://www.rubyist.net/~slagell/ruby/
26.1	http://www.faqs.org/docs/Linux-HOWTO/XWindow-Overview-HOWTO.html
26.2	http://www.gtk.org/tutorial

Contents

4. Processes in Linux

5. Shell Programming

6. Debian Linux Installation Guidelines

7. Redhat Fedora Core 4 Installation Guidelines

8. Installing Apache : The Web server

9. Samba Installation and Configuration

10. Installing SMTP Mail Server

11. Installing Common Unix Printing System (CUPS)

12. Installing Squid Proxy and Firewalls

13. Users and Account Management

14. A brief Introduction to Unix Devices and File System

15. Linux System Startup and Shutdown

16. System Logging

17. Networks : A Brief Introduction

18. Compiling C and C++ Programs under Linux

19. GNU Debugger

20. Make

21. Revision Control System

22. Lex and Yacc

23. A brief tour of Python

24. Introduction to perl

25. A peep into Ruby

26. X Windows Architecture and GUI Programming

List of Figures

List of Tables

1 Introduction to Linux Operating System

1.1 Introduction to Operating System

In the annals of computer science, the most commendable development one could consider is the emergence of the operating system which enables even a lay man to avail the services of computers without joining computer science program! An Operating System is the software layer between the hardware and user (shown in Figure 1.1) giving a compact and convenient interface to the user.

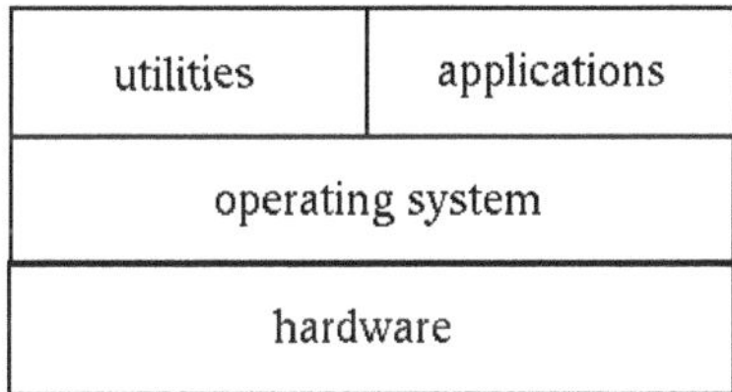

Figure 1.1 A Typical Operating System.

An Operating System is responsible for the following functions

- Device management using device drivers
- Process management using processes and threads
- Inter-process communication
- Memory management
- File systems

In addition, all operating systems come with a set of standard utilities. The utilities allow common tasks to be performed such as

- being able to start and stop processes
- being able to organize the set of available applications
- organize files into sets such as directories
- view files and sets of files
- edit files
- rename, copy, delete files
- communicate between processes

1.1.1 Kernel

The *kernel* of an operating system is the part responsible for all other operations. When a computer boots up, it goes through some initialization activities, such as checking memory. It then loads the kernel and switches control to it. The kernel then starts up all the processes needed to communicate with the users and the rest of the environment (e.g. the LAN). The kernel is always loaded into memory, and the kernel functions run continuously, handling processes, memory, files and devices. The traditional structure of a kernel is a *layered* system, as in Unix where all layers are part of the kernel, and each layer can talk to only a few other layers. Application programs and utilities lie above the kernel.

The Unix kernel looks like (Figure 1.2)

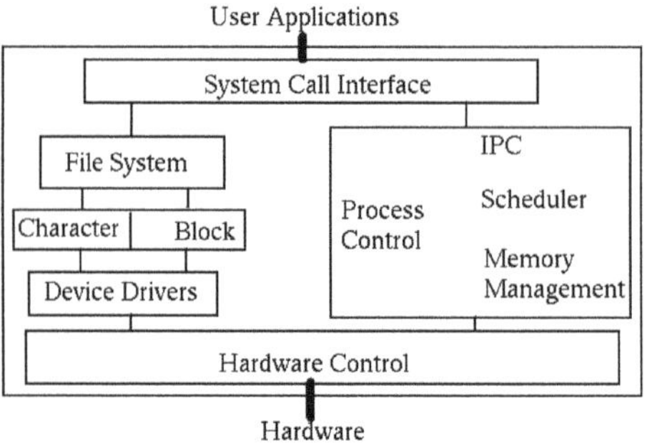

Figure 1.2 Unix Kernel.

Most of the currently prevalent Operating Systems use instead a *micro kernel*, of minimal size. Many traditional kernel operations are made into user level services. Communication bearing service is often carried out by an explicit *message passing* mechanism. Mach is one of the major micro-kernel operating systems whose concepts are used by many others (see Figure 1.3).

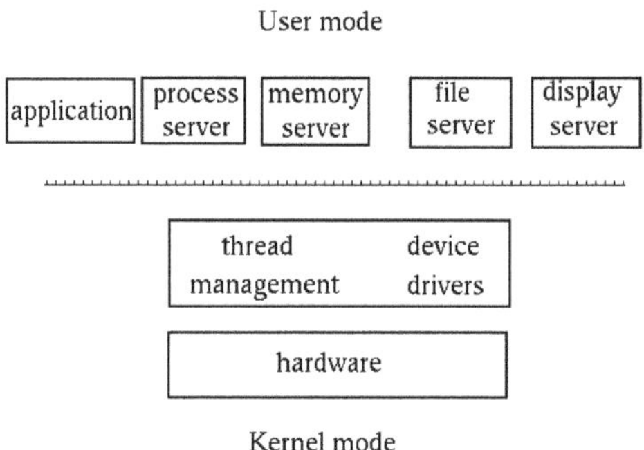

Figure 1.3 Micro Kernel Architecture.

Some systems, such as Windows NT (Figure 1.4) use a mixed approach [Gary Nutt].

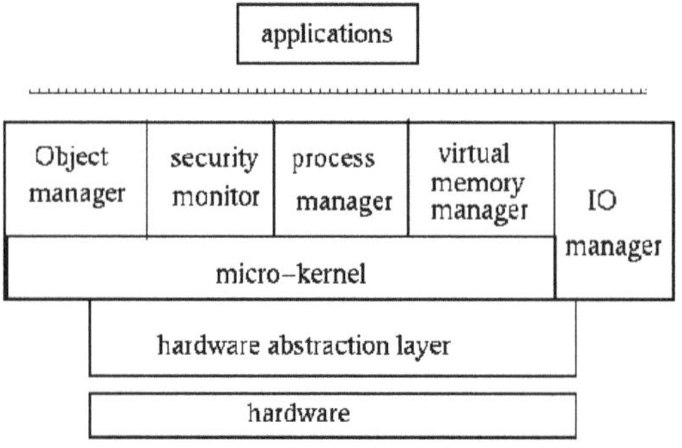

Figure 1.4 Windows NT Kernel.

1.1.2 Distinguished Applications

An Operating System has been described as an "application with no top" [Venkateswarlu]. *Other* applications interact with it, through a large variety of entry points. In order to use an O/S, you need to be supplied with at least some applications that already use these entry points.

All Operating Systems come bundled with a set of "utilities" which do this. For example

- Windows95 has a shell that allows programs to be started from the Start button. There is a standard set of applications supplied
- MSDOS starts up with COMMAND.COM to supply a command line prompt, and a set of utilities
- Unix has a set of command line shells and a huge variety of command line utilities
- X-Windows supplies a login shell (xdm). Others supply file managers, session managers, etc which can be used to provide a variety of interfaces to the underlying Unix/POSIX system.

1.1.3 Command Interpreter

Users interact with operating systems through the intermediary of a command interpreter. This utility responds to user inputs in the following ways :

- start or stop applications
- allow the user to switch control between applications
- allow control over communication between an application and other applications or the user.

The command interpreter may be character-based, as in the Unix shells or MSDOS COMMAND.COM, or can be a GUI shell like the Windows 3.1 Program Manager. The interpreter may be simple, or with the power of a full programming language. It may be imperative (as in the Unix shells), use message passing (as in AppleScript) or use visual programming metaphors such as drag-and-drop for object embedding (as in Microsoft's OLE). It is important to distinguish between the command interpreter and the underlying Operating System. The command interpreter may only use a subset of the capabilities offered by the Operating System; it may offer them in a clumsy or sophisticated way; it may require complex skills or be intended for novices

1.1.4 Differences between DOS and Unix

- Unix is multi user and multi tasking operating system whereas DOS is single user, single task system.
- All the commands in Unix should be given in lower case while the DOS commands are case insensitive.
- Unlike Unix, DOS is more virus prone.
- Processor will be in protected mode in Unix whereas DOS uses unprotected mode.
- DOS uses only 640KB of RAM during boot time unlike Unix which uses all the available RAM.
- Unix needs an administrator which is not the case with DOS.
- Unix employs time sharing operating system. Where as DOS supports a pseudo time sharing known as Terminate and Stay Resident (TSR) programs.
- Unix supports both character user interface and graphical interface (X Windows) unlike DOS which supports only character user interface.
- User requires legal username and password to use Unix machines. DOS systems can be used by any one without any username and password.

- Unix uses single directory tree (/) irrespective of how many drives or partitions are there. Where as in DOS, a separate directory tree exists for each partition.
- Unix supports NFS to share files.
- Till recently, DOS did not have proper WWW browser.

1.1.5 Linux and the Open Source Movement

Linus Torvalds [Matt Welsh], a student at the University of Helsinki, created the first version of "Linux" in August 1991. Released as an open-source software under the Free Software Foundation's GNU General Public License (GPL), Linux quickly grew into a complete operating-system package, with contributions from hundreds of programmers. Since the release of version 1.0 in 1994, organizations have been able to download free copies of Linux. One could also purchase commercial distributions of Linux from companies such as **Slackware**, **Red Hat** etc who also provide consultancy, services, and maintenance [Carla Schroder].

Many people raise a question about Linux "if it's released under the Free Software Foundation's GPL, shouldn't it be free?". The answer is **no**. A company can charge money for products that include Linux, as long as the source code is made available. The GPL allows people to distribute (and charge for) their own versions of free software [Carla Schroder]. According to the Free Software Foundation, the "free" in free software refers to *freedom* or ***liberty***, ***not price***. In the foundation's definition, organizations have the freedom to run software for any purpose, study how it works, modify, improve and re-release it.

Another common misconception about Linux is that it's a complete operating system. In reality Linux refers to the " kernel or core " of the operating system. Combining Linux with a set of open-source GNU programs from the Free Software Foundation turns it into what most people know as Linux "forming both the full operating system and the core of most Linux distributions". ***Distributions*** are the versions of Linux, GNU programs, and other tools that are offered by different companies, organizations, or individuals. Popular distributions include **Red Hat, Debian, SuSE, Caldera**, and others. Each distribution might be based on a different version of the Linux kernel, but all migrate forward over time, picking up core changes that are made to the kernel and keeping everything in somewhat loose synchronization.

Eric S. Raymond's famous essay, "The Cathedral and the Bazaar," argues that most commercial software is built like cathedrals by small groups of artisans working in isolation. Open-source software, like Linux, is developed collectively over the Internet, which serves as an electronic bazaar for innovative ideas. The first of the two programming styles is closed source - the traditional factory-production model of proprietary software, in which customers get a sealed block of computer binary that they cannot examine, modify, or evolve. The other style is open-source, the Internet engineering tradition in which software source code is generally available for inspection, independent peer review, and rapid evolution. Linux operating environment is the standard-bearer of the open source approach.

With Open Source products like Linux, new changes come through an open development model, meaning that all new versions are available to the public, regardless of their quality. "Linux' s versioning scheme is designed to let users understand whether they're using a stable version or a development version," says Jim Enright, director of Oracle's Linux program office. "Even decimal-numbered releases [such as 2.0, 2.2, and 2.4] are considered stable versions, while odd-numbered releases [such as 2.3 and 2.5] are beta-quality releases intended for developers only."

For much of the 1990s, Linux was primarily an experiment: something that developers fiddled with and used on local servers to see how well it worked and how secure it was. Then, with the internet boom of the late 1990s, many companies started using Linux for their Web servers, fueling the first wave of corporate Linux adoption leading to over 30 percent penetration of web server market by 2002.

Open source movement today is no more about just Linux, there are hundreds of thousands of software products being worked on in the Free/Open Source Software (FOSS) mode—*Apache, MySQL, Postgres, Firefox ,Jboss* etc are some of the other popular members of this growing family who have proved themselves in the real world. Also, its influence is no more confined to CSE/IT areas alone; Open Source solutions are today available for many of the simulation, computing, design and visualization needs of the entire Scientific and Engineering community.

It is for reasons such as the above that most of the major global players in the computing arena such as IBM, Intel, Oracle, HP etc all have started their own in-house FOSS initiatives.

1.1.6 So What Makes Linux So Popular?

Here are a few of the reasons - though obviously every Linux user will have his/her own reasons to add.

It's Free

Linux is free. Really and truly free. One can browse to any of the distributors of Linux , find the "download" link and download a complete copy of the entire operating system plus extra software without paying any thing. One can also buy a boxed version of course. For a nominal price, the CDs are available, manuals get door-delivered, plus there is telephone or online support. By comparison, "home" versions of popular commercial OS would cost thousands of rupees.

With Linux you also don't have to worry about paying again every time you upgrade the operating system - the upgrades are obviously free too. With commercial OS, upgrades also have to be paid for every time one is announced.

It's Open Source

This means two things: First, that the CDs (or the download site) contain an entire copy of the source code for Linux. Secondly, the user can legally make modifications to improve it.

While this might not mean much to non- programmers, there are thousands of people with programming capability who could improve the code or fix problems quickly. When a problem is found, it is sent off to the coordinating team in charge of the module in question, who will update the software and issue a patch. What all this boils down to is that bugs in Linux get fixed much faster than any other operating system.

It's Modular

Commercial Operating Systems normally get installed as a complete unit. One cannot, for example, install them without their Graphical User Interface, or without its printing support -- install everything or nothing.

Linux, on the other hand, is a very modular operating system. One could install or run exactly the bits and pieces of Linux that are needed. In most cases, the choice is on one of the predefined setups from the installation menu, but is not compulsory. In some cases this makes a lot of sense. For example, while setting up a server, one might want to disable the graphical user interface once it is set up correctly, thus freeing up memory and the processor for the more important task at hand.

It also allows the users to upgrade parts of the operating system without affecting the rest. For example, one could get the latest version of Gnome or KDE without changing the kernel.

It's got More Choices

Also due to its modularity, there is more choice of components to use. One example is the user interface. Many users choose KDE, which is very easy to learn for users with Windows experience. Others choose Gnome, which is more powerful but less similar to Windows. There are also several simple alternatives for less-powerful computers, which make less demands on the hardware available.

It's Portable

Linux runs on practically every piece of equipment which qualifies as a computer. It can be run on huge multiprocessor servers or a PDA. Apart from Pentiums of various flavors, there are versions of Linux (called "ports") on Atari, Amiga, Macintosh, PowerMac, PowerPC, NeXT, Alpha, Motorola, MIPS, HP, PowerPC, Sun Sparc, Silicon Graphics, VAX/MicroVax, VME, Psion 5, Sun UltraSparc, etc.

It's got lots of Extras

Along with the Linux CD, normally quite a lot of software gets thrown in, which is not usually included with operating systems. Using only the applications that come with Linux, one could set up a full web, ftp, database and email server for example. There is a firewall built into the kernel of the operating system, one or more office suites, graphics programs, music players, and lots more. Different distributions of Linux offer different "extra programs". Slackware, for example, is quite simple (though it still provides all the commonly needed programs), while SuSE Linux comes with seven CDs and a DVD-ROM!

It is Stable

All applications can crash, but in many systems, the only recourse is to switch off and reboot (and with some new "soft-switch" PCs, even that doesn't work - you have to pull out the power cable).

In comparison, Linux is rock-solid. Every application runs independently of all others - if one crashes, it crashes alone. Most Linux servers run for months on end, never shutting down or rebooting. Even the GUI is independent of the kernel of the operating system.

It's got Networking

The networking facilities offered by Linux are positively awe-inspiring. One can use terminal sessions, secure shells, share drives from across the world, run a wide variety of servers and much more. The user can, for example, connect XWindows to another Linux PC across a network. If there is more than one computer, one does not have to physically use the screen, keyboard and mouse connected to each computer - from any computer connect to any other computer, running applications etc. as if they were on the local system.

Multiple OS' s on a PC

Dual options like having Windows as well as Linux are possible and one could select which one of them to load every time you switch on. Linux can read Windows' files - it supports the FAT and FAT32 file system's, and sometimes NTFS, so it's quite easy to transfer files from one operating system to the other. The opposite, however, is not possible.

Generally, Windows applications cannot run under Linux, though there is a module called WINE which runs various small Windows programs in Linux. However, Open Office – an open source product loaded on to the Linux system-- can read and write MS-Office files. There are also other office suite options like Star Office, KOffice, GnomeOffice, WordPerfect Office, etc.

Can Windows and Linux machines interact via network? Definitely. You can use SAMBA to share files or connect to shared directories or printers. With SAMBA, the Linux computer could be set up function as a full NT server - complete with authentication, file/printer sharing and so on. Apart from that, Linux comes with excellent FTP, Web and similar services which are accessible to all computers.

Linux Configuration Tool

LinuxConf is a popular utility which allows the configuration of most parts of Linux and its applications from one place.

Salient Features of Linux

Here are some of the benefits and features that Linux provides over single-user operating systems and other versions of UNIX for the PC.

- **Full multitasking and 32-bit support** : Linux, like all other versions of UNIX, is a real multitasking system, allowing multiple users to run many programs on the same system at once. The performance of a 50 MHz 486 system running Linux is comparable to many low- to medium-end workstations, such as those from Sun Microsystems and DEC, running proprietary versions of UNIX. Linux is also a full 32-bit operating system, utilizing the special protected-mode features of the Intel 80386 and 80486 processors.
- **GNU software support** : Linux supports a wide range of free software written by the GNU Project, including utilities such as the GNU C and C++ compiler, gawk, groff, and so on. Many of the essential system utilities used by Linux are GNU software.
- **The X Window System** : The X Window System is the de facto industry standard graphics system for UNIX machines. A free version of The X Window System (known as "Xfree86") is available for Linux. The X Window System is a very powerful graphics interface, supporting many applications. For example, one can have multiple login sessions in different windows on the screen at once. Other examples of X Windows applications are Seyon, a powerful telecommunications program; Ghostscript, a PostScript language processor; and XTetris, an X Windows version of the popular game.
- **TCP/IP networking support** : TCP/IP ("Transmission Control Protocol/Internet Protocol") is the set of protocols which links millions of computers into a worldwide network known as the Internet. With an Ethernet connection, one can have access to the Internet or to a local area network from your Linux system. Or, using SLIP ("Serial Line Internet Protocol"), you can access the Internet over the phone lines with a modem.
- **Virtual memory and shared libraries**: Linux can use a portion of the hard drive as virtual memory, expanding the total amount of available RAM. Linux also implements shared libraries, allowing programs which use standard subroutines to find the code for these subroutines in the libraries at runtime. This saves a large amount of space, as each application doesn't store its own copy of these common routines.

Linux Distributions

Here are some of the more popular distributions of Linux.

* **Mandrake**
* **Red Hat**
* **SuSE**
* **Caldera**
* **Corel**
* **Debian**
* **Slackware**
* **TurboLinux**

1.2 Introduction to Linux File System

Files are stored on devices such as hard and floppy disks. O/S defines a *file system* on the devices. Many O/S use a *hierarchical* file system (See Figure 1.5).

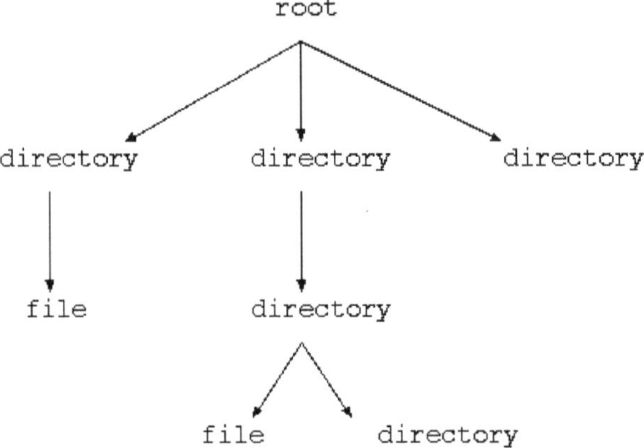

Figure 1.5 Hierarchical File System.

A directory is a file that keeps a list of other files. This list is the set of children of that directory node in the file system. A directory cannot hold any other kind of data.

On MSDOS a file system resides on each floppy or partition of the hard disk. The device name forms part of the file name [S. Prata].

On Unix there is a single file system. Devices are *mounted* into this file system. (Use the command mount for this.)

1.2.1 File and Directory Naming

An individual node of the file system has its own name. Naming conventions differ between O/S's. In MSDOS, a name is constructed of upto 8+3 characters. Windows95 uses some tricks on top of the MSDOS file system to give "long file names" of upto 255 characters. In "standard Unix" (POSIX) a name may consist of upto 256 characters.

The full file names are constructed by concatenating the directory names from the root down to the file, with some special separator between names. This is known as absolute path naming. In MSDOS, the full path name also includes the drive name.

Example : MSDOS

C:\expsys\lectures\search.txt

Example : Unix

/usr/usrs/os

/usr/usrs/os/myfile

Relative naming means that files are named from some special directory:

. current directory (Unix and MSDOS)

.. parent directory (Unix and MSDOS)

~ home directory (some Unix shells)

~user home directory of user (some shells)

Example : Unix

~fred/../bill/dir1/./../file1

If just the name itself is given without any special prefixes (such as /, ., .., ~) then it refers to the file in the current working directory.

1.2.2 Linux Directory Tree

Like all good operating systems, Linux allows the privilege of storing information indefinitely (or at least until the next disk crash [Chrish Drake]) in abstract data containers called files. The organization, placement and usage of these files comes under the general umbrella of the file hierarchy. As a system administrator, we need to be very familiar with the file hierarchy. To maintain the system, install software and manage user accounts we have to have better idea of it.

At a first glance, the file hierarchy structure of a typical Linux host the root directory contain something like:

```
bin     etc     lost+found  root    usr
boot    home    mnt         sbin    var
dev     lib     proc        tmp
```

Why was it done like this?

Historically, the location of certain files and utilities has not always been standard (or fixed). This has lead to problems with development and upgrading between different "distributions" of Linux. The Linux directory structure (or file hierarchy) was based on existing flavors of UNIX, but as it evolved, certain inconsistencies developed. These were often small things like the location (or placement) of certain configuration files, but it resulted in difficulties porting software from host to host.

To combat this, a file standard was developed. This is an evolving process, to date resulting in a fairly static model for the Linux file hierarchy. Here, we will examine how the Linux file hierarchy is structured, how each component relates to the overall OS and why certain files are placed in certain locations.

The root

The top level of the Linux file hierarchy is referred to as the root (or /) [Kernigham]. The root directory typically contains several other directories including the following given in Table 1.1.

Table 1.1 Major Linux Directories.

Directory	Contains
bin/	Required Boot-time binaries
boot/	Boot configuration files for the OS loader and kernel image
Dev/	Device files
etc/	System configuration files and scripts
home/	User/Sub branch directories
lib/	Main OS shared libraries and kernel modules
lost+found/	Storage directory for "recovered" files
mnt/	Temporary point to connect devices to
proc/	Pseudo directory structure containing information about the kernel, currently running processes and resource allocation
root/	Linux (non-standard) home directory for the root user. Alternate location being the / directory itself
sbin/	System administration binaries and tools
tmp/	Location of temporary files
usr/	Difficult to define - it contains almost everything else including local binaries, libraries, applications and packages (including X Windows)
var/	Variable data, usually machine specific. Includes spool directories for mail and news

Generally, the root should not contain any additional files - it is considered bad form to create other directories off the root, nor should any other files be placed there.

Why root?

The name "root" is based on the analogous relationship between the UNIX files system structure and a tree! Quite simply, the file hierarchy is an inverted tree.

Every part of the file system eventually can be traced back to one central point, the root. The concept of a "root" structure has now been (partially) adopted by other operating systems such as Windows NT. However, unlike other operating systems, UNIX doesn't have any concept of "drives". While this will be explained in detail in a later chapter, it is important to be aware of the following:

The file system may be spread over several physical devices; different parts of the file hierarchy may exist on totally separate partitions, hard disks, CD-ROMs, network file system shares, floppy disks and other devices.

This separation is transparent to the file system hierarchy, user and applications. Different "parts" of the file system will be "connected" (or mounted) at startup; other parts will be dynamically attached as required.

In the following pages, we examine some of the more important directory structures in the Linux file hierarchy.

/home Home for all users

The /home directory structure contains the home directories for most login-enabled users (some notable exceptions being the root user and (on some systems) the www/web user). While most small systems will contain user directories directly off the /home directory (for example, /home/jamiesob), on larger systems is common to subdivide the home structure based on classes (or groups) of users, for example:

```
/home/admin         # Administrators
/home/finance       # Finance users
/home/humanres      # Human Resource users
/home/mgr           # Managers
/home/staff         # Other people
```

One must be extremely careful when allowing a user to have a home directory in a location other than the /home branch. The problem occurs when the system administrator has to back-up the system - it is easy to miss a home directory if it isn't grouped with others in a common branch such as /home.

/root is the home directory for the root user. That is, when he log's in with username as root he will be placed in his directory. If, for some strange reason, the /root directory doesn't exist, then the root user will be logged in the / directory - this is actually the traditional location for root users.

It is advisable that a system administrator should **never** use the root account for day to day user-type interaction; the root account should only be used for system administration purposes only.

/usr and /var

It is often slightly confusing to see that /usr and /var both contain similar directories:

```
/usr

X11R6    games              libexec   src
bin      i486-linux-libc5   local     tmp
dict     include            man
doc      info               sbin
etc      lib                share

/var
catman   local   log   preserve   spool
lib      lock    nis   run        tmp
```

It becomes even more confusing when you start examining the maze of links which intermingle the two major branches.

To put it simply, /var is for **VAR**iable data/files. /usr is for **US**e**R** accessible data, programs and libraries. Unfortunately, history has confused things - files which should have been placed in the /usr branch have been located in the /var branch and vice versa. Thus to "correct" things, a series of links have been put in place.

The following are a few highlights of the /var and /usr directory branches:

/usr/local

All software that is installed on a system after the operating system package itself should be placed in the /usr/local directory. Binary files should be located in the /usr/local/bin (generally /usr/local/bin should be included in a user's PATH setting). By placing all installed software in this branch, it makes backups and upgrades of the system far easier - the system administrator can back-up and restore the entire /usr/local system with more ease than backing-up and restoring software packages from multiple branches (i.e.. /usr/src, /usr/bin etc.).

An example of a /usr/local directory is listed below:

bin	games	lib	rsynth	cern
man	sbin	volume-1.11	info	
mpeg	speak	www	etc	java
netscape	src			

As you can see, there are a few standard directories (bin, lib and src) as well as some that contain installed programs.

Linux is a very popular platform for C/C++, Java and Perl program development. As we will discuss in later chapters, Linux also allows the system administrator to actually modify and recompile the kernel. Because of this, compilers, libraries and source directories are treated as "core" elements of the file hierarchy structure.

The /usr structure plays host to three important directories:

/usr/include holds most of the standard C/C++ header files - this directory will be referred to as the primary include directory in most Makefiles.

/usr/lib holds most static libraries as well as hosting subdirectories containing libraries for other (non C/C++) languages including Perl and TCL. It also plays host to configuration information for ldconfig.

/usr/src holds the source files for most packages installed on the system. This is traditionally the location for the Linux source directory (/usr/src/linux), for example:

linux linux-2.6.31 redhat.

/var/spool

This directory has the potential for causing a system administrator a bit of trouble as it is used to store (possibly) large volumes of temporary files associated with printing, mail and news. /var/spool may contain something like:

at	lp	lpd	mqueue	samba	uucppublic
cron	mail	rwho	uucp		

In this case, there is a printer spool directory called lp (used for storing print request for the printer lp) and a /var/spool/mail directory that contains files for each user's incoming mail.

Keep an eye on the space consumed by the files and directories found in /var/spool. If a device (like the printer) isn't working or a large volume of e-mail has been sent to the system, then much of the hard drive space can be quickly consumed by files stored in this location.

/var/log

Linux maintains a particular area in which to place logs (or files which contain records of events). This directory is /var/log.

This directory usually contains:

cron	lastlog	maillog.2	samba-log.	secure.2	uucp
cron.1	log.nmb	messages	samba.1	sendmail.st	wtmp
cron.2	log.smb	messages.1	samba.2	spooler	xferlog
dmesg	maillog	messages.2	secure	spooler.1	xferlog.1
httpd	maillog.1	samba	secure.1	spooler.2	xferlog.2

/usr/X11R6

X-Windows provides UNIX with a very flexible graphical user interface. Tracing the X Windows file hierarchy can be very tedious, especially when your are trying to locate a particular configuration file or trying to removed a stale lock file.

Most of X Windows is located in the /usr structure, with some references made to it in the /var structure.

Typically, most of the action is in the /usr/X11R6 directory (this is usually an alias or link to another directory depending on the release of X11 - the X Windows manager). This will contain:

bin doc include lib man

The main X Windows binaries are located in /usr/X11R6/bin. This may be accessed via an alias of /usr/bin/X11 .

Configuration files for X Windows are located in /usr/X11R6/lib. To really confuse things, the X Windows configuration utility, xf86config, is located in /usr/X11R6/bin, while the configuration file it produces is located in /etc/X11 (XF86Config)!

Because of this, it is often very difficult to get an "overall picture" of how X Windows is working - my best advice is read up on it before you start modifying (or developing with) it.

bin's

A very common mistake amongst first time UNIX users is to incorrectly assume that all "bin" directories contain temporary files or files marked for deletion. This misunderstanding comes about because :

- People associate the word "bin" with rubbish
- Some unfortunate GUI based operating systems use little icons of "trash cans" for the purposes of storing deleted/temporary files.

However, bin is short for binary - binary or executable files. There are four major bin directories (none of which should be used for storing junk files :)

- /bin
- /sbin
- /usr/bin
- /usr/local/bin

All of the bin directories serve similar but distinct purposes; the division of binary files serves several purposes including ease of backups, administration and logical separation. Note that while most binaries on Linux systems are found in one of these four directories, not all are.

/bin

This directory must be present for the OS to boot. It contains utilities used during the startup; a typical listing would look something like:

mail	df	gzip	mount	stty
arch	dialog	head	mt	su
ash	dircolors	hostname		mt-GNU
sync				
bash	dmesg	ipmask	mv	tar
cat	dnsdomainname	kill	netstat	tcsh
chgrp	domainname	killall	ping	telnet
chmod	domainname-yp	ln	ps	touch
chown	du	login	pwd	true
compress	echo	ls	red	ttysnoops
cp	ed	mail	rm	umount
cpio	false	mailx	rmdir	umssync
csh	free	mkdir	setserial	uname
cut	ftp	mkfifo	setterm	zcat
date	getoptprog	mknod	sh	zsh
dd	gunzip	more	sln	

Note that this directory contains the shells and some basic file and text utilities (ls, pwd, cut, head, tail, ed etc). Ideally, the /bin directory will contain as few files as possible as this makes it easier to take a direct copy for recovery boot/root disks.

/sbin

/sbin Literally "System Binaries". This directory contains files that should generally only be used by the root user, though the Linux file standard dictates that no access restrictions should be placed on normal users to these files. It should be noted that the PATH setting for the root user includes /sbin, while it is (by default) not included in the PATH of normal users.

The /sbin directory should contain essential system administration scripts and programs, including those concerned with user management, disk administration, system event control (restart and shutdown programs) and certain networking programs.

As a general rule, if users need to run a program, then it should not be located in /sbin. A typical directory listing of /sbin looks like :

adduser
ifconfig
mkfs.minix
rmmod
agetty
init
mklost+found rmt
arp
insmod
mkswap
rootflags
badblocks
installpkg
mkxfs
route
bdflush
kbdrate
modprobe

runlevel
chattr
killall5
mount setup
clock
ksyms
netconfig
setup.tty
debugfs
ldconfig
netconfig.color
shutdown
depmod
lilo
netconfig.tty
swapdev
dosfsck
liloconfig

pidof swapoff
dumpe2fs
liloconfig-color
pkgtool
swapon
e2fsck
lsattr
pkgtool.tty telinit
explodepkg
lsmod
plipconfig
tune2fs
fdisk
makebootdisk
ramsize

umount
fsck
makepkg
rarp update
fsck.minix
mkdosfs
rdev
vidmode
genksyms
mke2fs
reboot xfsck
halt
mkfs remov
pkg

We should note that :

/usr/sbin - used for non-essential admin tools.

/usr/local/sbin - locally installed admin tools.

/usr/bin

This directory contains most of the user binaries - in other words, programs that users will run. It includes standard user applications including editors and email clients as well as compilers, games and various network applications.

/usr/local/bin

To this point, we have examined directories that contain programs that are (in general) part of the actual operating system package. Programs that are installed by the system administrator after that point should be placed in /usr/local/bin. The main reason for doing this is to make it easier to back up installed programs during a system upgrade, or in the worst case, to restore a system after a crash.

/etc is one place where the root user will spend a lot of time. It is not only the home to the all important passwd file, but contains just about every configuration file for a system (including those for networking, X Windows and the file system).

The /etc branch also contains the skel, X11 and rc.d directories.

/etc/skel contains the skeleton user files that are placed in a user's directory when their account is created.

/etc/X11 contains configuration files for X Windows.

/etc/rc.d is contains rc directories - each directory is given by the name rcn.d (n is the run level) - each directory may contain multiple files that will be executed at the particular run level. A sample listing of a /etc/rc.d directory looks something like:

```
init.d   rc.local    rc0.d   rc2.d   rc4.d   rc6.d
rc       rc.sysinit  rc1.d   rc3.d   rc5.d
```

/proc

The /proc directory hierarchy contains files associated with the *executing* kernel. The files contained in this structure contain information about the state of the system's resource usage (how much memory, swap space and CPU is being used), information about each process and various other useful pieces of information.

/dev

We will be discussing /dev in detail in the next chapter, however, for the time being, you should be aware that this directory is the primary location for special files called **device files**.

1.3 man pages

All the Unix command information are organized in a special fashion like the following [Shelley Powers].

- The user-level commands are all in Section One.

- Section Two is the Unix Application Programmer's Interface, API (i.e. C functions directly supported by Unix).
- Section Three is library extensions to these.
- Section Four defines devices known to Unix.
- Section Five defines common file formats.
- Sections Local and New are for stuff we have added to our local system.

If we run **man** command with a name first it will check for commands with that name.

Example :

```
man  sleep
```

```
man 2 sleep
```

This displays details of sleep library function if available

```
man 3 sleep
```

This displays details of sleep system call if exists any.

apropos command can be used to displays names of all the commands whose manual page contains a search pattern.

Example :

```
apropos TERM
```

This displays names of the Unix commands, system calls or library functions whose manual page contains the search pattern TERM.

1. 4 The first command 'cat '

In order to login from Unix/Linux machines, you have to first get username and password. Approach your system administrator. Once you get them, power on the machine and you may find boot loader options from which you can select Linux or Unix. Wait for a while and if possible go through the system messages appearing on the screen. After loading all the necessary drivers you may find 'login' prompt either in character mode or in graphical mode. Now enter your username and password.

You may be interested to create a file or view a file. The simplest command available in Unix system to create and view files is 'cat'. Follow the following exercise to create and see the files.

To create files.

Example :

```
cat > ABC
```

This is a test file.

I wish you find happy to create first file.

```
^d
```

This is also used to see the file(s) content. If the file contains more lines then it simply scrolls the matter of that file.

Example :

```
cat ABC
```

This command is also used to create duplicates to a file.

Example :

```
cat ABC >XYZ
```

or

```
cat <ABC >XYZ
```

XYZ becomes duplicate copy of file ABC.

This cat command can be used to see the content of more than one file.

Example :

```
cat ABC XYZ
```

This cat command can be used to join the content of two or more files and create another file.

Example :

```
cat ABC XYZ > MNO
```

Now MNO file contains the content of both file XYZ and ABC.

While joining two or more files and creating a combined file we can add interactive input also.

Example :

```
cat ABC - XYZ > PPP
```

You type what ever you wanted followed by control D at the end.

```
^d
```

Now file PPP contains content of ABC, the interactive input and the content of file XYZ in the same order. By changing the location of -, we can add interactive input between any two files.

1.5 Command History

The shell, bash has a command history for convenience, i.e. most recently executed commands are stored in history buffer which users can browse through any time without retyping the same. For example, the list of previous commands may be obtained by executing the following command.

```
history
```

```
!n
```

(n is an integer) will re-execute the nth command.

```
!!
```

This executes the most recent command

```
!cp
```

This executes the most recent command which starts with cp.

Up arrow, down arrows can be used in some shells to recollect the commands from command history buffer.

1.6 Conclusions

This chapter explores operating system concepts. The reasons that have made Linux as popular is also examined, along with its file system organization and architecture. Some numerical examples were also included to demonstrate the capabilities of the Linux/Unix file system.

2 Basic Unix Commands

2.1 vi Editor

A popular Unix[1] editor since 1970s, **vi** is a screen editor which is based on an earlier editor known as ***elvis*** [Richard L Peterson]. The editor has three modes: In the **Input Mode,** whatever user keys in will be written into the document. **Command Mode** allows the user to enter commands. It is reached from the Input mode by pressing the ESC key and hence is also referred to as ESC mode. If the ESC key is pressed while in command mode one will get a beep sound. In the third mode, called the **colon mode**, users can run commands and also do some document editing. Thus it is not considered a separate mode but a mixture by some users!!.

In a nutshell, the following is the summary of useful commands to immediately work under UNIX:

1. **vi *filename*** -- opens the vi editor to work with the given filename.
2. Initially, a screen will be opened with the command mode.
3. To enter text, press **i**. The input mode will be displayed at bottom right part of the screen.
4. On pressing **Esc** key, the command mode reemerges. One could press

   :w to save the matter and resume editing.

   :wq to save the matter and quit the vi editor.

   :q! to quit the editor without saving.
5. The three modes present in vi editor are: i) Command mode ii) input mode iii) Colon mode
6. In command mode, commands can be entered.

   A. press **i** to insert text before the current cursor position.

   B. press **I** to insert text at the beginning of the line.

   C. press **a** to insert text after the cursor position.

   D. press **A** to insert text at the end of the current line.

   E. press **o** to open a new line below the current line.

   F. press **O** to open a new line above the current line.

   G. press **r** to replace the present character with a character.

   H. press **R** to replace a group of characters from current cursor position.

   I. press **x** to delete present character.

   J. press **J** to join the next line to the end of the current line.

   K. press **dd** to delete the current line.

   L. press **4dd** to delete 4 lines from the current line.

   M. press **dw** to delete the current word.

   N. press **7dw** to delete 7 words from the current word onwards.

   O. press **30i*Esc** (invisible command) to insert 30 *'s at the cursor position.

   P. press **u** to undo the effect of the previous command on the document.

---

[1]In this book we assume Unix and Linux are synonymous

Q. press **.** to repeat the previous command.

R. press **yy** to copy the entire line in to the buffer.

S. press **yw** to copy the entire word in to buffer.

T. press **p** to place the copied or deleted information below the cursor.

U. press **P** to place the copied or deleted information above the cursor.

7. **Colon mode commands**

Search and substitute commands

1. **:/raja** searches for the string "raja" in the forward direction. Press **n** to repeat the search.
2. **:?raja** search for the string in the backward direction. Press **n** to repeat the above search.
3. **:s/raja/rama** replaces the first occurrence of "raja" with "rama".
4. **:s/raja/rama/g** replaces all "raja"'s with rama in the present line.
5. **:g/raja/s/raja/rama/g** replaces all "raja"'s by "rama" in the entire file.

Block delete commands

1. **:1d** delete the line 1.
2. **:1,5d** deletes the lines from 1 to 5.
   $ Means last line of the file.
   . Means present line (i.e.) present line.
3. **:10,$d** deletes lines from 10th line to the last line of the file.
4. **:1,$d** deletes lines from 1 to last line of the file.
5. **:.,$d** deletes lines from present line to the last line.
6. **:.-3,.d** deletes the lines from present line and above 2 lines (deletes 3 lines including the cursor line).
7. **:.,.+4d** deletes the lines from the present cursor line followed 3 lines(total 4 lines).
8. **:-1,. +3d** deletes the lines one above the cursor line followed by it 3 lines.
9. **:18** cursor goes to 18 th line of the file.

Block copy commands

1. **:1,5 co 10** copies the lines from 1 to 5 after 10th line
2. **:1,$ co $** copies the lines from 1 to last line after last line
3. **:.,.+5 co 8** copies lines from present line to 5 lines after 8th line
4. **:-3,. co 10** copies the lines from present cursor line and above 3 lines after 10 th line.

Block moving commands

1. **:1,5 mo 9** moves lines from 1 to 5 after 9th line.
2. **:1,$ mo $** moves lines from 1 to $ after last line.
3. **:.,.+5 mo 10** moves lines from present line and next 5 lines after 10 th line onwards.
4. **:.-3,. mo 10** moves present line and above 3 lines after 10 th line.

Importing & **Exporting the files**

1. **:1,5 w filename** writes lines 1 to 5 in the specified filename.
2. **:1,5 w! filename** overwrites lines 1 to 5 in the specified filename.
3. **:r filename** Adds the content of filename after the current line.

8. **Book mark command**

   Bookmarks (markers) are not visible and are useful to jump from one line to another quickly. Markers should be in lower case. To have the marker on a specified line press **m** followed by a lower case alphabet (say a) then marker for that line is set as a. To go to the marked line press **`a** (` back quote)followed a. e.g.: go to 500th line, press mb (b is the marker). To go to the 500th line from anywhere in the document press **`b**. Then the cursor goes to the 500th line.

2.2 Redirection Operators

For any program whether it is developed using C, C++ or Java, by default three streams are available known as input stream, output stream and error stream. In programming languages, to refer to them some symbolic names are used (i.e. they are system defined variables).

For example

- *In C, stdin, stdout and stderr.*
- *In C++, cin, cout, and cerr.*
- *In Java, System.in, System.out and System.err.*

By default is input is from keyboard and output and error are sent to monitor. With the help of redirection operators, we can send them to a file or to a device.

Unix, supports the following redirection operators are available.

- ***standard output operator***
- ***< standard input operator***
- ***<< here the document***
- ***>> appending operator***

2.2.1 Standard Input, Output Redirection operators

Unix supports input, output redirection. We can send output of any command to a file by using > operator.

Example :

```
command >aaa
```

Output of the given command is sent to the file. First, file aaa is created if not existing otherwise its content is erased and then output of the command is written.

```
cat aa >aaaa
```

Here, aaaa file contains the content of the file aa.

We can let a command to take necessary input from a file with < operator (standard input operator).

```
cat<aa
```

This displays output of file aa on the screen.

```
cat aa aa1 aa3>aa12
```

This creates the file aa12 which contains the content of all the files aa, aa1 and aa3 in order.

```
cat <aa >as
```

This makes cat command to take input from the file aa and write its output to the file as. That is, it works like a cp command.

Unix has a nice (intelligent) command line interface. Thus, all the following commands works in the same manner.

```
cat <aa >as
cat >as <aa
<aa cat >as
<aa >as cat
>as cat <aa
>as <aa cat
```

This discussion is meaningful with any command. For example, consider the following C program which takes three integers and writes their values.

```
#include<stdio.h>
void main()
{
int x,y,z;
scanf("%d%d%d", &x, &y, &z);
printf("%d\n%d\n%d\n", x, y, z);
}
```

Let the file name be a.c and by using the either of the following commands, its machine language file a is created.

```
gcc -o a a.c
cc -o a a.c
```

When we start this program a by simply typing a at the dollar prompt, it takes 3 values and displays given values on the screen.

```
a>res
```

This program takes three values interactively and writes the same into file res. You can check by typing cat res.

```
a<res
cat <aa >as
cat >as <aa
<aa cat >as
<aa >as cat
>as cat <aa
>as <aa cat
```

This command takes necessary input from the file res and displays the results on the screen.

```
a <res >as
a >as <res
<res a >as
<res >as a
>as a <res
>as <res a
```

All, of these commands takes three values from the file res and write the same in the file as.

2.2.2 The >> and << Operators

Similarly, >> operator can be used to append standard output of a command to a file.

Example

```
command>>aaa
```

This makes, output of the given command to be appended to the file aaa. If the file aaa is not existing, it will be created afresh and then standard output is written.

Here the document operator(<<)

This is used with shell programs. This signifies that the data is here rather in a separate file.

Example :

```
grep Rao<<end
I like PP Reddy
I know Mr. PN Rao since 1987
I wanted to see Raj today
Mr. Rao, please see me today
end
```

The above sequence of commands when executed at the dollar prompt, we will get those lines having rao as output of grep command. Here, by using << operator we are mentioning that the data is directly available here. The command takes input till we enter 'end'.

```
cat<<END
This will display
Whatever we type
Interactively on the screen again
END
```

The above workout displays whatever we have typed till the string "END". Make sure that we enter the string "END" on a fresh line.

```
cat<<END  >outputfile
This will display
Whatever we type
Interactively on the screen again
END
```

The above command writes whatever we have typed at till "END" string into the file "outputfile".

2.3 Some Unix Commands

2.3.1 more command

This command is used to see the content of the files page by page or screen by screen fashion. This is very useful if the file contains more number of lines.

Example :

```
more filenames(s)

more file1 file2
```

This displays content of the files file1 and file2 one after another.

```
more <file1
```

This also displays the content of the file1 in screen by screen fashion.

```
more file1 file2 ... filen > XXX
```

This command creates file XXX such that it contains the content of all the given files in the strictly same order.

```
more +/rao filename
```

This command displays the content of the given file starting from the line which contains the string "rao".

```
more +10 filename
```

This command displays the content of the file from 10'th line.

2.3.2 pg command

This command is also used to see the content of the files in page by page fashion. However, this is not available in recent versions. Rather more command is in wide use and is more flexible.

2.3.3 nl command

This command is used to display the content of the file along with line numbers.

Example :

```
nl filename
```

2.3.4 tail command

```
tail filename(s)
```

This command displays last 10 lines of the given file(s).

```
tail -1 filename(s)
```

This command displays last 1 line of the given file(s).

```
tail +2 filename(s)
```

This command displays second line to last line of the given file(s)

2.3.5 head command

```
head filename(s)
```

This command displays first 10 lines of the given file(s).

```
head -2 filename(s)
```

This command displays first 2 lines of the given file(s)

2.3.6 mkdir command

This is used to create a new directory.

```
mkdir rao
```

This creates rao directory in the current directory.

```
mkdir /tmp/rao
```

This creates rao directory in /tmp directory.

```
mkdir /bin/rao
```

This fails for normal users because of permissions (/bin belongs to super user).

2.3.7 rmdir command

This is used to remove empty directory only.

```
rmdir rao
```

This removes rao directory of current working directory.

```
rmdir /tmp/rao
```

This removes rao directory in /tmp directory.

2.3.8 pwd command

displays where currently we are located.

2.3.9 cd directoryname

This changes the current working directory to the given directory.

```
cd
```

This command takes you to your home directory.

2.3.10 ls command

This command displays names of the files and directories of current directory.

```
a1
a2
a3
a4
a5
```

The following command displays names of files and directories of current directory in long fashion. That is, file permissions, owner name, group, links, time stamps, size and names.

```
ls -l
total 4
-rw-r--r--   1 root   root      0 Feb 13 23:55 a1
-rw-r--r--   1 root   root      0 Feb 13 23:55 a2
-rw-r--r--   1 root   root      0 Feb 13 23:56 a3
-rw-r--r--   1 root   root      0 Feb 13 23:55 a4
-rw-r--r--   1 root   root    290 Feb 13 23:59 a5
```

In Unix, files whose names starts with . are called as hidden files. If we want to see their details also then we have to use -a option (Of course either alone or with other options).

For example, the following command displays other files also whose names starts with '.' .

```
ls -al
total 12
drwxr-xr-x    2 root   root   4096 Feb 14 00:01 .
drwxr-x---   29 root   root   4096 Feb 14 00:01 ..
-rw-r--r--    1 root   root      0 Feb 13 23:55 a1
-rw-r--r--    1 root   root      0 Feb 13 23:55 a2
-rw-r--r--    1 root   root      0 Feb 13 23:56 a3
-rw-r--r--    1 root   root      0 Feb 13 23:55 a4
-rw-r--r--    1 root   root    882 Feb 14 00:01 a5
-rw-r--r--    1 root   root      0 Feb 14 00:01 .aa1
```

A Note on File types

UNIX supports a small number of different file types. The following Table 2.1 summarizes these different file types. What the different file types are and what their purpose is will be explained as we progress. File types are signified by a single character.

Table 2.1 UNIX file types

File type	Meaning
-	a normal file
d	a directory
l	symbolic link
b	block device file
c	character device file
p	a fifo or named pipe

For current purposes one can think of these file types as falling into three categories [Richard Stevens]

- "normal" files,

  Files under UNIX are just a collection of bytes of information. These bytes might form a text file or a binary file.

  When we run ls –l command we will see some lines starts with – indicating they are normal files.

- directories or directory files,

  Remember, for UNIX a directory is just another file which happens to contain the names of files and their I-node. An I-node is an operating system data structure which is used to store information about the file (explained later).

  When we run ls –l command we will see some lines starts with d indicating they are normal files.

- special or device files.

  Explained in more detail later on in the text these special files provide access to devices which are connected to the computer. Why these exist and what they are used for will be explained.

  Run the following commands.

```
ls –l /dev/ttyS*
```

We will see that every line to start with 'c' indicating they are character special files; it is acceptable to us as they refer to terminals which are character devices.

```
ls –l /dev/hda*
```

We will see that every line to start with 'b' indicating they are block special files; it is acceptable to us as they refer to disk partitions which are block devices.

The following command displays details of the files in chronological order.

```
ls -alt

total 12
drwxr-xr-x   2 root   root     4096 Feb 14 00:03 .
drwxr-x---  29 root   root     4096 Feb 14 00:03 ..
-rw-r--r--   1 root   root     1451 Feb 14 00:03 a5
-rw-r--r--   1 root   root        0 Feb 14 00:01 .aa1
-rw-r--r--   1 root   root        0 Feb 13 23:56 a3
-rw-r--r--   1 root   root        0 Feb 13 23:55 a2
-rw-r--r--   1 root   root        0 Feb 13 23:55 a1
-rw-r--r--   1 root   root        0 Feb 13 23:55 a4
```

```
ls -l filename
```

It displays only that file details if it exists.

```
ls -l directoryname
```

It displays the files and directory details in the given directory.

All the options -a, -t etc can be also used. Moreover, Unix commands will be having excellent command line interface. Thus, all the following commands are equivalent.

```
ls -a -l -t
ls -alt
ls -a -t -l
ls -atl
ls -l -a -t
ls -lat
ls -l -t -a
ls -lta
ls -t -l -a
ls -tla
ls -t -a -l
ls -tal
```

-R option with ls command displays details of files and subdirectories recursively.

Example :

ls -alR / (Of course you can go for a cup of coffee and come back before you see the prompt again!!).

This command displays all the files in Unix system.

2.3.11 find command

A common task for a Systems Administrator is searching the UNIX file hierarchy for files which match certain criteria. Some common examples of what and why a Systems Administrator may wish to do this include

- searching for very large files
- finding where on the disk a particular file is
- deleting all the files owned by a particular user
- displaying the names of all files modified in the last two days.

Given the size of the UNIX file hierarchy and the number of files it contains this isn't a task that can be done by hand. This is where the find command becomes useful.

The find command

The find command is used to search through the directories of a file system looking for files that match a specific criteria. Once a file matching the criteria is found the find command can be told to perform a number of different tasks including running any UNIX command on the file.

find command format

The format for the find command is

find [*path-list*] [*expression*]

path-list is a list of directories in which the find command will search for files. The command will recursively descend through all sub-directories under these directories. The expression component is explained in the next section.

Both the path and the expression are optional. If you run the find command without any parameters it uses a default path as the current directory, and a default expression as printing the name of the file. Thus, when we run find command we may get all the entries of current directory.

find expressions

A find expression can contain the following components

- options,

  These modify the way in which the find command operates.
- tests,

  These decide whether or not the current file is the one you are looking for.
- actions,

  Specify what to do once a file has been selected by the tests.
- and operators.

  Used to group expressions together.

find options

Options are normally placed at the start of an expression. Table 2.2 summarizes some of the find commands options.

Table 2.2 find options

Option	**Effect**
-daystart	for tests using time measure time from the beginning of today
-depth	process the contents of a directory before the directory
-maxdepth *number*	*number* is a positive integer that specifies the maximum number of directories to descend
-mindepth *number*	*number* is a positive integer that specifies at which level to start applying tests
-mount	don't cross over to other partitions
-xdev	don't cross over to other partitions

For example

The following are two examples of using find's options. Since I don't specify a path in which to start searching the default value, the current directory, is used.

find -mindepth 2

./Adirectory/oneFile

In this example the mindepth option tells find to only find files or directories which are at least two directories below the starting point.

find -maxdepth 1

.

This option restricts find to those files which are in the current directory.

find tests

Tests are used to find particular files based on

- when the file was last accessed
- when the file's status was last changed
- when the file was last modified
- the size of the file
- the file's type
- the owner or group owner of the file
- the file's name
- the file's inode number
- the number and type of links the file has to it
- the file's permissions

Table 2.3 summarizes find's tests. A number of the tests take numeric values. For example, the number of days since a file was modified. For these situations the numeric value can be specified using one of the following formats (in the following *n* is a number)

- +*n*

  greater than *n*
- -*n*

  less than *n*
- *n*

  equal to *n*

For example

Some examples of using tests are shown below. Note that in all these examples no command is used. Therefore the find command uses the default command which is to print the names of the files.

- find . -user david

  Find all the files under the current directory owned by the user david
- find / -name *.html

  Find all the files one the entire file system that end in .html. **Notice** that the * must be quoted so that the shell doesn't interpret it (explained in more detail below). Instead we want the shell to pass the *.html to the find command and have it match filenames.
- find /home -size +2500k -mtime −7

  Find all the files under the /home directory that are greater than 2500 kilobytes in size and have been in modified in the last seven days.

The last example shows it is possible to combine multiple tests. It is also an example of using numeric values. The +2500 will match any value greater than 2500. The -7 will match any value less than 7.

find actions

Once the files are found, some operations have to be done on them.. The find command provides a number of actions most of which allow to either

- execute a command on the file, or
- display the name and other information about the file in a variety of formats

For the various find actions that display information about the file you are urged to examine the manual page for find

Executing a command

find has two actions that will execute a command on the files found. They are -exec and -ok.

The format to use them is as follows

> -exec *command* ;
>
> -ok *command* ;
>
> *command* is any UNIX command.

The main difference between exec and ok is that ok will ask the user before executing the command. exec just does it.

Table 2.3 find tests

Test	Effect
-amin *n*	file last access *n* minutes ago
-anewer *file*	the current file was access more recently than *file*
-atime *n*	file last accessed *n* days ago
-cmin *n*	file's status was changed *n* minutes ago
-cnewer *file*	the current file's status was changed more recently than *file*'s
-ctime *n*	file's status was last changed *n* days ago
-mmin *n*	file's data was last modified *n* minutes ago
-mtime *n*	the current file's data was modified *n* days ago
-name *pattern*	the name of the file matches *pattern* -iname is a case insensitive version of –name -regex allows the use of REs to match filename
-nouser-nogroup	the file's UID or GID does not match a valid user or group
-perm *mode*	the file's permissions match *mode* (either symbolic or numeric)
-size *n*[bck]	the file uses *n* units of space, b is blocks, c is bytes, k is kilobytes
-type *c*	the file is of type *c* where *c* can be block device file, character device file, directory, named pipe, regular file, symbolic link, socket
-uid *n* -gid *n*	the file's UID or GID matches *n*
-user *uname*	the file is owned by the user with name *uname*

For example

Some examples of using the exec and ok actions include

- find . -exec grep hello \{\} \;

  Search all the files under the local directory for the word hello.

- find / -name *.bak -ok rm \{\} \;

  Find all files ending with .bak and ask the user if they wish to delete those files.

{} and ;

The exec and ok actions of the find command make special use of {} and ; characters. Since both {} and ; have special meaning to the shell they must be quoted when used with the find command.

{} is used to refer to the file that find has just tested. So in the last example rm \{\} will delete each file that the find tests match.

The ; is used to indicate the end of the command to be executed by exec or ok.

For example :

This command is used to locate files in the Unix directory tree.

find directoryname -name filenametobefound

Example

find / -name core

This command displays all the occurrences of the file named core under / directory.

```
find . -ctime 2 -name
```

This command displays names of those files which are created in the last two days and are in the current directory.

```
find . -mtime 2 -name
```

This command displays names of those files which are modified in the last two days and are in the current directory.

```
find . -size 10 -name
```

This command displays names of those files whose size is greater than 10 blocks of size 512 bytes and are in the current directory.

```
find . -type d -name
```

This command displays names of directories in the current directory.

2.3.12 cp command

cp command is used to duplicate a file(s).

Syntax

cp source destination

cp a1.c /tmp	*creates a1.c file in /tmp directory which contains same content as that of file a1.c of current working directory.*
cp /bin/ls /tmp/AA	*Creates a new file AA in /tmp directory with the content of /bin/ls*
cp /tmp/a1.c .	*Creates a1.c file in current working directory with the content of file /tmp/a1.c*
cp a1.c a2.c	*Creates a2.c in current working direct with the content of a1.c*
*cp *.c /tmp*	*Copies all files with extension c in current directory to /tmp directory*
cp /tmp/.c .*	*Copies all files with extension c in /tmp directory to current working directory*
cp /bin/ /tmp*	*Copies all files of /bin directory to /tmp*
cp -r sourcedirectory destinationdirectory	*Copies all files, subdirectories and files in them of the source directory to detination directory.*
*cp *.c /bin*	*This command will fail if you are a normal user as we do not have permissions usually on /bin directory. However, it will work for super (root) user.*

2.3.13 mv command

mv command is used to move file(s) from one directory to another directory or to rename the file.

The options include

-i interactive confirmation of overwrites

-f force a copy

-R recursively copy to a directory

Syntax

mv source destination

mv a1.c /tmp	*creates a1.c file in /tmp directory while file a1.c of current working directory is removed.*
mv a1.c a2.c	*Creates a2.c in current working direct with the content of a1.c while a1.c is disappeared*
*mv *.c /tmp*	*Moves all files with extension c in current directory to /tmp directory*
mv /tmp/.c .*	*Moves all files with extension c in /tmp directory to current working directory*
mv /bin/ /tmp*	*Moves all files of /bin directory to /tmp*

The options include

-i interactive confirmation of overwrites

-f force a move

2.3.14 wc command

wc filename or wc<filename

These command displays number of lines, words and characters in the given file.

wc -l filename

This displays number lines in the given file.

wc -w filename

This displays number words in the given file.

wc -c filename

This displays number characters in the given file.

2.3.15 Link Files

Unix supports to types of links (shortcuts) for files and directories known as hard links and symbolic links.

Example :

```
ln a1 a6
```

Here, a6 becomes hard link to the file a1. Whatever operations we do on a6 is really seen from a1 also. The reverse also is true. In fact, a6 will not take extra disk space. If we delete a1 (or a6) yet the file content is accessible through other name.

Hard links can not be created to directories. Moreover, they can not be created to the files of other partitions.

```
ls -l a1 a6 gave the following result

-rw-r--r--   2 root   root        20 Feb 14 00:13 a1
-rw-r--r--   2 root   root        20 Feb 14 00:13 a6

ln a1 a7
ls -al a1 a6 a7 gave the following result

-rw-r--r--   3 root   root        20 Feb 14 00:13 a1
-rw-r--r--   3 root   root        20 Feb 14 00:13 a6
-rw-r--r--   3 root   root        20 Feb 14 00:13 a7
```

We can observe that link count is increasing whenever a new hard link is created for a file. Similarly, whenever we remove a hard link file link count is reduced.

```
rm a6
ls -l a1 a7  gives results

-rw-r--r--   2 root   root        20 Feb 14 00:13 a1
-rw-r--r--   2 root   root        20 Feb 14 00:13 a7
```

I-node numbers or hard link and original files are same.

```
ls -li a1 a7
264826 -rw-r--r--  2 root  root       20 Feb 14 00:13 a1
264826 -rw-r--r--  2 root    root     20 Feb 14 00:13 a7
```

Symbolic Links

```
ln -s a1 a8
ls -l a1 a8
-rw-r--r--   1 root   root        20 Feb 14 00:13 a1
lrwxrwxrwx   1 root   root         2 Feb 14 00:20 a8 -> a1
```

We can see the difference. Though, whatever operations we do on symbolic link really takes place on the original file yet if we delete original file the information of the file can not be accessible through symbolic link unlike hard link files. Of course, if we delete symbolic link yet the information is accessible through original name. Moreover, inode numbers or original file and symbolic link files are different. In fact, symbolic link file will take separate disk block in which path of the original file is saved.

```
ls -li a1 a8
264826 -rw-r--r--   3 root   root        20 Feb 14 00:13 a1
264831 lrwxrwxrwx   1 root   root         2 Feb 14 00:20 a8 -> a1
```

Main advantages of symbolic link files is that they can be used to create links for directories and also to the files of other partitions. In fact, symbolic links are used for SW fine tuning. For example check for file 'X' in Linux system, which is normally symbolic link to the appropriate X server (Check in /usr/X11R6/bin).

```
ls -l /usr/X11R6/bin/X  gave me the following results
lrwxrwxrwx   1 root   root       7 Feb  7 06:31 /usr/X11R6/bin/X -> XFree86
```

If we want to change to some other X server, simply we change X to point to that and start the X server.

2.3.16 Wildcards

Unix has special meaning for some characters such as *, ?, ., /, [,]. Words in the commands that contain these characters are treated as patterns (model) for filenames. The word is expanded into a list of file names, according to the type of pattern. If we want that the shell not to expand these characters then we have to pre-pend \ before them. This way we can make these characters to get escape from shells normal interpretation and is known as escaping and thus these characters are called as escape characters.

The following expansions are made by most shells, including bash:

* matches any string (including null)

? matches any single character As a special case, any . beginning a word must be matched explicitly.

/ root directory

. any character

Example :

The directory contains the files

tmp
tmp1
tmp2
tmp10
tmpx

The pattern *1* matches the files tmp1 and tmp10.

The pattern t??? matches tmp1 and tmp2

The pattern tmp[0-9] matches with tmp1 and tmp2

The pattern tmp[!0-9] matches with tmpx only

The pattern tmp[a-z] matches with tmpx only

The pattern tmp* matches with all files.

This models can be used with any command.

For example

ls -l tmp[0-9] displays details of files tmp1 and tmp2 only

rm tmp* deletes all files whose names starts with tmp.

2.3.17 Printing

lpr [options] files...

lpr -#2 filename	prints two copies of the given file
lpq	prints the printer queue status along with printer process job id.
lprm jobid	removes specified printer job id from printer queue (only legal owner can do this. Exception for super user).

2.2.18 Mtools

Mtools are used to copy files from/to floppy's.

mcopy rao a:	copies file rao of PWD to floppy.
mcopy a:\rao .	copies file rao from floppy to C.W.D
mdel a:\rao	removes file rao from floppy
mdir	displays content of floppy
mcd	changes directory in floppy

2.4 Conclusions

This chapter gives overview of most commonly used Linux commands. It starts with popular editor in Unix family, vi and then explains redirection operators. It explores link files and also printing under Linux/Unix.

3 File Filters

3.1 Introduction

Linux/Unix operating system supports a variety of file processing utilities called filters. This chapters explores the filters along with some other useful commands.

3.1.1 uniq command

This command displays uniq lines of the given files. That is if successive lines of a file are same then they will be removed. By default output will be on to the screen. This can be used to remove successive empty lines to the given file.

```
cat list-1 list-2 list-3 | sort | uniq final.list
```

Concatenates the list files, sorts them, removes duplicate lines, and finally writes the result to an output file.

The useful -c option prefixes each line of the input file with its number of occurrences.

Let the file "testfile" contains the following lines.

```
This line occurs only once.
This line occurs twice.
This line occurs twice.
This line occurs three times.
This line occurs three times.
This line occurs three times.
```

Then, the following command is executed the result is as displayed below.

```
uniq -c testfile
```

```
1 This line occurs only once.
2 This line occurs twice.
3 This line occurs three times.
```

Similarly, when the following command is executed the result is displayed as below.

```
sort testfile | uniq -c | sort -nr
```

```
3 This line occurs three times.
2 This line occurs twice.
1 This line occurs only once.
```

3.1.2 grep command

This command is used to select lines from a file having some specified string.

```
grep "rao"  xyz
```

This displays those lines of the file xyz having string rao.

```
grep "[rR]ao"  xyz
```

This displays those lines of the file xyz having strings either "Rao", or "rao".

```
grep "[rR]a[uo]"  xyz
```

This displays those lines of the file xyz having strings either "Rao", or "Rau", or "rao", or "rau".

```
grep "^rao"  xyz
```

This displays those lines of the file xyz which starts with string "rao"

```
grep "rao$"  xyz
```

This displays those lines of the file xyz which ends with string "rao".

```
grep "^rao$"  xyz
```

This displays those lines of the file xyz which contains the string "rao" only. No more characters in the line.

```
grep "^$"  xyz
```

This displays empty lines of the file xyz.

```
grep "^[rR]ao"  xyz
```

This displays those lines of the file xyz which starts with either "Rao" or "rao".

```
grep "[rR]ao$"  xyz
```

This displays those lines of the file xyz which ends with "Rao" or "rao".

-n option if we use with grep command it displays line numbers also.

```
grep -n "rao" xyz
```

This displays those lines of file xyz which are having the string "rao" along with their line numbers.

-v option if we use with grep command it displays those lines which does not have the given search pattern.

```
grep -v "rao" xyz
```

This displays those lines of the file xyz which does not contain the string "rao".

3.1.3 fgrep (fixed grep) and egrep (extended grep) commands

fgrep is used search for a group of strings. One string has to be separated from other by a new line.

```
$fgrep 'rao
>ram
>raju' filename
```

This command displays those lines having either rao or ram or raju.

fgrep will not accept regular expressions.

egrep is little more different. It also takes a group of strings. while specifying strings piping (|) can be used as separator.

Example :

```
egrep 'rao|ram|raju' filename
```

In addition it accepts regular expressions also.

3.1.4 cut command

This is used to split files vertically.

```
cut -f1,3 filename
```

This displays 1'st and 3'rd words of each line of the given file. Between word to word TAB should be available.

```
cut -d":" -f1,3 /etc/passwd
```

This displays username, UID of each legal user of the machine. Here, with -d option we are specifying that : is the field separator between word to word.

Cut command can not change the natural order of the fields. That is, the following command also gives same result as that of the above command.

```
cut -d":"  -f3,1 /etc/passwd
```

```
cut -d":"  -f1-3 filename
```

This displays first word to third word from each line of the given file.

```
cut -f":" -f3- filename
```

This displays third word to till last word of each line of the given file.

```
cut -c3-5 filename
```

This displays 3'rd character to 5'th character of each line of the given file.

```
cut -d":" -f1 /etc/passwd > a1
```

File a1 contains usernames of legal users of the machine.

```
cut -d":"  -f3 /etc/passwd > a3
```

File a3 contains UID's of each legal user of the machine.

3.1.5 paste command

This is used to join files vertically.

```
paste a3 a1 >a31
```

```
cat a31
```

This displays

```
0  root
1  bin
2  daemon
3  adm
4  lp
5  sync
6  shutdown
7  halt
```

```
8  mail
9  news
10 uucp
11 operator
12 games
13 gopher
14 ftp
99 nobody
38 ntp
32 rpc
69 vcsa
28 nscd
74 sshd
37 rpm
47 mailnull
51 smmsp
25 named
42 gdm
80 desktop
101        rao
39 canna
78 fax
57 nut
```

```
paste -d"|" a3 a1 >a13
```

This command places the given field separator while joining the files contents vertically.

```
cat a13
```

```
0|root
1|bin
2|daemon
3|adm
4|lp
5|sync
6|shutdown
7|halt
8|mail
9|news
10|uucp
```

```
11|operator
12|games
13|gopher
14|ftp
99|nobody
43|xfs
25|named
42|gdm
39|canna
49|wnn
78|fax
57|nut
```

3.1.6 join command

This is used to join files. Unlike paste it works similar to join operation of DBMS.

Let the files content are :

File aa1 contains

```
111|NBV Rao
121|PP Raj
116|Teja
119|Rani
```

File aa2 contains

```
111|Prof
112|Asst Prof
121|lecturer
116|Prof
```

```
join -t"|" -j 1 1 aa1 aa2
```

This command produces the following result:

```
111|NBV Rao|Prof
121|PP Raj|lecturer
116|Teja|Prof
```

```
join -t"|" -j 1 1 -o 1.1 2.2 aa1 aa2
```

This command produces output such as the following. That is, first field from the first file and second field from the second file is displayed.

```
111|Prof
121|lecturer
116|Prof

join -t"|" -a1 -o 1.1 2.2 aa1 aa2
```

This command gives the following results.

```
111|Prof
121|lecturer
116|Prof
119|

join -t"|"  -a2 -o 1.1 2.2 aa1 aa2
```

This command gives the following results.

```
111|Prof
|Asst Prof
121|lecturer
116|Prof
```

3.1.7 tr command

This command can be used for transliteration. That is replacing a character with another character. It accepts standard input and gives standard output.

```
tr '*' '-' <xyz
```

This command replaces all the occurrences of character * with - in the given file xyz.

```
tr '*/' '-?' <xyz
```

This command replaces all the occurrences of * with - and / with ? in the given file. In both the situations output appears on the screen. By standard redirection operator output can be stored in a file.

Example

```
tr '*' '-' <xyz >pqr

tr '[a-z]' '[A-Z]' < xyz
```

This command replaces all lower case characters of the file xyz to uppercase.

```
tr -d '*' <xyz
```

This command removes all occurrences of * in the given file xyz.

```
tr -s '*' <xyz
```

This command replaces multiple consecutive *'s with a single * in the given file.

3.1.8 df command

This command displays details about the each of the mounted partition, percentage of free ness, percentage of occupation etc.

```
Filesystem      1K-blocks    Used Available Use% Mounted on
/dev/hdb5         6048288  5163420    577632  90% /
none                62520        0     62520   0% /dev/shm
```

3.1.9 du command

This command displays disk usage(usually in multiples of 1K blocks).

du command without any argument displays disk usage of all files, subdirectories of current working directory.

```
du  directoryname
```

This displays disk usage of all files sub-directories of the given directory.

Please note that du command will not display the actual size of the file in bytes. Rather, number of 1K blocks assigned for the file. Try the following and find out the difference.

```
du filename
ls -l filename
du -b filename
```

3.1.10 who command

This displays details about the users such as user name, terminal on which working and since when they are working.

```
root    :0        Feb  9 00:22
root    pts/0     Feb  9 00:25 (:0.0)
root    pts/1     Feb  9 20:25 (:0.0)
```

3.1.11 w command

This displays details about the users in addition to what command they are working now.

w

Presents who users are and what they are doing in the following fashion.

```
USER   TTY    FROM          LOGIN@   IDLE   JCPU   PCPU  WHAT
root   :0     -             12:22am  ?      0.00s  1.66s /usr/bin/gnome-
root   pts/0  :0.0          12:25am  0.00s  0.81s  0.03s w
```

```
w username
```

Displays what that user is doing.

```
w -i
```

displays details sorted by idle time

3.1.12 rm command

This is used to remove file(s)

Example :

```
rm xyz
```

This command removes file xyz (If it is not write protected).

Only legal owner of the file can remove file (Exception for super user).

```
rm f1 f2 f3 .... fn
```

Removes all files f1, f2, ... fn.

```
rm a*.c
```

Removes all files with extension c and primary name starts with a.

```
rm a?.c
```

Removes all files with extension c and primary is two characters length with first character as a.

```
rm a[0-9]*.c
```

Removes all files with extension c and primary name starting with a and second character as digit.

```
rm a[!a-zA-Z0-9]*.c
```

Removes all files with extension c and primary name starting with a and second character is other than alphanumeric.

```
rm -R directoryname
```

Removes all files, sub-directories of the given directory recursively.

```
rm -i file(s)
```

Interactive deletion. That is, it prompts before deleting the file(s).

```
rm -F file(s)
```

File(s) are deleted forcibly (ignoring permissions).

3.1.13 unlink filename

This command also removes the given file.

3.1.14 ulimit command

Unix system has resource limits such as limits on number of processes, maximum allowed file size, etc.

Example :

```
ulimit -a

core file size          (blocks, -c) 0
data seg size           (kbytes, -d) 231122
file size               (blocks, -f) 231122
max locked memory       (kbytes, -l) unlimited
max memory size         (kbytes, -m) unlimited
open files              (-n) 1024
pipe size               (512 bytes, -p) 8
stack size              (kbytes, -s) 8192
cpu time                (seconds, -t) unlimited
max user processes       (-u) 1016
virtual memory          (kbytes, -v) unlimited
```

```
ulimit
```

This command displays file size limit on the system currently.

```
ulimit -f 121212
```

This changes file size limit to 121212.

Similarly, we can change resource limits such as max data, text segment sizes etc.

3.1.15 chmod command

With the help of chmod command we can change permissions of a file or a directory.

For any file or directory which is available in Unix system there exists three types of owners given as :

- Owner (real user)
- Group Member
- Others

For the purpose of administration, users are grouped such that resources can be appropriated. For example, the administrator can appropriate for all second year B.Tech students 1 hour CPU time, 20 hours of Terminal time, 3 pages of hard copy and 10MB of space. Except the disk space others are allocated on weekly basis. These appropriations can be different for final year students. Also, groups makes users to share the files.

Similarly, for any file or a directory three types of operations can be carried out known as:

- Read
- Write
- Execute

If we have reading permissions on a file we can see the content of the file or some other command such as cat which wants to read the file on behalf of us also works. Similarly if we have writing permissions on a file we can modify the content of the file (please note the file can be deleted by only legal owner of the file and super user even if you have writing permissions). Similarly, if we have execution permissions for a file then it can be loaded into RAM and executed if it is executable file. If the file is not executable and having executable permissions will have no effect on the file. You will be knowing in the next chapters that if we want to run a shell script (a simple text file) it has to be given executable permissions.

Similarly, if we have reading permissions on a directory we can run ls command on it. If we have writing permissions on a directory we can create file or directory in it (try to create a file in /bin). If we have executable permissions then we can enter into it.

For example create a file xyz and run the following command.

```
ls –l xyz
```

The result may look like this:

```
-rw-r--r--          ___________ xyz
```

The first string in the above commands output is called as mode string or permissions string which indicates what permissions are available to the file for user, group and others. The first character in the above string is – indicates that xyz is file. There are some characters such as d,b,c,p,l to indicate that xyz is directory, character special file (character device), block special file (block device), pipe file or link file respectively which are explained later.

The next three characters "rw-" indicated that the user can read, write but not execute. Similarly "r—" for group and others indicates that group members and others can only read the xyz.

The chmod command supports two ways of changing file/directory permissions.

- Octal Approach
- Symbol ic Approach

Octal approach of changing File Permissions

In octal approach, we specify three digit octal number to change permissions such as:

chmod 700 xyz

ls –l xyz

Output of the above command looks like:

-rw-------- ____________ **xyz**

In this approach, we have to specify the required permissions without what are the previous permissions. Thus this technique is called as absolute approach.

Here, we assume (no answer for why and why not other numbers)

- Read - 4
- Write - 2
- Execute - 1

If we want all the three permissions then we use 7 (sum of 4+2+1) and vice versa . Like this in the above example 700 we have used as we want all the permissions to be available for the user and none to others and group.

chmod 000 xyz

ls –l xyz

--------- ____________ **xyz**

Now if we try to run the following commands, we can not succeed as there is no reading permission for us.

cat xyz

vi xyz

chmod 400 xyz

ls –l xyz

-r-------- ____________ **xyz**

Now if we try to run the following commands, we can succeed as there is reading permission for us. However, we can not modify the file content using vi command as we do not have writing permissions.

```
cat xyz

vi xyz

chmod 200 xyz

ls -l xyz

---------          ___________ xyz
```

Now if we try to run the following commands, we can not succeed as there is no reading permission for us.

```
cat xyz

vi xyz
```

However, the following command may succeed.

```
cat>>xyz
Asas
Asas
Asa
Aas
^d
```

Symbolic way of changing File Permissions

Similarly, we can change permissions with symbolic approach.

Here, we use the following symbols

- All –a
- User –u
- Group –g
- Others –o
- Read – r
- Write –w
- Execute – x
- = to assign permissions
- + to add permissions
- to remove permissions

For example run the following command.

```
chmod u=rwx  xyz

ls –l xyz
```

We will see

-rwx------ ___________ xyz

```
chmod u-x,go+r   xyz

ls –l xyz
```

We wil see

-rw-r--r-- ___________ xyz

A Note on Sticky bit, setgid bit, setuid bit

Sticky bit on a file

In the past having the sticky bit set on a file meant that when the file was executed the code for the program would "stick" in RAM. Normally once a program has finished its code was taken out of RAM and that area used for something else [Robert Love].

The sticky bit was used on programs that were executed regularly. If the code for a program is already in RAM the program will start much quicker because the code doesn't have to be loaded from disk.

However today with the advent of shared libraries and cheap RAM most modern Unix's ignore the sticky bit when it is set on a file.

Sticky bit on a directory

The /tmp directory on UNIX is used by a number of programs to store temporary files regardless of the user. For example when you use elm (a UNIX mail program) to send a mail message, while you are editing the message it will be stored as a file in the /tmp directory. Please note that every user will have his own privacy rules on the files stored in such directories.

Modern UNIX operating systems (including Linux) use the sticky bit on a directory to make /tmp directories more secure [David Evans]. Try the command ls -ld /tmp what do you notice about the file permissions of /tmp.

If the sticky bit is set on a directory you can only delete or rename a file in that directory if you are

- the owner of the directory,
- the owner of the file, or
- the super user

Changing passwords—setuid bit??

When you use the passwd command to change your password the command will actually change the contents of either the /etc/passwd or /etc/shadow files. These are the files where your password is stored. However, we can not directly edit /etc/passwd as we don't have permissions for the same.

Check the file permissions on the /etc/passwd file?.

```
ls -l /etc/passwd
-rw-r--r--   1 root    root         697 Feb  1 21:21 /etc/passwd
```

Now the file belongs to root and others do not have write permission thus we are unable to modify through vi. Then how do does the passwd command change my password in /etc/passwd file?

The answer is setuid and setgid.

Let's have a look at the permissions for the passwd command (first we find out where it is).

```
ls -l /usr/bin/passwd
-rws--x--x   1 root    bin    7192 Oct 16 06:10 /usr/bin/passwd
```

Notice the s symbol in the file permissions of the passwd command, this specifies that this command is setuid.

When we execute the passwd command a new process is created. The real UID and GID of this process will match my UID and GID. However the effective UID and GID (the values used to check file permissions) will be set to that of the command. Thus, we are able to modify the file /etc/passwd which belongs to root.

Similarly, setgid bit is useful while enforcing locks on files.

3.1.16. umask command

This command when executed without any argument it displays the current value of the umask. This umask value is used to change the default permissions of any file or directory created. By changing the umask value we can change default permissions of a file or directory created.

Example :

```
cat>p1
add
adjda
^d
ls -l p1
-rw-r--r--   1 root    root          4 Feb 10 00:32 p1
umask 000
cat>p3
ads
sad
sdsd
^d
ls -l p3
-rw-rw-rw-   1 root    root          9 Feb 10 00:35 p3
```

We can see that permissions of files p1 and p3 are different.

Unix Kernel uses a mask known as file creation mask (octal 666) [Kernigham]. While a file is created this mask and umask jointly plays role in deciding the permissions of a file. Default umask value is 022. Thus, when file p1 is created this is used. Whereas while p3 is created umask value is taken as 000, which we have specified.

	P1	P3
File Mask (Binary)	110110110	110110110
Umask	000010010 (022)	000000000 (000)
Exclusive-OR	110100100	110110110
Permissions	rw-r--r--	rw-rw-rw-

The same is applicable to default directory permissions also. Unix Kernel uses default directory creation mask as 777.

Directory l1 is created after changing the umask where as directory l2 is created before changing. We can see the difference in the permissions.

```
drwxrwxrwx   2 root   root    4096 Feb 10 00:43 l1
drwxr-xr-x   2 root   root    4096 Feb 10 00:44 l2
```

3.1.17 chown command

With the help of chown command, we can change owner ship of a file or directory. Only real owner (exception for the super user) of the file or directory can change owner ship of a file or directory. Once it is changed, he/she will not have any authority revert it back.

```
chown   username   filename
```

Example

```
chown   rao    xyz.c
```

3.1.18 chgrp command

With the help of chgrp command we can change group membership of a file. For example:

```
chgrp   groupname   filename
```

3.1.19 id command

The id command can be used to discover username, UID, group name and GID of any user.

For example, when we have executed id command on our machine we got the following output.

```
uid=500(venkat) gid=100(users) groups=100(users)
```

3.1. 20 diff command

This is used to compare the contents of two files in general.

Example

```
diff p1 p2
```

If the content of p1 and p2 are exactly same it displays nothing. Otherwise it displays the difference information in a special format such as the following:

```
1c1
< ass
---
> add
3d2
< ass
```

3.1.21 sed command

Sed is a stream editor. A stream editor is used to perform basic text transformations on an input stream (a file or input from a pipeline). While in some ways similar to an editor which permits scripted edits (such as ed), sed works by making only one pass over the input(s), and is consequently more efficient. But it is sed's ability to filter text in a pipeline which particularly distinguishes it from other types of editors.

We have seen vi editor in previous chapters. Sed uses almost same commands while processing the files.

The following options are used with sed.

-n shows only those lines on which sed actually acted. Sed's default behavior is to display the line what it has read from the file and also to display the line after applying the command. However, if we specify the -n option it displays only the lines after applying the action.

-f Usually the commands are enclosed in between single quotes. However, if we want the sed command to be stored in a file (like shell or awk script) and sed to use it then we will use this option.

In the following pages, we use the file 'ABC' with the following content for experimentation purpose.

I am not happy with your Progress.

I think you have to improve a lot.

Why you are not serious?.

Make sure you take things with whole heart.

```
sed -n '' ABC
```

This command displays nothing.

```
sed '' ABC
```

This command gives the following output which we can find as the file content. Actually, sed's default behavior is displaying the lines what ii has read. Thus, we see the file content as it is. However, when we use -n option (above command), nothing is displayed as -n option displays lines content after applying our command; which is nothing is this case.

I am not happy with your Progress.
I think you have to improve a lot.
Why you are not serious?.
Make sure you take things with whole heart.

```
sed -n '1,2p' ABC
```

This command displays first two lines of the file as shown below.

I am not happy with your Progress.
I think you have to improve a lot.

```
sed  '1,2p' ABC
```

This command displays first two lines two times and next lines once. This is because, sed's default behavior is to display the lines read. In addition, we have asked two print first two lines. Thus, first two lines are printed twice.

I am not happy with your Progress.
I am not happy with your Progress.
I think you have to improve a lot.
I think you have to improve a lot.
Why you are not serious?.
Make sure you take things with whole heart.

```
sed  '1,2d' ABC
```

This command displays 3'rd and fourth lines of the files as shown below.

Why you are not serious?.
Make sure you take things with whole heart.

```
sed -n '1,2d' ABC
```

This command displays nothing. Why?.

Now, run the following commands and see the content of the file 'pp'.

```
sed '1,2d' ABC>pp

cat pp

Why you are not serious?.
Make sure you take things with whole heart.

sed '1,/Why/p' ABC
```

This command displays lines from 1'st line to the (first) line having the pattern 'Why'.

```
I am not happy with your Progress.
I am not happy with your Progress.
I think you have to improve a lot.
I think you have to improve a lot.
Why you are not serious?.
Why you are not serious?
Make sure you take things with whole heart.

sed -n '1,/Why/p' ABC

I am not happy with your Progress.
I think you have to improve a lot.
Why you are not serious?.

sed '1,/Why/w pp1' ABC
```

The above command writes the selected lines into the file pp1.

```
I am not happy with your Progress.
I think you have to improve a lot.
Why you are not serious?.
Make sure you take things with whole heart.

cat pp1
I am not happy with your Progress.
I think you have to improve a lot.
Why you are not serious?.
```

Run the following commands and check the difference.

```
sed -n '1,/Why/w pp2' ABC
cat pp2
I am not happy with your Progress.
I think you have to improve a lot.
Why you are not serious?.
```

```
sed '/not/s/not/NOT/g' ABC
```

The above command replaces all the occurrences of the string 'not' with 'NOT'. Remember, original file is not changed.

```
I am NOT happy with your Progress.
I think you have to improve a lot.
Why you are NOT serious?.
Make sure you take things with whole heart.
```

```
sed '1 r pp1' ABC
```

The above command reads the content from the file 'pp1'. That is, it displays 1'st line of the file ABC and then the content of the file pp1 and then remaining content of file ABC.

Thus, the result is as follows.

```
I am not happy with your Progress.
I am not happy with your Progress.
I think you have to improve a lot.
Why you are not serious?.
I think you have to improve a lot.
Why you are not serious?.
Make sure you take things with whole heart.
```

We can ask sed to take instructions from a file. To explain, we now create a file say, 'ff' with the sed command in it.

```
cat >ff
/not/s/not/NOT/g
^d
```

```
sed -f ff ABC
```

Now with the help of –f option, we are informing sed to take commands from the file 'ff'. The result is as follows.

```
I am NOT happy with your Progress.
I think you have to improve a lot.
Why you are NOT serious?.
Make sure you take things with whole heart.
```

```
sed -n '1,3 w pp2' ABC
```

This command prints first three lines to file pp2, which we can check by running the following command.

```
cat pp2
```

```
sed -n '1~2 w pp2' ABC
```

This command prints every alternative line from first line. We can check the same by running the following command.

```
cat pp2
```

```
sed  '1~2d' ABC
```

This command prints 2'nd and fourth lines while deleting 1'st, 3'rd, etc., line.

```
sed  '1,/Why/d' ABC
```

This command displays all the lines other than the lines from 1'st line to the line which contains the pattern 'Why'.

```
sed  '1,/Why/s/not/NOT/' ABC
```

This command replaces the pattern 'not' with 'NOT' in the lines starting from 1'st line to the line having the pattern 'Why'.

```
sed  '1,2s/not/NOT/' ABC
```

This command replaces the pattern 'not' with 'NOT' in the lines 1 to 2.

3.1.22 cmp command

The cmp utility compares two files of any type and writes the results to the standard output. By default, cmp is silent if the files are the same; if they differ, the byte and line number at which the first difference occurred is reported.

Bytes and lines are numbered beginning with one.

Example : cmp file1 file2

3.1.22 comm command

comm - compare two sorted files line by line

Compare sorted files LEFT_FILE and RIGHT_FILE line by line.

-1 suppress lines unique to left file

-2 suppress lines unique to right file

-3 suppress lines that appear in both files

Example : comm p1 p2

3.1.23 Software Patching

Normally SW products are supplied either as binary distribution or source distribution. In source distribution, all the source program files are supplied to the customer and the customer is required to compile on his target machine to get binary or executable code of the SW. Moreover, it is common that SW systems are released in incremental fashion. When a new release is made, a patch file (difference file) is prepared by comparing with the previous release files. This can downloaded by the customer who is having previous release and by applying the SW patching he can get recent version of the SW source which he can compile to get updated version of SW running on his machine.

Example :

diff p1 p2>p3

Here p3 can be called as patch file.

patch p1 <p3 will change the content of the file p1 as p2.
patch p2 <p3 will change the p2 file content as p1.

3.2 Introduction to Pipes

Unix operating system supports a unique approach through which we can join two commands and generate new command with the help of pipe concept.

For example

command1|command2

Here, whatever output first command generates becomes standard input for the second command. We can develop complex UNIX command sequences by joining many commands while maintaining this input output relation ships. Whenever left hand side of piping symbol does not generate we may get broken pipe error.

For example

```
ls -l|grep "^d"
```

This command displays details of only the directories of the current working directory. That is output of ls -l command becomes input to grep command which displays only those lines which starts with d (they are nothing but details of files).

```
ls -l|grep "^d"|wc -l
```

This command displays number of directories in the given file.

```
grep "bash$" /etc/passwd|wc -l
```

This command displays number of users of the machine whose default shell is bash.

```
cut -t":" -f 3 /etc/passwd|sort -n|tail -1
```

This command displays a number which is largest used UID number in the system. Here, cut command first extract UID's of all the users in the system from the /etc/passwd file, and the same becomes input to sort; which sorts these numbers in numerical order and sends to tail command as input which in turn displays the largest number (last one).

3.2.1 tee command

tee command is used to save intermediate results in a piping sequence. It accepts a set of filenames as arguments and sends its standard input to all these file while giving the same as standard output. Thus, use of this in piping sequence will not break the pipe.

For example if you want to save details of the directories of current working directory while knowing their using the above piping sequence we can use tee as follows. Here, the file xyz will have the details of directories saved.

```
ls -l|grep "^d"|tee xyz|wc -l
```

The following piping sequence writes the number of directories into the file pqr while displaying the same on the screen.

```
ls -l|grep "^d"|tee xyz|wc -l|tee pqr
```

3.3 Some Other Means of Joining Commands

Unix supports some other means of joining command such as the following.

```
Command1&&Command2
```

Here, if first command is successfully executed then second command is executed.

For example:

```
ls x1&&cat x1
```

Here, 'ls x1' command first checks whether x1 file is available or not. If it succeeds, i.e. it x1 exists then the second executes. That is, we will see the output of the file x1.

```
Command1||Command2
```

Here, if first command is failed then second command is executed.

For example :

```
ls x1||echo File x1 not found
```

Here, 'ls x1' command first checks whether x1 file is available or not. If it fails, i.e. it x1 does not exists then the second command is executed. That is, we will see that x1 file is not found

We can also enclose a set of commands which has to be executed one after another in between parenthesis. For example:

```
(ls; cat /etc/passwd)
```

We can send output of a group of file into a file or directory.

```
(ls; cat /etc/passwd) > outputfile
```

We can also enclose a set of commands which has to be executed one after another in between curly braces.

3.4 awk command

This facility is very much useful for small scale database applications requiring no precision.

Syntax of awk command

```
awk option 'BEGIN{}
            {

            }
            END{}' filename
```

Awk command considers the given file as database file; each line of the file is considered as a record, each word of a line is taken as field [Venkateswarlu]. Whatever operations we wanted to execute, we have write in the BEGIN section which are really executed before processing any record. The operations which are required to be executed after processing all the records has to be written in END section. Instructions which are required to be executed on every record has to be written in the middle block. It is not necessary that every awk command to have all the three blocks. However, opening curly braces should immediately follow the BEGIN and END words and should be on the same line as that of BEGIN, END words. Awk supports a limited amount of C style programming constructs. However, we can not say that it can be used in place of C though!. While running, instructions in the BEGIN block are executed, then instructions in the middle block are executed on every record and the instructions in END block are executed at the last.

Normally, awk assumed space or TAB as the field separator between word to word. However, if a file contains some other character as field separator, the same can be informed through -d option.

awk uses the following things:

NF= number of fields

NR= number of records

OFS=output field separator

$0 = current record as a whole

$1, $2, $3... = first, second, third etc., fields of current record

```
awk '{ print $0} ' filename
awk '{ printf "%s", $0 }'  filename
```

These commands displays the content of the file

```
awk -F":" '{ print $3, $1}'  /etc/passwd
awk -F":" '{ printf "%3d %s", $3, $1 }' /etc/passwd
```

These commands displays UID's and usernames of the legal users of the machine.

```
awk '{ printf "%3d  %s", NR, $0}' filename
```

This command displays file content along with line numbers. Here, NR value refers to the record number.

Like "grep", find string "fleece" (the {print} command is the default if nothing is specified)

```
awk '/fleece/' file
```

Select lines 14 through 30 of file

```
awk 'NR==14, NR==30' file
```

Select just one line of a file

```
awk 'NR==12' file
```

```
awk "NR==$1" file
```

Rearrange fields 1 and 2 and put colon in between

```
awk '{print $2 ":" $1}' file
```

All lines between BEGIN and END lines (you can substitute any strings for BEGIN and END, but they must be between slashes)

```
awk '/BEGIN/,/END/' file
```

Print number of lines in file (of course wc -l does this, too)

```
awk 'END{print NR}' file
```

We can use variables in awk wherever we wanted and their initial value will be taken as 0. The following prints no of lines, words, characters.

```
awk '{ w +=NF  c +=length($0) }  END{ print NR, w, c} ' filename
```

Substitute every occurrence of a string XYZ by the new string ABC: Requires nawk.

```
nawk '{gsub(/XYZ/,"ABC"); print}' file
```

Print 3rd field from each line, but the colon is the field separate

```
awk -F: '{print $3}' file
```

Print out the last field in each line, regardless of how many fields:

```
awk '{print $NF}' file
```

To print out a file with line numbers at the edge:

```
awk '{print NR, $0}' somefile
```

This is less than optimal because as the line number gets longer in digits, the lines get shifted over. Thus, use printf:

```
awk '{printf "%3d %s", NR, $0}' somefile
```

Print out lengths of lines in the file

```
awk '{print length($0)}' somefile
```

or

```
awk '{print length}' somefile
```

Print out lines and line numbers that are longer than 80 characters

```
awk 'length 80 {printf "%3d. %s\n", NR, $0}' somefile
```

Total up the lengths of files in characters that results from "ls -l"

```
ls -l | awk 'BEGIN{total=0} {total += $4} END{print total}'
```

Print out the longest line in a file

```
awk 'BEGIN {maxlength = 0} \
{ \ if (length($0) maxlength) { \
maxlength = length($0) \
longest = $0 \
} \
 } \
END {print longest}' somefile
```

How many entirely blank lines are in a file?

```
awk '/^$/ {x++} END {print x}' somefile
```

Print out last character of field 1 of every line

```
awk '{print substr($1,length($1),1)}' somefile
```

Comment out only #include statements in a C file. This is useful if you want to run "cxref" which will follow the include links.

```
awk '/#include/{printf "/* %s */\n", $0; next} {print}'  file.c | cxref -c $*
```

If the last character of a line is a colon, print out the line. This would be useful in getting the pathname from output of ls -lR:

```
awk '{ \
lastchar = substr($0,length($0),1) \
 if (lastchar == ":") \
print $0 \
}' somefile
```

Here is the complete thing....Note that it even sorts the final output

```
ls -lR | awk '{ \
lastchar = substr($0,length($0),1) \
if (lastchar == ":") \
dirname = substr($0,1,length($0)-1) \
else \
 if ($4 20000) \
printf "%10d %25s %s\n", $4, dirname, $8 \
}' | sort -r
```

The following is used to break all long lines of a file into chunks of length 80:

```
awk '{ line = $0
while (length(line) 80)
{
print substr(line,1,80) line = substr(line,81,length(line)-80)
}
if (length(line) 0) print line
}' somefile.with.long.lines>whatever
```

If you want to use awk as a programming language, you can do so by not processing any file, but by enclosing a bunch of awk commands in curly braces, activated upon end of file. To use a standard UNIX "file" that has no lines, use /dev/null.

Here's a simple example:

```
awk 'END{print "hi there everyone"}' < /dev/null
```

Here's an example of using this to print out the ASCII characters:

```
awk ' { for(i=32; i<127; i++) \
printf "%3d %3o %c\n", i,i,i \
}' </dev/null
```

Sometimes you wish to find a field which has some identifying tag, like X= in front. Suppose your file (playfile1) looked like:

```
50 30 X=10 Y=100 Z=-2
X=12 89 100 32 Y=900
1 2 3 4 5 6 X=1000
```

Then to select out the X= numbers from each do

```
awk '{ for (i=1; i <=NF; i++) \
if ($i ~ /X=.*/) \
print substr($i,3) \
}' playfile1
```

Note that we used a regular expression to find the initial part: /X=.*/

Pull an abbreviation out of a file of abbreviations and their translation. Actually, this can be used to translate anything, where the first field is the thing you are looking up and the 2nd field is what you want to output as the translation.

```
nawk '$1 == abbrev{print $2}' abbrev=$1 translate.file
```

Join lines in a file that end in a dash. That is, if any line ends in -, join it to the next line. This only joins 2 lines at a time. The dash is removed.

```
awk '/-$/ {oldline = $0 \
getline \
print substr(oldline,1,length(oldline)-1) $0 \
next} \
{print}' somefile
```

Function in nawk to round: function round(n) { return int(n+0.5) }

If you have a file of addresses with empty lines between the sections, you can use the following to search for strings in a section, and print out the whole section. Put the following into a file called "section.awk":

```
BEGIN {FS = "\n"; RS = ""; OFS = "\n"} $0 ~ searchstring { print }
```

Assume your names are in a file called "rolodex". Then use the following nawk command when you want to find a section that contains a string. In this example, it is a person's name:

```
nawk -f section.awk searchstring=Wolf rolodex
```

We assume the following data in the file EMPLOYEE having employee ID, name, designation, department, salary, no of dependents and age in each line.

```
111|NB Venkateswarlu|Professor|CSE|27000|2|42
121|GV Saradamba|Professor|CHEM|32000|2|46
122|PN Rao|Assistant Professor|Civil|26000|3|54
```

```
awk -F"|"  '{ printf "%s %d", $2 , $1}' EMPLOYEE
```

This command displays names of the employees and their ID's in a tabular fashion.

```
awk -F"|"  ' $2 ~ /Rao/{ printf "%s %d", $2 , $1}' EMPLOYEE
```

This command displays names of the employees and their ID's whose name contains the string "Rao".

```
awk -F"|"  ' $2 ~ /Ra[ou]/{ printf "%s %d", $2 , $1}' EMPLOYEE
```

This command displays names of the employees and their ID's whose name contains the string "Rao" or "Rau".

```
awk -F"|"  ' $2 ~ /^Rao/{ printf "%s %d", $2 , $1}' EMPLOYEE
```

This command displays names of the employees and their ID's whose name starts with the string "Rao".

```
awk -F"|"  ' $2 ~ /^Ra[ou]/{ printf "%s %d", $2 , $1}' EMPLOYEE
```

This command displays names of the employees and their ID's whose name starts with the string "Rao" or "Rau".

```
awk -F"|"  ' $2 ~ /Rao$/{ printf "%s %d", $2 , $1}' EMPLOYEE
```

This command displays names of the employees and their ID's whose name ends with the string "Rao".

```
awk -F"|"  ' $2 ~ /Ra[ou]$/{ printf "%s %d", $2 , $1}' EMPLOYEE
```

This command displays names of the employees and their ID's whose name ends with the string "Rao" or "Rau".

```
awk -F"|"  ' $2 ~ /^Ra[ou]$/{ printf "%s %d", $2 , $1}' EMPLOYEE
```

This command displays names of the employees and their ID's whose name contains the strings "Rao" or "Rau".

```
awk -F"|"  ' $2 ~ /^[rR]a[ou]$/{ printf "%s %d", $2 , $1}' EMPLOYEE
```

This command displays names of the employees and their ID's whose name contains the strings "Rao", "rao" , "Rau" or "rau".

```
awk -F"|"  ' $4 >10000 { printf "%s %d", $2 , $1}' EMPLOYEE
```

This command displays names of the employees and their ID's whose salary is more than 10000.

```
awk -F"|"'{ s+=$4  p+=$6} END { printf "%d %d", s/NR, p/NR}' EMPLOYEE
```

This command displays average salary and average number of dependents of the employees.

```
awk -F"|"'$4<5000{s+=$4  p+=$6}END{printf "%d %d",s/NR,p/NR}' EMPLOYEE
```

This command displays average salary and average number of dependents of the employees whose salary is less than 5000.

```
awk -F"|"'$6<50{s+=$4  p+=$6}END{printf"%d %d",s/NR,p/NR}' EMPLOYEE
```

This command displays average salary and average number of dependents of the employees whose age is more than 50.

```
awk -F"|" ' {
                If ($4 >5000)  n1++
                Else n2++
                }END{ printf "%d %d", n1, n2 }' EMPLOYEE
```

This command displays no of employees whose salary is greater than 5000 and less than 5000.

```
awk -F"|" ' {
                If ($4 >5000)
                {
                 n1++
                s1+=$4
                }
                else
                {
                  n2++
                s2+=$4
                }
                }END{ printf "%d %d", s1/n1, s2/n2 }' EMPLOYEE
```

This command displays average salary of employees whose salary is greater than 5000 and less than 5000.

We can use arrays also. Their initial values also taken as zeros.

```
awk -F"|" ' {
        if ($4 >5000)
        {
         s[1]++
         s[2]+=$4
        }
        else
        {
          s[3]++
          s[4]+=$4
        }
        }END{ printf "%d %d", s[2]/s[1], s[4]/s[3] }' EMPLOYEE
```

This command displays average salary of employees whose salary is greater than 5000 and less than 5000.

We can use content addressable arrays. That is, the element indexes for these arrays can be strings rather than usual integers.

```
awk -F"|" '{ s[$3]++}  END{ for(desig in s) printf "%s %d", desig, s[desig] }' EMPLOYEE
```

The above command displays designation and number of people having that designation.

```
awk '{ l=(80-length($0))/2
          I=0;
          While(I<l)
          {
          printf "%s", " "
          I++;
          }
     printf "%s", $0 }'  filename
```

This program prints every line of the program centered on the screen.

```
awk '{ l=(80-length($0))/2
          for(I=0;I<l; I++)
          {
          printf "%s", " "
          }
     printf "%s", $0 }'  filename
```

This program prints every line of the program centered on the screen.

3.5 Backup Commands

We sure that everyone know that "Data is more important than SW". After all, by paying some more salary, a SW system can be generated by trillions of SW programmers. However, the data can not be developed or created; especially time dependent data if it is lost. Thus, in all the applications at most importance is given to the safe data storage. One of the prime responsibilities of a system administrator is data safety. Normally, to safeguard against viruses, power failures, disk failures, backup's are taken. In UNIX, tar, cpio commands are in wide use.

3.5.1 tar command

This command is used to join a group of files and prepare a archive file.

```
tar -cvf  a.tar directoryname(s)orfilename(s)
```

This command creates a archive file a.tar by joining the given files or files in the given directories.

```
tar -cvZf a.tZ  directoryname(s)orfilename(s)
```

This command creates compressed tar archive.

```
tar -cvzf a.tgz  directoryname(s)orfilename(s)
```

This command creates gzipped tar archive.

```
tar -xvf a.tar
```

This command extracts all files from the archive.

```
tar -xvZf a.tZ
```

This command extracts all files from the compressed archive.

```
tar -xvzf a.tgz
```

This command extracts all files from the gzipped archive.

```
tar -xvf a.tar fileordirectoryname
```

This extracts the given file or directory from the archive.

```
tar -xvZf a.tZ fileordirectoryname
```

This extracts the given file or directory from the archive.

```
tar -xvzf a.tgz fileordirectoryname
```

This extracts the given file or directory from the archive.

3.5.2 cpio command

This is also used for backup purpose. Normally this command requires list of filenames as input and the result is archive file which appears on the standard output.

```
ls|cpio -o > archivefilename
```

The above command creates archive having all the files of current directory.

```
cpio -i <archivefilename
```

This command restores all the files from the archive file.

```
cpio -i abc <archivefilename
```

This command restored the file abc from the given archive file.

```
cpio -i "*.c" <archivefilename
```

This command restores all the files with extension c from the archive file.

We can create the archive on the tapes or other devices also.

```
find . -ctime 2 -print |cpio -ov > /dev/rmt0
```

This command creates backup file on magnetic tape rmt0 and stores all the files which are created in the recent 2 days.

3.5.3 Zip and Unzip Commands

In Windows world, pkzip and pkunzip (or Winzip) are in very wide use for archiving. Their counterparts in Unix world is zip and unzip. The archives created in Windows can be used on Unix system with these commands and vice-versa.

To Create Archive

```
zip  zipfilename    filestobezipped
```

Example

```
zip a.zip    /home/rao/progs
```

This command creates an archive file a.zip by joining all the files of directory /home/rao/progs.

To Extract files

```
unzip  a.zip
```

This commands extracts all file from a.zip file to current working directory.

```
unzip a.zip filename
```

This commands extracts file "filename" from a.zip file to current working directory.

3.5.4 File Compression

In Linux we compress files as and when required. Commands such as compress, gzip, bunzip.

```
compress filename creates filename.Z
uncompress filename.Z creates filename

gzip filename creates filename.gz
gzip -d filename.gz creates filename

bzip2 filename creates filename.bz2
bunzip filename.bz2 creates filename
```

3.5.4 mount and umount commands

Unix operating system supports mount and umount commands to mount devices such as HD's, FD's and CD's as and when required and do the operations. In order to carry out these operations, user should have super user privileges. When we mount a device then the directory tree available on that device becomes integral part of Unix directory tree such that whatever operations we can do on any Unix files or directories can be carried out on this mounted files and directories also. It is necessary that the device has to be mounted under an empty directory. More over, only some types of file systems a Unix kernel allow to mount under a directory. Please check the configuration files of your current kernel capabilities (check /etc/filesystems in the case of Redhat Linux).

For example if we assume that on /dev/hda1 partition Windows 95 is installed and we want the same to be available under directory /mnt (usually /mnt is empty directory), then execute the following command as a super user.

```
mount -t msdos /dev/hda1 /mnt
```

Check for command.com file to check whether partition is mounted or not.

To umount the partition

```
umount /mnt
```

Now check for command.com flle!.

Once a device is mounted, all the Unix commands such as cp, mv, rm can be executed on the files in it.

Please check for some messages such as "/dev/hda5 as mounted as /". Some of the partitions are mounted during the mount time. Check files such as: /etc/fstab, /etc/mtab or /etc/vsftab.

3.6 Conclusions

This chapter discusses about variety of commands for processing files such as awk, grep, cut, paste, diff, sed, etc.,. Also Unix permissions is explained in detail. Software patching is also explained with lucid examples. In addition, backup commands such as tar, cpio are explained in a lucid manner along with compression utilities.

4 Processes in Linux

4.1 Introduction

The boot process in Linux (in most of Unix variants) has two stages: the bootloader stage and the kernel stage. In the following pages we describe booting process in general in Unix and Linux specifically.

The main components of the bootloader stage are the hardware stage, the firmware stage, the first-level bootloader, and the second-level bootloader. The booting process begins when the hardware is powered on. after some initialization (power of self test, POST), control goes to the firmware. Firmware, also referred to as "BIOS" on some architectures, detects the various devices on the system, including memory controllers, storage devices, bus bridges, and other hardware. The firmware, based on the settings, hands over control to a minimal bootloader known as the master boot record, which could be on a disk drive, on a removable media, or over the network. The bootloader may be available in the boot block of bootable partition also. In BIOS setting, in what sequence drives are required to be checked for this bootloader is specified. On those systems in which multiple operating systems are installed, this bootloaders (such as LILO, GRUB, Windows NT loader, OS/2 Loader) will be displaying a menu from which user can select which OS they want to load now. Normal usage is that if only one OS is installed on the system bootstrap program is said to be available in the MBR or boot block. Otherwise they are said to be having bootloader. For example, if we install only DOS on a disk it contains 446 bytes long bootstrap program is seen in the boot block. Where as if Linux is installed, bootloader such as LILO or GRUB is available in boot area of the bootable partition [Chris Drake]. The actual job of transferring control to the operating system is performed by the second-stage bootloader (commonly referred to as simply the "boot loader"). This bootloader allows the user to choose the kernel to be loaded, loads the kernel and related parameters onto memory, initializes the kernel, sets up the necessary environment, and finally "runs" the kernel [G. Nutt].

The next stage of booting is the kernel stage, when the kernel takes control. It sets up the necessary data structures, probes the devices present on the system, loads the necessary device drivers, and initializes the devices.

The kernel will begin initializing itself and the hardware devices for which support is compiled in. The process will typically include the following steps.

- Detect the CPU and its speed, and calibrate the delay loop
- Initialize the display hardware
- Probe the PCI bus and build a table of attached peripherals and the resources they have been assigned
- Initialize the virtual memory management system, including the swapper kswapd
- Initialize all compiled-in peripheral drivers; these typically include drivers for IDE hard disks, serial ports, real-time clock, non-volatile RAM, and AGP bus. Other drivers may be compiled in, but it is increasingly common to compile as stand-alone modules those drivers that are not required during this stage of the boot process. Note that drivers must be compiled in if they are needed to support the mounting of the root filesystem. If the root filesystem is an NFS share, for example, then drivers must be compiled in for NFS, TCP/IP, and low-level networking hardware.

- The kernel can then run the first true process (called /sbin/init. Depending on your vendor and system, the *init* utility is located in either /etc or /sbin.) to the root filesystem (strictly speaking, kswapd and its associates are not processes, they are kernel threads)., although the choice can be overridden by supplying the boot= parameter to the kernel at boot time. The init process runs with uid zero (i.e., as root) and will be the parent of all other processes. Note that kswapd and the other kernel threads have process IDs but, even though they start before init, init still has process ID 1. This is to maintain the Unix convention that init is the first process.
- This init process uses the configuration file /etc/inittab information and creates terminal handling activity (process) and checks the integrity of file systems, mounts file systems, sets up swap partitions (or swap files), starts system services..

Content of /etc/inittab:

```
#
# inittab   This file describes how the INIT process should set up
#           the system in a certain run-level.
#
# Author:   Miquel van Smoorenburg,
#           Modified for RHS Linux by Marc Ewing and Donnie Barnes
#

# Default runlevel. The runlevels used by RHS are:
#   0 - halt (Do NOT set initdefault to this)
#   1 - Single user mode
#   2 - Multiuser, without NFS (The same as 3, if you do not have networking)
#   3 - Full Multiuser mode
#   4 - unused
#   5 - X11
#   6 - reboot (Do NOT set initdefault to this)
#
id:5:initdefault:

# System initialization.
si::sysinit:/etc/rc.d/rc.sysinit

l0:0:wait:/etc/rc.d/rc 0
l1:1:wait:/etc/rc.d/rc 1
l2:2:wait:/etc/rc.d/rc 2
l3:3:wait:/etc/rc.d/rc 3
l4:4:wait:/etc/rc.d/rc 4
l5:5:wait:/etc/rc.d/rc 5
l6:6:wait:/etc/rc.d/rc 6
```

```
# Things to run in every runlevel.
ud::once:/sbin/update

# Trap CTRL-ALT-DELETE
ca::ctrlaltdel:/sbin/shutdown -t3 -r now

# When our UPS tells us power has failed, assume we have a few minutes
# of power left.  Schedule a shutdown for 2 minutes from now.
# This does, of course, assume you have powered installed and your
# UPS connected and working correctly.
pf::powerfail:/sbin/shutdown -f -h +2 "Power Failure; System Shutting Down"

# If power was restored before the shutdown kicked in, cancel it.
pr:12345:powerokwait:/sbin/shutdown -c "Power Restored; Shutdown Cancelled"

# Run gettys in standard runlevels
1:2345:respawn:/sbin/mingetty tty1
2:2345:respawn:/sbin/mingetty tty2
3:2345:respawn:/sbin/mingetty tty3
4:2345:respawn:/sbin/mingetty tty4
5:2345:respawn:/sbin/mingetty tty5
6:2345:respawn:/sbin/mingetty tty6

# Run xdm in runlevel 5
# xdm is now a separate service
x:5:respawn:/etc/X11/prefdm -nodaemon
```

The above file contains records with specific structure. Here is an explanation of the them.

- The first field us just a descriptor or identifier and should kept as unique.
- The 2nd field is which runlevel(s) does this entry apply to.

A runlevel is a state for the system. Usually, you have runlevels 0,1,2,3,4,5,6 and additional levels are also supported in other systems.

For example, runlevel 1 (or S) usually means a single shell running, as few processes as possible, maybe no login, maybe just asking for root's password. While runlevel 5 may mean 6 logins in text mode, a graphical login, and a web server running. The system starts, when init loads in an undefined state (sometimes called N), and then will switch to one runlevel or another depending on what the runlevel argument to the bootloader to the kernel was, and the contents of /etc/inittab.

- The 3rd field seems to be some specific keyword that /sbin/init understands such as wait, respawn, once, etc given as:
    - boot — The process is started only on bootup and is not restarted if it dies. init doesn't wait for it to complete running before continuing to the next command and can run many processes simultaneously. This action is rarely used.
    - bootwait — The process is started only on bootup, and init waits for it to finish running and die before continuing. It doesn't restart the process once it finishes or dies. Notice that line 2 of the listing employs bootwait with a utility to mount and check file systems.
    - off — If the process is currently running, a warning signal is sent and after 20 seconds, the process is killed by the dreaded kill -9 command. Line 16 shows that when the run level is changed to 2 (multiple user), terminal 1 is killed. The user who was logged on is now logged off and must log on again — adding a level of security that keeps the root user from changing run levels and then walking away from the terminal, thereby giving access to anyone who happens to sit there.
    - once — When the specified run level comes, the process is started. init doesn't wait for its termination before continuing and doesn't restart it if it dies. Like boot, once isn't used very often.
    - ondemand — This action has same meaning as respawn but is used mostly with a, b, and c levels (user defined). See respawn, below, for more information.
    - powerfail — The action takes place only when a power failure is at hand. A signal 19 is the most common indication of a power failure. Usually, the only action called by a powerfail is a sync operation.
    - powerwait — When a power failure occurs, this process is run and init waits until the processing finishes before processing any more commands. Again, sync operations are usually the only reason for the action.
    - respawn — This action restarts the process if it dies after it has been started. init doesn't wait for it to finish before continuing to other commands. Notice in lines 8–15 that respawn is the action associated with the terminals. Once they are killed, you want them to respawn and allow another login.
    - syncinit — Not available on all systems, this action tells init to reset the default sync interval, which is the interval, in seconds, between times the modified memory disk buffers are written to the physical disk. The default time is 300 seconds, but it can be set to anything between 15 and 900.
    - sysinit — Before init tries to access the console, it must run this entry. This action is usually reserved for devices that must be initialized before run levels are ascertained. Line 1 shows that the TCB — used for user login and authentication — is initialized even before the console is made active, allowing any user to log on.
    - wait — This action starts the process at the specified run level and waits until it completes before moving on. It is associated with scripts that perform run-level changes. You want them to fully complete operation before anything else happens. Notice that lines 4–7 use this action for every run level change.
- The 4th field the program/script that is to be called along with any parameters.

Some the items in /etc/inittab are given and explained their use in the following paragraphs.

si::sysinit:/etc/rc.d/rc.sysinit

This line calls /etc/rc.d/rc.sysinit.

Also note that any "wait" lines will wait until the system has booted before they start.

This rc.sysinit loads hostname, starts system logs, loads keyboard keymap, mounts swap partitions, initializes usb ports, checks file system, and mount the filesystems read/write.

After /sbin/init finishes with /etc/rc.d/rc.sysinit (which was specified by the "sysinit" line), it then switches to the default runlevel (which is defined by the "initdefault" line in /etc/inittab).

Changing runlevels should leave any processes running that are in both the old and new runlevels.

Scripts prefixed with S will be started when the runlevel is entered, eg */etc/rc5.d/S99xdm*

- Scripts prefixed with K will be killed when the runlevel is entered, eg /etc/rc6.d/K20apache
- X11 login screen is typically started by one of S99xdm, S99kdm, or S99gdm.

1:2345:respawn:/sbin/getty 9600 tty1

- Always running in runlevels 2, 3, 4, or 5
- Displays login on console (tty1)

2:234:respawn:/sbin/getty 9600 tty2

- Always running in runlevels 2, 3, or 4
- Displays login on console (tty2)

l3:3:wait:/etc/init.d/rc 3

- Run once when switching to runlevel 3.
- Uses scripts stored in /etc/rc3.d/

ca:12345:ctrlaltdel:/sbin/shutdown -t1 -a -r now

- Run when *control-alt-delete* is pressed

Usually on those terminals which are defined in /etc/inittab, *getty* prompts for the user's login name. Then, *login* prompts the user to type his/her password by printing a prompt. If the user enters the password (which does not appear on the screen) and the password is incorrect, the system responds with a generic message. In reality, The *login* command accepts the password typed by the user and encrypts it using the same mechanism the *passwd* command uses to put the password in the /etc/passwd file. If the encrypted values match, the password is correct. Otherwise, the password the user types is incorrect. The *login* command can't decrypt the password once it has been encrypted. When the password is typed properly, the login process enters the next phase. The next phase of the process starts after the user has typed the correct password for the login. This phase establishes the environmental parameters for the user. For example, the user's login shell is started, and the user is placed in the home directory. The *init* command starts the user's login shell as specified in the /etc/passwd file. The user's initial environment is configured, and the shell starts executing. Once the shell is started, the user executes commands as desired. When the user logs off, the shell exits, *init* starts up *getty* again, and the process loops around.

To know What Is Running and How Do We Change It?

The *-r* parameter of the *who* command shows the run level at which your machine is currently operating as well as the two most recent previous run levels. For example,

```
who -r
run level 2 May 4 10:07 2   1   0
```

The above command shows that the current run level is 2 and has been since May 4 at 10:07. On some systems, the three numbers to the right show the current run level, the previous run level, and the next previous run level. On other systems, the three numbers represent the process termination status, process ID, and process exit status.

Changing run levels requires root permission and can be done with either the *init* or the *shutdown* command.

During system reboot, the bootloader stage is preceded by a shutdown of the previously running system. This involves terminating running processes, writing back cache buffers to disk, unmounting file systems, and performing a hardware reset.

The *shutdown* command, on the other hand, is usually in /usr/sbin. The *init* command is very simple. It lets you specify a number behind it and the machine then changes to that run level. For example

```
init 3
```

immediately begins changing the machine to run level 3.

The *shutdown* command interacts with *init* and offers more parameters and options. A *-g* option lets you specify a grace period of seconds to elapse before beginning the operation (the default is 60), *-i* signifies which run level you want to go to, and *-y* carries out the action without asking for additional confirmation. Thus, to change to run level 3 in 15 seconds, the command would be

```
shutdown -g15 -i3 -y
```

Once the command is typed, a warning message is broadcast telling users that the run level is changing (this is true with *init* as well). The system then waits the specified number of seconds — giving users the chance to save files and log off — before making the change. Contrast this with *init* command, which tells users that the run level is changing and immediately begins changing it without giving them time to prepare.

```
init 6
```

This command also make the system to shutdown properly.

4.2 Users Processes

As mentioned earlier, PID of the init process is 1. This process starts terminal handling processes (such as getty, mingetty, agetty, uugetty) on each of the lines mentioned in the /etc/inittab file. Thus, these processes becomes child processes to init process. In Unix system, child processes PID will be larger than parent. When a user log's in with legal user name and password, getty process will die in place of it shell will become active. Thus, on some terminals on which user is logged in shell processes will be running where as on other terminals getty process will be running. We can check by running the commands "ps –al" or "ps –Al".

The command "ps" displays details of the processes running on the current terminal and which belongs to the user.

```
PID TTY      TIME CMD
1175 tty1    00:00:00 bash
1283 tty1    00:00:00 ps
```

The command "ps -Al" displays details of all the processes running on the system. For brevity reasons, only few lines of the output only displayed here.

```
F S  UID  PID   PPID  C PRI NI ADDR SZ WCHAN  TTY    TIME     CMD
4 S  0    1     0     1 75  0  -    343  schedu  ?    00:00:04 init
4 S  0    1103  1     0 82  0  -    336  schedu  tty3 00:00:00 mingetty
4 S  0    1104  1     0 82  0  -    336  schedu  tty4 00:00:00 mingetty
4 S  0    1105  1     0 82  0  -    337  schedu  tty5 00:00:00 mingetty
4 S  0    1106  1     0 82  0  -    337  schedu  tty6 00:00:00 mingetty
4 S  0    1175  1101  0 76  0  -    1091 wait4   tty1 00:00:00 bash
4 S  0    1229  1102  1 85  0  -    1089 schedu  tty2 00:00:00 bash
4 R  0    1284  1175  0 81  0  -    791  -       tty1 00:00:00 ps
```

We can observe from the above output that on terminals tty1 and tty2, we have logged in. Thus, Shell (bash) is running. Where as on other terminals, mingetty is running. Also, please note that the command ps is also became as a process while gathering information about the processes. Also, note that bash is in sleeping state while "ps" is running. Also, note that PPID's of mingetty and bash are same. That is both of them are child processes of init process. When we login with valid user name and password mingetty will die and in place bash (shell) becomes active and is also child to init process whose PID is 1.

When we run any piping command, each command will be made as a process.

Run the following command.

```
ps -Al|more|tail -4|tee aa

4 S  0 1229 1102 0 85 0 - 1089 schedu tty2  00:00:00 bash
4 R  0 1326 1175 0 80 0 - 792 -       tty1  00:00:00 ps
0 S  0 1327 1175 0 76 0 - 926 pipe_w  tty1  00:00:00 more
0 S  0 1328 1175 0 76 0 - 926 pipe_w  tty1  00:00:00 tail
0 S  0 1329 1175 0 76 0 - 852 pipe_w  tty1  00:00:00 tee
```

The programs written by the users also becomes as processes when we start them. When a user enters a command at the dollar prompt it will be first received by the shell then it parses the command and identifies from where input has to be taken and to where output has to be sent. Then it calls a system call known as fork() which in turn returns PID of a new process which resembles the shell. Now shell assigns the duty to this new process to run the command typed by the user and goes to sleeping state while the new child process starts continuing the assigned duty. When it completes or encounters an error it indicates the same to the parent (shell) and then dies. Thus, in Unix systems processes will be getting created and completing the assigned duties.

For example, compile and run the following program "aa.c".

```
#include<stdio.h>
int main()
{
/* This program is an infinite loop program doing nothing. */

while(1);
}
```

To Compile

```
gcc -o aa aa.c
```

To Run

```
Aa  or  ./aa
```

As the above program is infinite loop program we will not see dollar prompt. By pressing* ALT + F2 or other function keys F3, F4, F5 or F6 we can get another terminal. Login into it and run the "ps -Al" command. We find the following line.

```
0 R    0 1371  1175 96  85   0    -   335 -     tty1     00:00:57 aa
```

The line shows that process "aa" is running on terminal tty1 since 57 seconds.

With the help of kill command we can kill any process. Of course, only legal owner of the process can kill his process, exception for super user.

For example, you can run from another terminal the following command to kill the process "aa". After executing command, press ALT + F1 to goto tty1 and their you will find the message "Killed".

```
kill -9 1371
```

In the above command, the number 9 is known as a signal number. Usually, when we press some key sequences such as ctrl +c or ctrl +d etc., some special SW signals are sent to the current process. They are called as SW interrupts. Please do not confuse with events of current days programming languages such as Java, etc.,. These SW interrupts or signals are like processor interrupts (which arrives from peripherals and which runs their service routines), and these signal's arrivals also makes processes to run some programs known as signal handlers. For example, when we press ctrl + c, the process terminates. In Unix

*We assume you are working character mode.

terminology, this ctrl + c is also called as SIGINT. Similarly, there are many signals available in Unix system and each signal has its default behavior. If one wants, we can make to run some other program when a signal arrives to a process and this is known as signal handling. We can make some signals to be ignored by a process. However, not all the signals to be made ignored by a process. One such a signal is signal number 9 or SIGQUIT which is called as uninterruptible signal. That is, it will be delivered to the process at any cost and the default action is going to take place. This signal's default action is to kill the process. Thus, when we run the above command, process "aa" which is an infinite loop program will be terminated.

We can logout by killing the bash (shell) process. For example,

```
kill -9 1229
```

4.2.1 Background and Foreground Processes

Unix supports background processes. To run any command in background, simply we have to append & while running the command. It displays terminal name and PID of the background process in responses.

For example execute :

```
ls &
aa &
```

We can checkup that the process "aa" is running by typing "ps -Al" command.

A process is said to be in background process, if its parent shell can accept another command to the user. That is its parent shell is Running state. Where as a process is said to be in foreground process if its parent shell is in sleeping state. That is it can not take any more commands from the user.

If we happened to have a dumb terminal (normally used in old Unix flavors) and you can have only one terminal we have in it then it is not possible to enjoy the benefit of multi tasking as shell can normally take one command at a time. Thus, by using background concept, we can start a program and put it in the background such that the shell can take another command from the user.

However, if we can not make a program which requires interactive input to be in background; we may get error message such as "stopped tty output".

Try at the command prompt the following command.

```
vi filename&
```

For a background process, key board (standard input) is not logically connected thus the programs which requires interactive input can be kept in the background. If we want them to be run in background, then we have to create a data file which contains the required data for this program and then start this program while specifying it is supposed to take necessary data from the data file. For example in the following manner.

```
program <datfile &
```

Also, output of a background process appears on to the same terminal to which it is invoked. It may be possible that this output may mingle with current foreground process on that terminal and may make the screen messy. In order to take care of this situation, the background process can started such that its output is sent to a file rather than to terminal such as:

```
program >output &
```

For example, consider the following program whose executable file name as "bb".

```
#include<stdio.h>
int main()
{
while(1) printf("1"); }
```

This program continuously prints 1's. To know the effect of the output of a background process, execute the following commands at command prompt one after another.

```
sleep 10
bb &
vi filename
```

We may find, even if we don't type anything, 1's will be coming on to the vi editor screen. We may find difficult to type anything into the file. Of course, when we save finally these 1's will not be saved into the file. However, vi editor working becomes clumsy because of this background process. Thus it is better to redirect output of a background process.

In total, if we want a process which requires to be kept in background and needs interactive input and gives standard output then the same can be started in the following manner.

```
program <inputfile >outputfile &
```

For example, consider the following C program which takes three integers and writes their values.

```
#include<stdio.h>
void main()
{
int x,y,z;
scanf("%d%d%d", &x, &y, &z);
printf("%d\n%d\n%d\n", x, y, z);
}
```

Let the file name be a.c and by using the either of the following commands, its machine language file a is created.

```
gcc -o a a.c
cc -o a a.c
```

When we start this program **a** by simply typing a at the dollar prompt, it takes 3 values and displays given values on the screen.

```
a>res &
```

We should get an error.

```
cat>res
10
20
11
^d
```

This program takes three values interactively and writes the same into file res. You can check by typing cat res.

```
a<res &
```

This should give results on the screen.

```
a <res >as &
```

This command takes necessary input from the file res and displays the results in the file "as".

If we want a piping command to be kept in background, then for each component of the piping sequence we have to append &.

```
command1&|command2&|command&
```

A background process gets killed if its parent (shell) dies. That if we logout. However, if we start a background process prepended with nohup it is continue to run even if logout.

For example

```
nohup  command &
```

Similarly, if we want a piping command we want run in background and continue to run even after we log out then we have start the same in the following manner.

```
nohup command1&| nohup command2&| nohup command&
```

4.2.2 at command

Unix also supports a facility known as at with the help of which we can instruct the Unix to start a program at a specified time on a specified date. It needs a file having the commands to be executed on that date and time.

For example, the file "xxx" contains the following statements.

```
aa>pp
lpr pp
rm pp
```

To run the above commands on Nov 30 at 4pm the following command can be used.

```
at -f xxx 4pm Nov 30
```

To see what jobs are submitted to at command we can execute command "atq".

With the help of "atrm" command we can remove a submitted job from at commands queue.

4.2.3 time command

Sometimes, we may need to know how much time a program is taking. This can be known with the help of "time" command.

Example

```
time ls
```

This command displays three times to name, user time, system time and elapsed time.

- User time is the actual CPU time consumed by the users program.
- System time is the CPU time consumed by the OS on behalf of the users program while administering the system such as allocating memory, resources, CPU etc.
- Elapsed time is the time elapsed between the instant of starting a program and till we seen dollar prompt again.

User time is most important one. When we want to compare two programs we may use their user times only.

A Note on Identification Numbers Used in Linux Systems

Process UID and GID

In order for the operating system to know what a process is allowed to do it must store information about who owns the process (UID and GID). The UNIX operating system stores two types of UID and two types of GID.

Real UID and GID

A process' real UID and GID will be the same as the UID and GID of the user who ran the process. Therefore any process you execute will have your UID and GID.

The real UID and GID are used for accounting purposes.

Effective UID and GID

The effective UID and GID are used to determine what operations a process can perform. In most cases the effective UID and GID will be the same as the real UID and GID.

However using special file permissions it is possible to change the effective UID and GID. How and why you would want to do this is examined later in this chapter.

4.3 Terminal Handling

Since its development, Unix systems are equipped with terminals which may be connected to machine via serial lines such as RS232. These terminals may use different control sequences while communicating with Unix system via serial line driver. This serial driver which may perform some low-level conversions (handling ^c, ^d characters for flow control and translating DEL and ERASE characters) on what we type from the terminal before it is passed to the program which we are running. As there is no standard among the plethora of terminals, a large part of satisfactory terminal emulation is carried out at the host operating system.

Both "termcap" and "terminfo" contain some features for allowing programs to know what Escape sequences to expect from a terminal type, although not every Unix program uses these features. For example /etc/termcap contains specifications about various terminals which users can use to log into the system. This information is used by terminal-emulation programs to adjust what the individual keys transmit.

The "term" and/or "TERM" environment variables are typically used to tell the system which records to look up in terminfo or termcap. The man page for your user shell should describe how these may be set.

You should be able to do at least

```
echo $TERM
```

to see the current setting.

To find out the serial-port/pseudo-terminal parameters, the "stty -a" command can be used, e.g.,

```
stty -a
speed 38400 baud;
rows = 25; columns = 80; ypixels = 0; xpixels = 0;
eucw 1:0:0:0, scrw 1:0:0:0
intr = ^c; quit = ^|; erase = ^?; kill = ^u;
eof = ^d; eol = <undef>; eol2 = <undef>; swtch = <undef>;
start = ^q; stop = ^s; susp = ^z; dsusp = ^y;
rprnt = ^r; flush = ^o; werase = ^w; lnext = ^v;
-parenb -parodd cs8 -cstopb -hupcl cread -clocal -loblk
-crtscts -crtsxoff -parext
-ignbrk brkint ignpar -parmrk -inpck -istrip -inlcr -igncr icrnl -iuclc
ixon -ixany -ixoff imaxbel
isig icanon -xcase echo echoe echok -echonl -noflsh
-tostop echoctl -echoprt echoke -defecho -flusho -pendin iexten
opost -olcuc onlcr -ocrnl -onocr -onlret -ofill -ofdel tab3
```

We can also use either of the following commands to know the terminal information.

```
stty
stty -everything
```

In the above commands output last line contains - before some words are see indicating the respective terminal characters are set. Where as others are not set.

If we wanted to change terminal behaviors we can use command stty. For example, the best way to set the number of rows and columns displayed is by using the "stty" command:

```
stty rows 24 cols 80
```

Also we can change "termcap" entry for a given terminal to achieve the same effect.

```
stty -echo
```

Now whatever we type at dollar prompt will not appear on the screen. If we enter the following command then terminal characteristics will return to previous style.

```
stty echo
```

For example try the following also.

```
stty -echo; cat >destfile; stty echo
```

Now you can type whatever you want and press at the end ^d as usual. The destfile contains what we have typed.

Try the following and identify what happens.

```
stty -echo; cat >destfile
```

Also, If we execute reset command (or stty sane) at the dollar prompt then terminal behavior returns to previous style.

Run the following command sequences to know the effect of cbreak mode.

```
tty cbreak
cat
<type whatever you wanted>
^d
```

We may find when we enter enter key afresh line will be appearing.

For example when we execute the following command at the dollar prompt then end of file (eof) become ^a.

```
stty eof  \^a
```

To see the effect try to create a file using cat command. By pressing ctrl + a we are able to stop giving input to cat command.

```
cat >filename
Adsdasds
Asdkjdsa
Asdkjds
Adsds
^a
```

Similarly, we can make ctrl + b as ctrl + c, we can run the following command.

```
stty intr \^b
```

4.3.1 Reading Verrrry Long Lines from the Terminal

Sometimes, you want a very long line of input to write a file. It might come from your personal computer, a device hooked to your terminal, or just an especially long set of characters that you have to type on the keyboard. Normally the UNIX terminal driver holds all characters you type until it sees a line terminator or interrupt character. Most buffers have room for 256 characters.

If you're typing the characters at the keyboard, there's an easy fix: Hit CTRL-d every 200 characters or so to flush the input buffer. You won't be able to backspace before that point, but the shell will read everything in.

Or, to make UNIX pass each character it reads without buffering, use stty to set your terminal to cbreak (or non-canonical) input mode.

For example :

% **stty cbreak**

% **cat > file**

enter the very long line.........

[CTRL-c]

% **stty -cbreak**

Run the following command sequences to know the effect of raw mode. You may find cat command not responding to ^d and ^c signals also!!

```
stty cbreak
cat
<type whatever you wanted>
^d
```

While you're in cbreak mode, special keys like BACKSPACE or DELETE won't be processed; they'll be stored in the file. Typing CTRL-d will not make cat quit. To quit, kill cat by pressing your normal interrupt key - say, CTRL-c.

4.4 Conclusions

This chapter explains about processes in Linux. How to make a processes as background and foreground is explained. How to kill a processes is explained giving emphasis to Linux signals. At the end commands such as at, and time are explained. A brief outline of terminal handling in Linux/Unix is also included.

5 Shell Programming

5. 1 Introduction

Why Shell Programming? A working knowledge of shell scripting is essential to everyone wishing to become reasonably adept at system administration, even if they do not anticipate ever having to actually write a script. Consider that as a Linux machine boots up, init process is initiated first then it executes the shell scripts in /etc/rc.d to restore the system configuration and set up services. A detailed understanding of these startup scripts is important for analyzing the behavior of a system, and possibly modifying it [Kernigham].

Writing shell scripts is not hard to learn, since the scripts can be built in bite-sized sections and there is only a fairly small set of shell-specific operators and options to learn. The syntax is simple and straightforward, similar to that of invoking and chaining together utilities at the command line, and there are only a few "rules" to learn. Most short scripts work right the first time, and debugging even the longer ones is straightforward. A shell script is a "quick and dirty" method of prototyping a complex application. Getting even a limited subset of the functionality to work in a shell script, even if slowly, is often a useful first stage in project development. This way, the structure of the application can be tested and played with, and the major pitfalls found before proceeding to the final coding in C, C++, Java, or Perl. Shell scripting hearkens back to the classical UNIX philosophy of breaking complex projects into simpler subtasks, of chaining together components and utilities. Many consider this a better, or at least more esthetically pleasing approach to problem solving than using one of the new generation of high powered all-in-one languages, such as Perl, which attempt to be all things to all people, but at the cost of forcing you to alter your thinking processes to fit the tool.

When we want to execute some set of commands one after another without users physical intervention and presence (batch operations), shell scripts are very handy.

Moreover, for small scale database applications where precision, speed and security is little botheration, shell scripts are very preferable and SW project cost may tremendously reduces.

Shell scripts are very much employed in developing automatic SW installation scripts and for fine tuning the SW's installed.

When not to use shell scripts

- resource-intensive tasks, especially where speed is a factor (sorting, hashing, etc.)
- procedures involving heavy-duty math operations, especially floating point arithmetic, arbitrary precision calculations, or complex numbers (use C++ or FORTRAN instead)
- cross-platform portability required (use C instead)
- complex applications, where structured programming is a necessity (need type checking of variables, function prototypes, etc.)
- mission-critical applications upon which you are betting the ranch, or the future of the company
- situations where security is important, where you need to guarantee the integrity of your system and protect against intrusion, cracking, and vandalism
- project consists of subcomponents with interlocking dependencies
- extensive file operations required (Bash is limited to serial file access, and that only in a particularly clumsy and inefficient line-by-line fashion)

- need multi-dimensional arrays
- need data structures, such as linked lists or trees
- need to generate or manipulate graphics or GUIs
- need direct access to system hardware
- need port or socket I/O
- need to use libraries or interface with legacy code
- proprietary, closed-source applications (shell scripts are necessarily Open Source)

If any of the above applies, consider a more powerful scripting language, perhaps Perl, Tcl, Python, or possibly a high-level compiled language such as C, C++, or Java. Even then, prototyping the application as a shell script might still be a useful development step.

Shell programs also called as shell scripts. In the simplest case, a script is nothing more than a list of system commands stored in a file. If we want to execute a set of commands many times repeatedly, we can write the same in a file and execute which saves the effort of retyping that particular sequence of commands each time they are needed.

5.1.1 Invoking the script

Having written the script, you can invoke it by sh scriptname, or alternately bash scriptname. (Not recommended is using sh < scriptname as this effectively disables reading from stdin within the script.)

Much more convenient is to make the script itself directly executable with chmod.

Either

chmod 555 scriptname (gives everyone read/execute permission)

or

chmod +rx scriptname (gives everyone read/execute permission)

chmod u+rx scriptname (gives only the script owner read/execute permission)

Having made the script executable, you may now test it by ./scriptname.

As a final step, after testing and debugging, you would likely want to move it to /usr/local/bin (as root, of course), to make the script available to yourself and all other users as a system-wide executable. The script could then be invoked by simply typing scriptname from the command line.

It is shell programming practice in which line starting with #! at the head of a script tells your system that this file is a set of commands to be fed to the command interpreter indicated. The #! is actually a two-byte "magic number", a special marker that designates a file type, or in this case an executable shell script . Immediately following the #! is a path name. This is the path to the program that interprets the commands in the script, whether it be a shell, a programming language, or a utility. This command interpreter then executes the commands in the script, starting at the top (line 1 of the script), ignoring comments.

```
#!/bin/sh
#!/bin/bash
#!/usr/bin/perl
#!/usr/bin/tcl
#!/bin/sed -f
#!/usr/awk -f
```

Each of the above script header lines calls a different command interpreter, be it /bin/sh, the default shell (bash in a Linux system) or otherwise. Using #!/bin/sh, the default Bourne Shell in most commercial variants of UNIX, makes the script portable to non-Linux machines, though you may have to sacrifice a few Bash-specific features (the script will conform to the POSIX sh standard).

#! can be omitted if the script consists only of a set of generic system commands, using no internal shell directives.

Variables are at the heart of every programming and scripting language. They appear in arithmetic operations and manipulation of quantities, string parsing, and are indispensable for working in the abstract with symbols - tokens that represent something else. A variable is nothing more than a location or set of locations in computer memory holding an item of data.

Unlike many other programming languages, Bash does not segregate its variables by "type". Essentially, Bash variables are character strings, but, depending on context, Bash permits integer operations and comparisons on variables. The determining factor is whether the value of a variable contains only digits

Shell programming supports prominently the following type of variables:

- Shell Variables
- Environment Variables
- Positional Variables

5.1.2 Shell Variables

X=Hello (no spaces before and after =)

The above statement at the bash prompt defines a shell variable X and assigns a value for it. Anywhere, $X indicates the value of the variable X.

Very often shell variables are used to reduce typing burden. For example, in the following examples after defining shell variable DIR the same can be used where ever we need to type /usr/lib.

```
DIR=/usr/lib

ls $DIR            displays listing of /usr/lib directory

cd $DIR            moves to /usr/lib directory

ls $DIR/libm*.so   displays all files /usr/lib which satisfies libm*.so  model
```

5.1.3 Environment Variables

Variables that affect the behavior of the shell and user interface Note In a more general context, each process has an "environment", that is, a group of variables that hold information that the process may reference. In this sense, the shell behaves like any other process. Every time a shell starts, it creates shell variables that correspond to its own environmental variables. Updating or adding new shell variables causes the shell to update its environment, and all the shell's child processes (the commands it executes) inherit this environment. *Caution:* The space allotted to the environment is limited. Creating too many environmental variables or ones that use up excessive space may cause problems.

If we execute "env" command at the dollar prompt we may find the details of all the environment variables defined in our current shell. The output may look like

```
PATH=/bin:/sbin:/usr/local/bin
MANPATH=/usr/man:/usr/man/man1:/usr/man/man2
IFS=
TERM=VT100
HOST=darkstar
USER=guest
HOME=/usr/guest
MAIL=/var/spool/mail/guest
MAILCHECK=300
```

Environment variables are used by shell and other application programs. For example, the value of MAILCHECK, i.e. 300 indicates that the mailer has to check for every 300 seconds for new arrivals and intimate the same to the user. A dynamic business user can set this variable value to a low value such that the mailer informs the user within the specified time period about new mails arrival.

Similarly, PATH environment variable is used by shell in locating the executable file of the commands typed by the user. System will check for the executable files in the directories of the PATH variable and if found it will be loaded and executed. Otherwise, we may get error "bad command or file not found".

Let the following C language file named "a.c":

```
#include<stdio.h>
main()
{
printf("Hello\n");
}
```

To compile:

```
gcc -o aa  a.c
```

The file a.c is the C language source file and "aa" will become executable file.

Very often (if PATH is set properly) by simply typing "aa" at the $ prompt we can run the above program. If in the value of PATH variable dot (".") is not available then we may get error "bad command or file not found" as the system is not in position to identify the file "aa". By typing ./aa we can run program (this problem is very much seen Redhat Linux distributions).

Similarly, if we created executable file name as "test" (normally, new users behavior) then if we type "test" at the dollar prompt the above program may not run. This is because, there exists a UNIX command "test". Thus when you try to start "test" command instead of running our developed program, Unix command test runs. This may be also attributed to PATH problem only. When we type test, the system will check first say program "test" in/bin or /usr/bin then system and the same is executed. Thus, never our can run. Thus, we can add . (dot) to PATH in the following manner such that the above problem is not seen.

```
PATH=.:$PATH
```

If a script sets environmental variables, they need to be "exported", that is, reported to the environment local to the script. This is the function of the export command.

Main difference between shell variables and environment variables is that the latter are inheritable to sub-shells. Environment variables defined in a shell or modified in a shell are visible in its sub-shells only. That is, parent shells do not see the environment variables defined in its sub-shell or the modifications done to environment variables in the sub-shells. Please note that when you see $ prompt, you are in bash shell.

```
X=Hello
Y=How
echo $PATH      // displays value of PATH environment variable
echo $X         // displays value of X shell variable
echo $Y         // displays value of X shell variable
export Y        // makes Y as environment variable

bash            // a sub-shell bash is created run ps -Al in other terminal to see
echo $PATH    // displays value of PATH environment variable which is same as above
echo $X         // displays nothing as X shell variable is not inherited
echo $Y         // displays how as Y is environment variable
Z=Raj
export Z
echo $Z         // displays Z variable value

csh            // another sub shell is initiated
echo $PATH     // displays value of PATH environment variable which is same as above
echo $X       // displays nothing as X shell variable is not inherited
echo $Y         // displays how as Y is environment variable
Z=Raj
export Z
echo $Z         // displays Z variable value
exit  or ^c           // to come out from C shell

^d                     // to come out from bash sub-shell

echo $PATH     // displays value of PATH environment variable which is same as above
echo $X        // displays  X shell variable value
echo $Y         // displays how as Y is environment variable
Z=Raj
export Z
echo $Z         // displays nothing as Z is not visible
```

Note

A script can export variables only to child processes, that is, only to commands or processes which that particular script initiates. A script invoked from the command line cannot export variables back to the command line environment. Child processes cannot export variables back to the parent processes that spawned them.

5.1.4 Positional Parameters

These parameters are arguments passed to the script from the command line - $0, $1, $2, $3... Here, $0 is the name of the script itself, $1 is the first argument, $2 the second, $3 the third, and so forth. After $9, the arguments must be enclosed in brackets, for example, ${10}, ${11}, ${12}.

Also, the following parameters can be also used in shell scripts

- $# number of command line arguments
- $* list of command line arguments
- $@ list of command line arguments
- $$ PID of the current shell
- $? Exit status of most recent command. Usually it is zero if the command is successful.
- $! PID of most recent background job

5.2 Programming Constructs

Like all programming languages, Shell also supports variety of programming constructs such as loops, if conditions, arrays, etc. In the following sections, we explain the same.

5.2.1 if-then-else-fi condition

Like high level languages Shell supports if condition. The syntax is as follows:

- ```
  if [ expr ]
  then
        statements
  fi
  ```

- ```
  if [ expr ]
  then
      statements
  else
      statements
  fi
  ```

- ```
  if [ expr ]
  then
      statements
  elif [ expr ]
  then
      statements
  elif [expr]
  then
      statements
  else
      statements
  fi
  ```
  ```

The expressions can be using the variables as described or numbers or filenames and relational operators. Any number of elif clauses can be used in third style which is commonly called as nested if statement. However, it has to terminate with an else block .

```
if [ $1 -gt $2 ]
then
    echo $1
else
    echo $2
fi
```

The above program takes two numbers along the command line and displays the maximum of them.

Similar to -gt we can also use -ge, -lt, -le, -ne, and -eq to compare numeric values of two arguments.

File testing operations

Some times, we may required to find our whether given file is having reading permissions or writing permissions, etc or we may required to check whether given name is a file or a directory etc. The following can be used if conditions expression with the argument.

-r true if the file/directory is having reading permissions
-w true if the file/directory is having writing permissions
-x true if the file/directory is having execution permissions
-f true if the given argument is file
-d true if the given argument is directory
-c true if the argument if character special file
-b true if the given argument is block special file

```
if [  -f   $1 ]
then
    echo Regular file
elif [ -d $1 ]
then
    echo Directory
elif [ -c $1 ]
then
    echo character special file
elif [ -b $1 ]
then
    echo Block special file
else
    echo others
fi
```

For the above shell script if we give /etc/passwd as argument we will get message "Regular file". If we give /etc as argument we will get message "Directory". If we give /dev/ttyS0 as argument we will get message "character special file". If we give /dev/hda1 as argument we will get message "block special file".

String comparison
= is equal to

Example :

if ["$a" = "$b"]

== is equal to

Example : if ["$a" == "$b"] This is a synonym for =.

Example : [$a == z*] # true if $a starts with an "z" (pattern matching)
Example : [$a == "z*"] # true if $a is equal to z*
Example : ["$a" == "z*"] # true if $a is equal to z*

!= is not equal to

Example :

if ["$a" != "$b"] #true if both the strings are different

This operator uses pattern matching within a [[...]] construct.

-z string is "null", that is, has zero length

Example : if [-z "$1"] #true if $1 is null

-n string is not "null".

Example : if [-n "$1"] # true if $1 is not null

- Write a shell program which takes two file names and if their contents are same then second one will be deleted.

  Ans :

```
if diff $1 $2
then
  rm $2
fi
```

- Write a shell script which says Good Morning, Good Evening, Good Afternoon depending on the present time.

```
x=`date|awk '{ print $4 }' |awk -F: '{ print $1 }'`

if [ $x -lt 3 ]
 then
  echo "Good Night"
elif [ $x -lt 12 ]
 then
  echo "Good Morning"
elif [ $x -lt 16 ]
 then
   echo "Good Evening"
elif [ $x -lt 22 ]
 then
  echo "Good Night"
fi
```

5.2.2 case construct

The following lines in file abc and is having world permissions and its name is entered in /etc/profile file. What happens?

```
case $LOGNAME in
guest) echo "It is common directory. don't disturb files”  ; ;
 root) echo "Don't be Biased"; ;
 *) echo "Don’t waste your time on internet" ; ;
esac
```

Ans :

If the username is guest first message will display at the login time, whereas root user logs in, the second message is displayed otherwise the third one is displayed.

- Explain what happen if you run this shell script?.

```
#!/bin/sh
usage="usage:
           —help   display help
         --opt    display options"
case $# in
   1)
    case “$1” in
     --help) echo "$usage"; exit 0; ;
      --opt) echo "1 for kill"; ;
            exit 0;;
             *) echo "$usage"; exit 0;-;
esac
```

Ans :

If the above shell program name is assumed as **XX,** if you enter XX at command line without arguments or with option **--help it** will display the following message.

```
--help   display help
--opt    display options
```

otherwise it will display the following message.

```
1 for kill
```

5.2.3 while loop

Like any other high level language, shell also supports loops which can be used to execute some set of instructions repeatedly, probably in given number of times.

The following styles of while loop are used to execute a group of statements eternally.

```
while :
do
---
--
done
or
while true
do
---
--
done
```

The following while loop structure is used execute a group of statements as long as the expression is true.

```
while [  expr ]
do
---
--
done
```

Here, the expr can be having relational or string comparison operations between command line arguments, environment variables, shell variables or literals both numbers or strings. As long as the expr is true the statements between do and done will be executed.

```
while  command
do
---
--
done
```

The above style of while loop execute the group of statements as long as the given command is executed successfully.

```
while test command
do
---
--
done
```

This version of while loop also behaves similar to the above while loop.

- Write a shell program which informs as soon as a specified user whose name is given along the command line is logged into the system.

```
while :
do
   if who|grep $1 >/dev/null
   then
      echo $1 is logged in
      exit
   else
      sleep 60
   fi
done
```

- Write a shell program which takes a source file name and other duplicate file names as command line arguments and creates the duplicate copies of the first file with the names given as subsequent command line arguments.

Solution 1 :

```
while [ "$2" ]
do
   cp $1 $2
   shift
done
```

Solution 2 :

```
X=$1
shift
while [ "$1" ]
do
   cp $X $1
   shift
done
```

Solution 3 :

```
X=$1
shift
while [ $# -ne 0 ]
do
    cp $X $1
    shift
done
```

- Write a shell program which takes a source file name and directories names as command line arguments and prints message yes if the file is found in any of the given directories.

Solution 1 :

```
X=$1
shift
while [ "$1" ]
do
if [  -f   $1/$X ]
             then
             echo Yes
          exit
   else
    shift
  fi
done
echo No
```

- The following program takes primary name of a C language program and it executes the same if it compiles successfully otherwise automatically it brings the vi editor to edit the C language program. This repeats till the program is corrected to have no compile time errors.

```
while true
gcc -o $1  $1.c
case "$?" in
0)echo executing
    $1
    exit ;;
*)vi $1.c ;;
esac
done
```

- Write a shell script to lock your terminal till you enter a password.

```
trap " "1 2 3
echo terminal locked
read key
pw=xxxxxx
while [ "$pw" = "xxxxxx" ]
do
echo Enter password
stty -echo
read pw
stty sane
done
```

5.2.4 until loop

```
until [ expr ]
do
---
--
done
```

Here, the expr can be having relational or string comparison operations between command line arguments, environment variables, shell variables or literals both numbers or strings. As long as the expr is false the statements between do and done will be executed.

```
until command
do
---
--
done
```

The group of statements between do and done will be executed as long the command is failure.

- Write a shell program which informs as soon as a specified user whose name is given along the command line is logged into the system.

```
until if who|grep $1 >/dev/null
do
sleep 60

done
echo $1 is logged in
```

- Write a shell program which takes a source file name and other duplicate file names as command line arguments and creates the duplicate copies of the first file with the names given as subsequent command line arguments.

Solution 1 :

```
until [ $# -eq 1 ]
do
    cp $1 $2
    shift
done
```

Solution 2 :

```
X=$1
shift
until [ $# -eq 0  ]
do
    cp $X $1
    shift
done
```

- Write a shell program which takes a source file name and directories names as command line arguments and prints message yes if the file is found in any of the given directories.

```
X=$1
shift
until [ $# -ne 0 ]
do
if [  -f   $1/$X ]
    then
            echo Yes
            exit
else
    shift
fi
done
echo No
```

- The following program takes primary name of a C language program and it executes the same if it compiles successfully otherwise automatically it brings the vi editor to edit the C language program. This repeats till the program is corrected to have no compile time errors.

```
until gcc -o $1  $1.c
vi $1.c
done
echo executing
$1
```

5.2.5 for loop

```
for var in list
   do
   ----
   ----
   done
```

- What is the **output** of

```
for x in  .
    do
    ls $x
done
```

Ans: lists all file names in P.W.D.

- What is the output of

```
for x in *
    do
       ls $x
done
```

Ans: lists all file names in P.W.D.

- What is the output of

```
for x in ..
do
  ls $x
done
```

Ans : lists all file names of parent directory of P.W.D..

- What is the output of the following program

```
IFS=#
for x in .#..
  do
      ls $x
done
```

Ans: lists file names in P.W.D and its parent directory.

- Write a shell program which takes a source file name and other duplicate file names as command line arguments and creates the duplicate copies of the first file with the names given as subsequent command line arguments.

```
X=$1
shift
for Y in $*
do
   cp $X $Y
   shift
done
```

- Write a shell program which takes a source file name and directories names as command line arguments and prints message yes if the file is found in any of the given directories else prints no.

```
X=$1
shift
for Y in $*
do
   if [  -f  $Y/$X ]
then
             echo Yes
             exit
   fi

done
echo No
```

- What does the following script does?.

```
a="$1"
shift
readonly a
for I in  $*
do
cp $a $I
shift
done
```

Ans: - makes the first command line argument as readonly. Then duplicates of the same will be created with the names $2 $3... and so on.

- What is the **output of following** shell script.

```
set `who am i`
for in i *
do
  mv $i  $i.$1
done
```

Ans: - it adds username as extension to files of **P.W.D.**

- What does the following shell script.

```
for x in `ls`
do
chmod  u=rwx  $x
done.
```

Ans: - changes permissions of files in **P.W.D** as **rwx** for users.

- What does the following shell script does.

```
for x in *.ps
do
compress $x
mv $x.ps.Z  /backup
done
```

Ans : - It compresses all postscript files in P.W.D and moves to /backup directory.

- What does the following shell script does.

```
for i in  $*
  do
  cc -C  $i.c
  done
```

Ans : -creates object files for those c program files whose primary names are given along the command line to the above shell script.

- What does the following shell script does.

```
for i in *.dvi
  do
dvips $i.dvi | lpr
done
```

Ans : - It converts all dvi files in P.W.D and converts to postscript and redirects to printer.

- Explain what happens if you run the following shell script.

```
I=1
    for i in $*
    do
    J=I
    for j in $*
    if [  $I -ne $J  ]
    then
      if diff $i $j
        then
          rm $j
      else
        J=`expr $J + 1`
      fi
    fi
    done
    I=`expr $I + 1`
    done
    echo $I
```

Ans : Takes a set of file names along the command line and removes if there exists duplicate files.

- Write a shell program such that files (only) of P.W.D will contain PID of the current shell (in which shell script is running) as their extension.

```
for x in `ls`

  do

   if [ ! -d $x ]
     then
        mv $x $x.$$
   fi
 done
```

- Two files contains a list of words to be searched and list of filenames respectively. Write a shell script which display search word and its number of occurrences over all the files as a tabular fashion.

```
echo "Word Filename Occurrences"
for x in `cat $file1`
 do
     for y in `cat $file2`
       do
          I=0
         for z in `cat $y`
             do
                 if [ "$x" == "$y" ]
                  then
                      I=`expr $I + 1`
                 fi
             done
         echo $x  $y $I
done
```

- Two files contains a list of words to be searched and list of filenames respectively. Write a shell script which display search word over all the files and display as a table with yes or no for each word and file combination respectively.

```
echo "Word Filename Occurrences"
for x in `cat $file1`
 do
     for y in `cat $file2`
       do

      done
       echo $x  $y $I
done
```

- Write a shell script which accepts in command line user's name and informs you as soon as he/she log into system.

```
uname=$1
while :
do
who | grep "$uname">/dev/null
if [ $? -eq 0 ]
  then
    echo $uname is logged in
    exit
    else
    sleep 60
done
```

- Write a shell script which lists the filenames of a directory_(reading permissions are assumed to be available) which contains more than specified no of characters.

```
read size
foreach x
do
y=`wc -c $x`
if [ $y -gt $size ]
echo $x
fi
done
```

- Write a shell script which displays names of c programs which uses a specified function.

```
read functname
for prog in *.c
do
if grep $functname $prog
then
echo $prog
fi
done
```

- Write a shell script which displays names of the directories in PATH one line each.

Ans :

```
IFS=:
set`echo $PATH`
for i in $*
do
  echo $i
done

IFS=:
for i in $PATH
do
  echo $i
done
```

- A file (ABC) having a list of search words. Write a program that takes a file name as command line argument and print's success if at least one line of the file contains all the search words of ABC otherwise display failure.

```
cat $1 |
while read xx
do
FLAG=1
for y in `cat ABC`
do
if ! grep $y $xx
then
FLAG=0
break
fi
done
if $FLAG -eq 1
then
echo "SUCCESS"
exit
fi
done
echo "FAILURE"
```

- Write a shell script which removes empty files from PWD and changes other files time stamps to current time.

```
for x in .
do
if [ -f $x ]
then
   if [ -s  $x ]
     then
        touch $x
   else
        rm $x
   fi
fi
done
```

* Write a program to calculate factorial value

```
#!/bin/sh

factorial()
{
  if [ "$1" -gt "1" ]; then
    i=`expr $1 - 1`
    j=`factorial $i`
    k=`expr $1 \* $j`
    echo $k
  else
    echo 1
  fi
}


while :
do
  echo "Enter a number:"
  read x
  factorial $x
done
```

- Write a program which reads a digit and prints its BCD code.

```
#!/bin/sh

convert_digit()
{
 case $1 in
  0) echo "0000 \c" ;;
  1) echo "0001 \c" ;;
  2) echo "0010 \c" ;;
  3) echo "0011 \c" ;;
  4) echo "0100 \c" ;;
  5) echo "0101 \c" ;;
  6) echo "0110 \c" ;;
  7) echo "0111 \c" ;;
  8) echo "1000 \c" ;;
  9) echo "1001 \c" ;;
  *) echo
    echo "Invalid input $1, expected decimal digit"
    ;;
 esac
}

decimal=$1
stringlength=`echo $decimal | wc -c`
char=1

while [ "${char}" -lt "${stringlength}" ]
do
 convert_digit `echo $decimal|cut -c ${char}`
 char=`expr ${char} + 1`
done
echo
```

* Write a program which reads a filename along the command line and prints frequency of the occurrence of words.

```
#!/bin/sh
# Count the frequency of words in a file.
# Syntax: frequency.sh textfile.txt
```

```
INFILE=$1
WORDS=/tmp/words.$$.txt
COUNT=/tmp/count.$$.txt

if [ -z "$INFILE" ]; then
  echo "Syntax: `basename $0` textfile.txt"
  echo "A utility to count frequency of words in a text file"
  exit 1
fi
if [ ! -r $INFILE ]; then
  echo "Error: Can't read input file $INFILE"
  exit 1
fi

> $WORDS
> $COUNT

# First, get each word onto its own line...
# Save this off to a temporary file ($WORDS)
# The "tr '\t' ' '" replaces tabs with spaces;
# The "tr -s ' '" removes duplicate spaces.
# The "tr ' ' '\n' replaces spaces with newlines.
# Note: The "tr "[:punct:]"" requires GNU tr, not UNIX tr.
cat $INFILE | tr "[:punct:]" ' ' | tr '\t' ' ' | tr -s ' ' | tr ' ' '\n' | while read f
do
  echo $f >> $WORDS
done

# Now read in each line (word) from the temporary file $WORDS ...
while read f
do
  # Have we already encountered this word?
  grep -- " ${f}$" $COUNT > /dev/null 2>&1
  if [ "$?" -ne "0" ]; then
    # No, we haven't found this word before... count its frequency
    NUMBER=`grep -cw -- "${f}" $WORDS`
    # Store the frequency in the $COUNT file
    echo "$NUMBER $f" >> $COUNT
  fi
done < $WORDS
```

```
# Now we have $COUNT which has a tally of every word found, and how
# often it was encountered. Sort it numerically for legibility.
# We can use head to limit the number of results - using 20 as an example.
echo "20 most frequently encountered words:"
sort -rn $COUNT  | head -20

# Now remove the temporary files.
#rm -f $WORDS $COUNT
```

5.2.6 Arrays

A useful facility in the C-shell is the ability to make arrays out of strings and other variables. The round parentheses `(..)' do this. For example, look at the following commands.

```
set array = ( a b c d )
echo $array[1]
a
echo $array[2]
b
echo $array[$#array]
d

set noarray = ( "a b c d" )
echo $noarray[1]
a b c d
echo $noarray[$#noarray]
a b c d
```

The first command defines an array containing the elements `a b c d'. The elements of the array are referred to using square brackets `[..]' and the first element is `$array[1]'. The last element is `$array[4]'. *NOTE: this is not the same as in C or C++ where the first element of the array is the zero'th element!*

The special operator `$#' returns the number of elements in an array. This gives us a simple way of finding the end of the array. For example

```
echo $#path
23

echo "The last element in path is $path[$#path]"
```

The last element in path is .

Bash arrays

The original Bourne shell does not have arrays. Bash version 2.x does have arrays, however. An array can be assigned from a string of words separated by white spaces or the individual elements of the array can be set individually.

```
colours=(red white green)
colours[3]="yellow"
```

An element of the array must be referred to using curly braces.

```
echo ${colours[1]}
white
```

Note that the first element of the array has index 0. The set of all elements is referred to by ${colours[*]}.

```
echo ${colours[*]}
red white green yellow
echo ${#colours[*]}
4
```

As seen the number of elements in an array is given by ${#colours[*]}.

5.3 Conclusions

In this chapter shell programming is explained in detail. It emphasizes the need for shell programming and its limitations. Shell constructs such as if, while, until and for loop etc., are explained. How arrays can be used in shell also dealt in a nutshell fashion. Also, user configuration is explained in detail.

6 Debian Linux Installation Guidelines

6.1 Installing Debian Linux

This material is taken from www.aboutdebian.com/install3.htm and is under GNU public license. Debian allows you to select from several different "flavors" of installs (compact, vanilla, etc.). We'll be using the vanilla flavor in this procedure because it offers the widest variety of driver support.

The procedure below does a very basic OS install. This keeps things simple, results in a more secure configuration, and allows you learn more. Another advantage is that it doesn't clutter up memory with unnecessary processes. The main knock against Debian over the years has been it's installation routine. They're working on making it better but it still has a ways to go before it compares with the install routines of the commercial distros.

Always **only try to install the latest stable release** of Debian. The second most important things is to gather the following details which are essential while configuring X windows.

- Monitor details (Horizontal Sync, Vertical Refresh, Resolutions permitted).
- Display card details (Video Memory supported, Video chipset, Other features).
- Keyboard type (PS/2, USB, Locale?).
- Mouse type (PS/2, USB, Scroll?).
- Also decide what resolutions and colour depth we want to run the system on.

We will need to know it to select the appropriate XFree86 video "server". A list of appropriate XFree86 servers for most supported video cards can be found at:

www.xfree86.org/4.1.0/Status.html

While it is possible to set up Debian on a second partition of an existing system and set up a dual-boot configuration, we wouldn't recommend it if this is our first time installing Linux. In order to set up a dual-boot we'll need to over-write the MBR (Master Boot Record) of our hard-drive, and if we mess that up we could lose access to our entire system.

The options we select in this procedure are more appropriate for a server system (external Internet server or internal file server). One thing we may want to check before we get started is in the BIOS setup of our system. Some systems have a "PnP OS" option in the BIOS. Make sure this is set to **No** before we get started.

Now that you've got everything you need you can go to the system you'll be installing Debian on and begin the installation procedure.

1. Insert CD #1 into the CD-ROM drive and boot the system off of it. The Welcome screen appears with a **boot:** prompt at the bottom. At this prompt, type in:

   vanilla

   and hit Enter. The Release Notes screen is displayed with **Continue** highlighted so hit Enter and the Installation Menu will appear.

The Installation Menu has two parts - upper area has a **Next:** and **Alternate:** and possibly an **Alternate1:** selection - lower part is the steps that we will progress through using the **Next:** selection.

2. **If our hard-disk has existing partitions** blow them away now

   - Arrow down to **Alternate1: Partition a Hard Disk** and press Enter to run the **cfdisk** partitioning utility. If we are installing Debian onto the first hard-drive, highlight **/dev/hda** (for IDE drives) or **/dev/sda** (for SCSI drives). If we only have one hard-drive it will already be highlighted. Pressing Enter will display a screen about Lilo limitations. If we have an older system (which will have an older BIOS) we should read this.
   - Pressing Enter with **Continue** highlighted will start cfdisk and the existing partitions will be displayed. (The up and down arrow keys will highlight partitions in the upper part of the cfdisk display. The left and right arrow keys highlight the available menu selections in the lower part of the display.) Use the arrow keys to highlight them and select **Delete**. After all partitions have been deleted, **be sure to select the Write selection to update the partition table or nothing will change.**
   - After writing the updates to the drive's partition table we will be back at caddis's main screen. Highlight the **Quit** selection and press Enter to return to the installation menu.
   - When you use cfdisk to remove existing partitions you "jump ahead" in the installation steps so you'll have to take a step back at this point. Back at the installation menu, arrow down to **Configure the Keyboard** and press Enter. This will put you back at the correct place in the installation routine so go to the next step in this procedure.

3. With the **Next: Configure the Keyboard** highlighted, press Enter and **U.S. English (QWERTY)** will be highlighted. Just press Enter if this is your desired selection and you'll be returned to the installation menu with the **Next:** step highlighted.

4. This next step partitions the hard-drive. With the **Next: Partition a Hard Disk** selected press Enter.

   - The first screen displays the list of connected hard-drive(s). Usually there's only one drive and it's already highlighted. If you have more than one IDE drive select **/dev/hda** for IDE drives or **/dev/sda** for SCSI drives and press Enter.
   - The LILO warning about 8-gig or larger drives on older systems with an older BIOS is displayed with **Continue** highlighted so just hit Enter to start cfdisk.

Note: The top part of the cfdisk display lists the partitions and free space and you use the **up** and **down** arrow keys to select those. The lower part of the display are the available menu options and you use the **left** and **right** arrow keys to select those.

   - You should have a single line that says **Pri/Log Free Space** with the total free space on the disk displayed on the right. Right arrow over to the **New** selection and press Enter.

Note: You need to create a root partition and a swap partition (for virtual memory). You typically want a swap partition with a size that is double the amount of RAM in your system. For example, if you have 64 meg of RAM, you'll want a swap partition that's 128 meg in size. **Be sure to set a <u>root</u> partition size which leaves enough free space for the desired-size <u>swap</u> partition.**

Note also: If you have a large disk, you may want to leave a gig or two free for partitioning as other file types. As you will see, cfdisk can create a huge variety of partitions and you may want to try creating a FAT16 (DOS), Win95 (FAT32), or NTFS partition later to experiment with exchanging files with other platforms.

- With **Primary** highlighted press Enter but **don't accept the default partition size value**. This default is the entire disk and you won't have any room left for a swap partition. Enter a size in megabytes using the considerations mentioned above (3000 MB in my example).
- Once you've entered a value and press Enter you'll be given options as to where to locate the primary partition. Accept the default **Beginning** option and press Enter and the new partition will be displayed.
- Press the down arrow key to highlight the free space and use the right arrow key to highlight the **New** selection and press Enter and again accept the **Primary** selection by pressing Enter.
- The default partition size value is whatever disk space remains. Enter the desired size of your **swap** partition (I used 256 due to my system having 128 meg of RAM) and press Enter. You will again be presented with the location selection and you can just accept **Beginning** and press Enter.
- With this new partition highlighted, arrow over to the menu selection **Type** and press Enter which will display some of the different partition types cfdisk supports. Note at the bottom of the screen is a prompt that says **Press a key to continue** and when you do even more partition types will be displayed.
- At the bottom of this second screen of partition types you'll see the **Enter file system type:** with the value defaulted to **82**. This is the Linux Swap type which is what we want to just hit Enter.
- You should now have listed the root partition, the swap partition, and any free space remaining. **Be sure to arrow over to the Write menu selection** and press Enter so that all your changes get written to the disk's partition table.
- Once the partition table is updated arrow over to the **Quit** selection and press Enter to exit out of cfdisk and return to the installation menu.

5. The installation menu will automatically highlight the **Initialize and Activate a Swap Partition** (hda2) so you can just press Enter. If you want to scan for bad blocks (a good idea even with new drives) Tab to **Yes** and press Enter, and then answer **Yes** at the **Are you sure?** prompt.
6. You are then prompted to initialize the Linux **Native** partition (the first partition you created - hda1). When you select to do this you are asked if you want to **scan for bad blocks**. If you do, Tab to **Yes** (this could take quite a long time with a large partition) or you can accept the default **No** and press Enter. Then answer **Yes** at the **Are you sure?** prompt. Then answer **Yes** to the prompt to mount the root filesystem.
7. The next item in the installation menu is **Install Kernel and Driver Modules**. The installation routine detects that you are doing a CD-ROM install and asks you if you want to use this drive as the default installation medium. Accept the default **Yes** to this by pressing Enter.
8. **Configure Device Driver Modules** is where you are given the chance to load additional drivers. A message about loaded drivers appears with **Continue** already highlighted so just press Enter.

   You are then presented with a list of module (driver) categories. Each category has a bunch of modules listed and you have to highlight them and press Enter to install them. If you are prompted for any "Command line arguments" just leave it blank and press Enter.

Install the listed modules from the following categories. Don't try and install any hardware drivers for hardware that isn't installed and ready.

- **net** - select **ppp** support (useful for more than just modems) and if you're connecting your system to a network **select your NIC driver** if it's listed. Many times it's easy to figure out which driver you need because the driver name coincides with the name of the NIC. However this is not always the case. The driver is often based on the chipset used by the card, not the card manufacturer or model. In the table below (Table 6. 1) are some common NICs and the driver you need for them.

Note: Many drivers will prompt you for command line options. If you have a good hub or switch and a decent card, you should not have to enter any command-line options for the cards to work. They auto-negotiated a 100 mb, full-duplex connection.

Table 6.1 Common NIC cards and their drivers under Linux.

NIC	Driver
3C509-B (ISA)	**3c509**
3C905 (PCI)	**3c59x**
SMC 1211 SiS 900 Allied Telesyn AT2550	**rtl8139**
SMC 8432BT SMC EtherPower 10/100 Netgear FX31 Linksys EtherPCI Kingston KNT40T Kingston KNE100TX D-Link DFE500TX D-Link DFE340TX D-Link DE330CT	**tulip**

Many other cards use the **pcnet32** or **lance** drivers. If your NIC is not one of the ones listed above you may find it, and its corresponding driver name, in the Ethernet HOWTO list.

Note that We had problems using some SMC cards (9432 in particular) and got errors saying "too much work at interrupt" and the card does not work properly. Your safest bet is to use a 3Com 3C509-B (ISA) or 3C905 (PCI) card. They're widely supported,

ipv4 - The following modules are for a system which would be connected to the Internet for firewall or proxy capability (but not needed if this will be a network file server). For our purposes, select the following:

- **ip_masq_autofw** - kernel support for firewall functionality
- **ip_masq_ftp** - (same as above)
- **ip_masq_irc** - (same as above)
- **ip_masq_mfw** - (same as above)
- **ip_masq_portfw** - (same as above)
- **ip_masq_raudio** - (same as above)

9. **fs** - The following are modules you'd want if this would be a system which is **not** going to be directly connected to the Internet such as an internal file, print, or application server. For our purposes, select all of the following:
   - **binfmt_aout** - for backward compatibility
   - **binfmt_misc** - (same as above)
   - **nfs** - for UNIX/Linux network file storage
   - **nfsd** - (same as above)

   (Note that **lockd** is selected automatically with **nfs**.)

   Tip: If you didn't see the above ipv4 and fs selections listed it's likely because you didn't enter "vanilla" at the start of this procedure. You'll want to start the installation over at Step 1.

10. Because you selected **net** modules, the next step in the installation menu is to **Configure the Network**.
   - Enter a hostname for your system. If this is going to be an Internet server, use a name that describes its function (ex: "www" or "mail"). If it's going to be in an internal domain in your company, use a name that uniquely identifies it. If this is going to be a home Web/e-mail server using dynamic DNS you'll want to pick something that's <u>really</u> unique (something that isn't already being used by anyone else using the same dynamic DNS service). If none of these apply, you can just accept the default "debian" name.
   - Select the **No** response to the question asking you if you want to use DHCP or BOOTP.

   Next you have to enter an IP address for your system. If you're installing this machine on an existing network, MAKE SURE IT'S AN AVAILABLE IP ADDRESS!. If you choose an IP address that's used by another system you'll cause all kinds of problems. (You can use a different system to try and ping the address you plan to use to make sure there are no replies to it.) If you don't know what IP address to use **don't** accept the default since it's commonly assigned in home networks.

   Note: If you're installing this machine on an existing network, even a home network, try this:
   - Go to a Windows machine that's also on the network
   - Open a DOS window
   - At the DOS prompt type in **winipcfg** or **ipconfig** (one of them should work) and see what the IP address of the machine is
   - Think of an address for your Linux system where the **first three** "octets" are the same. For example, if the Windows machine has an address of 192.168.10.23, the address for you Linux machine should be 192.168.10.xxx (you make up a number for "xxx" from 1 to 254)
   - Try to ping the number you come up with. For example, if the number you come up with for xxx is 45, at the DOS prompt type in **ping 192.168.10.45** and make sure there are no responses to the ping. This means the address isn't being used by another system so you can use it for your Linux system.
     - The subnet mask will be automatically calculated for you based on the class of the IP address you entered and it should be OK as long as you're not on a subnetted LAN.
     - Enter a gateway address if you know what it is (the default route off your network). If it's a home network you probably not have a gateway (unless you have a cable/DSL router). Don't just accept the default entry

as a system that's not a gateway may already have this address. The procedure above using a Windows system already on the network may display a default gateway address. If not, just back-space out the default value and press Enter leaving the field blank.

- You will then be prompted for a domain name. Enter your domain name if you already have one. If you're just playing around, use your last name (for example smith.net). You'll see why on the Internet Servers page. If you accepted the default "debian" host name earlier, your system will then be referred to as "debian.smith.net". Don't worry about conflicting with a real domain that may have that name since this machine won't have a DNS record created on any ISP's DNS server.

Note : There are up to three types of "domains" to consider when you are asked for a domain name in Linux. If this will be a system in your **Internet domain** space, naturally you would use that name. Companies can also set up an **internal domain** space which has the same type of naming hierarchy as the Internet domain naming system. This type of domain name can be anything you want because it is not visible to the outside world nor do you have to "register" the name with any domain naming authority. In other words, a company can have a public (Internet) domain name (registered through someone like Network Solutions) and a private (internal) domain name. They can be the same or they can be different.

The third type of domain are familiar to those who work with Windows NT networks. These domains only have a single-word domain, not the dotted hierarchy found on the Internet and in internal Linux/UNIX networks. Linux does not support these type of domains. However, starting with Windows 2000, Windows servers also started using the dotted hierarchy domain naming convention. If you have any such Windows servers on your network, your Linux system can be put into this domain space (i.e. be given the same dotted domain name as your Windows 2000 servers).

- At the prompt for a DNS address, enter the address of one of your ISP's DNS servers. (Most companies don't have heir own DNS servers and will usually use the DNS servers of their ISP or WAN service provider.) Here again you don't want to just accept the default because that address may be used by another machine on the network which isn't a DNS server. If you're not sure of your ISP's DNS server addresses, just backspace out the existing address and leave it blank.

Note : If you enter your ISP's DNS server address, some network-related functions (like establishing a telnet session) may operate slowly until your get your system connected to the Internet so it can "see" the ISP's DNS server. However, this is the only viable entry to use on networks that don't have their own DNS server.

11. Back at the installation menu **Install the Base System** is highlighted so just press Enter and the file copying and extraction will begin.
12. The next three selections refer to setting up the system to boot up.
    - Select **Make System Bootable**
    - Select the default **Install LILO in the MBR** and press Enter when the "Securing LILO" message appears
    - You **don't** need to Make a Boot Floppy so arrow down to **Alternate: Reboot the System** press Enter and answer **Yes** to the confirmation.

Be sure to remove the CD as the system reboots to force it to boot off hard-drive. This next phase of the OS installation will install some basic software and configure some basic OS operations. You may see some errors messages in all of the text that's displayed during the boot process. Don't worry about those at this point.

Once the system reboots you'll have to press Enter at the screen saying that Debian is installed and the configuration process begins.

13. Tab over to the **No** selection when the prompt appears asking you if your hardware clock is set to Greenwich Mean Time.

14. For the time zone select your geographic area (if you're in the US, choose "US" and not "America") and press Enter. Then select your correct time zone and press Enter.

15. The next series of dialogs will be password and account related. Note that the cursor will not move and nothing will be displayed when you enter passwords.

   - First you'll be asked if you want to use MD5 passwords. Use default **No** selection.
   - Next you'll be asked if you want to use shadow passwords. Use the default **Yes** selection.
   - You'll have to press Enter about an informational message about root passwords. Then you'll be prompted to enter, and re-enter, a password for the root (super-user) account. REMEMBER IT.
   - Finally you'll be asked to create a non-root user account entering the username, full name, and password. Create one for yourself using your first name.

16. When asked if you want to remove the PCMCIA files accept the default **Yes** answer.

17. When asked **Do you want to use PPP to install the system?** use the default **No** answer.

18. At this point the **apt** (package installer) configuration begins. Before continuing, **place the CD #1 back in the drive**. What apt is going to do is scan the CDs and create an inventory of the packages on them and store it in a database for later use.

19. After the CD #1 is scanned it will ask if you have another CD to scan. Pop in CD #2, Tab to the **Yes** selection and press Enter. Repeat this process until all seven CDs have been scanned.

20. Once CD #7 has been scanned, remove it and put CD #1 back in the drive. This time, accept the default **No** to the prompt asking if you have another CD to scan and press Enter.

21. When prompted to **add another apt source** accept the default **No** answer and press Enter.

22. Answer **No** to the prompt about using security updates from security.debian.org. (We'll take care of this later.)

23. The next window to appear is the System Configuration window where you are asked if you want to run the **tasksel** task selection utility. Accept the default **Yes** by pressing Enter.

24. The Task Installer appears with a list of task packages you can select using the space bar. **Only select following** at this time:

   - **X window system**
   - **C and C++**
   - Tab to **Finish** and press Enter.

25. Accept the default **No** to running dselect at this time.

26. At this point a list of packages to be installed are presented with a prompt asking "Do you want to continue?" with **Yes** being the default so just press Enter.

27. You'll be prompted to insert CD#1 but it should already be in the drive so just press Enter.

28. Just press Enter when the informational message about "kernel link failures".
29. Accept the default **No** answer to configuring less.
30. Accept the default **No** answer to adding a mime handler.
31. Next you'll have to select a locale for those applications that use this information. If you are in the US, arrow down to the **en_US ISO-8859-1** selection and press the Space Bar to select it. Then Tab to OK and press Enter.
32. Accept the default **Leave alone** for the default locale selection by pressing Enter
33. Press Enter at the informational message about statd using tcpwrappers.
34. When prompted to "Allow SSH protocol 2 only" Tab over to **No** and press Enter.
35. Press Enter at the informational message about privileged separation.
36. Accept the default **Yes** answer to install ssh-keysign SUID root by pressing Enter.
37. Answer **No** to the prompt to run the sshd server.
38. Accept the default path for the CVS repositories by pressing Enter and then press Enter again when the prompt to **Create** the repository directory appears.
39. CVS is a version control system that tracks changes to source files which is useful if you are going to use your system for development work - i.e. programming. For this install, press Enter at the CVS informational message and accept the default **No** answer to the prompt about starting the CVS pserver.
40. Accept the default **Yes** to the prompt about managing the X server wrapper using debconf.
41. Accept the default **Yes** to the prompt about managing the XFree86 configuration using debconf.
42. Select your video card's chipset manufacturer from the list presented and press Enter. If you're not sure what it is, use to the **vga** selection.
43. Accept the default **Yes** to the prompt about using the kernel's framebuffer interface.
44. Accept the indicated X rule set by pressing Enter.
45. Press Enter at the informational message about keyboard types.
46. Select the appropriate keyboard type based on what you read in the previous informational message and press Enter. The default **pc104** value is for the Windows types of keyboards most often found in the US.
47. Enter the appropriate keyboard layout based on your locale and press Enter.
48. Press Enter at the informational message regarding mice and trackballs.
49. On the mouse port selection screen, select **/dev/psaux** if you have a PS/2 mouse. For older serial-type mice, use **/dev/ttyS0** if it's conneted to COM1 or **/dev/ttyS1** if it's connected to COM2. Then Tab to **OK** and press Enter.
50. On the mouse selection screen, if you have a name-brand select the model which matches it, or simply select the generic model entry.
51. Answer appropriately to the prompt about whether you have an LCD monitor or not.
52. Press Enter at the informational screen about monitors. Then select **Simple** from the list of selection methods and press Enter.
53. Select your monitor's size and press Enter.
54. If you have a 15" monitor, you'll want **only** the **640x480** value for the resolution. If you have a 17" monitor have **only** the **800x600** value selected (i.e. de-select the 640x480 selection) using the Space Bar. Then Tab to **OK** and press Enter.

55. At the color depth selection, a recommended value based on your earlier selections will be at the top of the list (highlighted) so just press Enter.
56. At this point more packages will be installed. At some point during this installation you may be prompted to select an ispell dictionary from a list presented. Simply select the appropriate dictionary for your locale.
57. If you get a prompt about erasing the .deb files accept the default **Yes** by pressing Enter and then pressing Enter again to continue.
58. Next you see a message about helping you configure your mail system. Debian installs the **Exim** e-mail server software by default which is a shame. 99% of the UNIX/Linux world uses Sendmail. On the Internet Servers page we'll remove Exim and install Sendmail but for now:
    - Press Enter at the "Press Return" prompt
    - Select option **5** to not configure Exim

    THAT'S IT! The installation is complete. And you'll be sitting at a text-based shell prompt. Before we reboot the system there a couple commands we need to enter to compensate for the differences in the installation routines between woody and potato. This will put on the "same page" as the potato installation before moving on to the subsequent guide pages.
59. Start out by logging in as the 'root' super user (i.e. enter **root** at the **login:** prompt and then whatever you entered above for a root password. This will place you at a shell prompt.
60. Unfortunately, when you choose to install the X-Windows system in Woody it sets the system up to bring up a GUI login prompt when the system is booted. We don't want that.

    Recall that back on the Basics page we showed what files are involved in the Linux boot process, including the symbolic links in the **rc2.d** directory. You can disable the running of the GUI login routine by renaming the symbolic link to the shell script which runs the GUI login routine. Recall also that any symbolic link that starts with an upper-case 'S' causes its associated script to be run at startup. Use the following **mv** (move) command to rename this link so that it starts with an underscore character so its associated script won't be run when the system is booted:

    mv /etc/rc2.d/S99xdm /etc/rc2.d/_S99xdm

61. Next, we want to be able to telnet into the system. Potato takes care of this by default but Woody doesn't (defaulting to the more secure SSH instead) so we'll have to install the telnet server daemon. With CD#1 in the drive, enter the following command:

    apt-get install telnetd

    You'll find out more about **apt-get** on the Packages page. For now, we're pretty much at the same point system-wise as the end of the potato installation. So now you can reboot the system by removing the CD from the drive and pressing Ctrl-Alt-Del.

We're not actually done with the initial setup of the system yet. The rest will be covered on the Packages page. For now though, try taking your new Debian system out for a spin around the block in the next section.

As your system reboots a lot of messages will be displayed. With a faster system you won't be able to read them all. You can use the **Shift-PgUp** and **Shift-PgDn** key combos to scroll through this previously-displayed text to look for any error messages, etc. Don't be too concerned about error messages at this point. We still have to install and update the packages.

Once your system restarts you'll be presented with a login prompt. Because Linux is a multi-user OS you have to indentify yourself to the OS via a login. Log in using the **root** username and the root password you entered during the install.

Once you log in the shell prompt **debian:~#** is displayed. The **#** indicates you're logged in as root. (Non-root users get a **$** prompt.) The **debian** is the hostname you gave to the system during the install. The **~** indicates that you have been placed in root's home directory. Whenever you first log in you will see this prompt because every user defaults to their home directory at login. (User home directories are created automatically when the user accounts are created on the system.)

All non-root users have a sub-directory under the **/home** directory. The names of these home sub-directories for non-root users match the user names (ex: **/home/fred**). The root user is a little different. root's home directory is off the root of the file system. Instead of **/home/root** it's at **/root**. It's important to understand that **/root** is the root user's home directory. Don't confuse it with the "root" of the file system, which is denoted by a single slash (**/**).

Since you're in the root user's home directory, look at the files the install routine created by typing in **ls** and pressing Enter. You won't see anything because there's nothing there. Kind of. There are no <u>user</u> files there. However, there are some system files there. Try typing in **ls -laF** and pressing Enter. You'll see two files that start with a period, the **.bashrc** and **.profile** files. They're both kind of the same thing, like a config.sys file on DOS systems.

The **.bashrc** file sets certain environment defaults when you use the bash shell. The **.profile** does the same thing, regardless of which shell you use. You can look at the contents of the **.profile** file by typing in

cat .profile

('cat' is the equivalent of the DOS TYPE command which just "types out" the contents of a text file on the screen.) As you can see, it's mainly just the setting of the PATH variable and you can see what the value of your path is set to. Notice I said **your** path. In UNIX/Linux each user gets their own path.

Now lets look at the **.bashrc** file. Type in

cat .bashrc

There's a little more here but most of it is commented out. In most UNIX/Linux configuration files **any line that begins with a pound character (#) are comments** (or are commands that have been commented out as in the case of numerous **alias** commands in the **.bashrc** file).

#!/bin/sh

This is known as the "bang" or "shebang" line. It specifies the path to the shell that the script should be run in. (You can run a shell script under a different shell than the one you're currently using.)

alias commands let you substitute one command for another, or "create" your own command. Note the line in the **.bashrc** file:

alias rm='rm -i'

This just substitutes the standard **alias** command with itself but using the **-i** command-line switch. The **-i** command-line switch is **i**nteractive mode, which means it will prompt you for a confirmation whenever you use the **rm** command to delete a file (a safety measure).

You can also "create" your own commands by aliasing existing commands with a different name. For example, you could enter the following line in the **.bashrc** file:

alias zapfilz='rm -i'

to "create" a **zapfilz** command.

Linux defaults it's "virtual terminal" sessions (what you use when you are working at a shell prompt) to the "tty" (teletype) specification. However, some text editors don't get along with the tty terminal type very well. They work better with a "VT100" type of terminal. (The term "terminal" refers to the old "green screen" keyboard/screen devices that were commonly used with mainframes.) Since you tend to work with text files quite a bit in Linux, it would be beneficial to set our virtual terminal sessions to use the VT100 terminal type.

Lets use the infamous **vi** text editor to edit the **.bashrc** file to change our default terminal type to VT100. We'll do this using an **export** statement.

1. At the shell prompt type in vi .bashrc to open the file in the editor and the contents will be displayed.

   Note that there already is one export statement in the .bashrc file. This statement is what sets our shell prompt to display the hostname and current working directory.
2. Press the down arrow key until you get to a blank line in a file (the position of the command in the file isn't important).
3. Press the 'a' key (for append).

   Note : If you screw things up and you want to quit without saving, just press the following keys in the given order:

   Esc : q ! Enter

4. Type in the following line (**don't** start the line with a pound sign):

   export TERM='vt100'

5. Now press the following keys in the given order to save the changes and exit vi:

   Esc : w q Enter

   Note that what we just did changes a <u>startup</u> file. It won't have any effect until the next time you log in. However, just enter that same command at the shell prompt and it will take effect immediately. Once your enter it at the shell prompt, you can make sure it took effect by entering this command at the shell prompt:

echo $TERM

You can also try entering this command the next time you log in to make sure that the statement you entered into the **.bashrc** file is correct. **$TERM** is the environment variable which stores the current terminal value. All environment variables are upper-case. You use the **$** character in front of them to indicate you want to echo the *contents* of the variable. If you didn't use the **$** in the above command the word **TERM** would simply be echoed to the screen.

The **vi** editor is legendary in it's difficulty to master. For one, it's a line editor, not a full-screen editor. For another, it has an "edit" mode and a "command" mode. (We went into edit mode above when we pressed the 'a' key above, and went back to command mode when we hit the Esc key.) There are entire books written on vi. It's only fair to mention though, that vi's keystroke combinations were devised in such a manner that once you get really good with vi, you'll rarely have to take your fingers off the "home" positions on the keyboard. The reason you want to at least become familiar with vi is because **every** Linux and UNIX system will have it, no matter how old or eccentric a distro it is. That can't be said about any other editor.

Keep in mind that changes made to the **.profile** only take effect when you're logged in as the same user that you are logged in as when you make the changes. Each user has their own **.profile** file located in their home directory (but as the root super-user you can edit everyone's **.profile** file if you want to set up a standard).

The same is true of the **.bashrc** file, except that, in addition to it only being valid for the current login, it is also only valid if you choose to run the bash shell. Likewise, every user that is set up to use the bash shell by default (which is the default shell in Linux) will have a **.bashrc** file in their home directory.

If you type in:

echo $SHELL

you'll see that you are using the Linux-default **bash** shell.

Here's something you can try. Log out of the system using the **exit** command. Start to log back in as root, but this time use the wrong password. You'll simply get an error message saying it was incorrect and another login prompt. At this second login prompt, use the correct password. Right above the shell prompt you'll see the message:

1 failure since last login

The "failure" the system is referring to is a login failure for the user account you just logged in as (works for all users, not just root). This is good to know as it will let you know if someone has been trying to hack in using this particular username.

What's next? If your system is connected to a network you should try seeing if you can ping another workstation on your network. You can use the procedure in Step 11 of the installation above (using winipcfg or ipconfig) to find the IP address of any Windows system on your network. For example, if the address of another system on your network is 192.168.10.12 you'd type in

ping 192.168.10.12

and see if you get "64 bytes from" the address. Left on its own, Linux ping will just keep pinging so press **Ctrl-C** to end it.

If you don't get any ping responses or get errors indicating that the "Network is unreachable" you can enter the **ifconfig** (not ipconfig as with Windows) and check the settings for your **eth0** interface (this is the NIC). The **lo** interface is the local loopback which is only used for testing.

If no eth0 interface is listed, you want to check to see if the kernel driver module got loaded at boot up. Enter the **lsmod** command. You should see **3c59x** or whatever driver you specified during the install listed.

If the module IS loaded (but eth0 doesn't show up in the ifconfig list) it means that the kernel "sees" the NIC. It's just not being brought up automatically at bootup. Check to see if it's set to be brought up automatically by typing out the contents of the interface configuration file with the command:

cat /etc/network/interfaces

and look for the line:

auto eth0

If there is no line like this, or if "eth0" isn't on the line, or if it has a pound character (**#**) at the beginning of the line (commented out) that's the problem. On the Packages we'll install a text editor called ee. You can wait until this editor is installed to open this file and correct the problem or you can try to edit it using the vi editor.

If the module ISN'T loaded try loading it with the command:

modprobe 3c59x

Substitute the "3c59x" for the name of the NIC module you selected during the installation. After doing this you may also need to bring the interface up manually. Use the **ifconfig** command to see if **eth0** is now listed. If not, bring it up with the command:

ifconfig eth0 up 192.168.10.50 netmask 255.255.255.0

substituting an address and subnet mask appropriate for your network. If you couldn't load the module you may have specified the wrong driver module during the installation or your NIC may be bad or, if this is a used non-PCI NIC, may have had the default IRQ, etc. settings changed at some point.

While the above installation procedure got you an operational system, it's pretty much bare-bones at this point.

Like any other Linux distributions Debian packages are also available both as source distributions and binary distribution. Binary Debian packages are called debs and end with the deb extension. Package name is generally in the following format:

PACKAGE VERSION-RELEASE ARCH.deb - Eg.
enlightenment 0.16.6-3 i386.deb

Library packages always being with lib - Eg.
libldap2_2.1.30-3_i386.deb

Development binaries or libraries always have -dev after the package name - Eg.
libldap2-dev 2.1.30-3 i386.deb

All the debian packages can be downloaded from ftp.debian.org or any of its mirrors.

6.2 Installing Additional Packages

Using **dpkg** and **apt-get** of package management tools are a very versatile collection for every aspect related to Debian packages. They can be used to build, extract, inspect, remove, debug and list packages!. Some common options are:

dpkg -l - Lists the installed packages in the system along with their status and version information.
dpkg -I - Shown information related to the package
dpkg -i - Installs the package(s) specified as arguments
dpkg -s - Shows information about an installed package
dpkg –S - Shows the package to which a file belongs
dpkg –r - Removes a package from the system
dpkg –P - Purges all files related to the package
dpkg –x - Extracts a package into its contents

Other utilities :

dpkg-reconfigure - Re-configures an installed package. This can be used to generate the configuration of the package again. Eg. Reconfiguring X Windows after a hardware upgrade

apt-cache search - Lets you run a search for a package in your current APT cache
apt-cache show - Shows information about a queried package from the current APT cache

The apt-get command also can be used to install, configure packages under Debian Linux.
apt-get install <package name>

6.2.1 dmesg command

The messages which crop-up during booting are very important and useful. At any time if we want to see the bootup messages we can use dmesg command. For example on my machine the following output is given.

```
Linux version 2.6.9-1.667 (bhcompile@tweety.build.redhat.com) (gcc version 3.4.2 20041017 (Red Hat 3.4.2-6.fc3)) #1 Tue Nov 2 14:41:25 EST 2004
BIOS-provided physical RAM map:
BIOS-e820: 0000000000000000 - 000000000009fc00 (usable)
BIOS-e820: 000000000009fc00 - 00000000000a0000 (reserved)
BIOS-e820: 00000000000f0000 - 0000000000100000 (reserved)
BIOS-e820: 0000000000100000 - 000000000f7f0000 (usable)
BIOS-e820: 000000000f7f0000 - 000000000f7f3000 (ACPI NVS)
BIOS-e820: 000000000f7f3000 - 000000000f800000 (ACPI data)
BIOS-e820: 00000000fec00000 - 00000000fec01000 (reserved)
BIOS-e820: 00000000fee00000 - 00000000fee01000 (reserved)
BIOS-e820: 00000000ffb00000 - 0000000100000000 (reserved)
0MB HIGHMEM available.
247MB LOWMEM available.
zapping low mappings.
On node 0 totalpages: 63472
DMA zone: 4096 pages, LIFO batch:1
Normal zone: 59376 pages, LIFO batch:14
HighMem zone: 0 pages, LIFO batch:1
DMI 2.2 present.
ACPI: RSDP (v000 IntelR) @ 0x000f6cd0
ACPI: RSDT (v001 IntelR AWRDACPI 0x42302e31 AWRD 0x00000000) @ 0x0f7f3000
ACPI: FADT (v001 IntelR AWRDACPI 0x42302e31 AWRD 0x00000000) @ 0x0f7f3040
ACPI: MADT (v001 IntelR AWRDACPI 0x42302e31 AWRD 0x00000000) @ 0x0f7f6d40
ACPI: DSDT (v001 INTELR AWRDACPI 0x00001000 MSFT 0x0100000c) @ 0x00000000
ACPI: PM-Timer IO Port: 0x408
Built 1 zonelists
Kernel command line: ro root=LABEL=/12 rhgb quiet
mapped 4G/4G trampoline to ffff4000.
Initializing CPU#0
CPU 0 irqstacks, hard=023d5000 soft=023d4000
PID hash table entries: 1024 (order: 10, 16384 bytes)
Detected 2794.983 MHz processor.
Using tsc for high-res timesource
Console: colour VGA+ 80x25
Dentry cache hash table entries: 32768 (order: 5, 131072 bytes)
Inode-cache hash table entries: 16384 (order: 4, 65536 bytes)
```

```
Memory: 247368k/253888k available (2068k kernel code, 5836k reserved, 647k data, 144k init, 0k highmem)
Calibrating delay loop... 5521.40 BogoMIPS (lpj=2760704)
Security Scaffold v1.0.0 initialized
SELinux:  Initializing.
SELinux:  Starting in permissive mode
There is already a security framework initialized, register_security failed.
selinux_register_security:  Registering secondary module capability
Capability LSM initialized as secondary
Mount-cache hash table entries: 512 (order: 0, 4096 bytes)
CPU: After generic identify, caps: bfebfbff 00000000 00000000 00000000
CPU: After vendor identify, caps:  bfebfbff 00000000 00000000 00000000
monitor/mwait feature present.
using mwait in idle threads.
CPU: Trace cache: 12K uops, L1 D cache: 16K
CPU: L2 cache: 1024K
CPU: After all inits, caps:        bfebf3ff 00000000 00000000 00000080
Intel machine check architecture supported.
Intel machine check reporting enabled on CPU#0.
CPU0: Intel P4/Xeon Extended MCE MSRs (12) available
CPU: Intel(R) Pentium(R) 4 CPU 2.80GHz stepping 04
Enabling fast FPU save and restore... done.
Enabling unmasked SIMD FPU exception support... done.
Checking 'hlt' instruction... OK.
ACPI: IRQ9 SCI: Level Trigger.
checking if image is initramfs... it is
Freeing initrd memory: 387k freed
NET: Registered protocol family 16
PCI: PCI BIOS revision 2.10 entry at 0xfb4c0, last bus=1
PCI: Using configuration type 1
mtrr: v2.0 (20020519)
ACPI: Subsystem revision 20040816
ACPI: Interpreter enabled
ACPI: Using PIC for interrupt routing
ACPI: PCI Root Bridge [PCI0] (00:00)
PCI: Probing PCI hardware (bus 00)
PCI: Ignoring BAR0-3 of IDE controller 0000:00:1f.1
PCI: Transparent bridge - 0000:00:1e.0
ACPI: PCI Interrupt Routing Table [\_SB_.PCI0._PRT]
ACPI: PCI Interrupt Routing Table [\_SB_.PCI0.HUB0._PRT]
ACPI: PCI Interrupt Link [LNKA] (IRQs 3 4 5 7 9 *10 11 12 14 15)
```

```
ACPI: PCI Interrupt Link [LNKB] (IRQs 3 4 *5 7 9 10 11 12 14 15)
ACPI: PCI Interrupt Link [LNKC] (IRQs 3 4 5 7 *9 10 11 12 14 15)
ACPI: PCI Interrupt Link [LNKD] (IRQs 3 4 5 7 9 10 *11 12 14 15)
ACPI: PCI Interrupt Link [LNKE] (IRQs 3 4 5 7 9 10 11 12 14 15) *0, disabled.
ACPI: PCI Interrupt Link [LNKF] (IRQs 3 4 5 7 9 10 *11 12 14 15)
ACPI: PCI Interrupt Link [LNK0] (IRQs 3 4 5 7 9 10 11 12 14 15) *0, disabled.
ACPI: PCI Interrupt Link [LNK1] (IRQs *3 4 5 7 9 10 11 12 14 15)
Linux Plug and Play Support v0.97 (c) Adam Belay
usbcore: registered new driver usbfs
usbcore: registered new driver hub
PCI: Using ACPI for IRQ routing
ACPI: PCI Interrupt Link [LNKA] enabled at IRQ 10
ACPI: PCI interrupt 0000:00:02.0[A] -> GSI 10 (level, low) -> IRQ 10
ACPI: PCI interrupt 0000:00:1d.0[A] -> GSI 10 (level, low) -> IRQ 10
ACPI: PCI Interrupt Link [LNKD] enabled at IRQ 11
ACPI: PCI interrupt 0000:00:1d.1[B] -> GSI 11 (level, low) -> IRQ 11
ACPI: PCI Interrupt Link [LNKC] enabled at IRQ 9
ACPI: PCI interrupt 0000:00:1d.2[C] -> GSI 9 (level, low) -> IRQ 9
ACPI: PCI Interrupt Link [LNK1] enabled at IRQ 3
ACPI: PCI interrupt 0000:00:1d.7[D] -> GSI 3 (level, low) -> IRQ 3
ACPI: PCI interrupt 0000:00:1f.1[A] -> GSI 9 (level, low) -> IRQ 9
ACPI: PCI Interrupt Link [LNKB] enabled at IRQ 5
ACPI: PCI interrupt 0000:00:1f.3[B] -> GSI 5 (level, low) -> IRQ 5
ACPI: PCI interrupt 0000:00:1f.5[B] -> GSI 5 (level, low) -> IRQ 5
ACPI: PCI Interrupt Link [LNKF] enabled at IRQ 11
ACPI: PCI interrupt 0000:01:06.0[A] -> GSI 11 (level, low) -> IRQ 11
apm: BIOS version 1.2 Flags 0x07 (Driver version 1.16ac)
apm: overridden by ACPI.
audit: initializing netlink socket (disabled)
audit(1129580303.823:0): initialized
Total HugeTLB memory allocated, 0
VFS: Disk quotas dquot_6.5.1
Dquot-cache hash table entries: 1024 (order 0, 4096 bytes)
SELinux:  Registering netfilter hooks
Initializing Cryptographic API
ksign: Installing public key data
Loading keyring
- Added public key 6ECDA687281A73E5
- User ID: Red Hat, Inc. (Kernel Module GPG key)
pci_hotplug: PCI Hot Plug PCI Core version: 0.5
vesafb: probe of vesafb0 failed with error -6
```

```
ACPI: Fan [FAN] (on)
ACPI: Processor [CPU0] (supports C1, 2 throttling states)
ACPI: Thermal Zone [THRM] (56 C)
isapnp: Scanning for PnP cards...
isapnp: No Plug & Play device found
Real Time Clock Driver v1.12
Linux agpgart interface v0.100 (c) Dave Jones
agpgart: Detected an Intel 845G Chipset.
agpgart: Maximum main memory to use for agp memory: 196M
agpgart: Detected 8060K stolen memory.
agpgart: AGP aperture is 128M @ 0xd8000000
serio: i8042 AUX port at 0x60,0x64 irq 12
serio: i8042 KBD port at 0x60,0x64 irq 1
Serial: 8250/16550 driver $Revision: 1.90 $ 8 ports, IRQ sharing enabled
ttyS0 at I/O 0x3f8 (irq = 4) is a 16550A
RAMDISK driver initialized: 16 RAM disks of 16384K size 1024 blocksize
divert: not allocating divert_blk for non-ethernet device lo
Uniform Multi-Platform E-IDE driver Revision: 7.00alpha2
ide: Assuming 33MHz system bus speed for PIO modes; override with idebus=xx
ICH4: IDE controller at PCI slot 0000:00:1f.1
ACPI: PCI interrupt 0000:00:1f.1[A] -> GSI 9 (level, low) -> IRQ 9
ICH4: chipset revision 2
ICH4: not 100% native mode: will probe irqs later
    ide0: BM-DMA at 0xf000-0xf007, BIOS settings: hda:DMA, hdb:DMA
    ide1: BM-DMA at 0xf008-0xf00f, BIOS settings: hdc:pio, hdd:pio
Probing IDE interface ide0...
hda: SAMSUNG SP0411N, ATA DISK drive
hdb: SAMSUNG CDRW/DVD SM-352F, ATAPI CD/DVD-ROM drive
Using cfq io scheduler
ide0 at 0x1f0-0x1f7,0x3f6 on irq 14
Probing IDE interface ide1...
Probing IDE interface ide1...
Probing IDE interface ide2...
ide2: Wait for ready failed before probe !
Probing IDE interface ide3...
ide3: Wait for ready failed before probe !
Probing IDE interface ide4...
ide4: Wait for ready failed before probe !
Probing IDE interface ide5...
ide5: Wait for ready failed before probe !
```

```
hda: max request size: 1024KiB
hda: 78242976 sectors (40060 MB) w/2048KiB Cache, CHS=16383/255/63, UDMA(100)
hda: cache flushes supported
 hda: hda1 hda2 < hda5 hda6 hda7 hda8 hda9 >
hdb: ATAPI 52X DVD-ROM CD-R/RW drive, 2048kB Cache, UDMA(33)
Uniform CD-ROM driver Revision: 3.20
ide-floppy driver 0.99.newide
usbcore: registered new driver hiddev
usbcore: registered new driver usbhid
drivers/usb/input/hid-core.c: v2.0:USB HID core driver
mice: PS/2 mouse device common for all mice
input: AT Translated Set 2 keyboard on isa0060/serio0
input: PS/2 Generic Mouse on isa0060/serio1
md: md driver 0.90.0 MAX_MD_DEVS=256, MD_SB_DISKS=27
NET: Registered protocol family 2
IP: routing cache hash table of 512 buckets, 16Kbytes
TCP: Hash tables configured (established 16384 bind 4681)
Initializing IPsec netlink socket
NET: Registered protocol family 1
NET: Registered protocol family 17
ACPI: (supports S0 S1 S4 S5)
ACPI wakeup devices:
SLPB PCI0 HUB0 UAR1 USB0 USB1 USB2 USB3 MODM
Freeing unused kernel memory: 144k freed
kjournald starting.  Commit interval 5 seconds
EXT3-fs: mounted filesystem with ordered data mode.
SELinux:  Disabled at runtime.
SELinux:  Unregistering netfilter hooks
inserting floppy driver for 2.6.9-1.667
Floppy drive(s): fd0 is 1.44M
FDC 0 is a post-1991 82077
sis900.c: v1.08.07 11/02/2003
ACPI: PCI interrupt 0000:01:06.0[A] -> GSI 11 (level, low) -> IRQ 11
divert: allocating divert_blk for eth0
eth0: SiS 900 Internal MII PHY transceiver found at address 1.
eth0: Using transceiver found at address 1 as default
eth0: SiS 900 PCI Fast Ethernet at 0xc000, IRQ 11, 00:11:5b:02:06:9f.
ACPI: PCI interrupt 0000:00:1f.5[B] -> GSI 5 (level, low) -> IRQ 5
PCI: Setting latency timer of device 0000:00:1f.5 to 64
intel8x0_measure_ac97_clock: measured 49426 usecs
intel8x0: clocking to 48000
```

```
hw_random hardware driver 1.0.0 loaded
ACPI: PCI interrupt 0000:00:1d.7[D] -> GSI 3 (level, low) -> IRQ 3
ehci_hcd 0000:00:1d.7: EHCI Host Controller
PCI: Setting latency timer of device 0000:00:1d.7 to 64
ehci_hcd 0000:00:1d.7: irq 3, pci mem 1212e000
ehci_hcd 0000:00:1d.7: new USB bus registered, assigned bus number 1
PCI: cache line size of 128 is not supported by device 0000:00:1d.7
ehci_hcd 0000:00:1d.7: USB 2.0 enabled, EHCI 1.00, driver 2004-May-10
hub 1-0:1.0: USB hub found
hub 1-0:1.0: 6 ports detected
USB Universal Host Controller Interface driver v2.2
ACPI: PCI interrupt 0000:00:1d.0[A] -> GSI 10 (level, low) -> IRQ 10
uhci_hcd 0000:00:1d.0: UHCI Host Controller
PCI: Setting latency timer of device 0000:00:1d.0 to 64
uhci_hcd 0000:00:1d.0: irq 10, io base 0000d800
uhci_hcd 0000:00:1d.0: new USB bus registered, assigned bus number 2
hub 2-0:1.0: USB hub found
hub 2-0:1.0: 2 ports detected
ACPI: PCI interrupt 0000:00:1d.1[B] -> GSI 11 (level, low) -> IRQ 11
uhci_hcd 0000:00:1d.1: UHCI Host Controller
PCI: Setting latency timer of device 0000:00:1d.1 to 64
uhci_hcd 0000:00:1d.1: irq 11, io base 0000d000
uhci_hcd 0000:00:1d.1: new USB bus registered, assigned bus number 3
hub 3-0:1.0: USB hub found
hub 3-0:1.0: 2 ports detected
ACPI: PCI interrupt 0000:00:1d.2[C] -> GSI 9 (level, low) -> IRQ 9
uhci_hcd 0000:00:1d.2: UHCI Host Controller
PCI: Setting latency timer of device 0000:00:1d.2 to 64
uhci_hcd 0000:00:1d.2: irq 9, io base 0000d400
uhci_hcd 0000:00:1d.2: new USB bus registered, assigned bus number 4
hub 4-0:1.0: USB hub found
hub 4-0:1.0: 2 ports detected
md: Autodetecting RAID arrays.
md: autorun ...
md: ... autorun DONE.
NET: Registered protocol family 10
Disabled Privacy Extensions on device 02369a00(lo)
IPv6 over IPv4 tunneling driver
divert: not allocating divert_blk for non-ethernet device sit0
ACPI: Power Button (FF) [PWRF]
ACPI: Sleep Button (CM) [SLPB]
```

```
EXT3 FS on hda1, internal journal
device-mapper: 4.1.0-ioctl (2003-12-10) initialised: dm@uk.sistina.com
cdrom: open failed.
EXT2-fs warning (device hda7): ext2_fill_super: mounting ext3 filesystem as ext2

Adding 522072k swap on /dev/hda8.  Priority:-1 extents:1
parport0: PC-style at 0x378 (0x778) [PCSPP,TRISTATE,EPP]
parport0: irq 7 detected
ip_tables: (C) 2000-2002 Netfilter core team
ip_conntrack version 2.1 (1983 buckets, 15864 max) - 356 bytes per conntrack
eth0: Media Link On 100mbps full-duplex
i2c /dev entries driver
parport0: PC-style at 0x378 (0x778) [PCSPP,TRISTATE,EPP]
parport0: irq 7 detected
lp0: using parport0 (polling).
lp0: console ready
eth0: no IPv6 routers present
ACPI: PCI interrupt 0000:00:02.0[A] -> GSI 10 (level, low) -> IRQ 10
[drm] Initialized i915 1.1.0 20040405 on minor 0:
mtrr: base(0xd8020000) is not aligned on a size(0x258000) boundary
ISO 9660 Extensions: Microsoft Joliet Level 3
ISOFS: changing to secondary root
```

6.2.2 lspci command

This command displays all the PCI buses in the system and all devices connected to them. The information is very useful while debugging drivers. For example the following output is given on my machine.

```
00:00.0 Host bridge: Intel Corp. 82845G/GL[Brookdale-G]/GE/PE DRAM Controller/Host-Hub Interface (rev 03)
00:02.0 VGA compatible controller: Intel Corp. 82845G/GL[Brookdale-G]/GE Chipset Integrated Graphics Device (rev 03)
00:1d.0 USB Controller: Intel Corp. 82801DB/DBL/DBM (ICH4/ICH4-L/ICH4-M) USB UHCI Controller #1 (rev 02)
00:1d.1 USB Controller: Intel Corp. 82801DB/DBL/DBM (ICH4/ICH4-L/ICH4-M) USB UHCI Controller #2 (rev 02)
00:1d.2 USB Controller: Intel Corp. 82801DB/DBL/DBM (ICH4/ICH4-L/ICH4-M) USB UHCI Controller #3 (rev 02)
00:1d.7 USB Controller: Intel Corp. 82801DB/DBM (ICH4/ICH4-M) USB2 EHCI Controller (rev 02)
00:1e.0 PCI bridge: Intel Corp. 82801 PCI Bridge (rev 82)
00:1f.0 ISA bridge: Intel Corp. 82801DB/DBL (ICH4/ICH4-L) LPC Interface Bridge (rev 02)
```

00:1f.1 IDE interface: Intel Corp. 82801DB (ICH4) IDE Controller (rev 02)

00:1f.3 SMBus: Intel Corp. 82801DB/DBL/DBM (ICH4/ICH4-L/ICH4-M) SMBus Controller (rev 02)

00:1f.5 Multimedia audio controller: Intel Corp. 82801DB/DBL/DBM (ICH4/ICH4-L/ICH4-M) AC'97 Audio Controller (rev 02)

01:06.0 Ethernet controller: Silicon Integrated Systems [SiS] SiS900 PCI Fast Ethernet (rev 02)

6.2.3 lsmod command

lsmod command shows the status of all the modules currently available in the Linux kernel. The device driver modules are loaded during the bootup time or after the booting. However, this command displays all the modules currently seen in kernel space. For example lsmod command gave the following output.

```
Module              Size  Used by
nls_utf8            1985  1
i915               76869  2
parport_pc         24705  1
lp                 11565  0
parport            41737  2 parport_pc,lp
autofs4            24005  0
i2c_dev            10433  0
i2c_core           22081  1 i2c_dev
sunrpc            160421  1
ipt_REJECT          6465  1
ipt_state           1857  3
ip_conntrack       40693  1 ipt_state
iptable_filter      2753  1
ip_tables          16193  3 ipt_REJECT,ipt_state,iptable_filter
dm_mod             54741  0
button              6481  0
battery             8517  0
ac                  4805  0
md5                 4033  1
ipv6              232577  8
uhci_hcd           31449  0
ehci_hcd           31557  0
hw_random           5589  0
snd_intel8x0       34829  2
snd_ac97_codec     64401  1 snd_intel8x0
snd_pcm_oss        47609  0
snd_mixer_oss      17217  2 snd_pcm_oss
```

```
snd_pcm              97993  2 snd_intel8x0,snd_pcm_oss
snd_timer            29765  1 snd_pcm
snd_page_alloc        9673  2 snd_intel8x0,snd_pcm
gameport              4801  1 snd_intel8x0
snd_mpu401_uart       8769  1 snd_intel8x0
snd_rawmidi          26725  1 snd_mpu401_uart
snd_seq_device        8137  1 snd_rawmidi
snd                  54053  11
snd_intel8x0,snd_ac97_codec,snd_pcm_oss,snd_mixer_oss,snd_pcm,snd_timer,snd
mpu401_uart,snd_rawmidi,snd_seq_device
soundcore             9889  2 snd
sis900               18629  0
floppy               58609  0
ext3                116809  1
jbd                  74969  1 ext3
```

rmmod command can be used to remove a driver from memory

modprob command can be used to load and remove drivers to/from memory. It has lot of options. For example **modprob –l** will display all modules currently available in kernel space along with their location details.

6.2.4 mii-tool

command can be used to view and set properties of network interface. For example the same gave the following output on machine.

```
eth0: negotiated 100baseTx-FD, link ok
```

cdrecord command can be used to use CD on your machine.

discover command

Discover is a set of libraries and utilities for gathering and reporting information about system's HW by using OS-specific modules and provides system-independent interface for querying XML data sources about this HW. We can find the same at http://alioth.debian.org/projects/pkg-discover .

6.3 Configuring X

Debian also has a post-install system for configuring XFree86-running the dpkg-reconfigure. xserver-xfree86 command will let you reconfigure the X

The XF86Config File is the main config file is used by XFree86. This configuration file requires many sections which are required to be filled by us. Important sections are:

"Files" - configures file paths for fonts etc.
"Module" - for enabling X server extensions
"InputDevice" - for handling keyboard, mouse etc
"Monitor" - for monitor hardware configuration
"Device" - configures the display card
"Screen" - defines the resolution and colours to use
"ServerLayout" - aggregates all configuration

Configuring Input Devices

Keyboard section supports:
Model (vendor, extensions)
Layout (language, locale)
Geometry (number of keys etc)
Other for support special keys

For example this is a sample for specifying about our keyboard.

```
Section "InputDevice"
Identifier "Keyboard0"
Driver "Keyboard"
Option "XkbModel" "pc104"
Option "XkbLayout" "us,cz,de"
Option "XKbOptions" "grp:alt_shift_toggle"
Option "XkbGeometry" "pc(pc104)"
EndSection
```

Mouse section supports:
Device - Serial, Bus, PS/2, USB
Protocol - Logitech, (IM)PS/2, Intellimouse etc.
ZAxisMapping - for mouse wheel
Emulate3Buttons

For example the following is seen in my configuration file.

```
Section "InputDevice"
Identifier "Mouse0"
Driver "mouse"
```

```
Option "Protocol" "IMPS/2"
Option "Device" "/dev/psaux"
Option "ZAxisMapping" "4 5"
Option "Emulate3Buttons"
EndSection
```

Configuring the Monitor

Main options:
HorizSync
VertRefresh
Other options

The following is seen in my X configuration file. Actually if your X windows is not running then gather horizontal and vertical frequencies from your monitors documentation and enter the same here.

```
Section "Monitor"
Identifier "Samtron"
VendorName "Monitor Vendor"
ModelName "Monitor Model"
HorizSync 30.0 - 55.0
VertRefresh 50.0 - 120.0
EndSection
```

X Drivers

XFree86 ships with drivers for most low and high end video cards; out of which vesa driver can run a basic X display on all video cards. Most common drivers that ship with XFree86 are

ATI ati
Cirrus Logic cirrus
Intel i810 i810
Matrox mga
NVidia nv
SiS sis
S3 s3

Configuring the Display Card
Driver - driver to use
BusID - PCI / AGP bus ID
VideoRam - (optional)
Hardware-specific options

The following type information has to be entered in device section.

```
Section "Device"
Identifier "Card0"
Driver "radeon"
VendorName "ATI Technologies Inc"
BusID "PCI:1:0:0"
EndSection
```

"Screen" section is used to write information about the monitor and video card are combined to define colour and resolutions to use

Device - which display device to use

Monitor - which monitor to use

DefaultColorDepth - default colour depth

Display subsection - to configure resolution

Depth - configured colour depth

Modes - resolution to use

An example Screen Section.

```
Section "Screen"
Identifier "Screen0"
Device "Card0"
Monitor "Samtron"
DefaultColorDepth 24
SubSection "Display"
Depth 24
Modes "1024x768"
EndSubSection
EndSection
```

The following steps can be used to configure X Windows when you are unable to configure the same during normal installations.

- Have XFree86 automatically generate the skeletal config file
- Command: XFree86 -configure
- This should generate the /root/XF86Config.new config file
- Move this to /etc/X11/XF86Config-4 and customise the following sections:

InputDevice - for mouse

Screen - for colour depth and resolution

(The keyboard, monitor and device defaults should work just fine)

- Test out whether X starts correctly by running: XFree86
- Launch desktop using startx

Configuring X Clients

- Simple example: **exec gnome-session**

This will start the Gnome Desktop.

To start KDE, we can use the following **exec startkde**

6.3.1 X Windows across the Network

Since X Windows is based a client server protocol, it is possible to attach a X client to another X Server over the network.

On the server :

Ensure that the X Server is listening on its TCP ports. Debian does not configure the X Server to listen on its TCP ports by default. This can be changed by editing the /etc/X11/xinit/xserverrc file and removing the -nolistentcp option.

X Server must *allow* other clients to connect to it. The xhost command can be used for this. Eg. Running "xhost +" turns off all access control.

On the client end set the DISPLAY variable. This is used by any X Client to determine which X server to connect to. Generally it is set to "0:0" - meaning the 0th display on the local machine. To connect to a X Server over the network using its IP address, we can use:

```
export DISPLAY=x.x.x.x:0
```

where x.x.x.x is the IP address of the server machine. :0 specifies that we want to use the 0th display. This is the default can be over-written if you are running multiple X servers on your system.

Start the client. Once this environment is set, all subsequent X clients will be shown on the server. Note that the client application is still running on the client machine and would use its resources - the server is just its display

6.4 Conclusions

This chapter details Debian Linux installation in step by step fashion. In addition, how to install packages after installing the basic Linux is emphasized. Also, it explains how X windows can be configured manually.

7 Redhat Fedora Core 4 Installation Guidelines

7.1 Introduction

The following information is extracted from Stanton finley.net/fedora_core_4_installation_notes_nocss.html and is under GNU license. We assume an i386 to i686 system (32 bit) with, an "always on" LAN or broadband connection configured "DHCP" and at least 10 GB of free disk space for the Fedora partition. Instructions for dual booting Windows and Fedora are included as well as a section on setting up an graphics card. For the most part the steps should be followed in the order that they were written as certain programs should be installed and certain configurations made in order to facilitate later steps. However after the base installation is complete additional user selected program installations are, of course, optional.

1. Download and burn the five Fedora Core 4 CDs from iso images or the DVD iso image from fedora.redhat.com/download. (You should get FC4-i386-disc1.iso, FC4-i386-disc2.iso, FC4-i386-disc3.iso, FC4-i386-disc4.iso and FC4-i386-rescuecd.iso.) The CD iso images or the DVD iso image are also available using bittorrent.
2. Partition your hard disk with one of the disk partition creation/editing tools on the System Rescue CD available at http://www.sysresccd.org/. We could also use a commercial product such as PartitionMagic (www.symantec.com/partitionmagic). The
3. Configure your bios settings to boot first from the CD drive.
4. Insert the first Fedora Core 4 CD or the DVD and reboot your machine.
5. We will get the following screen (Figure 7.1). We can select the "boot" prompt hit enter.

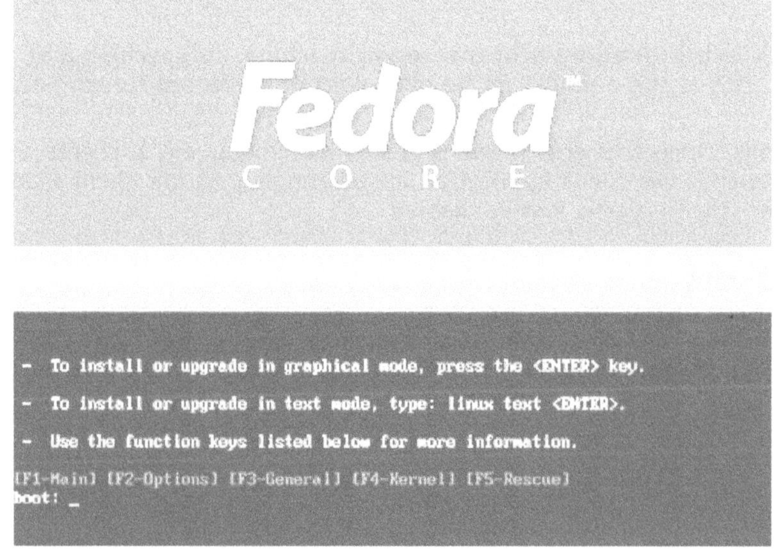

Figure 7.1 Boot up Menu of Redhat Linux.

5. We will get the following screen (Figure 7.1). We can select the "boot" prompt hit enter.
6. Hit enter for "ok" and enter again for "Test" to test your CD or DVD media or the right arrow key to select the "Continue" box and hit enter to skip this test. (We recommend testing your media to determine if your CDs or DVDs are properly burned). If your media passes you will be given an opportunity to check additional CDs or DVDs. When you are finished testing hit enter for "ok", right arrow to the "Continue" box and hit enter to continue.
7. When Anaconda, the Fedora Core installer loads click "Next" at the "Welcome.." page.
8. Click "Next" at the "Language Selection" page for default English or select your language.
9. Click "Next" at the "Keyboard Configuration" page for default U. S. English or select your language.
10. Select "custom" on the "Installation Type" page. Click "Next".
11. Select "automatically partition" on the "Disk Partitioning Setup" page (see Figure 7.2). Click "Next". If you elect to manually edit your partition with Disk Druid, double click on the partition, select the "swap" file type, and configure your swap space size to equal about twice your computer's physical memory size. Double click on the remainder of the partition to configure it as a Linux ext3 file system. At minimum you must designate this remaining space (probably /dev/hda2 or /dev/sda2) as the root "/" partition mount point. Refer the chapter on "Devices and File systems".

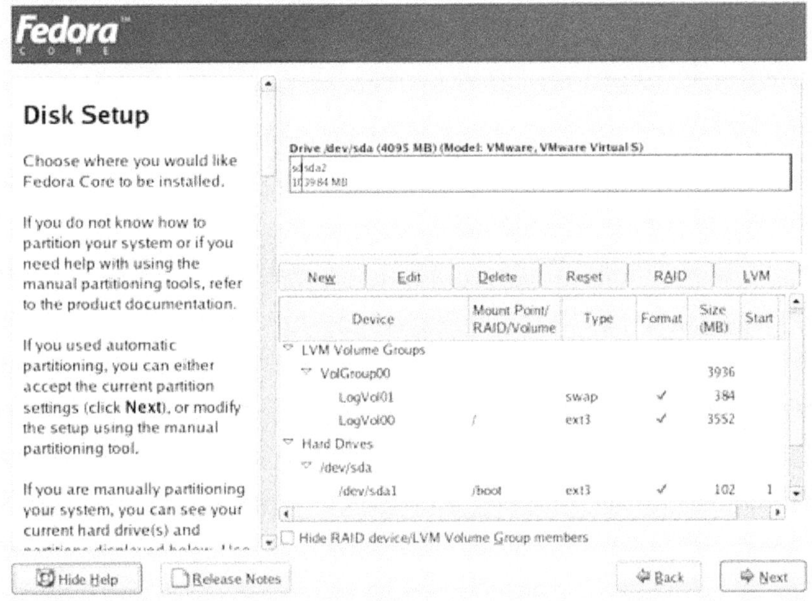

Figure 7.2 Disk Setup Screen.

12. If you are going to dual boot Windows and Fedora and you already have Windows installed on another partition select "keep all partitions and use existing free space" on the "Automatic Partitioning" page. Otherwise select "Remove all partitions on this system" to use all of your hard disk for Fedora or choose "Remove all Linux partitions on this system" for a fresh install over any existing Linux partitions. Click "Next".

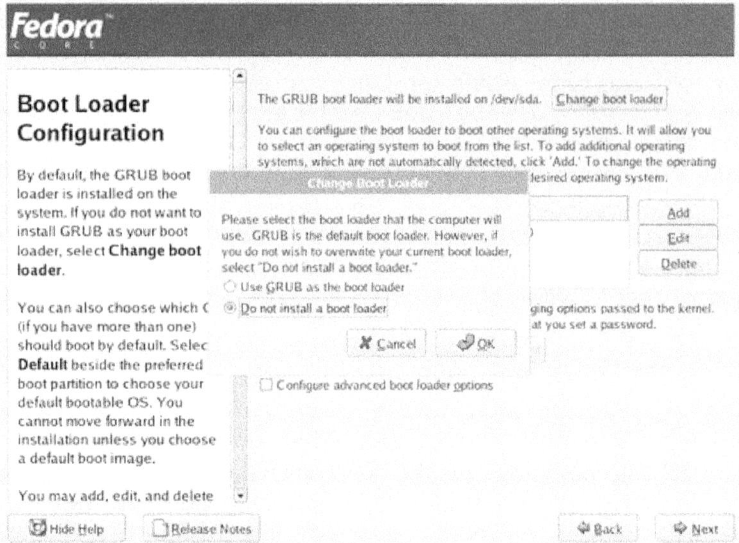

Figure 7.3 Boot Loader Setting Screen.

13. Click "Next" on the "Disk Setup" page.
14. If you are dual booting Windows and Fedora Check the "other" check box on the "Boot Loader Configuration" page. Click "edit". Type "Windows" in the "label" box and uncheck the "default boot target" check box. Click "ok".
15. Click the "default" check box next to "Fedora Core" to make it your default boot operating system. Click "Next".
16. Leave "eth0" and hostname "automatically via DHCP" on the "Network Configuration" page. Click "Next".

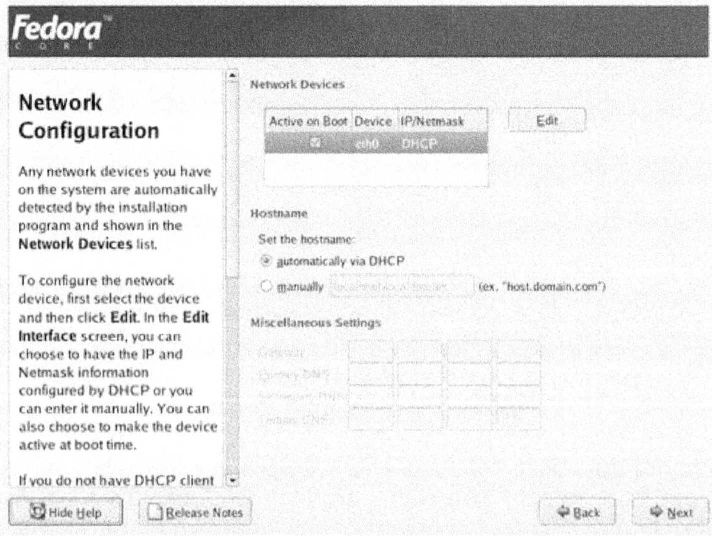

Figure 7.4 Network Settings screen.

17. Leave "Enable firewall" selected on the "Firewall Configuration" page and click the check boxes for "ssh", "http", "https", "ftp" and "smtp". Leave "Enable SELinux" "active". Click "Next".
18. Click on the map for your location on the "Time Zone Selection" page. Click "Next".
19. Set your preferred root password on the "Set Root Password" page. Click "Next".
20. You will see a message "Reading package information...".
21. Scroll down the "Package Group Selection" page and click in the "everything" box under "miscellaneous". Click "Next".

    (There has been some criticism from some quarters regarding the fact that I recommend doing an "everything" installation. From my point of view there are several good reasons to do so. There are many wonderful packages in a Fedora Core "everything" installation including a web server and all the packages needed to make it work with modern scripting language support. Installing everything supplies the novice with a huge Linux playground containing hundreds of great programs to explore. If you install everything there will be no question that package dependencies and inter-dependencies are met. Everything will be there and everything will "just work" including the kernel development packages in case you need to compile something such as a proprietary driver for your video card. Why not install everything? In this day and age bandwidth and disk space are cheap and plentiful.)
22. You will see a message "Checking dependencies..."
23. Click "Next" on "About to Install" page.
24. Click "continue" to get to the "Installing Packages" page. You will see a "Formatting / file system..." message, a "Starting install process..." message, a "Preparing to install..." message, and you will eventually be prompted to insert the remainder of the installation CDs unless you are using the DVD. (It took about an hour to install "everything" on my system.)
25. When the installation is complete remove the last CD or the DVD and click "reboot" for the first boot screen.
26. After Fedora reboots click "Next" on the "Welcome" page.
27. Click the appropriate radio button to agree to the license agreement and Click "Next".
28. If you are already connected to an "always on" LAN or broadband connection click on the "Network Time Protocol" tab, click in the "Enable Network Time Protocol" check box, click the down arrow in the "Server" box, select "clock.redhat.com" , click "Add" and click "Next". You will see a message "Contacting NTP Server. Please wait"...".
29. On the "Display" page select your preferred screen resolution and color depth based upon the capabilities of your monitor. If your monitor's screen resolution is not available in the dialog box or if Fedora did not recognize your monitor or graphics card you will have an opportunity to configure them later. Click "Next".
30. On the "System User" page choose a user name (in lower case, not "root"), a full name (any case), and a password for that default user. Click "Next".
31. Click "play test sound" on the "Sound Card" page to test your sound system. Your should hear three chords in sequence. If you don't you can try to configure your sound card later. Click "No" or "Yes" in the "Did you hear the sample sound?" dialog box. Click "Next".
32. Click "Next" on the "Additional CDs" page.
33. Click "Next" on the "Finish Setup" page.
34. Log in as "root" with the root password you selected earlier.

35. Click "log in anyway" if a Gnome error message appears on first boot. We will correct this later.
36. When Fedora finishes booting to the graphical interface click on the top panel, hold your left mouse button down, drag the top panel to the bottom of the screen, and release the mouse button.
37. Click "Applications" > "System Tools". Right click on "Terminal" and select "Add this launcher to panel".
38. Right click on the terminal icon on the bottom panel and select "move". Move the icon to the left near the other icons and click to position it there.
39. Click on the terminal icon. This will open the terminal.
40. Type:

    gedit /boot/grub/grub.conf
41. Hit enter and gedit will open. Revise the "hiddenmenu" and "kernel" lines in grub.conf so that your file looks like this:

```
# grub.conf generated by anaconda
#
# Note that you do not have to rerun grub after making changes to this file
# NOTICE:  You have a /boot partition.  This means that
#          all kernel and initrd paths are relative to /boot/, eg.
#          root (hd0,1)
#          kernel /vmlinuz-version ro root=/dev/VolGroup00/LogVol00
#          initrd /initrd-version.img
#boot=/dev/hda
default=0
timeout=5
splashimage=(hd0,1)/grub/splash.xpm.gz
#hiddenmenu
title Fedora Core 4 (2.6.11-1.1369_FC4)
                root (hd0,0)
        kernel  /vmlinuz-2.6.11-1.1369_FC4  ro  root=/dev/VolGroup00/LogVol00
        vga=788 selinux=0
                initrd /initrd-2.6.11-1.1369_FC4.img
title Windows
rootnoverify (hd0,0)
chainloader +1
```

Disabling the "hiddenmenu" with the "#" comment and removing "rhgb quiet" from the kernel line will cause the operating system selection menu to display immediately upon boot and will also disable the graphical boot screens so that you will see the boot sequence scroll by in text. You may also choose to disable SELinux here by including "selinux=0" on the kernel line. Leave out the "selinux=0" if you wish to keep SELinux enabled. If you choose to use SELinux (Security Enhanced Linux) you should search the web for information about it and how it impacts a Linux installation. Click on the "save" icon in gedit and close it. Close the terminal.

42. Click on "Desktop" > "System Settings" > "Server Settings" > "Services" and deselect system services that you will not immediately use. When you click on each of them you will see a description as to what they are for. If you're not sure, leave them in there. (I deselected "anacron", "apmd", "atd", "canna", "cpuspeed", "cups", "cups-config-daemon", "hpoj", "mDNSResponder", "mdmonitor", "nfslock", "nifd", "pcmcia", "rpcgssd", "rpcidmapd", and "sendmail".) Click the "save" icon. You should also select "Edit Runlevel" on the menu, select "Runlevel 3", deselect the same system services as you just did for run level 5, and save them as well by clicking the "save" icon. Then close the service configuration screen. (Run level 3 is for text mode only without X windows and we will use this run level later when configuring the nVidia driver.)
43. If a Gnome error message appeared on first boot and you had to click "log in anyway", open the terminal and type:

    gedit /etc/hosts

    Hit enter and gedit will open. Place your cursor after "localhost" and hit tab. Then type in the characters that appear on your root terminal screen after "root@" up to but not including the space and tilde (~). When you are finished, your hosts file should look something like this:

    ```
    # Do not remove the following line, or various programs
    # that require network functionality will fail.
    127.0.0.1          localhost.localdomain localhost x1-6-00-04-5a-5e-ac-83
    ```

    Click on the "save" icon in gedit and close it. This will eliminate the Gnome error message that appears on boot-up on some systems.
44. In the root terminal type:

    gedit /etc/modprobe.conf

    Hit enter and gedit will open. Add these lines to the bottom of the file:

    alias net-pf-10 off

    alias ipv6 off

    Add a carriage return if required. (There should be a blank line at the bottom of these files.) Click on the "save" icon in gedit and close it. This will speed up browsing and file transfers in some cases by decreasing DNS lookup time.
45. Click on "Desktop" > "System Settings" > "Login Screen". Under the "Timed Login" section click on the "Login a user automatically after a specified number of seconds" check box. Type or select your default user name that you selected during installation (lower case, not "root") in the "Timed login username:" box and type "5" in the "Seconds before login:" box . Click "close".
46. Click "Desktop" > "Log Out" > "Restart the computer" and click "ok".
47. After boot up you should be logged in as the default user. Click on the top panel, hold your left mouse button down, drag the top panel to the bottom of the screen, and release the mouse button.
48. Click the red flashing up2date icon in the lower right. Click "Forward". Click "Forward". Click "Forward". Click "Apply". Click on the up2date icon in the lower right again. Click on the "Launch up2date..." box. Type in your root password and click "ok". Click on the "Package Exceptions" tab, click on "kernel*" and click on

the "Remove" box. Click "ok" again. Click on "yes" to install the key. Click "Forward". Click "Forward" again. After the headers are downloaded click on the "select all packages" check box and click "Forward". You will see a progress dialog "Testing package set / solving RPM dependencies". Click "Yes" on each instance if you get messages "...not signed with a GPG signature..." When this is complete the updates will be downloaded. (This may take a very long time depending upon your connection speed the first time you run up2date and you may think that your installation has hung but it actually has not. If you don't have the patience for this configure yum as described below and do a "yum update" as root instead.) Click "Forward" to install the updates and "Forward" again to complete. Click "Finish". "Click "Close". Click "Activate" in the Subscription Alert box if it appears, launch up2date, and check for updates again as described above. Click "Desktop" > "Log Out">"Restart the computer" and click "ok" to reboot. Note: If you get errors with up2date or yum with error messages similar to "file /usr/share/doc/HTML/en /common/xml.dcl conflicts between attempted installs of kdelibs-3.4.2-0.fc4.1 and kde-i18n-Polish-3.4.2-0.fc4.1" do as root a "yum remove kde-i18n-Polish", then a "yum update", and finally a "yum install kde-i18n-Polish".

7.2 Configuring X Windows

Run the following command and modify the section as explained in previous chapter.

```
gedit /etc/X11/xorg.conf
```

Hit enter and gedit will open. Scroll down to the "Monitor" section. Find the "HorizSync" line and enter your monitor's supported horizontal frequency range. The line should look something like "HorizSync 30.0 - 70.0". Enter your monitor's supported vertical frequency range opposite "VertRefresh". The line should look something like "VertRefresh 50.0 - 160.0". Scroll down to the "Screen" section and opposite each instance of "modes" enter you monitor's supported pixel resolution, starting with the highest. The line should look something like "Modes "1024x768" "800x600" "640x480"". You should be able to get these values from your monitor's manual or from a search for your monitor by manufacturer and model number on the Internet. Hit the "save" button in gedit and exit gedit. Log out and log back in.

Click "Desktop" > "System Settings" > "Display". Type your root password in the dialog box presented and hit enter. Click the down arrow on the right of the "Resolution:" box and select your preferred pixel resolution. Click the down arrow on the right of the "Color Depth:" box and select your preferred color depth. Click "OK". Log out and log back in.

Click "Desktop" > "Preferences" > "Screen Resolution". Click the down arrow on the right of the "Resolution:" box and select your preferred pixel resolution. Click the down arrow on the right of the "Refresh rate:" box and select the highest refresh rate available. A refresh rate of 85 Hz or more will decrease noticeable flicker significantly and may eliminate it completely. Click "Apply". Log out and log back in.

7.2.1 Installing Other Packages under Redhat distributions after Installing base system

To Install

rpm –ivh packagefile

for example

rpm –ivh apache-1.3-12.rpm

The options mean: -i=install, -v =verify, –h=print hash marks as a progress meter.

The installation may fail because some other package(s) are needed to resolve dependencies: install them first.

A package may be removed using the command rpm –e packagename, e.g.

rpm –e apache

Notice that the *package name* is used, not the name of the *file* which contained the package: that file probably isn't around any more.

Upgrading to a new version is just like installing, using

rpm –Uvh packagefile

Again the operation may fail because of a dependency that would be broken. If significant changes to the form of configuration files have taken place between versions of the software, RPM will normally save the older configuration file, and advise where. The differences between the files must be investigated and resolved.

What is installed?

RPM has facilities to:

To list the installed packages:

rpm –qa (pipe this through more, or grep)

To find the package a file belongs to:

rpm –qf filename

This later option is useful to find out what some cryptic filename actually means:

rpm –qf imrc

There are numerous options to specify exactly how much information these commands return.

Verifying package integrity

RPM is useful for verifying that a system is in pristine condition: checking for accidents or even cracking. This compares the current state of files with the same information from the original, pristine, sources.

rpm –Va verifies all installed packages. Again, pipe this to more

rpm –Vf filename verifies the package containing a file, for example rpm -Vf /bin/vi

verifies the vi editor package.

If there is no problem nothing is displayed. If there are any discrepancies, a string of 8 characters is displayed, the letter "c" if the file is possibly a configuration file (which you *might* have modified) and then the file name.

The string of characters denotes the failure of certain tests: if the character is displayed a test has failed; a "." means the test passed.

The tests are:

5 - an MD5 checksum D - a device has changed in some way

S - the file size U - the user who "owns" the file

L - a link to, or from, the file G - the group owning the file

T - the file modification time M - the file mode - including permissions

If a test fails investigation is called for: the change may be innocuous and deliberate, or may be a symptom of a more serious problem

7.3 Conclusions

This chapter explore how to install Redhat Fedora core version 4. It explains how to partition the disk, how to select key board, language and packages while installing the Redhat release. In addition, it illustrates how to configure X windows manually if we encounter any difficulty during automatic installation.

8 Installing Apache : The Web Server

8.1 Introduction

Web pages, web hosting, web page development, web server etc., became normal usage words these days. . It's old news that the internet has made information available on a scale never before seen in human history. It's old news that the most popular way to provide this information is HTML. It's even old news that Apache serves more than 60% of all web pages, thus making it more popular than all other web servers combined.

Most distributions of Linux include pre-compiled versions of Apache, and many include the source code as well. Usually the easiest thing to do is just install Apache from your CD's. But if you want the latest version of Apache or insist on pristine sources, you're going to want to download. Everything Apache can be found at http://www.apache.org/ including source code, documentation, helper applications, and (for the code-head) more information about the Apache API than you can take in one sitting, and of course, binaries for Linux..

Download the file **httpd-2_0_54.tar.bz2** from www.apache.org

Now uncompress the file using bunzip2 command.

bunzip2 httpd-2-0_54.tar.bz2

Now extract the files from tar archives using:

tar –xvf httpd-2_0_54.tar

Now decide about the apache directory organization. Table 8.1 demonstrates the possible directory structure for apache.

Table 8.1 Possible directory structure apache SW distribution.

Basic config.layout options	
Option	**Meaning**
prefix	This is the basic top level directory of most things apache.This option is almost purely at your discretion
execprefix	The prefix for binary files.Typically */usr*
bindir	Where apache places binary files.Typically *$execprefix/bin*
sbindir	Where apache places system binaries.Typically *$execprefix/sbin*
libexecdir	Where apache looks for what can best be described as apache-specific helper files. These include such things as dynamic modules, which we'll discuss later. Typically */usr/lib/apache*
mandir	Where apache will install the manpage(s)Typically */usr/man*
sysconfdir	Where apache looks by default for the runtime config files. Typically */etc/httpd/conf*
datadir	Used to mark the top level of the directory tree containing the data to be served. Typically the same as *$prefix*

Table 8.1 ***Contd...***

Basic config.layout options	
Option	**Meaning**
iconsdir	Where apache looks for icons representing various mime-types when serving ftp directories as web-pages. Typically *$datadir/icons*
htdocs	This is the "document root", where your main "index.html" lives. Typically *$datadir/htdocs*
cgidir	The default location for cgi executables. Typically *$datadir/cgi-bin*
includedir	Location for include files for compiling apache add-ons. Typically *$prefix/incluce /apache*
localstatedir	Where apache stores state files. Typically */var*
runtimedir	Where apache will store runtime state files. Typically *$localstatedir/run*
logfiledir	Default location of apache log files. Typically *$localstatedir/log/apache*
proxycachedir	Where apache will store cached files if you've included the proxy module as part of the configuration. Typically *$localstatedir/cache/apache*

Now that you've decided your file layout structure, you need to consider what capabilities you want your web server to have. Several things that we take for granted about web servers may not be default behavior. In general, the apache team included the most useful modules (see Table 8.2) as part of the source distributions default configuration, but you should probably take a good look at *src/Configuration.tmpl*. Most modules can either be included statically in the binary or can be loaded dynamically by the server as needed (DSO -- Dynamic Shared Object).

Both methods have their pros and cons, and in general the normal guidelines for static vs. dynamic apply. The static method is the easiest, and makes for faster servers. The downside is that your web server can suffer "Microsoft Syndrome" and can begin to take on swiss army knife features at the expense of memory efficiency and executable size. Using dynamic shared modules makes your overall executable size smaller, meaning less resources are required to handle multiple instances (apache uses the fork-ahead server model for those C coders keeping score at home) and children spawn faster. The downsides are that there is a measurable latency to loading/linking the module into apache on the fly, and DSO's don't execute quite as fast as static modules. Since benchmarking these tradeoffs is highly traffic-pattern dependant, and patterns tend to change over time, it's a real tough call at design time.

Table 8.2 Short list of loadable modules for apache web server.

Mod Name	**Description**
actions	Executing CGI script based on media type or request method
autoindex	Automatic directory listings
cgi	Invoking CGI scripts
env	Altering the environment passed to CGI and SSI pages
imap	Improved support for server side image maps
include	Support for **S**erver **S**ide **I**ncludes
log_config	Configurable logging support.

Table 8.2 *Contd...*

Mod Name	Description
mime_magic	Support for media types based on file contents (type).
mime	Support for media types based on common but braindead MIME type.
negotiation	Support for content negotiation.
proxy	Provides for HTTP 1.0 caching proxy support.
rewrite	URI to filename rewriting on the fly.
setenvif	Allows setting env variables based on request attributes. This is useful to deal with buggy browsers, or to deny cool features to MSIE users just for the fun of it.
so	Supports loading shared modules at runtime.
status	Provides information on server status and performance.
userdir	Supports user-specific directories (member home pages).
vhost_alias	Dynamically configured mass virtual hosting.

Once you have decided your layout, and made your decisions about modules, you're ready to configure the source code for compilation. This important step sets up the makefiles to be compatible with Linux and also sets up the proper linking options for your modules. **Go to the root of the apache source tree**, and enter the command

./configure --with-layout= ***MyLayoutName*** \
--enable-module= ***module_name*** \
--enable-module= ***module_name2*** \
--enable-shared= ***shared_module_name*** \
--enable-shared= ***shared_module_name2*** \
--disable-module= ***unwanted_module_name***

In our case we have simply used **./configure** to let everything to be default.

To build apache just enter the command

make

If our Linux box has a proper development environment set up (and it should, or you probably would have already skipped ahead to the configuration section) everything should go smoothly. Once the build has completed, installing apache is just a matter of typing

make install

We now need a way to start and stop apache on our system. Most distro's have a fairly good SYSV init template to copy somewhere in the /etc/rc directories, but apache provides a program called apachectl to start and stop the server if you want to use it.

In principle we may have to edit the file httpd.conf to make apache to meet our needs. However, we can simply test the bare version with the following steps.

/usr/local/apache2/bin/acpachectl start

Now start a web browser such as Fire Fox and then enter the web page as http://localost. If web page is displayed indicating apache web server is running.

8.2 Basic Configuration

In order to configure the apache web server we have modify/edit the file **/etc/httpd/conf/ httpd.conf**. The config file is broken up into three sections, the Global Section, the Main (or default server) section, and the Virtual Hosts section.

8.2.1 Global Section

This section controls behavior that is global to all instances of apache running on your system. The example configuration file contains excellent documentation for each of the options. Below is a table (Table 8.3) containing some general guidance for use when modifying the options.

Table 8.3 Description of global section items.

Directive	Hints
ServerRoot	If you configured sysconfdir to be */etc/httpd/conf* then make this *"/etc/httpd"*
LockFile	This file is used by apache to decide if it's running or not. If the path does not start with a leading /, apache will assume the path is relative to the **ServerRoot** defined above. (RedHat */var/lock/httpd.lock*)
pidfile	This file is where apache stores the process id of the server. If the path does not start with a leading "/" apache will assume the path is relative to the **ServerRoot** defined above. (Redhat */var/run/httpd.pid*)
ScoreBoardFile	This file stores internal server information, but is not needed on most Linux configurations. Just to be safe, create a place for it. (RedHat */var/run/httpd.scoreboard*)
TimeOut	This is the number of seconds before net traffic times out. The default on this is 300, which is 5 minutes. It can be set much lower, but values below 30 tend to cause problems.
KeepAlive	Allows persistant connections. Unless you have a good reasons to not want them, set this to "on".
MaxKeepAliveRequests	This determines the maximum number of Requests allowed on a persistant channel before it closes. 100 is a reasonable number
KeepAliveTimeout	Determines how long a KeepAlive channel will remain open if idle. 15 is a good number.
MinSpareServers	Sets the desired number of servers that are idle, awaiting requests. If there are ever less than this many of idle child processes, apache will start spawning more until this number is reached. Too many wastes resources. Too few and spikes in server hits could degrade performance. 2 is a good number for home or SOHO, 3 - 5 for a business or small university.
MaxSpareServers	Sets the maximum desired number of idle servers. If there are more idle servers than desired, apache will begin to kill off children, reclaiming their resources. 10 is the default, while for the hobbyist or SOHO user, a value of 5 can be used to save resources.

Table 8.3 ***Contd...***

Directive	Hints
StartServers	The number of children to spawn at startup. The default is 5. Busy sites should set this higher, but not too high or you'll spend your first minute and a half spawning children and not serving requests. Apache will dynamically adjust the number of processes later, so setting this value very high is almost never useful.
MaxClients	This sets a ceiling on the number of child processes that can be spawned. It can be set up to 256 without modifying source code.
MaxRequestsPerChild	This sets the maximum number of requests that a child process will handle before dying. It is mainly useful on IRIX and SunOS where there are noticeable memory leaks in the libraries. A vaule of 0 will allow unlimited requests per child, and is claimed to be safe on Linux. I recommend a value of 1000, or 10000 for heavily loaded sites.
Listen	Determines the address and port number that apache will bind. This can be used to limit apache to a specific address. For instance, you can use **Listen 127.0.0.1:80** to cause apache to respond only to requests from the localhost. The usual value is 80, which tells apache to listen on the HTTP port of all interfaces. Multiple **Listen** directives can be used.
BindAddress	Detemines which IP addresses apache will respond to. This is used on machines with multiple IP addresses (either through multiplexing or using multiple interfaces). The normal value is *, which causes apache to listen on all addresses.
ExtendedStatus	This is only useful if you have loaded mod_status, and tells apache to keep track of extended information on a per request basis. It cannot be used on a virtualhost by virtualhost basis. Set this value to "on" if you've decided to compile mod_status as a built-in module (recommended).
ClearModuleList	Apache has a list of modules that should be active. This directive clears that list. It is assumed that you will then turn on what you want using the **AddModule** directive.
AddModule	Modules are sort of complicated. When you compile apache, it gets a list of included modules, not all of which are "turned on". This directive is used to activate a built-in module. It can be used even if you haven't used the **ClearModuleList** directive.
LoadModule	This directive is used to load a dynamically loaded module (as oppossed to a built-in module. Order of execution can be important, so pay close attention to the example configuration and the documentation for any alternative modules you load.
<IfDefine></IfDefine>	This is used to conditionally execute directives based on whether or not a specific value is defined, usually by means of a command line switch (-D foo). One use for this is for a startup script to check for the existance of a module, and load/configure it if it exists (RedHat's startup script does this, for example).

8.2.2 Main (Default Server) Section

Section 2 of the configuration file deals with the default server. The default server (or main server) is the one that will handle any requests not captured by a <VirtualHost> stanza in your configuration. Directives and instructions that you set in this section (given in Table 8.4) are, in general, inherited by virtual hosts as well, so you can set some good default behaviors here rather than duplicating a lot of effort. Settings inside <VirtualHost> stanzas will override these options for that particular virtual host only.

Table 8.4 Directives in main section and their explanations.

Directive	Notes
Port	Here for historical reasons, and for setting the **SERVER_PORT** environment variable for CGI and SSI. Set this to whatever your HTTP port will be (usually 80). Note: This does NOT apply to virtual hosts.
User	Sets the user that apache will handle requests as. For security reasons, apache changes its effective UID before handling requests, so all of your documents must be accessible to this user. For this reason, it is useful to create a user called *www* or *apache* to use with your web server. Running as the user *nobody* or as UID -1 does not work on all systems or with all libraries.
Group	Just as apache changes its UID, it also changes its GID. This is the group to change to. Once again, *nobody* can cause you some difficult to track-down problems, so it's probably a good idea to create a group.
ServerAdmin	Set this to the e-mail address that should receive all error notifications.
ServerName	Set this to the fully qualified domain name of the server. Also used when setting up name-based virtual hosts. If you don't set this, you will likely encounter problems on startup.
DocumentRoot	Set this to the directory to search for the main index file for this server. Apache will search for a file that matches your **DirectoryIndex** in this directory to display when no other page is requested (as when you request http://www.example.com)
UserDir	When using the mod_userdir module, this allows you to map requests to user's home directories instead of to the document root tree. Set this to "www" to map requests for *http://example.org/~foo* to *~foo/www* on the example.org server, for example. For security reasons, if you use this, also use **UserDir Disabled root.**
DirectoryIndex	Used with mod_dir, this option sets the search order for files when a user requests a directory listing by specifying a "/" at the end of a directory name or for the document root. Normally this will just return "index.html", but you could specify **DirectoryIndex index.html index.php index.pl index.cgi** to have apache search for each of these files, returning the first one it found.

Table 8.4 ***Contd...***

Directive	Notes
HostNameLookups	Generally set to "off" to save the latency time of the DNS lookup, you can set this to either "on" or "double". "On" is useful to pass the hostname as **REMOTE_HOST** to CGI/SSI's and "Double" is the ultra-paranoid setting to detect spoofed requests. On heavily loaded sites this can cause some real slowdown, and most poeple don't need it.
ErrorLog	Sets the name of the file to use for error logging. As of version 1.3, you can also direct errors to the syslog facility.
LogLevel	Sets the level of information that apache will send to the error log. Defaults to "error". Possible options are "emerg", "alert", "crit", "error", "warn", "notice", "info", and "debug". These options follow the general content guidelines for syslog(3).
LogFormat	When using mod_log_config (recommended), this directive allows you to customize the format of the log file. The options are many and various. Read the documentation. The most commonly used is **LogFormat "%h %l %u %t \"%r\" %>s %b"** for main host, and **LogFormat "%v %l %u %t \"%r\" %>s %b"** for virtual hosts.
Alias	Allows for transparent redirection of requests. Typically used for icon, library image, and cgi directory redirection on a wholesale basis. Aliases are processed after <Location> stanzas and before <Directory> stanzas.
ScriptAlias	Has the same result as **Alias**, but also marks the directory as containing cgi scripts, so apache will process them as such.
AddHandler	If using mod_mime (recommended) this directive maps file extensions to handlers. An example of this is using **AddHandler cgi-script .cgi** to cause any file with the extension .cgi to be treated as a cgi file. This overrides any previous mappings.
AddType	If using mod_mime (recommended) this directive maps file extensions to MIME types. One particularly forward looking use for this directive is mapping the ".xhtml" extension to text/html. An example of this is using **AddType text/html .xhtml** to cause any file with the extension .xhtml to be treated as html by the client. Converting your html to xhtml will generally only have small impacts on presentation, which can almost always be mediated with proper adjustments to CSS. While it isn't fully desirable to treat xhtml as html, no major browser is fully XHTML aware as of yet, so waddayagonnadoo?
ErrorDocument	Allows you to set custom pages or scripts to handle HTTP exceptions and errors. This lets you get away from the canned error messages and allows for a more friendly and effective way to handle things like broken links and access denial. Example: **ErrorDocument 404 errordocs/404.cgi** would invoke a custom error script when a file is not found on the server (bad typing or broken/obsolete link).

8.2.3 Virtual Servers

Virtual servers are a way for a single invocation of apache to serve multiple domain names. There are three ways to go about it, named based, port based, and address based. Port based is commonly used to serve HTTP and HTTPS from the same server. Address based virtual hosting is used primarily for backward compatibility to HTTP 1.0 clients, which don't transmit the desired hostname as part of the request. The most commonly used method of virtual hosting is named based, where multiple domain names share the same IP address (CNAME aliasing) and is commonly used by web hosting services to preserve IP space, and by SOHO's who wish to serve something like www.my_business.com and www.my_personal_page.net from the same server. One caveat is that named based virtual hosting cannot be used with SSL secure servers because of the way the SSL protocol works.

The third section of the apache configuration file deals with virtual servers. Virtual servers are defined in a <VirtualHost> *stanza*. Stanzas are almost like HTML tags.... they start with a *<keyword>* in angle braces, and end with *</keyword>*. Other common examples of stanzas are **<Location>**, **<Directory>**, and **<IfDefine>**. Directives inside stanzas only apply within the scope defined by that stanza. For instance, if you added

```
<Directory /home/foouser/public_html/*>
  Order Deny, Allow
  Deny from Joe
  Allow from All
</Directory>
```

then the user Joe would have no access to files located under /home/foouser/public_html, but his access would remain unaffected for all other areas of your server.

Let's give an example of setting up a name based virtual host. We will assume that www.example.com and www.foo.org point to the same IP address. In your **httpd.conf** file you would add the following:

```
NameVirtualHost *
<VirtualHost>
  ServerAdmin webmaster@example.com
  DocumentRoot /www/docs/example.com
  ServerName example.com
  ErrorLog logs/example.com_error
</VirtualHost>

<VirtualHost>
  ServerAdmin webmaster@foo.org
  DocumentRoot /www/docs/foo.org
  ServerName foo.org
  ErrorLog logs/foo.org_error
</VirtualHost>
```

This is about all you need to get started. Of course, you may want to enable or disable certain features for each virtual host, like disabling cgi or enabling paranoid DNS lookups for logging purposes. Simply place the appropriate directives in the virtual hosts stanza, and you're done.

But what if you want to host hundreds of virtual hosts? Your **httpd.conf** would grow quick huge, be slow to load, and consume a lot of resources. The answer comes from dynamically configured mass virtual hosting provided by mod_vhost_alias. If you enable this module, either as a dynamic module or built-in, you can use something like this:

```
# Turn off Canonical Names so CGI/SSI works properly
UseCanonicalName off

# Set the logging format for all virtual hosts
LogFormat "%V %h %l %u %t \"%r\" %s %b" vcommon
CustomLog logs/access_log vcommon

# Dynamically include server names in file requests
VirtualDocumentRoot /www/vhosts/%0/htdocs
VirtualScriptAlias  /www/vhosts/%0/cgi-bin
```

With this setup, a request to http://www.virtualhost.com/foo/bar.html would map to a request for the file /www/vhosts/www.virtualhost.com/htdocs/foo/bar.html. You can still use **<Directory>** and other stanzas to control things on a directory by directory basis.

One interesting thing you can do with virtual hosts is make your own web server perform differently by how you access it. For instance, on my web server at home, I have my DNS set up with several aliases to the web server, like "docs", "weather", "mirror", "daily", "rfc", and "howto". I then access my web server by different name, like "http://rfc" or "http://weather" to access the right sets of pages.

8.2.4 Logging Options

Apache offers a very well rounded set of logging options, including options to place logs from virtual hosts into separate files. Using configurable logs via mod_log_config, you can accomplish just about any type of logging you desire, including logging cookies, conditional logging, or passing logs to a logging host via syslog. Maintaining a separate logging host is almost always beneficial to large sites.

8.2.5 Authorization Options

Another issue that garnered some interest was Apache authorization methods. There are dozens of ways to authorize and authenticate access in apache.

8.2.6 Dynamic Content

Dynamic content is a fairly fun thing to play with. It includes things like negotiated content (for folks who want their web-pages gif-free and in French), CGI, PHP, Perl generated pages, and SSI (Server Side Includes).

8.2.7 Negotiated Content

Beginning with HTTP 1.1, compliant browsers have been able to send information to the server specifying additional information and preferences along with their requests for web documents. The browser can, for example, inform the web server that it will accept GIF images, but would really prefer PNG or JPEG if they're available. Apache can parse these preferences and react to them. The common request headers that Apache understands are Accept, Accept-Language, Accept-Charset, and Accept-Encoding.

Apache's negotiation rules can be quite complex, so it's a real good idea to read the documentation if you really want to fine-tune your website, but basic negotiation is actually quite easy. First, ensure that mod_negotiation is enabled for your server (since it is compiled in by default, unless you changed that, your're OK). Second, add a handler for type-map, usually by including the configuration directive

AddHandler type-map .var

and third by setting up the type-map files themselves. Then instead of hyper-linking to an image file or web-page, you hyperlink to the .var file, and let Apache sort out what should get served. An example file that would serve a page in a preferred language might be helpful here. If you create a file called foo.var, and create a hyperlink to it, and fill in the contents like this:

```
URI: foo.english.html
Content-type: text/html
Content-language: en

URI: foo.french.html
Content-type: text/html
Content-language: fr

URI: foo.german.html
Content-type: text/html
Content-language: de
```

Now when the user clicks on the link, Apache looks for a which language the browser says it prefers (the **Accept-language** header), and will return the right file. You can do the same thing with images. If you had a link like **<IMG SRC=./foo.var>** and the foo.var file contained

```
URI: foo.jpeg
Content-type: image/jpeg; qs=0.8

URI: foo.gif
Content-type: image/gif; qs=0.5

URI: foo.png
Content-type: image/png; qs=0.3
```

then apache would look for the **Accept-encoding** header in the request, and return the type of image that was 1) in the list of acceptable encodings, and 2) had the highest qs value (these range from 1.000 to 0.000)

Now lets say you have a case where *none* options in your .var file are acceptable to the browser. Apache will return error 406 (NOT ACCEPTABLE), and a hyperlinked list of the possible options. This can be a cool feature with translated pages, but tends not to work too well with images, as you can probably imagine.

8.2.8 Transparent Content Negotiation

Now, it's often not that much fun to do all of this work.... setting up the .var files, checking all the links for validity, reconfiguring your browser's preferences for each test run, etc. So Apache offers what is called "transparent content negotiation". If you enable Multiviews in the Options directive, have files like foo.en.html, foo.fr.html, foo.de.html, and foo.html, and simply hyper-link to "foo", with no extension, Apache will fake up a type-map on the fly, and serve the best match. It's often a good idea to have a "default", like foo.html which, since it has no encoding or language specified at all, is always acceptable to the browser.

http://hoohoo.ncsa.uiuc.edu/cgi/

8.2.9 CGI

CGI refers to the Common Gateway Interface, and is the most common method of executing external programs or scripts on the server side to generate content. Even things like PHP make use of the concepts of CGI to perform their functions and features. CGI can also be your worst security nightmare, so use it carefully, and pay close attention to your server configuration. Probably the best instructions on enabling CGI in Apache ever written is the CGI HOWTO included with the Apache documentation (Table 8.5). Look it over carefully. For those who don't want to click the mouse, be aware that the default setting for the **Options** directive is "All", which allows executing CGI's from anywhere they are found. This can be a big security hole in and of itself, so if your web server will be visible from the internet *pay close attention to your server configuration*.

Table 8.5 Getting CGI to Work.

Modules	Configuration Directives
mod_alias	AddHandler
mod_cgi	Options
mod_mime	ScriptAlias

If you wish to allow execution of CGI on your web server, you should include **mod_cgi**, **mod_mime**, and **mod_alias** in your server. You may also want to add a couple lines to your configuration file:

```
AddModule mod_mime.c
AddModule mod_cgi.c
AddModule mod_alias.c
ScriptAlias /cgi-bin/ /home/httpd/cgi-bin/
AddHandler cgi-script cgi
```

ScriptAlias maps requests for **http://www.example.com/cgi-bin/foo** to the script **/home/httpd/cgi-bin/foo**, and tells Apache that every file in the cgi-bin directory should be treated as a CGI script. The **AddHandler** directive tells apache that files that ends with .cgi should be treated as a CGI program; that is, if the file exists and is executable, Apache should run it. This example will work anywhere in the document tree, not just the cgi-bin directory. You only need this line if you wish to allow execution of CGI's outside the ScriptAlias'ed directory. You could drop this directive into < VirtualHost> or <Directory> stanzas to limit its scope. No matter how you choose to configure your CGI access, you may want to consider security along every step of the way.

```
Options -ExecCGI
<Directory /foo/bar/ >
  Options +ExecCGI
<Directory>
<Directory /home/httpd/*/www/cgi-bin/ >
  Options +ExecCGI
<Directory>
```

This disables CGI execution globally , but allows it for the /foo/bar directory and any directory with a name that matches /home/httpd/*/www/cgi-bin. This might be useful to allow execution of CGI's from user's home directories. Interaction between **ScriptAlias**, **Options**, and the **AddHandler** directives can be tricky, (ScriptAlias and ScriptAliasMatch override Options, for example, while Options and the Handler work hand in hand) so it will require some experimentation on your part until you are comfortable with the way things work.

Since this is strictly an Apache tutorial, we're not going to cover how to write CGI scripts, but if there is enough interest, KPLUG will do a CGI HOWTO in the future.

8.2.10 Configuring Apache for PHP

Simply add the following lines to your httpd.conf file.

```
# Use the next line if PHP is a DSO, omit it otherwise
LoadModule php4_module /path/to/php3/module/libphp4.so

# These lines need to go in for both DSO and static
AddModule mod_php4.c
AddType application/x-httpd-php4 .php4 .php
```

8.2.11 Configuring Apache for mod_perl

```
# for Apache::Registry Mode
Alias /perl/  "/home/httpd/cgi-bin/"
# for Apache::Perlrun Mode
Alias /cgi-perl/  "/home/httpd/cgi-bin/"

# For /perl/* as apache modules written in perl
<Location /perl>
  Perlrequire  /path/to/apache/modules/perl/startup.perl
  PerlModule   Apache::Registry
  SetHandler   perl-script
  PerlHandler  Apache::Registry
  Options      ExecCGI
  PerlSendHeader On
```

```
</Location>
# For /cgi-perl/*  handling as embedded perl
<Location /cgi-perl>
  SetHandler   perl-script
  PerlHardler  Apache::PerlRun
  Options      ExecCGI
  PerlSendHeader On
</Location>

# For mod_perl status information
<Location /perl-status>
  SetHandler   perl-script
  PerlHandler  Apache::Status
  order        deny, allow
  deny from all
  allow from localhsot
</Location>

# Include the next line if mod_perl is a DSO
LoadModule perl_module  /path/to/apache/modules/libperl.so

AddModule mod_perl.c
```

8.2.12 Server Side Includes (SSI)

Much like html pages with embedded scripts, SSI is just another set of what can be thought of as almost HTML tags. SSI allows for an easy way to include right in the middle of a web page such things as file modification time, values of environment variables, current date and time, and even the output of programs and scripts. It differs from standard CGI in that the "included" information is parsed right into an html file, rather than the entire content being generated by a program or script. The apache documentation carries a quite good tutorial. Probably the most common use for SSI's is including a standard footer or header on web pages.

8.2.13 Configuring Apache for SSI

There isn't much to do, really. Just configure and compile mod_include (either as DSO or static), and add a few lines to the config file:

```
# Use this to allow SSI in files.  This can go in stanzas, too.
Options +Includes
# Or you can have SSI but disable executing scripts via SSI with
Options +IncludesNOEXEC

# Use this if mod_include is a DSO
 LoadModule includes_module
/path/to/apache/modules/mod_include.so
```

```
AddModule mod_include.c
  AddType text/html .shtml
  AddHandler server-parsed .shtml

  # Optionally, you could run *all* html files through the SSI parser.
  # This does no harm to non SSI html files, but slows you down a bit
  AddHandler server-parsed .html
```

8.3 Conclusions

This chapter deals with installation and configuration of Apache, a popular Web server. It explains how the same can be built from the sources. In addition, it deals with how to make the web server to work for perl, CGI, PHP scripts.

9 Samba Installation and Configuration

9.1 Introduction to File Sharing and Samba

It is not uncommon to have intranets with different types of operating systems. Thus, a user needs to handle files generated on machines different from the one on which he or she is currently working. File sharing is employed to solve this need. Main objectives of file sharing are:

- to share files on your machine with others on the network
- to access files that are shared by others
- to enable organizations to create and maintain central data stores
- to run File servers with complex access control on stored data, so that access privileges and restrictions could be incorporated
- to enable a file server to share data with networks running different operating systems, e.g., Windows or Unix. Linux contains software to do both these things

File sharing services on Linux is provided through two methods namely.

1. Linux-with-Linux file sharing is implemented with a set of protocols called NFS (Network File Service). NFS is basically a UDP based protocol that allows Linux and Unix systems to access files stored on other machines. Nowadays, NFS supports TCP-based file services also.
2. Linux-with-Windows file sharing is implemented using the Samba package. Samba is Free Software that implements the SMB and NetBIOS protocols. It lets a Linux user create shareware so that the files can be accessed over the network from a Windows machine.

Introduction to Samba

Samba can be used with Linux to provide transparent access between machines running Linux and machines running Windows. Samba itself runs on a Linux machine and makes shared files and printers available to Windows machines, as if they are available on a Window machine or server. Thus, Samba has several practical applications which can generally be categorized as follows:

1. Using a Linux server as a simple **peer-to-peer server.** There is no user authentication involved and no need for passwords.
2. Using a Linux server as a **member server** on an existing Windows NT domain. The existing Windows domain controller will use NT authentication tools to control file permissions and access.
3. Using a Linux server as a **primary domain controller** with its own user authentication and control mechanisms.

Which of these three applications of Samba is used, determines how Samba is configured on the Linux machine.

9.2 Compiling Samba from source

Installing Samba - From Source:

- Download source code from a Samba mirror (details at www.samba.org)
- Uncompress source code and read the README file and other required documents
- Using the configure utility, configure Samba -e.g., change the prefix to /usr/local/samba/ so that you have all Samba related files in one directory

After downloading samba, the following commands are to be run:

gunzip samba-3.x.x.tar.gz
tar –xvf samba-3.x.x
./configure
cd samba-3.x.x/source
make
make install

If needed, PATH environment variable should be changed so as to contain samba binaries path.

Samba has to be manually started – E.g., smbd -D, nmbd -D

9.3 Installing Samba

Some useful Samba binaries are :

- smbd - The SMB / CIFS daemon [samba]
- nmbd - The NetBIOS server daemon [samba]
- smbpasswd - The Samba Password tool [samba-common]
- net - Multipurpose tool for administering Samba [samba-common]
- smbclient - Linux-based Samba client [smbclient]
- testparm - Tests whether the Samba config files are correct [samba-common]
- nmblookup - Resolves a NetBIOS name into its IP address [samba-common]

By executing the command *apt-get,* install samba smbclient samba-doc swat can be also done assuming binaries are available with Linux distribution.

We can also start Samba using: /etc/init.d/samba start

9.3.1 Configuring Samba Server

The Main configuration is smb.conf. Binaries expect to find this file as /etc/samba/smb.conf. Samba maintains its configuration in /var/lib/samba/ and other cached configuration in /var/cache/samba/.

Default Samba logs - log.smbd and log.nmbd - can be found in /var/log/samba/. Samba also maintain a file called smbpasswd which stores information about SMB user accounts and their passwords

There is a browser-based utility called SWAT (Samba Web Administration Tool) that one can use over a network to configure and monitor Samba. From the local browser, one can initiate the same by typing http://localhost:901 .

The **smb.conf** file supplied with Debian has six sections:

1. **[global]** - contains many subsections for network-related things such as the domain/workgroup name, WINS, some printing settings, authentication, logging and accounting, etc.
2. **[homes]** - for file sharing of user home directories
3. **[netlogon]** - commented out by default, for setting the server to act as a domain controller
4. **[printers]** - for printer sharing of locally-attached printers
5. **[print$]** - to set up a share for Windows printer drivers

6. [cdrom] - commented out by default, to optionally share the server's CD-ROM drive

Each section has a series of statements that follow the:

option = value

format and these statements are typically unique to each section (i.e. one has to put the right statements in the right section).

- Minimal Options include: (M = Mandatory, O = Optional, s = string, m = multiple options, b = boolean)
- workgroup : M,s : The workgroup or domain that the Samba server will be a part of
- netbios name : O,s : How the server will be known on the network
- server string : O,s : Description of the Samba server
- security : O,m : The server role that the Samba server will perform-can be one of user (domain controller is enabled), share (only per-share level access control and authentication is enabled), domain (authentication information is picked up from another domain controller or server).

- encrypt passwords : M,b : Whether passwords sent by a client should be encrypted or not
- passdb backend: M,s : What type of database to use for picking up user accounts
- printing: O,m : Printing system to use
- log level : O,s : Verbosity of the log messages
- preferred master : M,b : Is the server going to be the master browser of the workgroup?
- local master : M,b : Should nmbd try to become the local master of the workgroup?
- domain master : M,b : Primary domain controller?
- domain logons : M,b : Enable domain logons?
- logon home : M,s : The network path for the logon home share

Sample Samba Global Configuration

```
[global]
workgroup = NRCFOSS
netbios name = laptop
server string = Samba Test Server
security = user
encrypt passwords = yes
passdb backend = smbpasswd:/etc/samba/smbpasswd
printing = cups
log level = 1
preferred master = yes
local master = yes
domain master = yes
domain logons = yes
logon home = \\laptop\homes
logon drive = x:
```

9.3.2 Configurating Samba Shares

Samba share section can be used to write instructions to export Linux files / directories and make them available on other machines. Basic Samba share options are:

comment - Description of what the share is about

path - Absolute path of the directory being shared

read only - Whether the share is read-only or read-write

guest ok - Should unauthenticated users be allowed to view the share?

browseable - Should the share show up while "browsing" the Samba server?

valid users - List of users who are allowed to see this share

force user - The user on whose behalf all directory operations are done

read list - Users with read-only access to the share's data; this is generally used in conjugation with the force user option. If this option is given, filesystem based access control is not used.

write list - Users who have full read-write access to the share's data

Sample Samba Share

```
[mydata]
comment = MyData Share
path = /mydata
read only = no
guest ok = no
browseable = yes
[homes]
comment = Home Directory of %U
path = /home/%U
read only = no
guest ok = no
browseable = no
force user = %U
```

Another Sample Samba Share

```
[test]
comment = Test Share for Force User
path = /usr/local/test
read only = no
guest ok = yes
browseable = yes
force user = admin
read list = userone usertwo admin
write list = userone userthree admin
valid users = userone usertwo userthree admin
```

9.3.4 Managing Samba Users

Samba can only authenticate users against passwords stored in its own database; it can not authenticate users again the Linux passwd file. However, it is necessary to have a mapping between Linux system users and Samba users-for each Samba user, a valid system user with the same name should also exist; otherwise Samba will not be able to lookup the user. In the simplest of scenarios, Samba can store its accounts in the smbpasswd file. The smbpasswd utility can be used to manipulate the smbpasswd file.

- To add a user: smbpasswd -a <username>
- To change a user's password: smbpasswd <username>
- To delete a user: smbpasswd -x <username>
- Lookup man smbpasswd for help

9.3.3 Samba Clients

To test out Samba authentication and configuration, run the smbclient utility

smbclient –Llocalhost -U<username>

smbclient \\\\<machine>\\<share-name> -U<username>

Testing out Samba from Windows

- Log on as a local user
- Open up "Network Neighbourhood" and browse the complete network
- Locate the "Workgroup" of interest that is setup on the Linux machine and click on it
- Inside the workgroup, select the machine and test the accessibility
- There will be a prompt for a password and, if authenticated, the shares defined in the Samba server will be shown
- Try doing some operations on the share to validate whether the access control is happening correctly or not

9.4 Introduction to NFS

NFS is a file sharing protocol primarily used on the Linux/Windows world. NFS is completely transparent for a user or application-there is no change in the way a user or application would access a file on disk or over NFS. NFS is commonly implemented over UDP; it depends on RPC to perform most of its functions. On Debian, the NFS server package is called: ***nfs-kernel-server***. Installing this package will install NFS on the Linux system.

The **nfs-common** package is installed by default. This package contains files needed by both NFS servers and NFS clients. To set up an NFS server one has to install the server package with the command:

apt-get install nfs-kernel-server

When the installation is over, the following message will appear:

Not starting NFS kernel daemon: No exports.

Installing this package creates the **/etc/exports** file. The user has to enter at least one line in the file for each directory that is to be "exported" (shared), specifying who have permissions to access it and what are the permission level. If there are no lines in this file, the NFS server will not start as there is nothing to export.

As an example using NFS server as a file server storing user files, let us assume that a user with the username 'bgates' uses a workstation with the hostname 'woody5'. The NFS server is to be set up so that the users can store their files on it. A home directory is to be created for the users and the a line to be entered in the **/etc/exports** file to make it available to them.

/home/bgates woody5(rw,sync)

Thereafter, one has to either reboot the system or manually start the NFS server with the commands in the order listed:

/etc/init.d/nfs-common

/etc/init.d/nfs-kernel-server

The **/etc/exports** file follows the format:

/directory-to-share client(permissions,sync-type)

Note that there is **no space** between the client and the permissions/sync values. The **client** can be specified using one of the following:

- a resolvable host name (i.e. there is an entry in the server's **/etc/hosts** file for the client or DNS page is used to set up a LAN DNS server)
- the IP address of a client
- a network or subnet address (with the subnet mask provided) to specify all the clients on the network or subnet
- an internal domain name with the wildcard character * to specify all the computers in the domain (***.yourdomain.com**)

Among the variety of permissions, the three most common ones are:

- **ro** - Read Only (this is the default if none is specified)
- **rw** - Read/Write
- **no_access** - blocks inheritance

"Inheritance" means that if someone is given certain permissions to a directory, the same permissions "flow down" to apply to all subdirectories under it. If the permission is to be given to the director, **but not to some or all of the subdirectories,** an entry is to be added to the **/etc/exports** file for each subdirectory specifying the **no_access** permission.

The **sync-type** can either be **sync** or **async.** Generally, **sync** is recommended as it flushes writes to the disk more often. If no option is chosen, there will be a message when the NFS server starts that it's defaulting to **sync** operation. If there is a message that a "*<hostname>* has non-inet address" when the NFS server starts, it usually means the hostname specified in the **/etc/exports** file is not resolvable (no entry in the **/etc/hosts** file).

For example:

/export/docs 172.16.0.0/255.255.0.0(ro,sync)

would give all users with machines on the 172.16.0.0 network read-only access to a shared documents directory.

If there is a second Linux or UNIX system on the network, one could use it to test drive NFS. Towards this, the following action is to be taken on the Debian server:

- Edit the **/etc/exports** file as follows:
  - Recall that during the Debian OS installation a user account is created. This user's home directory is the one to be specified for share.
  - Enter the hostname of the other Linux or UNIX system for the client.
  - Specify **rw** permissions and **sync** operation.
  - Exit the editor saving the file.
- If necessary, edit the **/etc/hosts** file on the Debian server so that it contains the hostname and IP address for the second Linux or UNIX system.
- If necessary, start the NFS server processes by entering the following commands in the order shown:

```
/etc/init.d/nfs-common start
/etc/init.d/nfs-kernel-server start
```

(The **nfs-common** script is so named because it is run on both NFS clients and servers.)

- Go to the second Linux or UNIX system and try and mount the shared directory on the Debian server. The steps to do this will vary depending on which Linux distribution or flavor of UNIX on the second system. If the "second Linux or UNIX system" is also a Debian system, do the following:
  - Make sure the Debian server (which we're assuming is named "sarge") is in the second system's **/etc/hosts** file
  - Enter the following commands to enable client NFS, create a local "mount point", and mount the remote server's share to the local mount point:

```
/etc/init.d/nfs-common start
mkdir /mnt/private
mount sarge:/home/bgates /mnt/private
```

Naturally, the **bgates** has to be replaced with the name of the user account created on the server during the OS installation.

Note the syntax of the **mount** command above. It's:

mount server-name:/path-to-share-on-server /path-to-local-mount-point

As a result, one can access the remote shared directory on the server by going to its mount point on the local system like :

```
cd /mnt/private
```

To unmount the share, you use the local mount point like so:

```
umount /mnt/private
```

NFS has many other features : to see what shares are available, show what shares have been mounted, auto-mounting when a client boots up, etc. The user could play around and explore the various features.

It should be noted that an NFS server does keep ports open. If a system is going to be connected to the Internet, NFS functionality should be disabled to close those ports.

Unlike NFS, Samba is implemented completely in user space and does not depend on the kernel at all.

9.5 Conclusions

This chapter explains file sharing through Samba and NFS. It explains how Samba can be compiled from the sources and configured. In addition, it explores how NFS sharing can be done under Linux.

10 Installing SMTP Mail Server

10.1 Introduction

Now a days every one is habituated to use emails while communicating with others. Unlike good old postal system, this is more reliable, inexpensive and fast in delivery. In addition, we can easily find out whether the message is delivered or not.

One could claim that the email is the first fruit to be enjoyed by the people because of the developments in computer network and Internet. This also uses the client server concept and TCP/IP protocol. In the following sections, first we try to explain some terms and then explore how emailing practically takes place.

Mail-boxes

A mail-box is a file, or possibly a directory of files, where incoming messages are stored.

User Agents

A mail user agent, or MUA, is an application run directly by a user. User agents are used to compose and send out-going messages as well as to display, file and print messages which have arrived in a user's mail-box. Examples of user agents are elm, mailx, mh, zmail, Netscape.

Transfer Agents

Mail transfer agents (MTAs) are used to transfer messages between machines. User agents give the message to the transfer agent, who may pass it onto another transfer agent, or possibly many other transfer agents. Users may give messages to transfer agents directly, but this requires some expertise on the part of the user and is only recommended for experts.

Transfer agents are responsible for properly routing messages to their destination. While their function is hidden from the average user, theirs is by far the most complex part of getting messages from their source to their destination. The most common transfer agent is sendmail(1m).

Delivery Agents

Delivery agents are used to place a message into a user's mail-box. When the message arrives at its destination, the final transfer agent will give the message to the appropriate delivery agent, who will add the message to the user's mail-box. The standard delivery agent for Solaris, starting with 2.5, is mail.local(1m).

Mailing Lists and Aliases

A mailing list is an e-mail address like any other, except that whereas a typical e-mail address represents a single recipient, a mailing list typically represents many recipients.

Each recipient address on a mailing list or alias can be an ordinary user or another mailing list or alias. These recipients can be at different hosts or all at the same; it doesn't matter.

History of SMTP

SMTP, which stands for Simple Mail Transfer Protocol, is the *de facto* standard for email receipt and delivery. SMTP used TCP/IP protocol to exchange email messages between two MTA's via intermediate MTA's using store and forward principle. Many SMTP servers are available for Linux such as Sendmail, Postfix, qmail, Exim. Today SMTP servers not only accept, relay and deliver email, but also perform other functions like Authentication, SPAM filtering and Access Control

10.1.1 How mail is delivered?

- Mail client connects to the SMTP server saying that it has an email to send
- SMTP server authenticates the client to ensure that it is allowed to relay through it
- SMTP server accepts the message and give a success code to the mail client as well as a message ID
- SMTP server checks the recipient(s) of the message and does a local delivery if the recipient(s) are local; if the recipient(s) are not local, then the SMTP server initiates a remote mail delivery
- SMTP server connects to the remote mail server and tries to deliver the email
- Remote mail server authenticates the delivery and accepts the email if it is authorized to receive email for the recipient(s)
- The remote mail server delivers the email to the recipient(s) mailbox
- Recipient(s) open the mailbox (using protocol like IMAP or POP3 or locally on the shell) and read the email.

10.1.2 Role of DNS in Mail Delivery

DNS plays a very important role in delivering email Mail eXchanger (**MX**) records are maintained by domain name servers (DNS) to tell MTAs where to send mail messages. An MX record can be specified for a specific host, or a wild-card MX record can specify the default for a specific domain. The MX record tells an MTA where a message, whose ultimate target is a given host in a given domain, should be sent to next, *i.e.*, which intermediate hosts should be used to ultimately deliver a message to the target host. These MX records vary depending on the domain. To illustrate, here is an example of how a message from a.eng.sun.com destined for b.ucsb.edu might be routed:

MX records are maintained by DNS only (*i.e.*, not hosts files or NIS). If no MX records are available for a given host, sendmail will try to send to that host directly. Once sendmail determines which host to attempt to send the message to: an intermediate host as indicated by an MX record, or a direct connection to the target host, it uses gethostbyname() to determine the IP-address of the target machine in order to make a connection. The gethostbyname() library routine may use DNS, an /etc/hosts file, or some other name service (*e.g.*, NIS, LDAP, ...) to perform its name-to-IP-address look-up.

Thus, to be able to deliver an email to a remote mail server, a SMTP server first has to use DNS to query the mail server of a specific recipient.

- On receiving information of the destination mail server from the MX record, a SMTP server will initiate a connection as soon as possible
- If the connection fails, then the SMTP server will keep trying again and again until it get a "permanent" error. The SMTP server can also query the DNS to get information about other mail servers that are available for the recipient and then try to initiate a mail delivery through them.

10.1.3 POP3 Server

Post office Protocol (POP3) runs on a server continuously sends and receives emails. When a user connects to this server, user's local MUA will read the users email's into his local machine (which are automatically removed from POP3 server).

10.1.4 IMAP4 Server

The Internet Message Access Protocol version 4 allows users to see their MUA's to read, send emails. Unlike POP3 the email messages are not deleted or downloaded to user's local machines. Moreover, we can login from any where to see emails.

10.2 Postfix as an MTA

Postfix is a SMTP server written as replacement for Sendmail and is designed to be secure and easy-to-use yet powerful SMTP server ships under the IBM Public License version 1.0. It is available as source code as well as binary packages under most distributions. It is a very flexible and advanced SMTP server-can be used to run a simple single domain mail server as well as very busy and high traffic mail servers

10.2.1 Installing Postfix

If the binary has been downloaded, then use the Debian repository:

```
apt-get install postfix
```

If the source code has been downloaded, then execute the following commands to install postfix. However, before compiling, it should be ensured that libdb-dev (Berkley DB development package) is installed which is needed by Postfix.

```
uncompress the source code
cd  to the source directory
Configure the software and generate the Makefiles.

make -f Makefile.in MAKELEVEL= Makefiles

make
make install
```

The Postfix Directory Structure

Postfix uses the following directories for storing configuration, data and binaries:

```
/etc/postfix - for configuration files
/usr/sbin - for server / system binaries
/usr/bin - for user level binaries (like mailq)
/var/spool/postfix - for storing the mail queue
```

As usual, the Postfix, by default, delivers email into /var/spool/mail/<username> file.

10.2.2 Postfix Configuration Files

- /etc/postfix/main.cf - This is the major Postfix configuration file. It controls all the settings and details of the Postfix MTA
- /etc/postfix/master.cf - Master process configuration file; controls how different Postfix components are initiated and run
- /etc/aliases - Email and system aliases for email delivery
- /etc/postfix/access - The Postfix access table; configures Postfix to selectively accept or reject email
- /etc/postfix/relocated - Handles bounce messages for users who have moved

Basic Postfix Configuration

Configure the main.cf file for the following options:

myorigin - Value = Domain; will be used for all outgoing email

mydestination - Value = Domains; what domains to receive emails for. These domains are considered to be "hosted" on Postfix and Postfix will accept all email meant for these domains

mynetworks - Value = Network subnets; what networks can clients relay from - emails from these networks configured here are accepted unconditionally - irrespective to whom they are addressed

relayhost - Value = host ; This configuration is not mandatory - configures Postfix to relay outgoing email through the configured host.

Configure the main.cf file for the following options:

smtpd banner - Value = string ; Specifies what sort of banner to show for SMTP connections

myhostname - Value = hostname ; Specifies what the

machine running postfix will be identified as

home mailbox - Value = Mailbox / Maildir ; Specifies the format and location of a user's mailbox

local recipient maps - configures how to look up valid local recipients and deliver email to them; empty value disables recipient lookups

The Maildir Mailbox Format

Maildir mailbox format replaces the mbox format. Unlike mbox format where all mail messages are stored in a single file such that each message is separated by a delimiter, Maildir format stores all messages in a directory with each message being stored in a separate file with the filename is a timestamp - the time at this the message was delivered. Maildir mailboxes are fast, don't need to be locked during operation, can be operated on simultaneously, are NFS-safe and very easy to use!. Using latest filesytems such as ReiserFS, which can efficiently store thousands of files in a single directly, Maildir becomes even more useful

Testing Mail Delivery

- The socket / telnet method

```
telnet  lcoalhost 25
```

- Using the mail command
- Logs are collected in /var/log/mail.*
- Log paths can be further customized by changing the syslog configuration in /etc/syslog.conf

10.2.3 Installing & Running Courier-IMAP/POP3

To install POP3 and IMAP server run the following.

```
apt-get install courier-pop courier-imap
```

There is no need for elaboration configuration required and configuration is stored in /etc/courier directory.

To start the IMAP & POP3 Services:

```
/etc/init.d/courier-authdaemon start
/etc/init.d/courier-imap start
/etc/init.d/courier-pop start
```

We can test out using a mail client or by telnetting to ports 143 (IMAP) or 110 (POP3)

10.3 Conclusions

This chapter explains about how to install and configure postfix, a SMTP MTA under Linux. Also, it explains how to install POP3 and IMAP4 services under Debian Linux.

11 Installing Common Unix Printing System

11.1 Introduction

Printing within UNIX has historically been done using one of two printing systems - the Berkeley Line Printer Daemon ("LPD") [RFC1179] and the AT&T Line Printer system. These printing systems were designed in the 70's for printing text to line printers; vendors have since added varying levels of support for other types of printers.

Replacements for these printing systems have emerged [LPRng, Palladin, PLP], however none of the replacements change the fundamental capabilities of these systems.

Over the last few years several attempts at developing a standard printing interface have been made, including the draft POSIX Printing standard developed by the Institute of Electrical and Electronics Engineers, Inc. ("IEEE") [IEEE-1387.4] and Internet Printing Protocol ("IPP") developed by the Internet Engineering Task Force ("IETF") through the Printer Working Group ("PWG") [IETF-IPP]. The POSIX printing standard defines a common set of command-line tools as well as a C interface for printer administration and print jobs, but has been shelved by the IEEE.

The Internet Printing Protocol defines extensions to the HyperText Transport Protocol 1.1 [RFC2616] to provide support for remote printing services. IPP/1.0 was accepted by the IETF as an experimental Request For Comments [RFC] document in October of 1999. Since then the Printer Working Group has developed an updated set of specifications for IPP/1.1 which have been accepted by the IETF and are awaiting publication as proposed standards. Unlike POSIX Printing, IPP enjoys widespread industry support and is poised to become the standard network printing solution for all operating systems.

Linux printing systems

- All printing systems on Linux make use of the excellent PostScript system called GhostScript (www.ghostscript.org).
- Ghostscript is a PostScript interpreter that is most commonly used on Linux
- Implements an excellent PostScript engine that can take as inputs formats like JPEG, TIFF, PS & Text and output data in formats like X Windows output, raster formats and PDF
- Also handles conversion of PS output for non-PS printers;
- can also be used a basic, spooler less printing system
- Most printing systems today use a combination of multiple tools (postscript interpreters, filters, rasterises etc) to process and print documents
- The printing system converts PostScript into a raster format and then converts that into a printer specific language to send commands to the printer

CUPS uses IPP/1.1 to provide a complete, modern printing system for UNIX that can be extended to support new printers, devices, and protocols while providing compatibility with existing UNIX applications. CUPS is free software provided under the terms of the GNU General Public License and GNU Library General Public License

CUPS Features

- IPP/1.1 Support
- Supports banner pages, authentication, print accounting and quota

- Supports parallel, serial, usb, IPP and JetDirect-based printers as also printers shared through other printing systems such as CUPS, lpd and Windows
- TLS (encryption) support
- Portable command set compatible with LPRng and LPD
- Excellent web-based interface for printer administration, configuration and management
- PPD-based drivers, rich API and imaging libraries
- Foomatic Printer database (from linuxprinting.org) has good support for CUPS

CUPS Architecture (see Figure 11.1)

- The scheduler is a server application that handles HTTP requests - the HTTP server servers print requests as well as printer / CUPS administration requests
- Filters are what convert input into intermediate formats and finally to a printer specific format (like texttops)
- Backend are what allow CUPS to communicate to the actual printer - through a hardware port or the network

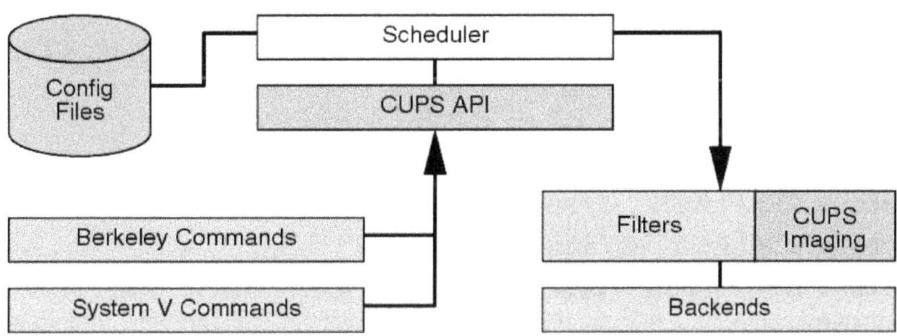

Figure 11.1 CUPS architecture.

11.2 Building and Installing CUPS

This chapter shows how to build and install the Common UNIX Printing System. If you are installing a binary distribution from the CUPS web site, proceed to the section titled, Installing a Binary Distribution.

Installing from Source

This section describes how to compile and install CUPS on your system from the source code.

Requirements

You'll need ANSI-compliant C and C++ compilers to build CUPS on your system. As its name implies, CUPS is designed to run on the UNIX operating system, however the CUPS interface library and most of the filters and backend supplied with CUPS should also compile and run under Microsoft Windows.

For the image file filters and PostScript RIP, you'll need the JPEG, PNG, TIFF, and ZLIB libraries. CUPS will build without these, but with significantly reduced functionality. Easy Software Products maintains a mirror of the current versions of these libraries at:

ftp://ftp.easysw.com/pub/libraries

The documentation is formatted using the HTMLDOC software. If you need to make changes you can get the HTMLDOC software from:

http://www.easysw.com/htmldoc

Finally, you'll need a make program that understands the include directive - FreeBSD, NetBSD, and OpenBSD developers should use the gmake program.

Compiling CUPS

CUPS uses GNU autoconf to configure the makefiles and source code for your system. Type the following command to configure CUPS for your system:

```
./configure
```

The default installation will put the CUPS software in the */etc* , */usr*, and */var* directories on your system, which will overwrite any existing printing commands on your system. Use the --prefix option to install the CUPS software in another location:

```
./configure --prefix=/some/directory
```

If the PNG, JPEG, TIFF, and ZLIB libraries are not installed in a system default location (typically */usr/include* and */usr/lib*) you'll need to set the CFLAGS, CXXFLAGS, and LDFLAGS environment variables prior to running configure:

```
setenv CFLAGS "-I/some/directory"
setenv CXXFLAGS "-I/some/directory"
setenv LDFLAGS "-L/some/directory"
setenv DSOFLAGS "-L/some/directory"
./configure ...
or:
CFLAGS="-I/some/directory"; export CFLAGS
CXXFLAGS="-I/some/directory"; export CXXFLAGS
LDFLAGS="-L/some/directory"; export LDFLAGS
DSOFLAGS="-L/some/directory"; export DSOFLAGS
./configure ...
```

To enable support for encryption, you'll also want to add the "--enable-ssl" option:

```
./configure --enable-ssl
```

SSL and TLS support require the OpenSSL library, available at:

http://www.openssl.org

If the OpenSSL headers and libraries are not installed in the standard directories, use the --with-openssl-includes and --with-openssl-libs options:

```
./configure --enable-ssl \
--with-openssl-includes=/foo/bar/include \
--with-openssl-libs=/foo/bar/lib
```

Once you have configured things, just type:

make

to build the software.

Use the "install" target to install the software:

make install

Once you have installed the software you can start the CUPS server by typing:

/usr/sbin/cupsd

Installing from Binaries

CUPS comes in a variety of binary distribution formats. Easy Software Products provides binaries in TAR format with installation and removal scripts ("portable" distributions), and in RPM and DPKG formats for Red Hat and Debian-based distributions. Portable distributions are available for all platforms, while the RPM and DPKG distributions are only available for Linux.

Installing a Portable Distribution

To install the CUPS software from a portable distribution you will need to be logged in as root; doing an su is good enough. Once you are the root user, run the installation script with:

./cups.install

After asking you a few yes/no questions the CUPS software will be installed and the scheduler will be started automatically.

Installing an RPM Distribution

To install the CUPS software from an RPM distribution you will need to be logged in as root; doing an su is good enough. Once you are the root user, run RPM with:

rpm -e lpr

rpm -i cups-1.1-linux-M.m.n-intel.rpm

After a short delay the CUPS software will be installed and the scheduler will be started automatically.

Installing an Debian Distribution

To install the CUPS software from a Debian distribution you will need to be logged in as root; doing an su is good enough. Once you are the root user, run dpkg with:

dpkg -i cups-1.1-linux-M.m.n-intel.deb

After a short delay the CUPS software will be installed and the scheduler will be started automatically.

11.3 Managing Printers

This chapter describes how to add your first printer and how to manage your printers.

The Basics

Each printer queue has a name associated with it; the printer name must start with any printable character except " ", "/", and "@". It can contain up to 127 letters, numbers, and the underscore (_). Case is not significant, e.g. "PRINTER", "Printer", and "printer" are considered to be the same name.

Printer queues also have a device associated with them. The device can be a parallel port, a network interface, and so forth. Devices within CUPS use Uniform Resource Identifiers ("URIs") which are a more general form of Uniform Resource Locators ("URLs") that are used in your web browser. For example, the first parallel port in Linux usually uses a device URI of parallel:/dev/lp1.

You can see a complete list of supported devices by running the lpinfo(8) command:

```
lpinfo -v
network socket
network http
network ipp
network lpd
direct parallel:/dev/lp1
serial serial:/dev/ttyS1?baud=115200
serial serial:/dev/ttyS2?baud=115200
direct usb:/dev/usb/lp0
network smb
```

The -v option specifies that you want a list of available devices. The first word in each line is the type of device (direct, file, network, or serial) and is followed by the device URI or method name for that device. File devices have device URIs of the form file:/directory/filename while network devices use the more familiar method://server or method://server/path format.

Finally, printer queues usually have a PostScript Printer Description ("PPD") file associated with them. PPD files describe the capabilities of each printer, the page sizes supported, etc., and are used for PostScript and non-PostScript printers. CUPS includes PPD files for HP LaserJet, HP DeskJet, EPSON 9-pin, EPSON 24-pin, and EPSON Stylus printers.

Adding First Printer

CUPS provides two methods for adding printers: a command-line program called lpadmin(8) and a Web interface. The lpadmin command allows you to perform most printer administration tasks from the command-line and is located in */usr/sbin*. The Web interface is located at:

http://localhost:631/admin

and steps you through printer configuration. If you don't like command-line interfaces, try the Web interface instead.

Adding Your First Printer from the Command-Line

Run the lpadmin command with the -p option to add a printer to CUPS:

/usr/sbin/lpadmin -p *printer* -E -v *device* -m *ppd*

For a HP DeskJet printer connected to the parallel port this would look like:

/usr/sbin/lpadmin -p DeskJet -E -v parallel:/dev/lp1 -m deskjet.ppd

Similarly, a HP LaserJet printer using a JetDirect network interface at IP address 11.22.33.44 would be added with the command:

/usr/sbin/lpadmin -p LaserJet -E -v socket://11.22.33.44 -m laserjet.ppd

As you can see, deskjet.ppd and laserjet.ppd are the PPD files for the HP DeskJet and HP LaserJet drivers included with CUPS. You'll find a complete list of PPD files and the printers they will work with in Appendix C, "Printer Drivers".

For a dot matrix printer connected to the serial port, this might look like:

**/usr/sbin/lpadmin -p DotMatrix -E -m epson9.ppd **
-vserial:/dev/ttyS0?baud=9600+size=8+parity=none+flow=soft

Here you specify the serial port (e.g. S0,S1, d0, d1), baud rate (e.g. 9600, 19200, 38400, 115200, etc.), number of bits, parity, and flow control. If you do not need flow control, delete the "+flow=soft" portion.

Administering CUPS through Web

Cups can be administered very easily through its web based administration page. To configure CUPS, just type: http://localhost:631/ in your web browser to open the CUPS management interface (see Figure 11.2).

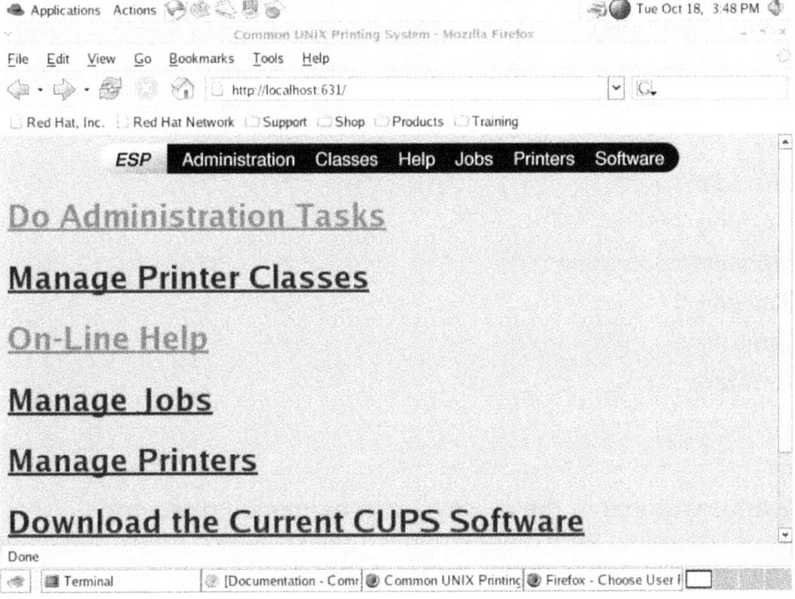

Figure 11.2 Web based CUPS administration tool.

Using CUPS Configured Printers

To use a printer configured through CUPS, we can use the lpr command:

```
lpr -P <destination> <filename>
<filename> can be any text, PostScript or graphic file
```

A destination is the name of the printer that you want to print to. If you want to print to the default printer, then it is not necessary to give a destination; the default printer will be automatically selected

CUPS Configuration Files

- CUPS is configured through the /etc/cups/cupsd.conf config file
- The file format is very similar to the Apache configuration file format
- This file manages the following things:
  - Server Identity
  - Server Options
  - Network and Browsing Options
  - Security and Access Control Options
- CUPS will function just fine with the default server options
- Printer configuration is stored in the /etc/cups/printers.conf file - we will look at this file in detail

```
printers.conf Sample
<Printer myprinter>
Info Laser Printer
Location anokha
DeviceURI parallel:/dev/lp0
State Idle
Accepting Yes
JobSheets none none
PageLimit 0
KLimit 0
</Printer>
```

CUPS Drivers

- CUPS drivers are stored in the /usr/share/cups/model/ directory
- This directory contains PPD (PostScript Printer Definition) files that define the specific features and details of a printer
- A new PPD downloaded from the Internet could be copied here and would be available for use inside CUPS after it is restarted.
- If the PPD is a foomatic-based PPD, then it will need the cupsomatic filter stored in the /usr/lib/cups/filter/ directory.

Sharing Printers

- Sharing printers is very easy with CUPS
- As long as network browsing support is enabled correctly in the configuration files, the printers on other machines will be detected automatically
- This simplifies the mapping of printers in a network – you just have to configure the printer in one machine and as long as all other machines support and enable the CUPS browse protocol, the configured printer will automatically show-up in the network nodes
- On the server where the printer is configured, you may wish to introduce a separate section to allow only specific machines to print to the attached printer

11.4. Conclusions

This chapter explores Common Unix Printing System (cups) with the main emphasis on its installation and administration. Web based and command line based administration of the same is explained.

12 Installing Squid Proxy and Firewall

12.1 Introduction

A firewall is a system or router that sits between an external network (i.e. the Internet) and an internal network. This internal network can be a large LAN at a business organization or our networked home PCs. Thus, a firewall has two network connections, one for the external network and one for the internal network. The purpose of the firewall is to protect what is on our side from (i.e. in our LAN) from the other side people. This is achieved by enforcing some security policies with which all Internet related services will be continued on our LAN. Decision based bridging of traffic between two connections is called "routing" or "IP forwarding". What this means is that any firewall, by its' very nature, is a router.

There are several tools which watch what packets are passing in and out of your Linux box: the most common one is `tcpdump' (which understands more than TCP these days), but a nicer one is `ethereal'. Such programs are known as `packet sniffers'.

Evidently three types of firewalls are in use known as packet-filtering firewall, application gateway (screened-host firewall) and proxy firewall (application level circuit gateway).

The packet filtering firewall is implemented in the OS itself and it makes decisions about routing to protect the system. An application gateway firewall is implemented at the network architecture and system configuration level. A proxy firewall is implemented as a separate program which establishes connections with remote servers on behalf of the client.

12.2 Setting Firewalls

Linux kernel contains advanced tools for packet filtering – the process of controlling network packets as they attempt to enter, move through, and exit your system.

Netfilter is a set of hooks inside the Linux kernel that allows kernel modules to register callback functions with the network stack. A registered callback function is then called back for every packet that traverses the respective hook within the network stack.

iptables is the userspace command line program used to configure the Linux 2.4.x and 2.6.x IPv4 packet filtering ruleset. It is targeted towards system administrators. Iptables can be used

- listing the contents of the packet filter ruleset
- adding/removing/modifying rules in the packet filter ruleset
- isting/zeroing per-rule counters of the packet filter ruleset

iptables is a generic table structure for the definition of rulesets. Each rule within an IP table consists of a number of classifiers (iptables matches) and one connected action (iptables target).

netfilter, ip_tables, connection tracking (ip_conntrack, nf_conntrack) and the Network Address Translation subsystem together build the major parts of the framework

The 2.4 kernel contains three tables also called rule lists namingly INPUT, OUTPUT, and FORWARD.

- Every packet being sent in or out of the machine is subject to one of these lists.

- When a packet enters the system via a network interface, the kernel decides if it is destined for the local system (INPUT) or another destination (FORWARD) to determine the rule list to use with it.
- If a packet originates on the system and attempts to leave the system, the kernel will check it against the OUTPUT list.
- Regardless of destination. when packet match a particular rule on one of the rule list, they are designated for a particular target or action to be applied to them.

A chain is a checklist of rules. Each rule says `if the packet header looks like this, then here's what to do with the packet'. If the rule doesn't match the packet, then the next rule in the chain is consulted. Finally, if there are no more rules to consult, then the kernel looks at the chain policy to decide what to do. In a security- conscious system, this policy usually tells the kernel to DROP the packet.

1. When a packet comes in (say, through the Ethernet card) the kernel first looks at the destination of the packet: this is called `routing'.
2. If it's destined for this box, the packet passes downwards in the diagram, to the INPUT chain. If it passes this, any processes waiting for that packet will receive it.
3. Otherwise, if the kernel does not have forwarding enabled, or it doesn't know how to forward the packet, the packet is dropped. If forwarding is enabled, and the packet is destined for another network interface (if you have another one), then the packet goes rightwards on our diagram to the FORWARD chain. If it is ACCEPTed, it will be sent out.
4. Finally, a program running on the box can send network packets. These packets pass through the OUTPUT chain immediately: if it says ACCEPT, then the packet continues out to whatever interface it is destined for.

Difference between ipchains & iptables

How does IPTables differ from IPChains?

There are many differences between iptables and ipchains. The most prominent of them are listed here:

Traversal of chains

In IPChains, all incoming packets pass through the input chain, irrespective of whether they are destined for the local machine or some other machine. Similarly, all outgoing packets are sent through the output chain, even if they are meant to be forwarded. iptables clearly classifies traffic into either the INPUT, OUTPUT or FORWARD chains, thus making packet filtering more efficient.

This feature of IPTables is perhaps the most significant improvement over ipchains. iptables can keep track of all the aspects of a TCP/IP connection like destination and source IP addresses, port numbers associated, timeouts, retransmissions, TCP sequencing etc. Thus, spurious packets which do not belong to an existing connection are easily recognized and can be conveniently logged/dropped. This stateful firewalling is more powerful than the simple packet filtering provided by ipchains.

IPTables provides advanced features like rate-limited packet matching, filtering based on a combination of tcp flags, MAC addresses, user, group and process ids. Unlike IPChains, IPTables handles tasks such as NAT and packet mangling with separate modules. There are many differences between the two in terms of syntax as well.

- In iptables , packets are applied against only one chain.
- In iptables, DROP is used instead of DENY.
- In iptables, the order in which rules appear matters.
- In iptables, interfaces must be used in the appropriate chains.

Incoming interfaces must be used in the INPUT or FORWARD chains, and OUTPUT interfaces must be used in FORWARD or OUTPUT chains.

For more specific information, consult the Linux 2.4 Packet Filtering HOWTO from http://www.netfilter.org web site.

When the iptables command is passed the L parameter, it lists the rules in a table. To view the current rules, type the following as the root user:

```
iptables L
```

The output will list all of the rules that are for the default table. These rules show IPTables that have not been configured. The default policy is to allow everything (as noted by policy ACCEPT, and there are no additional rules defined.)

Ideally the default policy of each table should be to deny traffic. that way, unless something specifically matches a rule in the list, it will be denied access to and from the network.

The order in which rules appear is very important! If a rule is listed first that accepts all traffic, other rules in the list will not be applied because the packets will have already been accepted.

IPTables command options

There are three built-in tables in the Linux kernel's netfilter, and each has built-in chains. the iptables command is used to configure these tables.

1. filter – A table that is used for routing network packets. This is default table, and is assumed by iptables if the t parameter is not specified.
   INPUT – Network packets that are destined for the server.
   OUTPUT – Network packets that originate on the server.
   FORWARD – Network packets that are routed through the server.
2. nat – A table that is used for NAT. NAT is a method of translating internal IP address to external IP addresses.
   PREROUTINGnetwork packets that can be altered when they arrive at the server.
   OUTPUTNetwork packets that originate on the server
   POSTROUTING – Network packets that can be altered right
3. mangle – A table that is used for altering network packets.
   INPUT – Network packets that are destined for the server.
   OUTPUT – Network packets that originate on the server.
   FORWARD – Network packets that are routed through the server.
   PREROUTINGnetwork packets that can be altered when they arrive at the server.
   POSTROUTING – Network packets that can be altered right before they are sent out.

Commands tell IPTables to perform a specific action, and only one command is allowed per iptables command string. Except for the help command, all commands are written in uppercase characters.

The iptables commands are:

A

- The specified rule is appended to the end of the chain.

C

- Checks a rule before adding to a userdefined chain.

D

- Deletes a rule from chain.

E

- Renames a userdefined rule.

F

- Flushes a chain, which deletes all rules inside a chain.

h

- Lists help for iptables command

I

- Inserts a rule into a chain.

L

- Lists the rules in a chain.

N

- Creates a new chain.

P

- Defines a default policy for a chain.

R

- Replaces a rule in a chain.

X

- Deletes a userspecified chain.

Z

- Sets the byte and packet counters in all chains for a table to zero.

Parameters are specified after commands when building a rule. The parameters specify certain aspects of a packet, such as packet's protocol, source, or destination.

p,

protocol

- Sets the IP protocol for the rule. The protocol can be tcp, udp, icmp, or all. The all option is default. A ! means not.

p

tcp - means where the protocol is tcp.

p

! udp - means that the protocol is not udp.

when p

tcp is used as a parameter, additional options are available that allow rules to be further defined. These match options are:

sport,

sourceport

- Sets the source port of packet. Either a service name, port number , or port range must follow the option.

dport,

destinationport

- Sets the destination port for packet. It is specified in the same way as –sport option.

tcpflags

- When this option is specified, flags on the packet may be analyzed to see if they match the rule. The available flags are

SYN, ACK, FIN, RST, URG, PSH, ALL, or NONE.

These match options are available for UDP protocol (p udp)

sport,

sourceport

- Sets the source port of packet. Either a service name, port number , or port range must follow the option.

dport,

destinationport

- Sets the destination port for packet. It is specified in the same way as –sport option.

Only one option may be specified when p

icmp is used

icmptype

- Sets the name or number of the ICMP type to match with the rule. The available types can be found by typing:

iptables p

icmp h

at the command line.

An example of using this rule is:

iptables A

p

icmp –icmptype

echorequest

DROP

This command will append a rule to the default table that will drop echo requests (pings).

s,

source

- Sets the source for particular packet. The parameter is followed by an IP address, a network address with a netmask, or a hostname as shown in following examples:

s

192.168.1.1

s

192.168.1.0/255.255.255

d,

destination

- The destination of the packet. The parameter is followed by an IP address, a network address with a netmask, or a hostname .

j,

jump

- A target is specified with the j parameter to tell the rule to send packet to that target. Targets may be value as ACCEPT, DROP, QUEUE, RETURN. If no target is specified, nothing is done with packet except that the counter is incremented by one.

i,

ininterface

- For INPUT, FORWARD, and PREROUTING

chains, the I parameter specifies the interface on which the packet is arriving at the server. A ! tells this parameter no to match. A + wild card character used to match all interfaces that match particular string.

o

-out—interface - For FORWARD, OUTPUT, and

POSTROUTING chains, the o parameter specifies the interface on which the packet is leaving the server. A ! tells this parameter no to match.

The final step in creating a rule is to tell IPTables what you want to do with a packet that matches the rest of rule. This is called defining a target, and once a packet matches a rule it is sent off to the target.

If the rule specifies an ACCEPT target for matching packet, the packet skips the rest of the rule checks and is allowed to continue to its destination.

If a rule specifies a DROP target, that packet is refused access to the system and nothing is sent back to the host that sent the packet.

If a rule specifies a REJECT target, The packet is dropped, but an error packet is sent to the packet's originator.

Every chain has a default policy to ACCEPT, DROP, REJECT, or QUEUE the packet to passed to user space. If none of the rules in the chain apply to the packet, then the packet is dealt with in accordance with the default policy.

DNAT This target modifies the destination address of a packet and can only be used in the PREROUTING & OUTPUT chains of the nat table.

todestination

ipaddress[ipaddress]

[:portport].

A destination IP address or address range can be specified. If the ports are specified, the destination port is modified.

MASQUERADEThis

extended target is used in the

POSTROUTING chain of the nat table. It is used for NAT when one of the connections has a dynamic address, like a dial up connection such as pointtopoint (PPP).

SNATThe

SNAT target is like the MASQUERADE extended target, but is used when doing NAT between two interfaces with static addresses. The SNAT target can only be defined in POSTROUTING chain of the nat table.

Here are some examples of some IPTables rules and what they do:

Allowing www

iptables A

INPUT p

tcp -dport www j

ACCEPT

This command appends a rule to the filter table since no table is defined with t. The rule is appended to the INPUT chain in the filter table, as noted by INPUT after A. This rule looks for packets where the protocol is tcp and the destination port is www service, or port 80 as listed in /etc/services file. The target for this rule is to let the packet pass through to its destination, which is accomplished by sending the packet to the ACCEPT target.

```
Forwarding
iptables A
FORWARD i
ppp0 o
eth0 m
state \
state
ESTABLISHED,RELATED j
ACCEPT
```

The lines above append (A) a new rule to the filter table to the forwarding chain (FORWARD) from the outside interface out to the internal interface where the packet's state is either a previously established connection or a related connection. As long as the default policy for the FORWARD chain is to DROP packets , a new connection from the outside will not match this rule and will be dropped.

```
Doing masquerading (NAT)
iptables t
nat A
POSTROUTING o
ppp0 j
MASQUERADE
Or, where x.x.x.x is a valid static IP address on the external interface.
iptables t
nat A
POSTROUTING o
    eth1 j
    SNAT to
    x.x.x.x
```

This examples are of doing NAT, or masquerading, and although they match the same packets they jump to different targets.

The first example matches all traffic that is going out on the outgoing interface. The target is MASQURADE which is used to do NAT on interfaces with dynamic IP addresses, such as ppp0 (dialup) interface.

The second example matches the same traffic, but forwards traffic to the SNAT target. The –to option is specified with the target, to the packets are modified to look as if they are coming from x.x.x.x IP address.

In this example
iptables A
OUTPUT p
icmp icmptype
echorequest
j
ACCEPT
iptables A
INPUT p
icmp icmptype
echoreply
j
ACCEPT

- iptables is being configured to allow the firewall to send ICMP echorequests (pings) and in turn, accept the expected ICMP echoreplies.
- set rules that allow telnet inside the network, but not outside:

iptables A
OUTPUT p
tcp destinationport
telnet d
198.168.0.0 j
ACCEPT
iptables A
OUTPUT p
tcp destinationport
telnet d
! 198.168.0.0
j
REJECT

Each rule specifies a set of conditions the packet must meet, and what to do if it meets them (a `target'). For example, you might want to drop all ICMP packets coming from the IP address 127.0.0.1. So in this case our conditions are that the protocol must be ICMP and that the source address must be 127.0.0.1. Our target is `DROP'. 127.0.0.1 is the `loopback' interface, which you will have even if you have no real network connection. You can use the `ping' program to generate such packets (it simply sends an ICMP type

8 (echo request) which all cooperative hosts should obligingly respond to with an ICMP type 0 (echo reply) packet). This makes it useful for testing.

```
# ping -c 1 127.0.0.1
PING 127.0.0.1 (127.0.0.1): 56 data bytes
64 bytes from 127.0.0.1: icmp_seq=0 ttl=64 time=0.2 ms

--- 127.0.0.1 ping statistics ---
1 packets transmitted, 1 packets received, 0% packet loss
round-trip min/avg/max = 0.2/0.2/0.2 ms
# iptables -A INPUT -s 127.0.0.1 -p icmp -j DROP
# ping -c 1 127.0.0.1
PING 127.0.0.1 (127.0.0.1): 56 data bytes

--- 127.0.0.1 ping statistics ---
1 packets transmitted, 0 packets received, 100% packet loss
#
```

You can see here that the first ping succeeds (the `-c 1' tells ping to only send a single packet).

Then we append (-A) to the `INPUT' chain, a rule specifying that for packets from 127.0.0.1 (`-s 127.0.0.1') with protocol ICMP (`-p icmp') we should jump to DROP (`-j DROP').

Then we test our rule, using the second ping. There will be a pause before the program gives up waiting for a response that will never come.

We can delete the rule in one of two ways. Firstly, since we know that it is the only rule in the input chain, we can use a numbered delete, as in:

```
# iptables -D INPUT 1
#
```

To delete rule number 1 in the INPUT chain.

The second way is to mirror the -A command, but replacing the -A with -D. This is useful when you have a complex chain of rules and you don't want to have to count them to figure out that it's rule 37 that you want to get rid of. In this case, we would use:

```
# iptables -D INPUT -s 127.0.0.1 -p icmp -j DROP
#
```

The syntax of -D must have exactly the same options as the -A (or –I or -R) command. If there are multiple identical rules in the same chain, only the first will be deleted.

12.3 Proxy Servers

A web proxy server is an intermediate server between local network and the internet. This is useful to provide better security and reduce network traffic for frequently accessed internet data by caching them locally.

A caching proxy is a server, which 'sits between' web browsers, such as Netscape or Internet Explorer and remote web sites. The proxy stores local copies of files as they are downloaded, and if a file is requested that has already been downloaded the local copy is supplied, rather than repeating the download. This save money (sometimes) and bandwidth (always). Squid is the leading caching proxy available: leading in terms of performance, reliability, versatility and scalability. Squid is an open-source project: its home is http://www.squid-cache.org. Squid is immensely scalable:all the large ISPs use it. It has provision for several servers ('neighbors') to share cached files. This scalability makes it look more complex to configure than it really is. Squid also has provision for restricting access in various ways. It isn't wise to leave squid security wide open: it can lead to unauthorized use of your server, and of your Internet connection.

Squid supports:

- proxying and caching of HTTP, FTP, and other URLs
- proxying for SSL
- cache hierarchies
- ICP, HTCP, CARP, Cache Digests
- transparent caching
- WCCP (Squid v2.3 and above)
- extensive access controls
- HTTP server acceleration
- SNMP caching of DNS lookups

12.4 Setting Proxy Server: SQUID

On a Debian Linux system, you can use the apt-get program to automatically download and install squid from the Internet, as follows:

apt-get install squid

Installing From Source If you prefer to install Squid from the source files, then you can do this on just about any Unix system. First, you will need to obtain the latest source code from the Squid web site, at http://www.squid-cache.org/ and read the INSTALL file which is provided with the Squid source code.

```
tar -xvzf squid-*-src.tar.gz
cd squid -*
```

(In the above * indicates the squid release number).

Now enter the following commands in order to configure, compile and install squid

```
./configure
make
make install
```

This will by default, install into "/usr/local/squid". Type ./configure --help to view all available options.

12.4.1 Configuring Squid

Everything in Squid is configured using a single configuration file, called squid.conf. The actual file is /etc/squid/squid.conf. By default, Squid comes with a configuration file that is mostly correct and almost usable It contains default settings for many of the options that require a setting, and should, by itself, allow access to your Squid configuration in a fairly secure manner from your local server only.

To allow Squid to be used as a proxy server for your entire network, we have to configure before we begin using Squid. Configuring squid can be a bit obscure: remember that there are thousands of options because the product is used by the largest ISPs in the world, with hundreds of servers in 'farms' all cooperating with each other.

By default, Debian Linux creates a user called 'proxy', in the group called 'proxy', and makes this user the owner of the /var/spool/squid directory which is where Squid stores its cache.

It makes sense to run the squid process as this (unprivileged) 'proxy' user, for security purposes. That way, anyone managing to hack the squid process using a buffer overflow or similar attack will not end up with root access to your machine.

Basic configuration

To the basic (as supplied) squid configuration file, add the following options:

The http_port is the port number on the local server that Squid binds itself to and listens for incoming requests, its default port is 3128 but can be changed if needed (8080 is also a common cache port).

```
http_port 192.168.1.1:8080
acl privatenet src 192.168.0.0/255.255.0.0
http_access allow privatenet
cache_effective_user proxy
cache_effective_group proxy
```

The acl privatenet src statement above needs to reflect your internal network. For example, allow the entire 192.168.x.x network to access squid since there are not any of these on the Internet, as all of them must be private.

The cache_dir tag specifies the location where the cache will reside in the filesystem. ufs identifies the storage format for the cache. The "100" specifies the maximum allowable size of the cache (in MB), and should be adjusted to suit your needs. The 16 and 256 specify the number1 of directories contained inside the first and second level cache store.

```
cache_dir ufs /var/spool/squid 100 16 256
```

When Squid proxies any FTP requests, this is the password used when logging in with an anonymous FTP account.

```
ftp_user Squid@example.com
```

The dns_nameservers specifies which DNS should be queried for name resolution. Squid will normally use the values located in the /etc/resolv.conf file, but can be overridden here.

```
dns_nameservers 127.0.0.1
```

If you need logs, uncomment the lines for cache_access_log and cache_log.

cache_store_log: enter 'none' here; you can't use the data so why waste the space.

emulate_httpd_log: change this to 'on', so common log analysis tools can work on the squid logs as well as http logs.

12.4.2 Setting Access Controls

The ACL's will help to avoid some of the more obscure problems, such as bandwidth-chewing loops, cache tunneling with SSL CONNECTs and other strange access problems. Access control is done on a per-protocol basis: when Squid accepts an HTTP request, the list of HTTP controls is checked. Similarly, when an ICP request is accepted, the ICP list is checked before a reply is sent.

Assume that you have a list of IP addresses that are to have access to your cache. If you want them to be able to access your cache with both HTTP and ICP, you would have to enter the list of IP addresses twice: you would have lines something like this:

```
http_access deny 10.0.1.0/255.255.255.0
http_access allow 10.0.0.0/255.0.0.0
icp_access allow 10.0.0.0/255.0.0.0
```

Rule sets like the above are great for small organizations: they are straight forward.

For large organizations, though, things are more convenient if you can create classes of users. We can then allow or deny classes of users in more complex relationships. Let's look at an example like this, where we duplicate the above example with classes of users:

```
# classes
acl mynetwork src 10.0.0.0/255.0.0.0
acl servernet src 10.0.1.0/255.255.255.0
# what HTTP access to allow classes
http_access deny servernet
http_access allow mynet
# what ICP access to allow classes
icp_access deny servernet
icp_access allow mynet
```

Acl-operators are checked in the order that they occur in the file (i.e. from top to bottom). The first acl-operator line that matches causes Squid to *drop out* of the acl list. Squid will not check through all acl-operators if the first denies the request.

In the previous example, we used a **src** acl: this checks that the source of the request is within the given IP range. The src acl-type accepts IP address lists in many formats, though we used the subnet/netmask in the earlier example. CIDR (Classless Internet Domain Routing) notation can also be used here.

Let see another example. The http_access allow http for all privatenet members in addition to localhost.

```
acl privatenet src 192.168.0.0/255.255.0.0
```

```
http_access allow localhost
http_access allow privatenet
http_access deny all
```

This rule defines an ACL called BADPC with a single source IP address of 192.168.1.25. It then denies access to the ACL.

```
acl BADPC src 192.168.1.25
http_access deny BADPC
```

Current day/time

Squid allows one to allow access to specific sites by time. Often businesses wish to filter out irrelevant sites during work hours. The Squid *time* acl type allows you to filter by the current day and time. By combining the *dstdomain* and *time* acls you can allow access to specific sites (such as your the sites of suppliers or other associates) during work hours, but allow access to other sites after work hours.

The layout is quite compact:

```
acl name time [day-list] [start_hour:minute-end_hour:minute]
```

Day list is a list of single characters indicating the days that the acl applies to. Using the first letter of the day would be ambiguous (since, for example, both Tuesday and Thursday start with the same letter). When the first letter is ambiguous, the second letter is used: *T* stands for Tuesday, *H* for Thursday. Here is a list of the days with their single-letter abbreviations:

S - Sunday *M* - Monday *T* - Tuesday *W* - Wednesday *H* - Thursday *F* - Friday *A* - Saturday

Start_hour and end_hour are values in military time (17:00 instead of 5:00). End_hour must always be larger than start_hour; this means (unfortunately) that you *cannot* do the following:

```
# since start_time must be smaller than end_time, this won't work:
acl darkness 17:00-6:00
```

The only alternative to the darkness example above is something like this:

```
acl night time 17:00-24:00
acl early_morning time 00:00-6:00
```

As you can see from the original definition of the *time* acl, you can specify the day of the week (with no time), the time (with no day), or both the time and day (?check!?). You can, for example, create a rule that specifies weekends without specifying that the day starts at midnight and ends at the following midnight. The following acl will match on either Saturday or Sunday.

```
acl weekends time SA
```

The following example is too basic for real-world use. Unfortunately creating a good example requires some of the more advanced features of the http_access line; these are covered in the next section of this chapter, and examples are included there.

Allowing Web access during the weekend only

```
acl myNet src 10.0.0.0/16
acl workdays time MTWHF
# allow web access only on the weekends!

http_access deny workdays
http_access allow myNet
```

The following is a mixed rule, it uses two ACLs to deny access. This rule denies PC during an ACL called CLEANTIME which is in effect MondayFriday 3 to 6PM.

```
acl PC src 192.168.1.25
acl CLEANTIME MTWHF 15:0018:00

http_access deny PC CLEANTIME
```

For example, consider this set of acl elements:

```
acl daytime time 09:00-16:00
acl subnet1 src 172.20.1.0/255.255.255.0
acl subnet2 src 172.20.2.0/255.255.255.0
acl all src 0/0

http_access allow subnet1
http_access deny subnet2 daytime
http_access allow subnet2
http_access deny all
```

The machines on subnet 1 can use the proxy (and therefore presumably the Internet) all the time; those on subnet 2 only during off-hours. Remember that acl elements are checked in order until one applies.

Destination Port

Web servers almost always listen for incoming requests on port 80. Some servers (notably site-specific search engines and unofficial sites) listen on other ports, such as 8080. Other services (such as IRC) also use high-numbered ports. Because of the way HTTP is designed, people can connect to things like IRC servers through your cache servers (even though the IRC protocol is very different to the HTTP protocol). The same problems can be used to tunnel telnet connections through your cache server. The major part of the HTTP specification that allows for this is the *CONNECT* method, which is used by clients to connect to web servers using SSL.

Since you generally don't want to proxy anything other than the standard supported protocols, you can restrict the ports that your cache is willing to connect to. The default Squid config file limits standard HTTP requests to the port ranges defined in the **Safe_ports** squid.conf acl. SSL **CONNECT** requests are even more limited, allowing connections to only ports 443 and 563.

Port ranges are limited with the **port** acl type. If you look in the default *squid.conf*, you will see lines like the following:

```
acl Safe_ports port 80 21 443 563 70 210 1025-65535
```

The format is pretty straight-forward: destination ports 443 OR 563 are matched by the first acl, 80 21 443, 563 and so forth by the second line. The most complicated section of the examples above is the end of the line: the text that reads "1024-65535".

The "-" character is used in squid to specify a *range*. The example thus matches any port from 1025 all the way up to 65535. These ranges are inclusive, so the second line matches ports 1025 and 65535 too.

The only low-numbered ports which Squid should need to connect to are 80 (the HTTP port), 21 (the FTP port), 70 (the Gopher port), 210 (wais) and the appropriate SSL ports. All other low-numbered ports (where common services like telnet run) do not fall into the 1024-65535 range, and are thus denied.

The following http_access line denies access to URLs that are not in the correct port ranges. You have not seen the *!* http_access operator before: it inverts the decision. The line below would read "deny access if the request does not fall in the range specified by acl Safe_ports" if it were written in English. If the port matches one of those specified in the Safe_ports acl line, the next http_access line is checked. More information on the format of http_access lines is given in the next section *Acl-operator lines*.

```
http_access deny !Safe_ports
```

Protocol (FTP, HTTP, SSL)

Some people may wish to restrict their users to specific protocols. The **proto** acl type allows you to restrict access by the URL prefix: the *http://* or *ftp://* bit at the front. The following example will deny request that uses the FTP protocol.

Denying access to FTP sites

```
acl ftp proto FTP
acl myNet src 10.0.0.0/16
acl all src 0.0.0.0/0.0.0.0

http_access deny ftp
http_access allow mynet
http_access deny all
```

The following rule will block all files that end in the file extensions ".mp3". The "i" means treat them as case insensitive which matches both upper and lower case.

```
acl FILE_MP3 urlpath_regex i
\.mp3$
http_access deny FILE_MP3
```

By default, Squid stores some information in a few log files as follows:

```
cache_access_log /var/log/squid/access.log
cache_log /var/log/squid/cache.log
cache_store_log none
```

With the above lines, Squid will store error messages in the file /var/log/squid/cache.log (this should be checked periodically), and access messages in the file /var/log/squid/access.log. There are a number of useful programs that can analyze the access log file, including SARG (Squid Analysis Report Generator).

We may want to allow access to your cache from a number of networks. This is accomplished by using various acl and http_access lines.

Note that an acl line defines a network or other access device, whereas the http_access (acl) (allow/deny) line grants or denies access to the acl that you have defined. Therefore, you should put your acl lines before the http_access lines in your configuration file.

Talking to an External (Upstream) Proxy

It may be advantageous to use an upstream proxy for Squid. This can speed Internet access up noticeably; for example, when your ISP also has a Squid cache that many users access. The ISP's cache can, over time, build up a large cache of many different sites, allowing faster access to those sites to your network.

For intercache communication, Squid supports a protocol known as 'ICP'. ICP allows caches to communicate to each other using fast UDP packets, sending copies of small cached files to each other within a single UDP packet if they are available.

To use an upstream proxy effectively, you should first determine what address it is (e.g.: proxyserver.yourisp.com), and what cache and ICP port (if any) it uses. Using an upstream proxy that supports ICP is simple, using a line like this one:

```
cache_peer proxy.yourisp.com parent 3128 3130
prefer_direct off
```

The cache_peer line specifies the host name, the cache type ("parent"), the proxy port (3128) and the ICP port (in this case, the default, which is 3130).

Sibling Proxies and Sharing Caches

Note that in a high volume situation, or a company with several connections to the Internet, Squid supports a multiparent, multisibling hierarchy of caches, provided that all of the caches support ICP. For example, your company may operate two caches, each with their own Internet connection but sharing a common network backbone. Each cache could have a cache_peer line in the configuration file such as:

```
cache_peer theotherproxy.yournetwork.com sibling 3128 3130
```

Note that the peer specification has changed to sibling, which means that we will fetch files from the other cache if they are present there, otherwise we will use our own Internet connection.

Denying Bad Files

There are a number of files that won't allow users to fetch, including the notorious WINBUGFIX. EXE file that was distributed with the Melissa virus. A simple ACL line to stop this file from being downloaded is as follows:

```
acl nastyfile dstdom_regex i
WIN[.*]BUG[.*]EXE

http_access deny nastyfile
```

To block some domains the blacklist is created, populated and secured, you place the appropriate "BAD_DOMAINS" access control policy in the configuration file.

```
acl BAD_DOMAINS dstdom_regex i
"/etc/squid/bad_domains"

http_access deny BAD_DOMAINS
```

19.2.3 Starting squid the first time

The first time squid runs it must build the cache directory tree in /var/spool. To ensure that this happens, run squid manually once: squid -z (to create the directories) then squid (to run the daemon).

Check squid is running by looking for two processes named squid and (squid) in the process table.

Starting squid at boot time

Use ntsysv to ensure that squid starts at boot.

12.5 Conclusions

This chapter explains about firewalls in general with specific emphasis on a popular proxy firewall, SQUID . It describes various types of firewalls and specifically packet filtering. How, Ipchains, and iptables are used in creating firewalls is explained in a lucid manner.

13 Users and Account Management

13.1 What is a UNIX account?

A UNIX account is a collection of logical characteristics that specify who the user is, what the user is allowed to do and where the user is allowed to do it. These characteristics include a

- login (or user) name,
- password,
- numeric user identifier or UID,
- a default numeric group identifier or GID,

Many accounts belong to more than one group but all accounts have one default group.

- home directory,
- login shell,
- possibly a mail alias,
- mail file, and
- collection of start-up files.

13.1.1 Login names

The account of every user is assigned a unique login (or user) name. The username uniquely identifies the account for people. The operating system uses the user identifier number (UID) to uniquely identify an account. The translation between UID and the username is carried out reading the /etc/passwd file (/etc/passwd is introduced below).

13.1.2 Login name format

On a small system, the format of login names is generally not a problem since with a small user population it is unlikely that there will be duplicates. However on a large site with hundreds or thousands of users and multiple computers, assigning a login name can be a major problem. With a larger number of users it is likely that you may get a number of people with names like David Jones, Darren Jones.

The following is a set of guidelines. They are by no means hard and fast rules but using some or all of them can make life easier for yourself as the Systems Administrator, or for your users.

- Unique
  This means usernames should be unique not only on the local machine but also across different machines at the same site. A login name should identify the same person and only one person on every machine on the site. This can be very hard to achieve at a site with a large user population especially if different machines have different administrators.

  The reason for this guideline is that under certain circumstances it is possible for people with the same username to access accounts with the same username on different machines.
- up to 8 characters
  UNIX will ignore or disallow login names that are longer. Dependent on which platform you are using.

- Lowercase
  Numbers and upper case letters can be used. Login names that are all upper case should be avoided as some versions of UNIX can assume this to mean your terminal doesn't recognise lower case letters and every piece of text subsequently sent to your display is in uppercase.
- Easy to remember
  A random sequence of letters and numbers is hard to remember and so the user will be continually have to ask the Systems Administrator "what's my username?"
- No nicknames
  A username will probably be part of an email address. The username will be one method by which other users identify who is on the system. Not all the users may know the nicknames of certain individuals.
- A fixed format
  There should be a specified system for creating a username. Some combination of first name, last name and initials is usually the best. Setting a policy allows you to automate the procedure of adding new users. It also makes it easy for other users to work out what the username for a person might be.

13.1.3 Passwords

An account's password is the key that lets someone in to use the account. A password should be a secret collection of characters known only by the owner of the account.

Poor choice of passwords is the single biggest security hole on any multi-user computer system. As a Systems Administrator we should follow a strict set of guidelines for passwords (after all if someone can break the root account's password, your system is going bye, bye). In addition we should promote the use of these guidelines amongst your users.

Password guidelines

An example set of password guidelines might include

- use combinations of upper and lower case characters, numbers and punctuation characters,
- don't use random combinations of characters if they break the following two rules,
- be easy to remember, If a user forgets their password they can't use the system and guess whom they come and see. Also the user SHOULD NOT have to write their password down.
- be quick to type, One of the easiest and most used methods for breaking into a system is simply watching someone type in their password. It is harder to do if the password is typed in quickly.
- a password should be at least 6 characters long, The shorter a password is the easier it is to break. Some systems will not allow passwords shorter than a specified length.
- a password should not be any longer than 8 to 10 characters, Most systems will look as if they are accepting longer passwords but they simply ignore the extra characters. The actual size is system specific but between eight and ten characters is generally the limit.
- do not use words from ANY language, Passwords that are words can be cracked.
- do not use combinations of just words and numbers, Passwords like hello1 are just as easy to crack as hello.
- use combinations of words separated by punctuation characters or acronyms of uncommon phrases/song lines, They should be easy to remember but hard to crack. e.g. b1gsh1p
- change passwords regularly, Not too often that you forget which password is currently set.
- never reuse passwords.

13.1.4 The UID

Every account on a UNIX system has a unique user or login name that is used by users to identify that account. The operating system does not use this name to identify the account. Instead each account must be assigned a unique user identifier number (UID) when it is created. The UID is used by the operating system to identify the account.

UID guidelines

In choosing a UID for a new user there are a number of considerations to take into account including

- choose a UID number between 100 and 32767 (or 60000), Numbers between 0 and 99 are reserved by some systems for use by system accounts. Different systems will have different possible maximum values for UID numbers. Around 32000 and 64000 are common upper limits.
- UIDs for a user should be the same across machines, Some network systems (e.g. NFS) require that users have the same UID across all machines in the network. Otherwise they will not work properly.
- you may not want to reuse a number. Not a hard and fast rule. Every file is owned by a particular user id. Problems arise where a user has left and a new user has been assigned the UID of the old user. What happens when you restore from backups some files that were created by the old user? The file thinks the user with a particular UID owns it. The new user will now own those files even though the username has changed.

13.1.5 Home directories

Every user must be assigned a home directory. When the user logs in it is this home directory that becomes the current directory. Typically all user home directories are stored under the one directory. Many modern systems use the directory /home. Older versions used /usr/users. The names of home directories will match the username for the account.

For example, a user rama would have the home directory /home/rama

In some instances it might be decided to further divide users by placing users from different categories into different sub-directories.

For example, all staff accounts may go under /home/staff while students are placed under /home/students. These separate directories may even be on separate partitions.

13.1.6 Login shell

Every user account has a login shell. A login shell is simply the program that is executed every time the user logs in. Normally it is one of the standard user shells such as Bourne, csh, bash etc. However it can be any executable program.

One common method used to disable an account is to change the login shell to the program /bin/false. When someone logs into such an account /bin/false is executed and the login: prompt reappears.

13.1.7 Dot files

A number of commands, including vi, the mail system and a variety of shells, can be customized using dot files [Kernigham]. A dot file is usually placed into a user's home directory and has a filename that starts with a . (dot). This files (see Table 13.1) are examined when the command is first executed and modifies how it behaves.

Dot files are also known as rc files, i.e., "run command".

Table 13.1 dot files for a number of shell or commands.

Filename	Command	Explanation
~/.cshrc	/bin/csh	Executed every time C shell started.
~/.login	/bin/csh	Executed after .cshrc when logging in with C shell as the login shell.
/etc/profile	/bin/sh	Executed during the login of every user that uses the Bourne shell or its derivatives.
~/.profile	/bin/sh	Located in user's home directory. Executed whenever the user logs in when the Bourne shell is their login shell
~/.logout	/bin/csh	executed just prior to the system logging the user out (when the csh is the login shell)
~/.bash_logout	/bin/bash	executed just prior to the system logging the user out (when bash is the login shell)
~/.bash_history	/bin/bash	records the list of commands executed using the current shell
~/.forward	incoming mail	Used to forward mail to another address or a command
~/.exrc	vi	used to set options for use in vi

Shell's dot files

These shell dot files, particularly those executed when a shell is first executed, are responsible for

- setting up command aliases, Some shells (e.g. bash) allow the creation of aliases for various commands. A common command alias for old MS-DOS people is dir, usually set to mean the same as ls -l.
- setting values for shell variables like PATH and TERM.

13.1.8 Skeleton directories

Normally all new users are given the same startup files. Rather than create the same files from scratch all the time, copies are usually kept in a directory called a skeleton directory. This means when you create a new account you can simply copy the startup files from the skeleton directory into the user's home directory.

The standard skeleton directory is /etc/skel. It should be remembered that the files in the skeleton directory are **dot** files and will not show up if you simply use ls /etc/skel. As mentioned earlier, we will have to use the -a switch for ls to see dot files.

13.1.9 The mail file

When someone sends mail to a user that mail message has to be stored somewhere so that it can be read. Under UNIX each user is assigned a mail file. All user mail files are placed in the same directory. When a new mail message arrives it is appended onto the end of the user's mail file.

The location of this directory can change depending on the operating system being used. Common locations are

- /usr/spool/mail,
- /var/spool/mail,

This is the standard Linux location in some Linux variants.

- /usr/mail
- /var/mail.

On some sites it is common for users to have accounts on a number of different computers. It is easier if all the mail for a particular user goes to the one location. This means that a user will choose one machine as their mail machine and want all their email forwarded to their account on that machine.

There are at least two ways by which mail can be forwarded

- the user can create a .forward file in their home directory (see Table 13.1), or
- the administrator can create an alias.

Mail aliases

If you send an e-mail message that cannot be delivered (e.g. you use the wrong address) typically the mail message will be forwarded to the postmaster of your machine. There is usually no account called postmaster (though recent distributions of Linux do). postmaster is a mail alias.

When the mail delivery program gets mail for postmaster it will not be able to find a matching username. Instead it will look up a specific file, usually /etc/aliases or /etc/mail/names (Linux uses /etc/aliases). This file will typically have an entry like

```
postmaster: root
```

This tells the delivery program that anything addressed postmaster should actually be delivered to the user root.

Site aliases

Some companies will have a set policy for e-mail aliases for all staff. This means that when you add a new user you also have to update the aliases file.

13.2 Account configuration files

Most of the characteristics of an account mentioned above are stored in two or three configuration files. All these files are text files, each account has a one-line entry in the file with each line divided into a number of fields using colons.

Table 13.2. lists the configuration files examined and their purpose. Not all systems will have the /etc/shadow file. On some platforms the shadow file will exist but its filename will be different.

Table 13.2 Account configuration files.

File	Purpose
/etc/passwd	the password file, holds most of an account characteristics including username, UID, GID, GCOS information, login shell, home directory and in some cases the password
/etc/shadow	the shadow password file, a more secure mechanism for holding the password, common on more modern systems
/etc/group	the group file, holds characteristics about a system's groups including group name, GID and group members

13.2.1 /etc/passwd

/etc/passwd is the main account configuration file. Table 13.3 summarizes each of the fields in the /etc/passwd file. On some systems the encrypted password will not be in the passwd file but will be in a shadow file.

Table 13.3 /etc/passwd.

Field Name	Purpose
login name	the user's login name
encrypted password *	encrypted version of the user's password
UID number	the user's unique numeric identifier
default GID	the user's default group id
GCOS information	no strict purpose, usually contains full name and address details, sometimes called the comment field
home directory	the directory in which the user is placed when they log in
login shell	the program that is run when the user logs in

**** not on systems with a shadow password file***

Everyone can read /etc/passwd

Every user on the system must be able to read the /etc/passwd file. This is because many of the programs and commands a user executes must access the information in the file. For example, when you execute the command ls -l command part of what the command must do is translate the UID of the file's owner into a username. The only place that information is stored is in the /etc/passwd file.

This is a problem

Since everyone can read the /etc/passwd file they can also read the encrypted password.

The problem isn't that someone might be able to decrypt the password. The method used to encrypt the passwords is supposedly a one way encryption algorithm. You aren't supposed to be able to decrypt the passwords.

The way to break into a UNIX system is to obtain a dictionary of words and encrypt the whole dictionary. You then compare the encrypted words from the dictionary with the encrypted passwords. If you find a match you know what the password is.

Studies have shown that with a carefully chosen dictionary, between 10-20% of passwords can be cracked on any machine.

An even greater problem is the increasing speed of computers. One modern super computer is capable of performing 424,400 encryptions a second. This means that all six-character passwords can be discovered in two days and all seven-character passwords within four months.

The solution to this problem is to not store the encrypted password in the /etc/passwd file. Instead it should be kept in another file that only the root user can read. Remember the passwd program is setuid root.

This other file in which the password is stored is usually referred to as the shadow password file. It can be stored in one of a number of different locations depending on the version of UNIX you are using. A common location, and the one used by the Linux shadow password suite, is /etc/shadow.

13.2.2 /etc/shadow file

Typically the shadow file consists of one line per user containing the encrypted password and some additional information including

- username,
- the date the password was last changed,
- minimum number of days before the password can be changed again,
- maximum number of days before the password must be changed,
- number of days until age warning is sent to user,
- number of days of inactivity before account should be removed,
- absolute date on which the password will expire.

The additional information is used to implement password aging.

13.2.3 Groups

As we understood earlier that a group is a logical collection of users. Users with similar needs or characteristics are usually placed into groups. A group is a collection of user accounts that can be given special permissions. Groups are often used to restrict access to certain files and programs to everyone but those within a certain collection of users.

/etc/group

The /etc/group file maintains a list of the current groups for the system and the users that belong to each group. The fields in the /etc/group file include

- the group name,

  A unique name for the group.
- an encrypted password (this is rarely used today) ,
- the numeric group identifier or GID, and
- the list of usernames of the group members separated by commas.

A user can in fact be a member of several groups. Any extra groups the user is a member of are specified by entries in the /etc/group file.

It is not necessary to have an entry in the /etc/group file for the default group. However if the user belongs to any other groups they must be added to the /etc/group file.

13.2.4 Special accounts

All UNIX systems come with a number of special accounts. These accounts already exist and are there for a specific purpose. Typically these accounts will all have UIDs that are less than 100 and are used to perform a variety of administrative duties. Table 13.4. lists some of the special accounts that may exist on a machine.

Table 13.4 Special accounts.

Username	UID	Purpose
root	0	The super user account. Used by the Systems Administrator to perform a number of tasks. Can do anything. Not subject to any restrictions
daemon	1	Owner of many of the system daemons (programs that run in the background waiting for things to happen).
bin	2	The owner of many of the standard executable programs

root

The root user, also known as the super user is probably the most important account on a UNIX system. This account is not subject to the normal restrictions placed on standard accounts. It is used by the Systems Administrator to perform administrative tasks that can't be performed by a normal account.

Restricted actions

Some of the actions for which you'd use the root account include

- creating and modifying user accounts,
- shutting the system down,
- configuring hardware devices like network interfaces and printers,
- changing the ownership of files,
- setting and changing quotas and priorities, and
- setting the name of a machine.

Be careful

We should always be careful when logged in as root. When logged in as root we must know what every command we type is going to do. Remember the root account is not subject to the normal restrictions of other accounts. If we execute a command as root it **will** be done, whether it deletes all the files on y\our system or not.

Adding a user is a fairly mechanical task that is usually automated either through shell scripts or on many modern systems with a GUI based program. However it is still important that the Systems Administrator be aware of the steps involved in creating a new account. If you know how it works you can fix any problems which occur.

13.3 Creating Users

In summary, the steps to create a user include

- adding an entry for the new user to the /etc/passwd file,
- setting an initial password,
- adding an entry to the /etc/group file,
- creating the user's home directory,
- creating the user's mail file or setting a mail alias,
- creating any start-up files required for the user,
- testing that the addition has worked, and
- possibly sending an introductory message to the user.

Other considerations

When adding a new account, user management tasks that are required include

- making the user aware of the site's policies regarding computer use,
- getting the user to sign an "acceptable use" form,
- letting the user know where and how they can find information about their system, and
- possibly showing the user how to work the system.

Adding an /etc/passwd entry

For every new user, an entry has to be added to the /etc/passwd file. There are a variety of methods by which this is accomplished including

- using an editor, This is a method that is often used. However it can be unsafe and it is generally not a good idea to use it.
- the command vipw, or Some systems (usually BSD based) provide this command. vipw invokes an editor so the Systems Administrator can edit the passwd file safely. The command performs some additional steps that ensures that the editing is performed consistently. Some distributions of Linux supply vipw.
- a dedicated **adduser** program [Richard L Peterson]. Many systems, Linux included, provide a program (the name will change from system to system) that accepts a number of command-line parameters and then proceeds to perform many of the steps involved in creating a new account. The Linux command is called adduser .

  useradd is an executable program which significantly reduces the complexity of adding a new user. A solution to the previous exercise using useradd looks like this

  useradd -c "David Jones" david

  useradd will automatically create the home directory and mail file, copy files from skeleton directories and a number of other tasks.
- With the help of GUI based facility for user management. On my machine, Applications -> system settings -> Users and Groups.

NEVER LEAVE THE PASSWORD FIELD BLANK.

If you are not going to set a password for a user put a * in the password field of /etc/passwd or the /etc/shadow file. On most systems, the * character is considered an invalid password and it prevents anyone from using that account.

If a password is to be set for the account then the passwd command must be used. The user should be forced to immediately change any password set by the Systems Administrator

/etc/group entry

While not strictly necessary, the /etc/group file should be modified to include the user's login name in their default group. Also if the user is to be a member of any other group they must have an entry in the /etc/group file.

Editing the /etc/group file with an editor should be safe.

The home directory

Not only must the home directory be created but the permissions also have to be set correctly so that the user can access the directory.

The permissions of a home directory should be set such that

- the user should be the owner of the home directory,
- the group owner of the directory should be the default group that the user belongs to,
- at the very least, the owner of the directory should have rwx permissions, and
- the group and other permissions should be set as restrictively as possible.

The startup files

Once the home directory is created the startup files can be copied in or created. Again you should remember that this will be done as the root user and so root will own the files. You must remember to change the ownership.

Setting up mail

A new user will either

- want to read their mail on this machine, or
- want to read their mail on another machine.

The user's choice controls how you configure the user's mail.

A mail file

If the user is going to read their mail on this machine then you must create them a mail file. The mail file must go in a standard directory (usually /var/spool/mail under Linux). As with home directories it is important that the ownership and the permissions of a mail file be set correctly. The requirements are

- the user must be able to read and write the file, After all, the user must be able to read and delete mail messages.
- the group owner of the mail file should be the group mail and the group should be able to read and write to the file, The programs that deliver mail are owned by the group mail. These programs must be able to write to the file to deliver the user's mail.
- no-one else should have any access to the file, No-one wants anyone else peeking at their private mail.

Mail aliases and forwards

If the user's main mail account is on another machine, any mail that is sent to this machine should be forwarded to the appropriate machine. There are two methods

- a mail alias, or
- a file ~/.forward

Both methods achieve the same result. The main difference is that the user can change the .forward file if they wish to. They can't modify a central alias.

Additional steps

Simply creating the accounts using the steps introduced above is usually not all that has to be done. Most sites may include additional steps in the account creation process such as

- sending an initial, welcoming email message, Such an email can serve a number of purposes, including informing the new users of their rights and responsibilities. It is important that users be made aware as soon as possible of what they can and can't do and what support they can expect from the Systems Administration team.
- creating email aliases or other site specific steps.

13.4 Testing an account

Once the account is created, at least in some instances, you will want to test the account creation to make sure that it has worked. There are at least two methods you can use

- login as the user
- use the su command.

The su command

The su command is used to change from one user account to another. To a certain extent it acts like logging in as the other user. The standard format is su *username*.

Su

Password:

Time to become the root user. su without any parameter lets you become the root user, as long as you know the password. In the following the id command is used to prove that I really have become the root user. You'll also notice that the prompt displayed by the shell has changed as well. In particular notice the # character, commonly used to indicate a shell with root permission.

id

```
uid=0(root) gid=0(root)
groups=0(root),1(bin),2(daemon),3(sys),4(adm),6(disk),10(wheel)
```

When you do use the "-" argument of the su command, it simulates a full login. This means that any startup files are executed and that the current directory becomes the home directory of the user account you "are becoming". This is equivalent to logging in as the user.

su – david

If you run su as a normal user you will have to enter the password of the user you are trying to become. If you don't specify a username you will become the root user (if you know the password).

The "-" switch

The su command is used to change from one user to another. By default, su david will change your UID and GID to that of the user david (if you know the password) but won't change much else. Using the - switch of su it is possible to simulate a full login including execution of the new user's startup scripts and changing to their home directory.

su as root

If you use the su command as the root user you do not have to enter the new user's password. su will immediately change you to the new user. su especially with the - switch is useful for testing a new account.

13.5 Removing an account

Deleting an account involves reversing the steps carried out when the account was created. It is a destructive process and whenever something destructive is performed, care must always be taken. The steps that might be carried out include

- disabling the account,
- backing up and removing the associated files
- setting up mail forwards.

Situations under which you may wish to remove an account include

- as punishment for a user who has broken the rules, or In this situation you may only want to disable the account rather than remove it completely.
- an employee has left.

Disabling an account

Disabling an account ensures that no-one can login but doesn't delete the contents of the account. This is a minimal requirement for removing an account. There are two methods for achieving this

- change the login shell, or Setting the login shell to /bin/false will prevent logins. However it may still be possible for the user to receive mail through the account using POP mail programs like Eudora.
- change the password.

The * character is considered by the password system to indicate an illegal password. One method for disabling an account is to insert a * character into the password field. If you want to re-enable the account (with the same password) simply remove the *.

Another method is to simply remove the entry from the /etc/passwd and /etc/shadow files all together.

Remove the user's files

All the files owned by the account should be removed from where ever they are in the file hierarchy. It is unlikely for a user to own files that are located outside of their home directory (except for the mail file). However it is a good idea to search for them. Another use for the find command.

Mail for old users

On some systems, even if you delete the user's mail file, mail for that user can still accumulate on the system. If you delete an account entirely by removing it from the password field, any mail for that account will bounce.

In most cases, a user who has left will want their mail forwarded onto a new account. One solution is to create a mail alias for the user that points to their new address.

userdel and usermod

userdel is the companion command to useradd and as the name suggests it deletes or removes a user account from the system. usermod allows a Systems Administrator to modify the details of an existing user account.

13.6 Allocating root privilege

Many of the menial tasks, like creating users and performing backups, require the access which the root account provides. This means that these tasks can't be allocated to junior members of staff without giving them access to everything else on the system. In most cases you don't want to do this.

There is another problem with the root account. If you have a number of trusted Systems Administrators the root account often becomes a group account. The problem with this is that since everyone knows the root password there is no way by which you can know who is doing what as root. There is no accountability. While this may not be a problem on your individual system on commercial systems it is essential to be able to track what everyone does.

sudo

A solution to these problems is the sudo command.

sudo allows you to allocate certain users the ability to run programs as root without giving them access to everything. For example, you might decide that the office secretary can run the adduser script, or an operator might be allowed to execute the backup script.

sudo also provides a solution to the accountability problem. sudo logs every command people perform while using it. This means that rather than using the root account as a group account, you can provide all your Systems Administrators with sudo access. When they perform their tasks with sudo, what they do will be recorded.

For example

To execute a command as root using sudo you login to your "normal" user account and then type sudo followed by the command you wish to execute. The following example shows what happens when you can and can't executable a particular command using sudo.

sudo ls We trust you have received the usual lecture from the local System Administrator. It usually boils down to these two things:

#1) Respect the privacy of others.

#2) Think before you type.

Password:

sudo cat

Sorry, user david is not allowed to execute "/bin/cat" as root on mc.

If the sudoers file is configured to allow you to execute this command on the current machine, you will be prompted for your normal password. You'll only be asked for the password once every five minutes.

/etc/sudoers

The sudo configuration file is usually /etc/sudoers or in some instances /usr/local/etc/sudoers. sudoers is a text file with lines of the following format

username hostname=command

An example sudoers file might look like this

```
Root      ALL=ALL
david     ALL=ALL
bob       cq-pan=/usr/local/bin/backup
jo        ALL=/usr/local/bin/adduser
```

In this example the root account and the user david are allowed to execute all commands on all machines. The user bob can execute the /usr/local/bin/backup command but only on the machine cq-pan. The user jo can execute the adduser command on all machines. The sudoers man page has a more detail example and explanation.

By allowing you to specify the names of machines you can use the same sudoers file on all machines. This makes it easier to manage a number of machines. All you do is copy the same file to all your machines (there is a utility called rdist which can make this quite simple).

sudo advantages

sudo offers the following advantages

- accountability because all commands executed using sudo are logged, Logging on a UNIX computer, as you'll be shown in a later chapter, is done via the syslog system. What this means is that on a Redhat machine the information from sudo is logged in the file /var/log/messages.
- menial tasks can be allocated to junior staff without providing root access,
- using sudo is faster than using su,
- a list of users with root access is maintained,
- privileges can be revoked without changing the root password.

Some sites that use sudo keep the root password in an envelope in someone's draw. The root account is never used unless in emergencies where it is required.

13.7 Conclusions

This chapter explores about users and account management. It emphasizes creating users with some specific privileges and assigning them to be able to run some commands to do a specific administration task. Also it explains how mail aliases can be done in Linux.

14 A brief Introduction to Unix Devices and File systems

14.1 Introduction

In Linux system devices also abstracted same as files. In this chapter first we try to explain about Linux devices notations, device drivers, major and minor number and physical organization of the data on the disk.

In the first chapter, we have examined the overall logical structure of the Linux file system. This was a fairly abstract view that didn't explain how the data was physically transferred on and off the disk. Nor in fact, did it really examine the concept of "disks" or even "what" the file system "physically" existed on.

14.2 Devices - Gateways to the kernel

A device is just a generic name for any type of physical or logical system component that the operating system has to interact with (or "talk" to).

Physical devices include such things as hard disks, serial devices (such as modems, mouse(s) etc.), CDROMs, sound cards and tape-backup drives.

Logical devices include such things as virtual terminals *[every user is allocated a terminal when they log in - this is the point at which output to the screen is sent (STDOUT) and keyboard input is taken (STDIN)]*, memory, the kernel itself and network ports.

14.2.1 Device files

Device files are special types of "files" that allow programs to interact with devices via the OS kernel. These "files" (they are not actually real files in the sense that they do not contain data) act as gateways or entry points into the kernel or kernel related "device drivers".

As explained in first chapter, **/dev** is the location where most device files are kept. A listing of /dev will output the names of hundreds of files. The following is an edited extract from the **MAKEDEV** (a Linux program for making device files - we will examine it later) man page on some of the types of device file that exist in /dev:

- std
  Standard devices. These include mem - access to physical memory; kmem - access to kernel virtual memory;null - null device; port - access to I/O ports;
- Virtual Terminals
  This are the devices associated with the console. This is the virtual terminal tty_, where can be from 0 though 63.
- Serial Devices
  Serial ports and corresponding dialout device. For device ttyS_, there is also the device cua_ which is used to dial out with.
- Pseudo Terminals
  (Non-Physical terminals) The master pseudo-terminals are pty[p-s][0-9a-f] and the slaves are tty[p-s][0-9a-f].

- Parallel Ports
  Standard parallel ports. The devices are lp0, lp1, and lp2. These correspond to ports at 0x3bc, 0x378 and 0x278. Hence, on some machines, the first printer port may actually be lp1.
- Bus Mice
  The various bus mice devices. These include: logimouse (Logitech bus mouse), psmouse (PS/2-style mouse), msmouse (Microsoft Inport bus mouse) and atimouse (ATI XL bus mouse) and jmouse (J-mouse).
- Joystick Devices
  Joystick. Devices js0 and js1.
- Disk Devices
  Floppy disk devices. The device fd_ is the device which autodetects the format, and the additional devices are fixed format (whose size is indicated in the name). The other devices are named as fd___. The single letter _ identifies the type of floppy disk (d = 5.25" DD, h = 5.25" HD, D = 3.5" DD, H = 3.5" HD, E = 3.5" ED). The number _ represents the capacity of that format in K. Thus the standard formats are fd_d360_fd_h1200_fd_D720_fd_H1440_and fd_E2880_
  Devices fd0_ through fd3_ are floppy disks on the first controller, and devices fd4_ through fd7_ are floppy disks on the second controller.
  Hard disks : The device hdx provides access to the whole disk, with the partitions being hdx[0-20]. The four primary partitions are hdx1 through hdx4, with the logical partitions being numbered from hdx5 though hdx20. (A primary partition can be made into an extended partition, which can hold 4 logical partitions).
  Drives hda and hdb are the two on the first controller. If using the new IDE driver (rather than the old HD driver), then hdc and hdd are the two drives on the secondary controller. These devices can also be used to access IDE CDROMs if using the new IDE driver.
  SCSI hard disks : The partitions are similar to the IDE disks, but there is a limit of 11 logical partitions (sd_5 through sd_15). This is to allow there to be 8 SCSI disks.
  Loopback disk devices : These allow you to use a regular file as a block device. This means that images of file systems can be mounted, and used as normal. There are 8 devices, loop0 through loop7.
- Tape Devices
  SCSI tapes. These are the rewinding tape devicest_ and the non-rewinding tape device nst_.
  QIC-80 tapes. The devices are rmt8, rmt16, tape-d, and tape-reset.
  Floppy driver tapes (QIC-117). There are 4 methods of access depending on the floppy tape drive. For each of access methods 0, 1, 2 and 3, the devices rft_ (rewinding) and nrft_ (non-rewinding) are created.
- CDROM Devices
  SCSI CD players. Sony CDU-31A CD player. Mitsumi CD player. Sony CDU-535 CD player. LMS/Philips CD player.
  Sound Blaster CD player. The kernel is capable of supporting 16 CDROMs, each of which is accessed as sbpcd[0-9a-f]. These are assigned in groups of 4 to each controller.
- Audio
  These are the audio devices used by the sound driver. These include mixer, sequencer, dsp, and audio.
  Devices for the PC Speaker sound driver. These are pcmixer. pxsp, and pcaudio.

- Miscellaneous
  Generic SCSI devices. The devices created are sg0 through sg7. These allow arbitrary commands to be sent to any SCSI device. This allows for querying information about the device, or controlling SCSI devices that are not one of disk, tape or CDROM (e.g. scanner, writable CDROM).

  While the /dev directory contains the device files for many types of devices, only those devices that have device drivers present in the kernel can be used or usable. For example, while your system may have a /dev/sbpcd, it doesn't mean that your kernel can support a Sound Blaster CD. To enable the support, the kernel will have to be recompiled with the Sound Blaster driver included.

14.2.2 Device Drivers

Device drivers are coded routines used for interacting with devices. They essentially act as the "go between" for the low level hardware and the kernel/user interface.

Device drivers may be physically compiled into the kernel (most are) or may be dynamically loaded in memory as required.

Popularly two types are devices and device drivers are available namingly character oriented and block oriented (In previous chapters we have discusses about them in brief).

If you were to examine the output of the **ls -al** command on a device file, something like:

ls -al /dev/ttyS*

```
crw--w--w-  1 james users     4,   0 Mar 31 09:28 /dev/ttyS0
crw--w--w-   1 james users     4,   0 Mar 31 09:28 /dev/ttyS1
```

In this case, we are examining the device file for the console. There are two major differences in the file listing of a device file from that of a "normal" file, for example:

ls -al iodev.html -rw-r--r-- 1 james users7938 Mar 31 12:49 iodev.html

The first difference is the first character of the "file permissions" grouping - this is actually the file type. On directories this is a "**d**", on "normal" files it will be blank but on devices it will be "**c**" or "**b**". This character indicates **c** for character mode or **b** for block mode. This is the way in which the device interacts - either character by character or in blocks of characters. Do remember that we have already discussed about this in previous chapters.

For example, devices like the console output (and input) character by character.

However, devices like hard disks read and write in blocks. You can see an example of a block device by the following:

ls -al /dev/had

```
brw-rw----  1 root    disk     3,   0 Apr 28  1995 /dev/hda
```

(hda is the first hard drive)

The second difference is the two numbers where the file size field usually is on a normal file. These two numbers (delimited by a comma) are the major and minor device numbers.

14.2.2.1 Major and minor device numbers

Major and minor device numbers are the way in which the kernel determines which device is being used, therefore what device driver is required. The kernel maintains a list of its available device drivers, given by the major number of a device file. When a device file is used (we will discuss this in the next section), the kernel runs the appropriate device driver, passing it the minor device number. The device driver determines which physical device is being used by the minor device number. For example:

ls -al /dev/had brw-rw---- 1 root disk 3, 0 Apr 28 1995 /dev/had
ls -al /dev/hdb brw-rw---- 1 root disk 3, 64 Apr 28 1995 /dev/hdb

What this listing shows is that a device driver, major number 3, controls both hard drives hda and hdb. When those devices are used, the device driver will know which is which (physically) because hda has a minor device number of 0 and hdb has a minor device number of 64.

Usually, other operating systems provide separate system calls to interact with each device. This means that each program needs to know the exact system call to talk to a particular device. With UNIX and device files, this need is removed. With the standard open, read, write, append etc., system calls (provided by the kernel), a program may access any device (transparently) while the kernel determines what type of device it is and which device driver to use to process the call. Here, major and minor number of the devices on which required the file is located are used by the kernel.

Using files also allows the system administrator to set permissions on particular devices and enforce security - we will discuss this in detail later.

The most obvious advantage of using device files is shown by the way in which as a user, you can interact with them. For example, instead of writing a special program to play .AU sound files, you can simply:

cat test.au > /dev/audio

This command pipes the contents of the test.au file into the audio device. Two things to note: **1)** This will only work for systems with audio (sound card) support compiled into the kernel (i.e. device drivers exist for the device file) and **2)** this will only work for .AU files - try it with a .WAV and see (actually, listen) what happens. The reason for this is that .WAV (a Windows audio format) has to be interpreted first before it can be sent to the sound card.

Creating device files

There are two ways to create device files - the easy way or the hard way!

The easy way involves using the Linux command MAKEDEV. This is actually a script that can be found in the /dev directory. MAKEDEV accepts a number of parameters (you can check what they are in the man pages. In general, MAKEDEV is run as:

/dev/MAKEDEV device

where device is the name of a device file. If for example, you accidentally erased or corrupted your console device file (/dev/console) then you'd recreate it by issuing the commend:

/dev/MAKEDEV console

NOTE! This must be done as the root user

We can use mknod command also for this purpose. With the mknod command you must know the major and minor device number as well as the type of device (character or block). To create a device file using mknod, you issue the command:

```
mknod device_file_name device_type major_number minor_number
```

For example, to create the device file for COM1 a.k.a. /dev/ttys0 (usually where the mouse is connected) you'd issue the command:

```
mknod /dev/ttyS0 c 4 240
ls -al /dev > /mnt/device_file_listing
```

Device files are used directly or indirectly in every application on a Linux system. When a user first logs in, they are assigned a particular device file for their terminal interaction. This file can be determined by issuing the command:

```
Tty
```

For example:

```
tty
/dev/ttyp1
ls -al /dev/ttyp1
crw-------   1 jamiesob tty4, 193 Apr  2 21:14 /dev/ttyp1
```

Notice that as a user, I actually own the device file! This is so I can write to the device file and read from it. When I log out, it will be returned to:

```
c--------- 1 root  root  4, 193 Apr  2 20:33 /dev/ttyp1
```

Try the following:

```
read X < /dev/ttyp1 ; echo "I wrote $X" echo "hello there" > /dev/ttyp1
```

You should see something like:

```
read X < /dev/ttyp1 ; echo "I wrote $X" hello
I wrote hello
echo "hello there" > /dev/ttyp1
hello there
```

A very important device file is that which is assigned to your hard disk. In my case /dev/hda is my primary hard disk, its device file looks like:

```
brw-rw----   1 root    disk      3,   0 Apr 28  1995 /dev/hda
```

Note that as a normal user, I can't directly read and write to the hard disk device file - why do you think this is?

Reading and writing to the hard disk is handled by an intermediary called the file system. We will examine the role of the file system in later sections, but for the time being, you should be aware that the file system decides how to use the disk, how to find data and where to store information about what is on the disk.

Bypassing the file system and writing directly to the device file is a very dangerous thing - device drivers have no concept of file systems, files or even the data that is stored in them; device drivers are only interested in reading and writing chunks of data (called blocks) to physical sectors of the disk. For example, by directly writing a data file to a device file, you are effectively instructing the device driver to start writing blocks of data onto the disk from where ever the disk head was sitting! This can (depending on which sector and track the disk was set to) potentially wipe out the entire file structure, boot sector and all the data. Not a good idea to try it. **NEVER** should you issue a command like:

```
cat some_file > /dev/hda1
```

As a normal user, you can't do this - but you can as root!

Reading directly from the device file is also a problem. While not physically damaging the data on the disk, by allowing users to directly read blocks, it is possible to obtain information about the system that would normally be restricted to them. For example, was someone clever enough to obtain a copy of the blocks on the disk where the shadow password file resided (a file normally protected by file permissions so users can view it), they could potentially reconstruct the file and run it through a crack program.

14.3 Disk Drives, Partitions and File systems

Device files and partitions

We can use variety of hard disks such as IDE, SCSI and RAID type. Normally, for a desktop systems IDE drives are sufficient and SCSI drives are used for server machines because of performance reasons. Whenever high level data safety and response times are needed RAID drives are.

Partitions are non-physical (I am deliberately avoiding the use of the word "logical" because this is a type of partition) divisions of a hard disk. IDE Hard disks may have 4 primary partitions, one of which must be a boot partition if the hard disk is the primary (modern systems have primary and secondary disk controllers) master (first hard disk) [this is the partition BIOS attempts to load a bootstrap program from at boot time].

Each primary partition can be marked as an extended partition which can be further divided into four logical partitions. By default, Linux provides device files for the four primary partitions and 4 logical partitions per primary/extended partition. For example, a listing of the device files for my primary master hard disk reveals:

```
brw-rw----  1  root disk  3,   0  Apr  28   1995  /dev/had   →  first IDE drive
brw-rw----  1 root  disk  3,   1  Apr  28   1995 /dev/hda1    →  first partition
```

(like C: in Windows)

```
brw-rw----   1 root   disk   3,  2 Apr 28  1995 /dev/hda2
brw-rw----   1 root   disk   3,  3 Apr 28  1995 /dev/hda3
brw-rw----   1 root   disk   3,  4 Apr 28  1995 /dev/hda4
brw-rw----   1 root   disk   3,  5 Apr 28  1995 /dev/hda5
brw-rw----   1 root   disk   3,  6 Apr 28  1995 /dev/hda6
brw-rw----   1 root   disk   3,  7 Apr 28  1995 /dev/hda7
brw-rw----   1 root   disk   3,  8 Apr 28  1995 /dev/hda8
brw-rw----   1 root   disk   3,  9 Apr 28  1995 /dev/hda9
```

Also, note the following notations.

/dev/hdb → second IDE drive
/dev/hdc → third hard disk
/dev/hdd → fourth hard disk
/dev/sd* → SCSI drives

Partitions are usually created by using a system utility such as fdisk. Generally fdisk will ONLY be used when a new operating system is installed or a new hard disk is attached to a system.

Why partitions are needed?

1. To have more then one OS installed on a same machine.
2. To organize the SW
3. To safeguard against viruses
4. If we use entire disk as a single partition we may see the following situation in which a small file (which is in physically stored in inner most tracks) taking more time than a large file (which is physically stored in outer most tracks). Main reasons for this differences in horizontal latency times, i.e. times required for the head to move to required track. In order reduce this effect disk partitions are used.
5. Certain directories will contain data that will only need to be read, others will need to be both read and written. It is possible (and good practice) to mount these partitions restricting such operations.
6. Directories including /tmp and /var/spool can fill up with files very quickly, especially if a process becomes unstable or the system is purposely flooded with email. This can cause problems. For example, let us assume that the /tmp directory is on the same partition as the /home directory. If the /tmp directory causes the partition to be filled no user will be able to write to their /home directory, there is no space. If /tmp and /home are on separate partitions the filling of the /tmp partition will not influence the /home directories.
7. By spreading the file system over several partitions and devices, the IO load is spread around. It is then possible to have multiple seek operations occurring simultaneously - this will improve the speed of the system.

How many partitions are recommended for a practical system?

1. One partition for swapping
2. One partition for users, i.e. for /home directory. Such that migration becomes easy.
3. One partition for /usr. Usually, in large organizations application SW takes more time for installing and fine tuning. Whenever, we wanted to upgrade the kernel, if we happened to have a separate partition for application programs, i.e. /usr then after installing new kernel this partition can be simply mounted.

4. One empty partition for experimental purpose. During migration this is very helpful.
5. One partition for /usr/local. That is, here we can install site specific, licensed SW and if required they can be made available for other systems through NFS.
    a. A separate partition for /boot.
    b. A separate partition for /tmp
    c. A separate partition for /var/spool

Every partition on a hard disk has an associated file system (the file system type is actually set when fdisk is run and a partition is created). It is quite possible that the file system structure is spread over multiple partitions and devices, each a different "type" of file system.

Linux can support (or "understand", access, read and write to) many types of file systems including: minix, ext, ext2, umsdos, msdos, proc, nfs, iso9660, xenix, Sysv, coherent, hpfs.

A file system is simply a set or rules and algorithms for accessing files. Each system is different; one file system can't read the other. Like device drivers, file systems are compiled into the kernel - only file systems compiled into the kernel can be accessed by the kernel.

To see what file systems our kernel supports can be known from /etc/filesystems file. If we want our kernel to use other file systems then we may have to recompile the same.

14.3.1 Unix File System Architecture

In Unix operating system point of view, a hard disk partition is considered as a 1-D array of disk blocks, where a disk block can be a physical sector or multiples of physical sector on the disk. It contains four important areas as shown in Figure 14.1; and to name boot block, super block, inode blocks and data blocks.

Boot Block	Super Block	Inode Blocks	Data Blocks

Figure 14.1 OS view of an Inode based file system.

- Boot block contains the bootstrap program with the help which operating system is loaded into RAM during the boot time. If the partition is not bootable partition then this block will be empty.
- Super block contains technical information such as
  The size of the partition
  The physical address of the first data block
  The number and list of free blocks
  Information of what type of file system uses the partition
  When the partition was last modified
- Inode area contains some set of blocks which contains inode's of the files and directories.
- Data Block area actually contains the files or directories content.

The inode is used to store all information about a file (which we call as meta data of the file but the content of the file), and there exists one inode per file for directory for every legal file and directory of the file system.. The inode contains: owner identification number, group identification number, time last modified, time last accessed, time created, size, file permissions, number of links, data blocks numbers (pointers) in which file information is stored, etc as shown in Figure 14.2. Some operating systems such as MINIX and XENIX file systems uses until second level indirection only .

- Inode is a 64 byte long data structure or record which contains file/directories meta-data.
- 0 is the inode no for root directory " / ". That is, first 64 bytes record in inode blocks of the disk belongs to root directory.
- The inode number of a file/directory refers to inode record number in the inode area of the disk.
- inode of a file/directory is also called as Binary name of a file or file descriptor or file handle of a file.
- Content of a directory is the names of the files and subdirectories and their inode numbers.

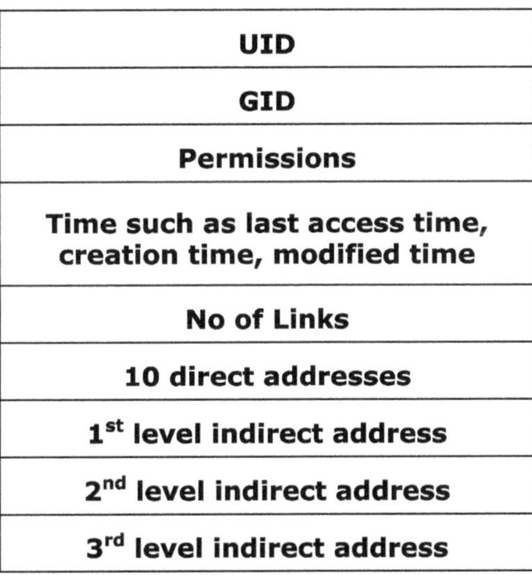

Figure 14.2 Inode Structure.

First 10 data block numbers of the file in which file information is available is stored directly in its inode. This allows direct accessing of the file information from the inode itself after knowing the block number in which the required data byte is located. If the file is bigger than 10 data blocks, then the next data block numbers of the file are stored in an index block and this index block number is stored in 1'st level indirection or in a *single* indirect block as shown below. If the file occupies still more number of data blocks *double indirect* block and a *triple indirect* block's are also used (See Figure 14.3 where only first two levels are shown for brevity reasons).

Let Block size = B

Block addresses = b bytes

Blocking factor = $N = B / b$

Thus in this data block allocation strategy which uses third level indirection, largest possible single file size $= 10 + N + N^2 + N^3$ blocks $= (10 + N + N^2 + N^3) * B$ bytes

How do know in which data blocks file **/home/rao/a.c** information is available.

- First, root directory (/) inode record (0'th inode) is read and the data block numbers in which that directory information is available is read.
- The data blocks are read and then inode number of **home** is identified.
- The inode record of **"home"** directory is read and then the data block numbers in which its contents are stored are identified.
- These data blocks are read and then inode number of directory "**rao**" is known.
- The inode record of "**rao**" directory is read and then the data block numbers in which its contents are stored are identified.
- These data blocks are read and then inode number of directory "**a.c**" is known.
- The inode record of "**a.c**" is read and then the data block numbers in which its contents are stored are identified and by accessing them from disk its content can be used.

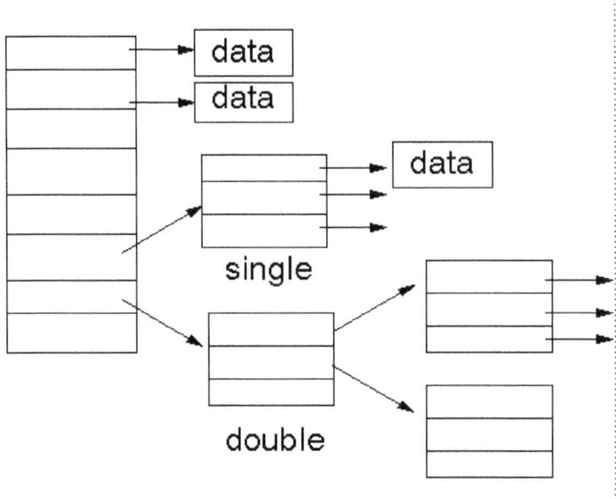

Figure 14.3 Indexed Allocation of Data Blocks.

Assuming that a file's inode is already available in RAM (i.e. , already located) and then to access any byte of the file, we require at most 4 disk accesses . where as to know the data block no which contains this required byte we may require at most 3 disk accesses .

Inode no's of a file and its hard link file will be same whereas a file and its soft link will not be same .

Whenever a hard link file is created , link count of the files inode will be incremented by 1 whenever either a hard link file or original file is deleted , link count value will be reduced by 1

When the link count value becomes 0 then all the data blocks consumed by that file will be marked as free and even the inode is marked as free .

Symbolic links are extensively used to fine tune the application software , they can be also used to link files in different partitions .

Whenever we open a file from a program such as C or C++, the file's info such as mode of opening , permissions , offset , pointer to the virtual node (which contains inode or other file system specific information) etc all are maintained in a row of a table known as Open file table. This row index is known as file descriptor of that file. This no is meaningful and is associated with that file as long as that process is running and the file is not closed in that process. This no is also known as binary name of that file and it can be called as dynamic no associated with that file . Where as inode number of a file is static number associated with the file.

Problem 1

A UNIX filesystem which uses 1K block size and 2 byte block addresses. Calculate what is the largest possible single file size .

Sol. : A = 1 KB

B = 2 bytes

N = 1024 / 2 = 512

So , Largest single file size = $10 + 512 + 512^2 + 512^3$ blocks

$\sim = 512^3$ blocks

= 128 X 2 X 512 X 2 X 512 X 1 KB

= 128 GB

Problem 2

A disk is formatted with 2 KB block size and 4 byte addresses, then find out the largest possible single file size ?

Sol. : N = 2 KB / 4 = 512

Max single file size = 256 GB

Problem 3

Calculate maximum possible disk space which can be spent on index blocks for a single file.

Sol. :

Max no of data blocks spend on Index blocks

$= 1 + (1 + N) + (1 + N + N^2)$ blocks

Inode in Unix :

Inode of a file doesn't contain the name of the file

14.3.2 The Virtual File System

The Linux kernel contains a layer called the VFS (or Virtual File System). The VFS processes all file-oriented IO system calls. Based on the device that the operation is being performed on, the VFS decides which file system to use to further process the call.

The exact list of processes that the kernel goes through when a system call is received follows along the lines of:

- A process makes a system call.
- The VFS decides what file system is associated with the device file that the system call was made on.

- The file system uses a series of calls (called Buffer Cache Functions) to interact with the device drivers for the particular device.
- The device drivers interact with the device controllers (hardware) and the actual required processes are performed on the device.
- Figure 14.4 Represents this.

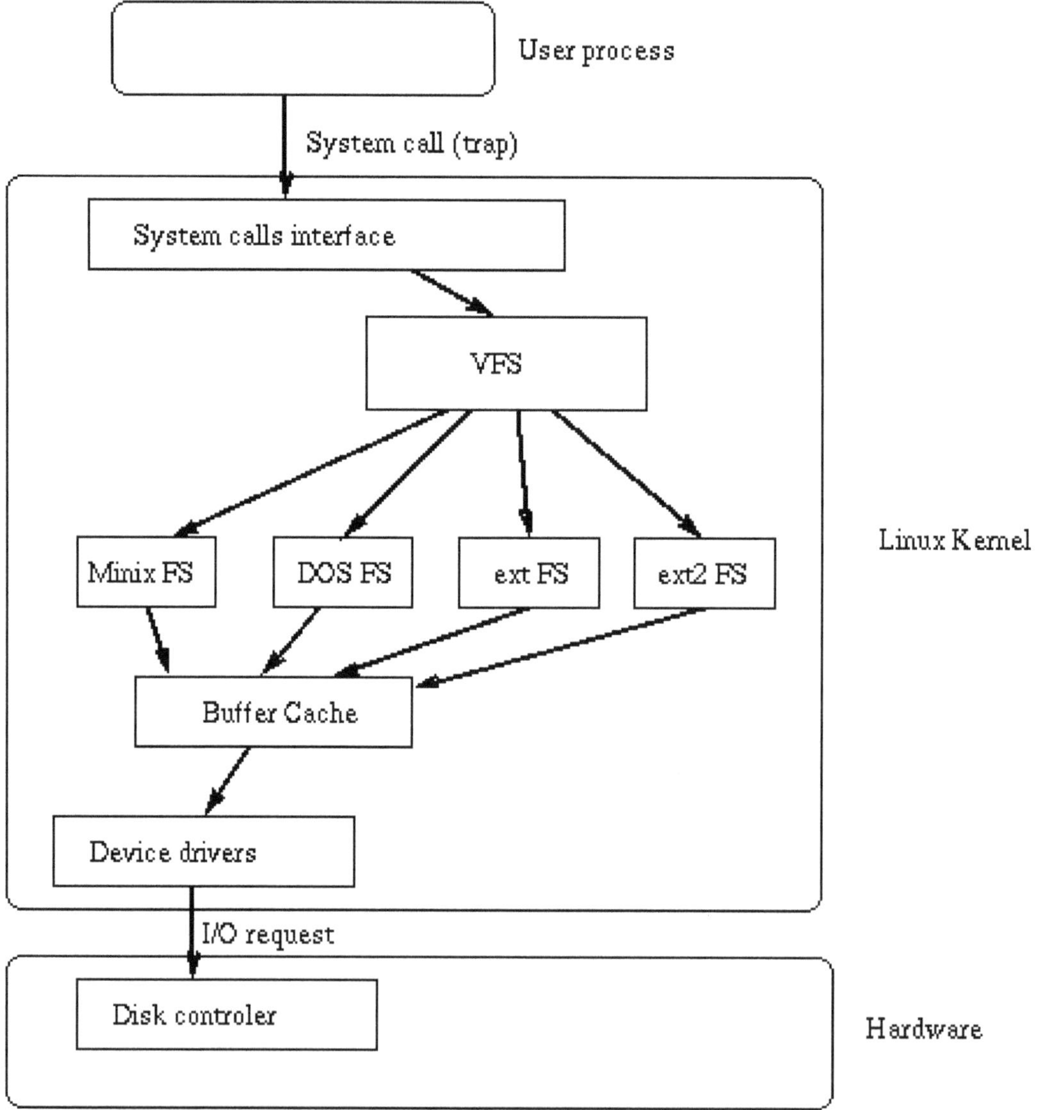

Figure 14.4 The Virtual File System.

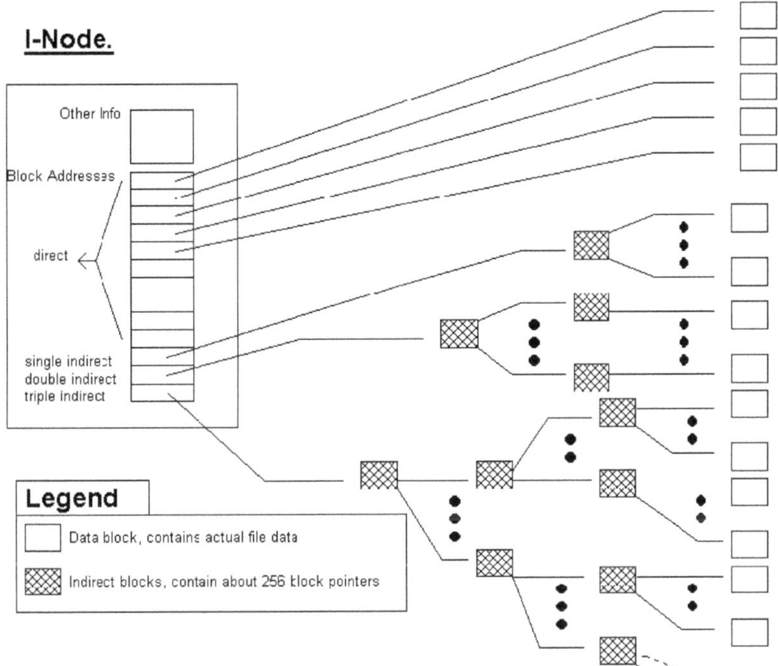

Figure 14.5 I-Node Structure.

See Figure 14.5 is a graphical representation on an I-Node.

Linux file system, ext2/ext3 uses a decentralized file system management scheme involving a "block group" concept. What this means is that the file systems are divided into a series of logical blocks. Each block contains a copy of critical information about the file systems (the super block and information about the file system) as well as an I-Node, and data block allocation tables and blocks. Generally, the information about a file (the I-Node) will be stored close to the data blocks. The entire system is very robust and makes file system recovery less difficult.

The ext2/ext3 file system also has some special features which make it stand out from existing file systems including:

- Logical block size - the size of data blocks can be defined when the file system is created; this is not dependent on physical data block size.
- File system state checks - the file system keeps track of how many times it was "mounted " (or used) and what state it was left in at the last shutdown.
- The file system reserves 5% of the file system for the root user - this means that if a user program fills a partition, the partition is still useable by root (for recovery) because there is reserve space.

14.3.3 Creating file systems

mkfs

Before a partition can be mounted (or used), it must first have a file system installed on it - with ext2, this is the process of creating I-Nodes and data blocks. This process is the equivalent of formatting the partition (similar to MSDOS's "format" command). Under Linux, the command to create a file system is called mkfs.

The command is issued in the following way:

mkfs [-c] [-t fstype] filesys [blocks] eg. mkfs -t ext2 /dev/fd0 # Make a ext2 file system on a disk

where:

- -c forces a check for bad blocks
- -t fstype specifies the file system type
- filesys is either the device file associated with the partition or device OR is the directory where the file system is mounted (this is used to erase the old file system and create a new one)
- blocks specifies the number of blocks on the partition to allocate to the file system
- Be aware that creating a file system on a device with an existing file system will cause all data on the old file system to be erased.

Assuming /dev/hdb1 is the 2GB partition and /dev/hdb2 is the 500 MB partition, we can create ext2 file systems using the commands:

```
mkfs -t ext2 -c /dev/hdb1
mkfs -t ext2 -c /dev/hdb2
```

This assumes the default block size and the default number of I-Nodes. If we wanted to be more specific about the number of I-Nodes and block size, we could specify them. mkfs actually calls other programs to create the file system - in the ext2 case, mke2fs. Generally, the defaults are fine - however, if we knew that we were only storing a few large files on a partition, then we'd reduce the I-Node to data block ratio. If we knew that we were storing lots of small files on a partition, we'd increase the I-Node to data block ration and probably decrease the size of the data blocks (there is no point using 4K data blocks when the file size average is around 1K).

14.3.4 Mounting and Un-mounting Partitions and Devices

Mount

To attach a partition or device to part of the directory hierarchy you must mount its associated device file.

First, we have to find a **mount point** - a directory where the device will be attached. This directory will exist on a previously mounted device (with the exception of the root directory (/) which is a special case) and will be empty. If the directory is not empty, then the files in the directory will no longer be visible while the device to mounted to it, but will reappear after the device has been disconnected (or unmounted).

To mount a device , you use the mount command:

```
mount [switches] device_file mount_point
```

With some devices, mount will detect what type of file system exists on the device, however it is more usual to use mount in the form of:

```
mount [switches] -t file_system_type device_file mount_point
```

Generally, only the root user can use the mount command - mainly due to the fact that the device files are owned by root. For example, to mount the first partition on the second hard drive off the /usr directory and assuming it contained the ext2 file system you'd enter the command:

```
mount -t ext2 /dev/hdb1 /usr
```

A common device that is mounted is the floppy drive. A floppy disk generally contains the msdos file system (but not always) and is mounted with the command:

```
mount -t msdos /dev/fd0 /mnt
```

Note that the floppy disk was mounted under the /mnt directory? This is because the /mnt directory is the usual place to temporally mount devices.

To see what devices you currently have mounted, simply type the command mount. Typing it on my system reveals:

```
/dev/hda3        on   /        type   ext2      (rw)
/dev/hda1        on   /dos     type   msdos     (rw)
none             on   /proc    type   proc      (rw)
/dev/cdrom       on   /cdrom   type   iso9660   (ro)
/dev/fd0 on /mnt type msdos (rw)
```

Each line tells me what device file is mounted, where it is mounted, what file system type each partition is and how it is mounted (ro = read only, rw = read/write). Note the strange entry on line three - the proc file system? This is a special "virtual" file system used by Linux systems to store information about the kernel, processes and current resource usages. It is actually part of the system's memory - in other words, the kernel sets aside an area of memory which it stores information about the system in - this same area is mounted onto the file system so user programs can easily gain this information.

To release a device and disconnect it from the file system, the **umount** command is used. It is issued in the form:

```
Umount device_file or umount mount_point
```

For example, to release the floppy disk, you'd issue the command:

```
umount /mnt or umount /dev/fd0
```

Again, you must be the root user or a user with privileges to do this. We can't unmount a device/mount point that is in use by a user (the user's current working directory is within the mount point. We may get **device busy** error message) or is in use by a process. Nor can you unmount devices/mount points which in turn have devices mounted to them.

Mounting with the /etc/fstab file

In true UNIX fashion, there is a file which governs the behavior of mounting devices at boot time. In Linux, this file is /etc/fstab. But there is a problem - if the fstab file lives in the /etc directory (a directory that will always be on the root partition (/)), how does the kernel get to the file without first mounting the root partition (to mount the root partition, you need to read the information in the /etc/fstab file!)? The answer to this involves understanding the kernel (a later chapter) - but in short, the system cheats! The kernel is "told" (how it is told doesn't concern us yet) on which partition to find the root file system; the kernel mounts this in read only mode, assuming the Linux native ext2 file system, then reads the fstab file and re-mounts the root partition (and others) according to instructions in the file.

An example line from the fstab file uses the following format:

```
device_file mount_point file_system_type mount_options [n] [n]
```

The first three fields are self explanatory; the fourth field, mount_options defines how the device will be mounted (this includes information of access mode ro/rw, execute permissions and other information) - information on this can be found in the mount man pages (note that this field usually contains the word "defaults"). The fifth and sixth fields will usually either not be included or be "1" - these two fields are used by the system utilities dump and fsck respectively - see the man pages for details.

As an example, the following is my /etc/fstab file:

```
/dev/hda3/ext2    defaults                 1  1
/dev/hda1/dos     msdos       defaults     1  1
/dev/hda2 swap     swap
none / proc proc  defaults                 1  1
```

As you can see, most of my file system exists on a single partition (this is very bad!) with my DOS partition mounted on the /dos directory (so I can easily transfer files on and off my DOS system). The third line is one which we have not discussed yet - swap partitions. The swap partition is the place where the Linux kernel keeps pages swapped out of virtual memory. Most Linux systems should access a swap partition - you should create a swap partition with a program such as fdisk before the Linux OS is installed. In this case, the entry in the /etc/fstab file tells the system that /dev/hda2 contains the swap partition - the system recognizes that there is no device nor any mount point called "swap", but keeps this information within the kernel (this also applies to the fourth line pertaining to the proc file system).

14.3.5 Checking the file system

It is a sad truism that anything that can go wrong will go wrong - especially if you don't have backups! In any event, file system "crashes" or problems are an inevitable fact of life for a System Administrator.

Crashes of a non-physical nature (i.e. the file system becomes corrupted) are non-fatal events - there are things a system administrator can do before issuing the last rites and restoring from one of their copious backups :)

You will be informed of the fact that a file system is corrupted by a harmless, but feared little messages at boot time, something like:

```
Can't mount /dev/hda1
```

If you are lucky, the system will ignore the file system problems and try to mount the corrupted partition READ ONLY.

It is at this point that most people enter a hyperactive frenzy of swearing, violent screaming tantrums and self-destructive cranial impact diversions (head butting the wall).

It is important to establish that the problem is logical, not physical. There is little you can do if a disk head has crashed (on the therapeutic side, taking the offending hard disk into the car park and beating it with a stick can produce favorable results). A logical crash is something that is caused by the file system becoming confused. Things like:

- Many files using the one data block.
- Blocks marked as free but being used and vice versa.
- Incorrect link counts on I-Nodes.
- Differences in the "size of file" field in the I-Node and the number of data blocks actually used.
- Illegal blocks within files.
- I-Nodes contain information but are not in any directory entry (these type of files, when recovered, are placed in the lost+found directory).
- Directory entries that point to illegal or unallocated I-Nodes. are the product of file system confusion. These problems will be detected and (usually) fixed by a program called fsck.

fsck

fsck is actually run at boot time on most Linux systems. Every x number of boots, fsck will do a comprehensive file system check. In most cases, these boot time runs of fsck automatically fix problems - though occasionally you may be prompted to confirm some fsck action. If however, fsck reports some drastic problem at boot time, you will usually be thrown in to the root account and issued a message like:

```
**************************************
fsck returned error code - REBOOT NOW!
**************************************
```

It is probably a good idea to manually run fsck on the offending device at this point (we will get onto how in a minute).

At worst, you will get a message saying that the system can't mount the file system at all and you have to reboot. It is at this point you should drag out your rescue disks (which of course contain a copy of fsck) and reboot using them. The reason for booting from an alternate source (with its own file system) is because it is quite possible that the location of the fsck program (/sbin) has become corrupted as has the fsck binary itself! It is also a good idea to run fsck only on unmounted file systems.

Using fsck

fsck is run by issuing the command:

```
fsck file_system
```

where file_system is a device or directory from which a device is mounted.

fsck will do a check on all I-Nodes, blocks and directory entries. If it encounters a problem to be fixed, it will prompt you with a message. If the message asks if fsck can SALVAGE, FIX, CONTINUE, RECONNECT or ADJUST, then it is usually safe to let it. Requests involving REMOVE and CLEAR should be treated with more caution.

In recent Linux versions such as Redhat Fedora, Debian when system finds problem with file system we will be given the choice of pressing Control-D for "normal startup" (which is actually just a reboot which won't help the problem at all) or entering the root password for system maintenance. When presented with these errors and this choice, do the following:

- Enter the root password.
- Run the command **fsck -fp /dev/hda1** (or whatever your root partition is).
- Repeat the above command until no errors are displayed.
- Reboot the system using the **init 6** command.
- Run the command **badblocks -sv /dev/hda1** (or whatever your root partition is). It will take awhile.

One way to tell if your hard-drive is starting to fail is to turn the system off for about 30 minutes. If you don't have problems for the first hour or so of using, but then problems start popping up, the hard-drive is failing. That's because failing hard-drives are more sensitive to heat and the hotter the drive gets the more likely it is to have problems. Replace these heat-sensitive drives ASAP

What caused the problem?

Problems with the file system are caused by:

- People turning off the power on a machine without going through the shutdown process - this is because Linux uses a very smart READ and WRITE disk cache - this cache is only flushed (or written to disk) periodically and on shutdown. fsck will usually fix these problems at the next boot.
- Program crashes - problems usually occur when a program is using several files and suddenly crashes without closing them. fsck usually easily fixes these problems.
- Kernel and system crashes - the kernel may become unstable (especially if you are using new, experimental kernels) and crash the system. Depending on the circumstances, the file system will usually be recoverable.

14.4 Conclusions

This chapter explains about UNIX devices with emphasis on how the system interacts with them. In addition, it explores disk drives, device drivers, disk partitioning and Linux file system organization. The meta data structure I-node is explained and some numerical examples are included to display the power of Linux system. Also, how file system checking can be done in Linux is explained.

15 Linux System Startup and Shutdown

15.1 Introduction

Being a multi-tasking, multi-user operating system means that Linux is a great deal more complex than an operating system like MS-DOS. Before the Linux operating system can perform correctly, there are a number of steps that must be followed, and procedures executed. The failure of any one of these can mean that the system will not start, or if it does it will not work correctly. It is important for the Systems Administrator to be aware of what happens during system startup so that any problems that occur can be remedied.

It is also important for the Systems Administrator to understand what the correct mechanism is to shut a Linux machine down. A Linux machine should (almost) never be just turned off. There are a number of steps to carry out to ensure that the operating system and many of its support functions remain in a consistent state.

15.2 A brief outline of the x86 Linux boot process

The most fundamental and obvious difference between x86 boards and embedded systems based on PPC, ARM, and others is that the x86 board will ship with one or more layers of manufacturer-supplied "black box" firmware that helps you with power-on initialization and the task of loading the operating system out of secondary storage. This firmware takes the system from a cold start to a known, friendly software environment ready to run your operating system. Figure 15.1 is a diagram of the typical PC boot process, with considerably more detail than you tend to find in PC-centric literature:

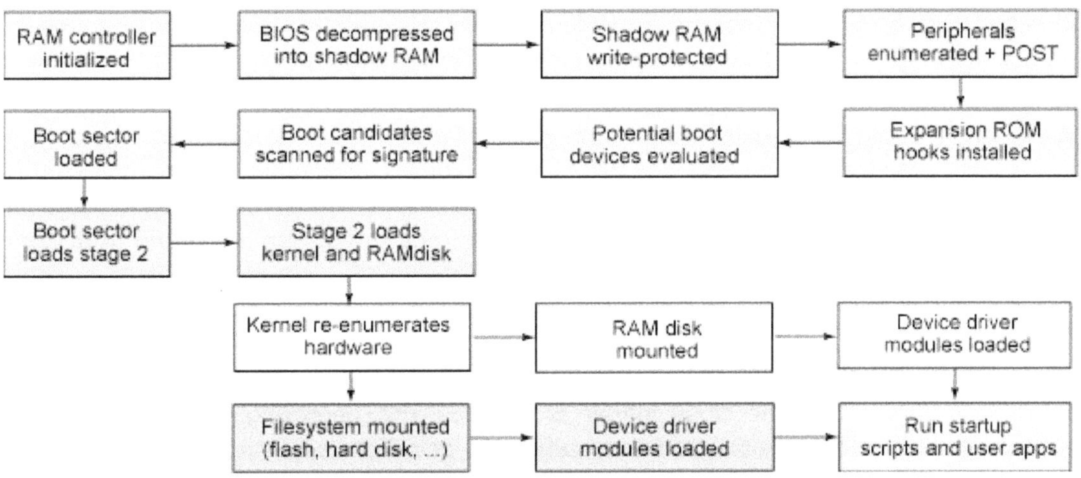

Figure 15.1 Typical start-up process for x86 based Linux.

For cost reasons, modern PC main board BIOS code is always stored compressed in flash. The only directly executable code in that chip is a tiny boot stub. Therefore, the first task on power-up is to initialize the main board chipset enough to get the DRAM controller working so that the main BIOS code can be decompressed out of flash into a mirror area in RAM, referred to as shadow RAM. This area is then write-protected and control is passed to the RAM-resident code. Shadow RAM is permanently stolen by the main board chipset; it cannot later be reclaimed by the operating system. For legacy reasons, special hardware mappings are set up so that the shadow RAM areas appear in the CPU's real-mode memory map at the locations where old operating systems like MS-DOS would expect to find them.

Keep in mind that the PC is an open architecture. This openness even extends down to firmware modules within the BIOS itself. Once the power-on initialization (POI) code has run, the next step it takes is to enumerate peripherals, and optionally install hooks provided by expansion ROMs in those peripherals. (Some of those expansion ROMs -- for instance, the video BIOS in a system that has onboard integrated video hardware -- will physically reside in the main BIOS image, but conceptually they are separate entities). The reasons the BIOS has to do this redundant initialization are:

1. The main BIOS itself needs basic console services to announce messages and allow the user to override default start-up behavior and configure system-specific parameters.
2. Historical issues limit the size of a user-supplied bootloader program to slightly less than 512 bytes. Since this isn't enough space to implement all the possible device drivers that might be required to access different displays and storage devices, it's necessary for the BIOS to install standardized software interfaces for all installed, recognized hardware that might be required by the bootloader.

Once all the BIOS-supported system peripherals are initialized, the main BIOS code will run through candidate boot devices (in accordance with a user-configurable preference list) looking for a magic signature word. Storage devices for IBM-compatible PCs have historically used a sector size of 512 bytes, and therefore the BIOS only loads the first 512 bytes from the selected boot device. The operating system's installation program is responsible for storing sufficient code in that zone to bootstrap the remainder of the IPL process.

Although it would be possible to write a minimalist Linux bootloader that would fit into such a space, practical Linux bootloaders for the PC consist of two stages: a small stub that lives in the boot sector, and a larger segment that lives somewhere else on the boot medium, usually inside the partition that contains the root file system. LILO and grub are the best-known boot loaders for mainstream Linux installations, and SYSLINUX is a popular choice for embedded distributions.

15.2.1 Using a RAM disk

The primary purpose of the boot loader is to load the operating system kernel from secondary storage into RAM. In a Linux system (x86 or otherwise), the boot loader can also optionally load an initial RAM disk image. This is a small file system that resides entirely in RAM. It contains a minimal set of modules to get the operating system off the ground before mounting the primary root file system. The original design purpose for initial RAM disk support in the kernel was to provide a means whereby numerous optional device drivers could be made available at boot time (potentially drivers that needed to be loaded before the root file system could be mounted).

You can get an idea of the original usage scenario for the RAM disk by considering a bootable Linux installation CD-ROM. The disk needs to contain drivers for many different hardware types, so that it can boot properly on a wide variety of different systems. However, it's desirable to avoid building an enormous kernel with every single option statically linked (partly for memory space reasons, but also to a lesser degree because some drivers "fight" and shouldn't be loaded simultaneously). The solution to this problem is to link the bare minimum of drivers statically in the kernel, and to build all the remaining drivers as separately loadable modules, which are then placed in the RAM disk. When the unknown target system is booted, the kernel (or start-up script) mounts the RAM disk, probes the hardware, and loads only those modules appropriate for the system's current configuration.

We can compress the boot copy of the root file system, and there is no run time performance hit. Although it's possible to run directly out of a compressed file system, there's obviously an overhead every time your software needs to access that file system. Compressed file systems also have other annoyances, such as the inability to report free space accurately (since the estimated free space is a function of the anticipated compression ratio of whatever data you plan to write into that space).

15.2.2 In a nutshell what is booting?

The process by which a computer is turned on and the UNIX operating system starts functioning – booting - consists of the following steps

- finding the kernel, The first step is to find the kernel of the operating system. How this is achieved is usually particular to the type of hardware used by the computer.
- starting the kernel, In this step the kernel starts operation and in particular goes looking for all the hardware devices that are connected to the machine.
- starting the processes. All the work performed by a UNIX computer is done by processes. In this stage, most of the system processes and daemons are started. This step also includes a number of steps which configure various services necessary for the system to work.

15.2.3 Finding the Kernel

For a UNIX computer to be functional it must have a kernel. The kernel provides a number of essential services which are required by the rest of the system in order for it to be functional. This means that the first step in the booting process of a UNIX computer is finding out where the kernel is. Once found, it can be started, but that's the next section.

In IBM PC, the ROM program typically does some hardware probing and then looks in a number of predefined locations (the first floppy drive and the primary hard drive partition) for a bootstrap program.

As a bare minimum, the ROM program must be smart enough to work out where the bootstrap program is stored and how to start executing it.

The ROM program generally doesn't know enough to know where the kernel is or what to do with it.

The bootstrap program

At some stage the ROM program will execute the code stored in the boot block of a device (typically a hard disk drive). The code stored in the boot block is referred to as a bootstrap program. Typically the boot block isn't big enough to hold the kernel of an operating system so this intermediate stage is necessary.

The bootstrap program is responsible for locating and loading (starting) the kernel of the UNIX operating system into memory. The kernel of a UNIX operating system is usually stored in the root directory of the root file system under some system-defined filename. Newer versions of Linux, including Redhat, put the kernel into a directory called /boot.

The most common bootstrap program in the Linux world is a program called LILO till recently. In the mean time other programs such as Grub also became available.

A boot loader generally examines the partition table of the hard-drive, identifies the active partition, and then reads and starts the code in the boot sector for that partition. This is a simplification. In reality the boot loader must identify, somehow, the sectors in which the kernel resides.

Other features a boot loader (under Linux) offers include

- using a key press to bring up a prompt to modify the boot procedure, and
- the passing of parameters to the kernel to modify its operation

Booting on a PC

The BIOS on a PC generally looks for a bootstrap program in one of two places (usually in this order)

- the first (A:) floppy drive, or
- the first (C:) hard drive.
- CDROM

By playing with your BIOS settings you can change this order or even prevent the BIOS from checking one or the other.

The BIOS loads the program that is on the first sector of the chosen drive and loads it into memory. This bootstrap program then takes over.

On the floppy

On a bootable floppy disk the bootstrap program simply knows to load the first blocks on the floppy that contain the kernel into a specific location in memory.

A normal Linux boot floppy contains no file system. It simply contains the kernel copied into the first sectors of the disk. The first sector on the disk contains the first part of the kernel which knows how to load the remainder of the kernel into RAM.

Making a boot disk

The simplest method for creating a floppy disk which will enable you to boot a Linux computer is

- insert a floppy disk into a computer already running Linux
- login as root
- change into the /boot directory
- copy the current kernel onto the floppy dd if=vmlinuz of=/dev/fd0 The name of the kernel, vmlinuz, may change from system to system. For my machines it vmlinux-2.6.31.
- tell the boot disk where to find the root disk rdev /dev/fd0 /dev/hda1

Where /dev/fd0 is the device for the floppy drive you are using and /dev/hda1 is the device file for your root disk. **You need to make sure you replace /dev/fd0 and /dev/hda1 with the appropriate values for your system.**

15.2.4 Starting the kernel

Okay, the boot strap program or the ROM program has found your system's kernel. What happens during the startup process? The kernel will go through the following process

- initialise its internal data structures, Things like ready queues, process control blocks and other data structures need to be readied.
- check for the hardware connected to your system, It is **important** that you are aware that the kernel will only look for hardware that it contains code for. If your system has a SCSI disk drive interface your kernel must have the SCSI interface code before it will be able to use it.
- verify the integrity of the root file system and then mount it, and
- create the process 0 (swapper) and process 1 (init).

The swapper process is actually part of the kernel and is not a "real" process. The init process is the ultimate parent of all processes that will execute on a UNIX system.

Once the kernel has initialized itself, init will perform the remainder of the startup procedure.

Kernel boot messages

When a UNIX kernel is booting, it will display messages on the main console about what it is doing. Under Linux, these messages are also sent to syslog and are by default appended onto the file /var/log/messages. The following is a copy of the boot messages on my machine with some additional comments to explain what is going on.

start kernel logging

Feb 2 15:30:40 beldin kernel: klogd 1.3-3, log source = /proc/kmsg started.

Loaded 4189 symbols from /boot/System.map.

Symbols match kernel version 2.0.31.

Loaded 2 symbols from 3 modules.

Configure the console

Console: 16 point font, 400 scans

Console: colour VGA+ 80x25, 1 virtual console (max 63)

Start PCI software

pcibios_init : BIOS33 Service Directory structure at 0x000f9320

pcibios_init : BIOS32 Service Directory entry at 0xf0000

pcibios_init : PCI BIOS revision 2.00 entry at 0xf0100

Probing PCI hardware.

Calibrating delay loop.. ok - 24.01 BogoMIPS

check the memory

Memory: 30844k/32768k available (736k kernel code, 384k reserved, 804k data)

start networking

Swansea University Computer Society NET3.035 for Linux 2.0

NET3: Unix domain sockets 0.13 for Linux NET3.035.

Swansea University Computer Society TCP/IP for NET3.034

P Protocols: IGMP, ICMP, UDP, TCP

FS: Diskquotas version dquot_5.6.0 initialized

check the CPU and find that it suffers from the Pentium bug

hecking 386/387 coupling... Hmm, FDIV bug i586 system

hecking 'hlt' instruction... Ok.

Lnux version 2.0.31 (root@porky.redhat.com) (gcc version 2.7.2.3) #1 Sun Nov 9 21:45:23 EST 1997

start swap

tarting kswapd v 1.4.2.2

start the serialdrivers

ty00 at 0x03f8 (irq = 4) is a 16550A

ty01 at 0x02f8 (irq = 3) is a 16550A

start drivers for the clock, drives

Real Time Clock Driver v1.07

Ramdisk driver initialized : 16 ramdisks of 4096K size

hda: FUJITSU M1636TAU, 1226MB w/128kB Cache, CHS=622/64/63

hdb: SAMSUNG PLS-30854A, 810MB w/256kB Cache, CHS=823/32/6

ide0 at 0x1f0-0x1f7,0x3f6 on irq 14

Floppy drive(s): fd0 is 1.44M

FDC 0 is a post-1991 82077

md driver 0.35 MAX_MD_DEV=4, MAX_REAL=8

scsi : 0 hosts.

scsi : detected total.

Partition check:

hda: hda1 hda2 < hda5 >

hdb: hdb1

mount the root file system an start swap

VFS: Mounted root (ext2 filesystem) readonly.

Adding Swap: 34236k swap-space (priority -1)

XT2-fs warning: mounting unchecked fs, running e2fsck is recommended ysctl: ip forwarding off

ansea University Computer Society IPX 0.34 for NET3.035

IPX Portions Copyright (c) 1995 Caldera, Inc.

Appletalk 0.17 for Linux NET3.035

eth0: 3c509 at 0x300 tag 1, 10baseT port, address 00 20 af 33 b5 be, IRQ 10.

3c509.c:1.12 6/4/97 becker@cesdis.gsfc.nasa.gov

eth0: Setting Rx mode to 1 addresses.

15.2.5 Starting the processes

So at this stage the kernel has been loaded, it has initialized its data structures and found all the hardware devices. At this stage your system can't do anything. The operating system kernel only supplies services which are used by processes. The question is how are these other processes created and executed. This discussion is already done in Chapter on Processes.

On a UNIX system the only way in which a process can be created is by an existing process performing a fork operation. A fork creates a brand new process that contains copies of the code and data structures of the original process. In most cases the new process will then perform an exec that replaces the old code and data structures with that of a new program.

But who starts the first process?

init is the process that is the ultimate ancestor of all user processes on a UNIX system. It always has a Process ID (PID) of 1. init is started by the operating system kernel so it is the only process that doesn't have a process as a parent. init is responsible for starting all other services provided by the UNIX system. The services it starts are specified by init's configuration file, /etc/inittab.

Run levels

init is also responsible for placing the computer into one of a number of run levels. The run level a computer is in controls what services are started (or stopped) by init. Table 15.1 summarizes the different run levels used by popular Linux releases. At any one time, the system must be in one of these run levels.

When a Linux system boots, init examines the /etc/inittab file for an entry of type initdefault. This entry will determine the initial run level of the system (see Table 15.1).

Table 15.1 Run levels.

Run level	Description
0	Halt the machine
1	Single user mode. All file systems mounted, only small set of kernel processes running. Only root can login.
2	multi-user mode , without remote file sharing
3	multi-user mode with remote file sharing, processes, and daemons
4	user definable system state
5	used for to start X11 on boot
6	shutdown and reboot
a b c	ondemand run levels
s or S	same as single-user mode, only really used by scripts

Under Linux, the telinit command is used to change the current run level. telinit is actually a soft link to init. telinit accepts a single character argument from the following

- 0 1 2 3 4 5 6

  The run level is switched to this level.

- Q q

  Tells init that there has been a change to /etc/inittab (its configuration file) and that it should re-examine it.

- S s

  Tells init to switch to single user mode.

/etc/inittab

/etc/inittab is the configuration file for init. It is a colon delimited field where # characters can be used to indicate comments. Each line corresponds to a single entry and is broken into four fields

- the identifier
  One or two characters to uniquely identify the entry.
- the run level
  Indicates the run level at which the process should be executed
- the action
  Tells init how to execute the process
- the process
  The full path of the program or shell script to execute.

What happens

When init is first started it determines the current run level (by matching the entry in /etc/inittab with the action initdefault) and then proceeds to execute all of the commands of entries that match the run level.

The following is an example /etc/inittab taken from a Redhat machine with some comments added.

Specify the default run level

```
id:3:initdefault:
# System initialisation.
si::sysinit:/etc/rc.d/rc.sysinit
```

when first entering various runlevels run the related start-up scripts before going any further

```
l0:0:wait:/etc/rc.d/rc 0
l1:1:wait:/etc/rc.d/rc 1
l2:2:wait:/etc/rc.d/rc 2
l3:3:wait:/etc/rc.d/rc 3
l4:4:wait:/etc/rc.d/rc 4
l5:5:wait:/etc/rc.d/rc 5
```

```
l6:6:wait:/etc/rc.d/rc 6
# Things to run in every runlevel.
ud::once:/sbin/update
```

call the shutdown command to reboot the system when the use does the three fingered salute

```
ca::ctrlaltdel:/sbin/shutdown -t3 -r now
```

A powerfail signal will arrive if you have a uninterruptible power supply (UPS) if this happens shut the machine down safely

```
pf::powerfail:/sbin/shutdown -f -h +2 "Power Failure; System Shutting Down"

# If power was restored before the shutdown kicked in, cancel it.
pr:12345:powerokwait:/sbin/shutdown -c "Power Restored; Shutdown Cancelled"
```

Start the login process for the virtual consoles

```
1:12345:respawn:/sbin/mingetty tty1
2:2345:respawn:/sbin/mingetty tty2
3:2345:respawn:/sbin/mingetty tty3
4:2345:respawn:/sbin/mingetty tty4
5:2345:respawn:/sbin/mingetty tty5
6:2345:respawn:/sbin/mingetty tty6
```

If the machine goes into runlevel 5, start X

```
x:5:respawn:/usr/bin/X11/xdm –nodaemon
```

The identifier

The identifier, the first field, is a unique two character identifier. For inittab entries that correspond to terminals the identifier will be the suffix for the terminals device file.

For each terminal on the system a getty process must be started by the init process. Each terminal will generally have a device file with a name like /dev/tty??, where the ?? will be replaced by a suffix. It is this suffix that must be the identifier in the /etc/inittab file.

Run levels

The run levels describe at which run levels the specified action will be performed. The run level field of /etc/inittab can contain multiple entries, e.g. 123, which means the action will be performed at each of those run levels.

Actions

The action's field describes how the process will be executed. There are a number of pre-defined actions that must be used. Table 15.2 lists and explains them.

Table 15.2 Inittab actions.

Action	Purpose
Respawn	restart the process if it finishes
wait	init will start the process once and wait until it has finished before going on to the next entry
once	start the process once, when the runlevel is entered
boot	perform the process during system boot (will ignore the runlevel field)
bootwait	a combination of boot and wait
off	do nothing
initdefault	specify the default run level
sysinit	execute process during boot and before any boot or bootwait entries
powerwait	executed when init receives the SIGPWR signal which indicates a problem with the power, init will wait until the process is completed
ondemand	execute whenever the ondemand runlevels are called (a b c). When these runlevels are called there is NO change in runlevel.
powerfail	same as powerwait but don't wait (refer to the man page for the action powerokwait)
ctrlaltdel	executed when init receives SIGINT signal (usually when someone does CTRL-ALT-DEL

15.2.6 Daemons and Configuration Files

Init is an example of a daemon. It will only read its configuration file, /etc/inittab, when it starts execution. Any changes you make to /etc/inittab will not influence the execution of init until the next time it starts, i.e. the next time your computer boots.

There are ways in which you can tell a daemon to re-read its configuration files. One generic method, which works most of the time, is to send the daemon the HUP signal. For most daemons the first step in doing this is to find out what the process id (PID) is of the daemon. This isn't a problem for init. Why?

It's not a problem for init because init always has a PID of 1.

The more accepted method for telling init to re-read its configuration file is to use the telinit command. **telinit q** or **init q** will tell init to re-read its configuration file.

15.2.7 System Configuration

There are a number of tasks which must be completed once during system startup which must be completed once. These tasks are usually related to configuring your system so that it will operate. Most of these tasks are performed by the /etc/rc.d/rc.sysinit script.

It is this script which performs the following operations

- sets up a search path that will be used by the other scripts
- obtains network configuration data
- activates the swap partitions of your system
- sets the hostname of your system
  Every UNIX computer has a hostname. You can use the UNIX command hostname to set and also display your machine's hostname.

- sets the machines NIS domain (if you are using one)
- performs a check on the file systems of your system
- turns on disk quotas (if being used)
- sets up plug'n'play support
- deletes old lock and tmp files
- sets the system clock
- loads any kernel modules.

Terminal logins

In a later chapter we will examine the login procedure in more detail. This is a brief summary to explain how the login procedure relates to the boot procedure.

For a user to login there must be a getty process (Redhat Linux uses a program called mingetty, slightly different name but same task) running for the terminal they wish to use. It is one of init's responsibilities to start the getty processes for all terminals that are physically connected to the main machine, and you will find entries in the /etc/inittab file for this.

Please note this does not include connections over a network. They are handled with a different method. This method is used for the virtual consoles on your Linux machine and any other dumb terminals you might have connected via serial cables. You should be able see the entries for the virtual consoles in the example /etc/inittab file from above.

15.2.8 Start-up scripts

Most of the services which init starts are started when init executes the system start scripts. The system startup scripts are shell scripts written using the Bourne shell (this is one of the reasons you need to know the Bourne shell syntax). You can see where these scripts are executed by looking at the inittab file.

```
l0:0:wait:/etc/rc.d/rc 0
l1:1:wait:/etc/rc.d/rc 1
l2:2:wait:/etc/rc.d/rc 2
l3:3:wait:/etc/rc.d/rc 3
l4:4:wait:/etc/rc.d/rc 4
l5:5:wait:/etc/rc.d/rc 5
l6:6:wait:/etc/rc.d/rc 6
```

These scripts start a number of services and also perform a number of configuration checks including

- checking the integrity of the machine's file systems using fsck,
- mounting the file systems,
- designating paging and swap areas,
- checking disk quotas,
- clearing out temporary files in /tmp and other locations,
- starting up system daemons for printing, mail, accounting, system logging, networking, cron and syslog.

In the UNIX world there are two styles for startup files: BSD and System V. Redhat Linux uses the System V style and the following section concentrates on this format. Table 15.3 summarizes the files and directories which are associated with the Redhat startup scripts. All the files and directories in Table 15.3 are stored in the /etc/rc.d directory.

Table 15.3 Linux start-up scripts.

Filename	Purpose
rc0.d rc1.d rc2.d rc3.d rc4.d rc5.d rc6.d	directories which contain links to scripts which are executed when a particular runlevel is entered
rc	A shell script which is passed the run level. It then executes the scripts in the appropriate directory.
init.d	Contains the actual scripts which are executed. These scripts take either start or stop as a parameter
rc.sysinit	run once at boot time to perform specific system initialisation steps
rc.local	the last script run, used to do any tasks specific to your local setup that isn't done in the normal SysV setup
rc.serial	not always present, used to perform special configuration on any serial ports

The Linux Process

When init first enters a run level it will execute the script /etc/rc.d/rc (as shown in the example /etc/inittab above). This script then proceeds to

- determine the current and previous run levels
- kill any services which must be killed
- start all the services for the new run level.

The /etc/rc.d/rc script knows how to kill and start the services for a particular run level because of the filenames in the directory for each run level. The following are the filenames from the /etc/rc.d/rc3.d directory on my system.

ls rc3.d

```
K10pnserver    K55routed     S40atd        S60lpd        S85postgresql
K20rusersd     S01kerneld    S40crond      S60nfs        S85sound
K20rwhod       S10network    S40portmap    S75keytable   S91smb
K25innd        S15nfsfs      S40snmpd      S80sendmail   S99local
K25news        S20random     S45pcmcia     S85gpm
K30ypbind      S30syslog     S50inet       S85httpd
```

You will notice that all the filenames in this, and all the other rcX.d directories, use the same format.

[SK]*numberService*

Where *number* is some integer and *Service* is the name of a service.

All the files with names starting with S are used to start a service. Those starting with K are used to kill a service. From the rc3.d directory above you can see scripts which start services for the Internet (S50inet), PCMCIA cards (S45pcmcia), a Web server (S85httpd) and a database (S85postgresql).

The numbers in the filenames are used to indicate the order in which these services should be started and killed. You'll notice that the script to start the Internet services comes before the script to start the Web server; obviously the Web server depends on the Internet services.

/etc/rc.d/init.d

If we look closer we can see that the files in the rcX.d directories aren't really files.

ls -l rc3.d/S50inet

```
lrwxrwxrwx   1 root   root  14 Dec 19 23:57 rc3.d/S50inet -> ../init.d/inet
```

The files in the rcX.d directories are actually soft links to scripts in the /etc/rc.d/init.d directory. It is these scripts which perform all the work.

Starting and stopping

The scripts in the /etc/rc.d/init.d directory are not only useful during the system startup process, they can also be useful when you are performing maintenance on your system. You can use these scripts to start and stop services while you are working on them.

For example, lets assume you are changing the configuration of your Web server. Once you've finished editing the configuration files (in /etc/httpd/conf on a Redhat machine) you will need to restart the Web server for it to see the changes. One way you could do this would be to follow this example

/etc/rc.d/init.d/httpd stop

Shutting down http:

/etc/rc.d/init.d/httpd start

Starting httpd: httpd

This example also shows you how the scripts are used to start or stop a service. If you examine the code for /etc/rc.d/rc (remember this is the script which runs all the scripts in /etc/rc.d/rcX.d) you will see two lines. One with $i start and the other with $i stop. These are the actual lines which execute the scripts.

Lock files

All of the scripts which start services during system startup create lock files. These lock files, if they exist, indicate that a particular service is operating. Their main use is to prevent startup files starting a service which is already running.

When you stop a service one of the things which has to occur is that the lock file must be deleted.

Damaged file systems

In the next two chapters we'll examine file systems in detail and provide solutions to how you can fix damaged file systems. The two methods we'll examine include

- the fsck command, and
- always maintaining good backups.

Shutting down

We should not just simply turn a UNIX computer off or reboot it. Doing so will usually cause some sort of damage to the system especially to the file system. Most of the time the operating system may be able to recover from such a situation (but NOT always).

Commands to shutdown

There are a number of different methods for shutting down and rebooting a system including

- the shutdown command

  The most used method for shutting the system down. The command can display messages at preset intervals warning the users that the system is coming down.

- the halt command

  Logs the shutdown, kills the system processes, executes sync and halts the processor.

- the reboot command

  Similar to halt but causes the machine to reboot rather than halting.

- sending init a TERM signal, init will usually interpret a TERM signal (signal number 15) as a command to go into single user mode. It will kill of user processes and daemons. The command is kill -15 1 (init is always process number 1). It may not work or be safe on all machines.
- the fasthalt or fastboot commands These commands create a file /fastboot before calling halt or reboot. When the system reboots and the start-up scripts find a file /fastboot they will not perform a fsck on the file systems.

The most used method will normally be the shutdown command. It provides users with warnings and is the safest method to use.

shutdown

The format of the command is

shutdown [-h | -r] [-fqs] [now | hh:ss | +mins]

The parameters are

- -h

  Halt the system and don't reboot.

- -r

  Reboot the system

- -f

  Do a fast boot.

- -q

  Use a default broadcast message.

- -s

  Reboot into single user mode by creating a /etc/singleboot file.

The time at which a shutdown should occur are specified by the now hh:ss +mins options.

- Now

  Shut down immediately.

- hh:ss

  Shut down at time hh:ss.

- +mins

  Shut down mins minutes in the future.

The default wait time before shutting down is two minutes.

The procedure for shutdown is as follows

- five minutes before shutdown or straight away if shutdown is in less than five minutes The file /etc/nologin is created. This prevents any users (except root) from logging in. A message is also broadcast to all logged in users notifying them of the imminent shutdown.
- at shutdown time. All users are notified. init is told not to spawn any more getty processes. Shutdown time is written into the file /var/log/wtmp. All other processes are killed. A sync is performed. All file systems are unmounted. Another sync is performed and the system is rebooted.

The other commands

The other related commands including reboot, fastboot, halt, fasthalt all use a similar format to the shutdown command. Refer to the man pages for more information.

Table 15.4 summarizes some of the commands that can be used to examine the current state of your machine. Some of the information they display includes

- amount of free and used memory,
- the amount of time the system has been up,
- the load average of the system, Load average is the number processes ready to be run and is used to give some idea of how busy your system is.
- the number of processes and amount of resources they are consuming.

Some of the commands are explained below in Table 15.4. For those that aren't use your system's manual pages to discover more.

Table 15.4 System status commands.

Command	Purpose
free	display the amount of free and used memory
uptime	how long has the system been running and what is the current load average
ps	one off snap shot of the current processes
top	continual listing of current processes
uname	display system information including the hostname, operating system and version and current date and time

top

ps provides a one-off snap shot of the processes on your system. For an on-going look at the processes Linux generally comes with the top command. It also displays a collection of other information about the state of your system including

- uptime, the amount of time the system has been up
- the load average,
- the total number of processes,
- percentage of CPU time in user and system mode,
- memory usage statistics
- statistics on swap memory usage

The top command displays the process on your system ranked in order from the most CPU intensive down and updates that display at regular intervals. It also provides an interface by which you can manipulate the nice value and send processes signals.

The nice value

The nice value specifies how "nice" your process is being to the other users of the system. It provides the system with some indication of how important the process is. The lower the nice value the higher the priority. Under Linux the nice value ranges from -20 to 19.

By default a new process inherits the nice value of its parent. The owner of the process can increase the nice value but cannot lower it (give it a higher priority). The root account has complete freedom in setting the nice value.

nice

The nice command is used to set the nice value of a process when it first starts.

renice

The renice command is used to change the nice value of a process once it has started.

15.3 Conclusions

This chapters explores Linux booting process. It outlines first Linux booting and then explains each task involved in a detailed manner. All the configurations files and how to modify them is explained in a lucid manner.

16 System Logging

16.1 Introduction

There will be times when you want to reconstruct what happened in the lead up to a problem. Situations where this might be desirable include

- you believe someone has broken into your system,
- one of the users performed an illegal action while online, and
- the machine crashed mysteriously at some odd time.
- We want to know who made un-successful login attempts in the last 24 hours.
- We want to continuously monitor the disk usage of users and warn them if it exceeds limits.

This is where

- l ogging, and
  The recording of certain events, errors, emergencies.
- accounting.
  Recording who did what and when. become useful.

This chapter examines the methods under Linux by which logging and accounting are performed. In particular it will examine

- the syslog system,
- process accounting, and
- login accounting.

Managing log and accounting files

Both logging and accounting tend to generate a great deal of information especially on a busy system. One of the decisions the Systems Administrator must make is what to do with these files. Options include

- don't create them in the first place,
  The head in the sand approach. Not a good idea.
- keep them for a few days, then delete them, and If a problem hasn't been identified within a few days then assume there is no reasons to keep the log files. Therefore delete the existing ones and start from scratch.
- keep them for a set time and then archive them. Archiving these files might include compressing them and storing them online or copying them to tape.

Centralize

If you are managing multiple computers it is advisable to centralize the logging and accounting files so that they all appear on the one machine. This makes maintaining and observing the files easier.

16.2 Logging

The ability to log error messages or the actions carried out by a program or script is fairly standard. On earlier versions of UNIX each individual program would have its own configuration file that controlled where and what to log. This led to multiple configuration and log files that made it difficult for the Systems Administrator to control and each program had to know how to log.

syslog

The syslog system was devised to provide a central logging facility that could be used by all programs. This was useful because Systems Administrators could control where and what should be logged by modifying a single configuration file and because it provided a standard mechanism by which programs could log information.

Components of syslog

The syslog system can be divided into a number of components

- default log file,
  On many systems messages are logged by default into the file /var/log/messages
- the syslog message format,
- the application programmer's interface,
  The API programs use to log information.
- the daemon, and
  The program that directs logging information to the correct location based on the configuration file.
- the configuration file.
  Controls what information is logged and where it is logged.

syslog message format

syslog uses a standard message format for all information that is logged. This format includes

- a facility,
  The facility is used to describe the part of the system that is generating the message. Table 16.1 lists some of the common facilities.
- a level,
  The level indicates the severity of the message. In lowest to highest order the levels are debug info notice warning err crit alert emerg and a string of characters containing a message.

Table 16.1 Common syslog facilities.

Facility	Source
kern	the kernel
mail	the mail system
lpr	the print system
daemon	a variety of system daemons
auth	the login authentication system

syslog's API

In order for syslog to be useful application programs must be able to pass messages to the syslog daemon so it can log the messages according to the configuration file..

There are at least two methods which application programs can use to send messages to syslog. These are:

- logger,
  logger is a UNIX command. It is designed to be used by shell programs which wish to use the syslog facility.
- the syslog API.
  The API (application program interface) consists of a set of the functions (openlog syslog closelog) which are used by programs written in compiled languages such as C and C++. This API is defined in the syslog.h file. You will find this file in the system include directory /usr/include.

syslogd

syslogd is the syslog daemon. It is started when the system boots by one of the startup scripts. syslogd reads its configuration file when it startups or when it receives the HUP signal. The standard configuration file is /etc/syslog.conf. syslogd receives logging messages and carries out actions as specified in the configuration file. Standard actions include

- appending the message to a specific file,
- forwarding the message to the syslogd on a different machine, or
- display the message on the consoles of all or some of the logged in users.

/etc/syslog.conf

By default syslogd uses the file /etc/syslog.conf as its configuration file. It is possible using a command line parameter of syslogd to use another configuration file.

A syslog configuration file is a text file. Each line is divided into two fields separated by one or more spaces or tab characters

- a selector, and
  Used to match log messages.
- an action.
  Specifies what to do with a message if it is matched by the selector

The selector

The selector format is facility.level where facility and level match those terms introduced in the syslog message format section from above.

A selector field can include

- multiple selectors separated by ; characters
- multiple facilities, separated by a , character, for a single level
- an * character to match all facilities or levels

The level can be specified with or without a =. If the = is used only messages at exactly that level will be matched. Without the = all messages at or above the specified level will be matched.

syslog.conf actions

The actions in the syslog configuration file can take one of four formats

- a pathname starting with /
  Messages are appended onto the end of the file.
- a hostname starting with a @
  Messages are forwarded to the syslogd on that machine.
- a list of users separated by commas
  Messages appear on the screens of those users if they are logged in. an asterix
  Messages are displayed on the screens of all logged in users.

For example

The following is an example syslog configuration file taken from the Linux manual page for syslog.conf

```
# Log all kernel messages to the console.
# Logging much else clutters up the screen.
#kern.*                                 /dev/console

# Log anything (except mail) of level info or higher.
# Don't log private authentication messages!
*.info;mail.none;authpriv.none          /var/log/messages
# The authpriv file has restricted access.
authpriv.*                              /var/log/secure

# Log all the mail messages in one place.
mail.*                                  /var/log/maillog
# Everybody gets emergency messages, plus log them on another
# machine.
*.emerg                                 *

# Save mail and news errors of level err and higher in
# special file.
uucp,news.crit                          /var/log/spooler
```

16.3 Accounting

Accounting was developed when computers were expensive resources and people were charged per command or CPU time. In today's era of cheap, powerful computers its rarely used for these purposes. One thing accounting is used for is as a source of records about the use of the system. Particular useful if someone is trying, or has, broken into your system.

In the following sections we will examine

- login accounting.
- process accounting

16.3.1 Login accounting

The file /var/log/wtmp is used to store the username, terminal port, login and logout times of every connection to a Linux machine. Every time you login or logout the wtmp file is updated. This task is performed by init.

last

The last command is used to view the contents of the wtmp file. There are options to limit interest to a particular user or terminal port.

last reboot

The above command displays log of all reboots since the log file is created.

lastb

This command displays details about un-successful login attempts.

ac

The last command provides rather rudimentary summary of the information in the wtmp file. As a Systems Administrator it is possible that you may require more detailed summaries of this information. For example, you may desire to know the total number of hours each user has been logged in, how long per day and various other information.

The command that provides this information is the ac command.

Installing ac

It is possible that you will not have the ac command installed. The ac command is part of the psacct package. If you don't have ac installed you will have to use rpm or glint to install the package.

16.3.2 Process accounting

Also known as CPU accounting, process accounting records the elapsed CPU time, average memory use, I/O summary, the name of the user who ran the process, the command name and the time each process finished.

Turning process accounting on

Process accounting does not occur until it is turned on using the accton command.

```
accton /var/log/acct
```

Where /var/log/acct is the file in which the process accounting information will be stored. The file must already exist before it will work. You can use any filename you wish but many of the accounting utilities rely on you using this file.

lastcomm

lastcomm is used to display the list of commands executed either for everyone, for particular users, from particular terminals or just information about a particular command. Refer to the lastcomm manual page for more information.

lastcomm –f /var/log/acct

The above command the following results.

```
Lastcomm    root    ttyp2    0.55 secs Sun Jan 25 16:21
ls          root    ttyp2    0.03 secs Sun Jan 25 16:21
ls          root    ttyp2    0.02 secs Sun Jan 25 16:21
accton      root    ttyp2    0.01 secs Sun Jan 25 16:21
```

The sa command

The sa command is used to provide more detailed summaries of the information stored by process accounting and also to summarize the information into other files.

Refer to the manual pages for the sa command for more information.

16.4 Available Graphical Tools

In the recent years, many Linux variants are supporting GUI facilities for viewing the logs. For example, on my desktop from the system tools option I have selected System log's option. The following window crapped up.

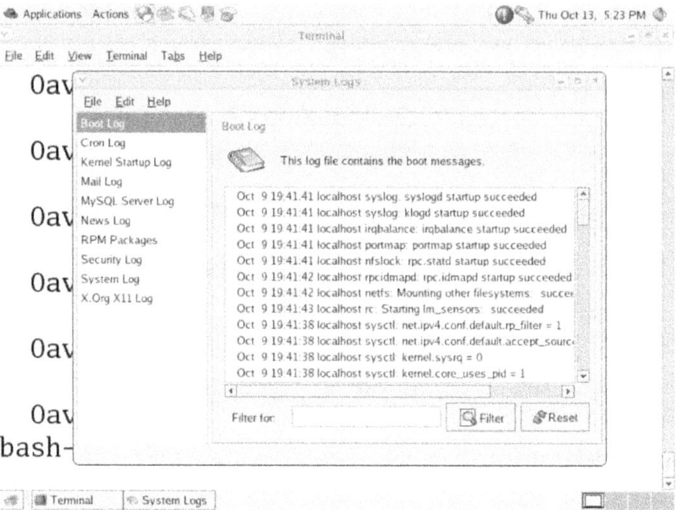

If we want to search for a specific thing also we can do here. For example, we wanted to check entries with venkat both Security log and System log (see Figure 16.1).

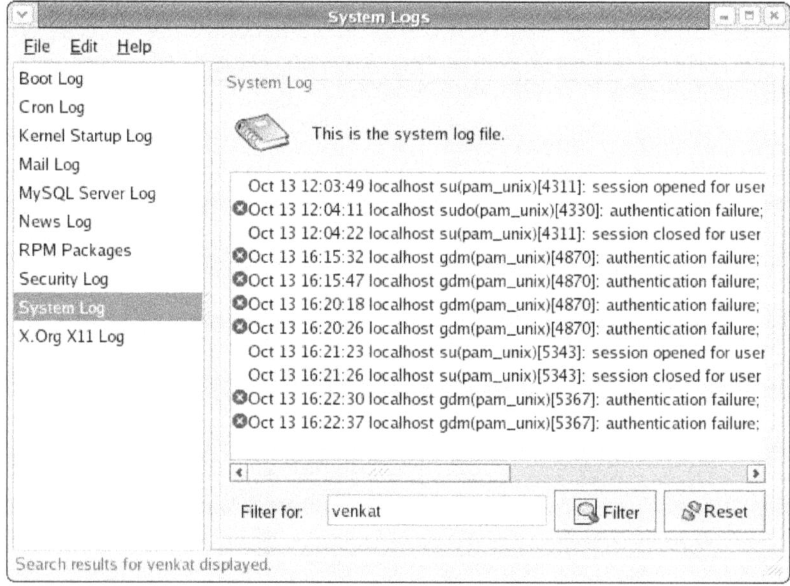

Figure 16.1 Security Log.

Also, from system tools we can select system monitor to see the details about memory usage of the system and also per process basis resource consumption (see Figures 16.2 and 16.3)

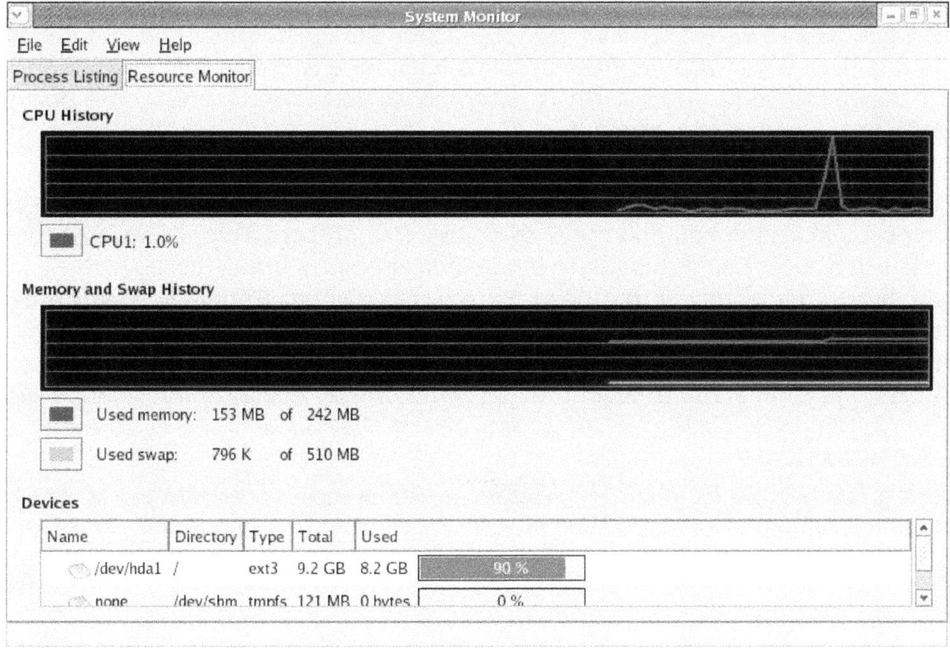

Figure 16.2 System Monitor.

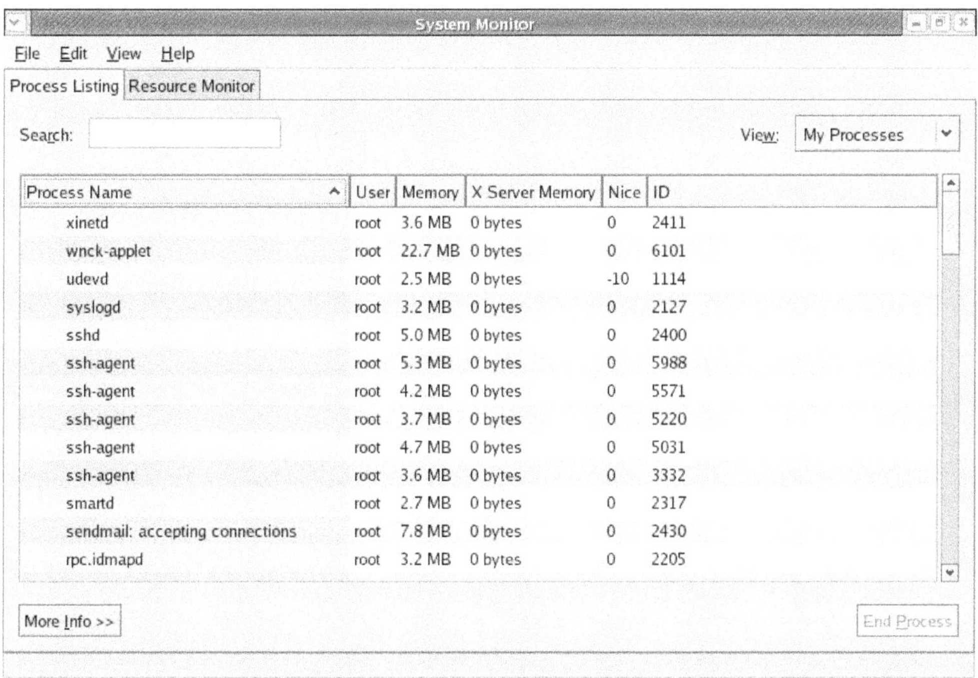

Figure 16.3 System Resources.

16.5 So what?

This section has given a very brief overview of process and login accounting and the associated commands and files. What use do these systems fulfill for a Systems Administrator? The main one is that they allow you to track what is occurring on your system and who is doing it. This can be useful for a number of reasons

- tracking which user's are abusing the system
  figuring out what is normal for a user If you know that most of your users never use commands like sendmail and the C compilers (via process accounting) and then all of a sudden they start using this might be an indication of a break in.
- justifying to management the need for a larger system Generally management won't buy you a bigger computer just because you want one. In most situations you will have to put together a case to justify why the additional expenditure is necessary. Process and login account could provide some of the necessary information.

16.6 Conclusions

This chapter explains how to monitor processes in the system with the help of syslog facility. Also, process accounting is explained and how it can be used to manage the users is explained.

17 Networks: A Brief Introduction

17.1 Introduction

Networks, connecting computers to networks and managing those networks are probably the most important, or at least the most hyped, areas of computing at the moment. This and the following chapter introduce the general concepts associated with TCP/IP-based networks and in particular the knowledge required to connect and use Linux computers to those networks.

This chapter examines how you connect a Linux machine and configure it to provide basic network connections and services for other machines. This chapter introduces the process and knowledge for connecting a Linux machine to a TCP/IP network from the lowest level up using the following steps

- network hardware
  Briefly looks at the hardware peripherals that allow network connections and in particular the network hardware which Linux supports.
- network support in the Linux kernel
  Many of the networking services require support from the kernel of the operating system. This section examines what support for network services the Linux kernel provides.
- configuring the network connection
  Once the hardware is installed and the kernel rebuilt the network connection must be configured. Linux/UNIX uses a number of specific commands to perform these tasks.

Each of these steps requires an understanding of the operation and basics of TCP/IP networks.

17.1.1 A brief overview of TCP/IP Model

Popularly three addresses are used in computer networks which are explained in detail later. They are:

- Network card or Ethernet address which is 48 bits long and is physical.
- IP address which is 32 bits (as of now) and is logical.
- Port address which is 16 bits and is logical.

A simply practical analogy

We can assume port number as person's name, Flat number in an apartment bldg and door number of the apartment as network card address, and postal code as IP address. With the help of PIN number (is logical like IP address as it is not written on a city!!) a postal packet is delivered to a city. Further, with the help of door number it will be delivered to the apartment watchmen; which is further delivered to a specific flat based on flat number (Probably door number and flat number can be considered as physical as they are written really!!). Then, with the help of person name the packet is really delivered to the actual person (name is considered as logical like port as it is not written on the face of a person!!).

In the same manner a packet (datagram) is delivered from destination machine router. In a nutshell steps involved in a packets delivery to an application (program) on a destination machine is as follows.

1. A packet is delivered to destination LAN with the help of network address (a portion of destination machine's IP address which is seen in the packet itself) of it. That is, all the packets which are bound to a machine will have same IP address irrespective of their source. Also, all the packets which are bound to machines of a LAN will be having their network part of their IP addresses as same.

2. Actually, LAN protocols are used to deliver a packet in a LAN and LAN protocols requires Ethernet address for this. When a packet arrives to destination router, using the **arp** protocol destination machines network card address is found and is used for actual delivery of packet to the machine.
3. When a packet arrives to a machine, with the help of **port** number available in it, the same will be hand overed to a program (running on that machine) which is looking for packets arrivals with this port number.

17.1.2 Network Hardware

The first step in connecting a machine to a network is to find out what sort of network hardware you will be using. The aim of this unit and this chapter is not to give you a detailed introduction to networking hardware. Before you can use a particular type of networking hardware, or any hardware for that matter, there must be support for that device in the Linux kernel. If the kernel doesn't support the required hardware then you can't use it. Currently the Linux kernel offers support for the networking hardware outlined in list below. For more detailed information about hardware support under Linux refer to the Hardware Compatibility HOWTO available from your nearest mirror of the Linux Documentation Project.

- arcnet
- ATM http://lrcwww.epfl.ch/linux-atm/
- AX25, amateur radio
- EQL

EQL allows you to treat multiple point-to-point connections (SLIP, PPP) as a single logical TCP/IP connection.

- FDDI
- Frame relay
- ISDN
- PLIP
- PPP
- SLIP
- radio modem, STRIP, Starmode Radio IP

http://mosquitonet.standford.edu/{mosquitonet.html|strip.html}

- token ring
- X.25
- WaveLan, wireless, card, and
- Ethernet

In most "normal" situations the networking hardware being used will be either

- Modem
  A modem is a serial device so your Linux kernel should support the appropriate serial port you have in your computer. The networking protocol used on a modem will be either SLIP or PPP which must also be supported by the kernel.
- Ethernet
  Possibly the most common form of networking hardware at the moment. There are a number of different Ethernet cards. You will need to make sure that the kernel supports the particular Ethernet card you will be using. The Hardware Compatibility HOW-TO includes this information.

17.1.3 Network devices

Only way a program can gain access to a physical device is via a device file. Network hardware is still hardware so it follows that there should be device files for networking hardware. Under other versions of the UNIX operating system this is true. It is not the case under the Linux operating system.

Device files for networking hardware are created, as necessary, by the device drivers contained in the Linux kernel. These device files are not available for other programs to use. This means I can't execute the command

```
cat < /etc/passwd > /dev/eth0
```

The only way information can be sent via the network is by going through the kernel.

Remember, the main reason UNIX uses device files is to provide an abstraction which is independent of the actual hardware being used. A network device file must be configured properly before you can use it send and receive information from the network. The process for configuring a network device requires a bit more background information than you have at the moment. The following provides that background and a later section in the chapter examines the process and the commands in more detail.

The installation process for most Linux variants will normally perform some network configuration for you. To find out what network devices are currently active on your system have a look at the contents of the file /proc/net/dev

cat /proc/net/dev

```
Inter-|              Receive           | Transmit
face |packets errs drop fifo frame|packets errs drop fifo colls carrier
lo:       91    0    0    0    0      91    0    0    0     0    0
eth0:      0    0    0    0    0      60    0    0    0     0   60
```

On this machine there are two active network devices. lo: the loopback device and eth0: an Ethernet device file. If a computer has more than one Ethernet interface (network devices are usually called network interfaces) you would normally see entries for eth1 eth2 etc.

IP aliasing (talked about more later) is the ability for a single Ethernet card to have more than one Internet address (why this is used is also discussed later). The following example shows the contents of the /proc/net/dev file for a machine using IP aliasing. *It is not normal for an Ethernet card to have multiple IP addresses, normally each Ethernet card/interface will have one IP address.*

cat /proc/net/dev

```
Inter-|  Receive                  | Transmit
face |packets errs drop fifo frame|packets errs drop fifo colls carrier
lo: 285968       0    0    0    0     285968   0   0   0          0   0
eth0:61181891   59   59    0   89   77721923   0   0   0  11133617  57
eth0:0:  48849   0    0    0    0        212   0   0   0          0   0
eth0:1:  10894   0    0    0    0        210   0   0   0          0   0
eth0:2: 481325   0    0    0    0        259   0   0   0          0   0
eth0:3:  29178   0    0    0    0        215   0   0   0          0   0
```

We can see that the device files for an aliased Ethernet device uses the format ethX:Y where X is the number for the Ethernet card and Y is the number of the aliased device. Since aliased devices use the same Ethernet card they must use the same network, after all you can't connect a single Ethernet card to two networks.

17.1.4 Kernel support for networking

Ensuring that the kernel includes support for your networking hardware is only the first step. In order to supply certain network services it is necessary for them to be compiled into the kernel. The following is a list of some of the services that the Linux kernel can support

- IP accounting

  IP accounting must be compiled into the kernel and is configured with the ipfwadm command. IP accounting allows you to track the number of bytes and packets transmitted over the network connection. This is useful in situations where you must track the network usage of your users. For example, if you are a Internet Service Provider.

- IP aliasing

  Essentially, IP aliasing allows your computer to pretend it is more than one computer. In a normal configuration each network device is allocated a single IP address. However there are times when you wish to allocate multiple IP addresses to a computer with a single network interface. The most common example of this is web sites, for example, the websites http://cq-pan.cqu.edu.au/, http://webclass.cqu.edu.au/, and http://webfuse.cqu.edu.au/ are all hosted by one computer. This computer only has one Ethernet card and uses IP aliasing to create aliases for the Ethernet card. The Ethernet card's real IP address is 138.77.37.37 and its three alias addresses are 138.77.37.36, 138.77.37.59 and 138.77.37.108.

  Normally the interface would only grab the network packets addressed to 138.77.37.37 but with network aliasing it will grab the packets for all three addresses.

  You can see this in action by using the arp command. Have a look at the hardware addresses for the computers cq-pan, webclass and webfuse. What can you tell?

/sbin/arp

```
Address                 Hwtype      HWaddress           Flags Mask    Iface
centaurus.cqu.EDU.AU    ether       AA:00:04:00:0B:1C        C         eth0
webfuse.cqu.EDU.AU      ether       00:60:97:3A:AA:85        C         eth0
cq-pan.cqu.EDU.AU       ether       00:60:97:3A:AA:85        C         eth0
science.cqu.EDU.AU      ether       00:00:F8:01:9E:DA        C         eth0
borric.cqu.EDU.AU       ether       00:20:AF:A4:39:39        C         eth0
webclass.cqu.EDU.AU     ether       00:60:97:3A:AA:85        C         eth0
138.77.37.46           (incomplete)                     eth0
```

- IP firewall

  This option allows you to use a Linux computer to implement a firewall. A firewall works by allowing you to selectively ignore certain types of network connections. By doing this you can restrict what access there is to your computer (or the network behind it) and as a result help increase security.
- The firewall option is closely related to IP accounting, for example it is configured with the same command, ipfwadm.
- IP encapsulation

  IP encapsulation is where the IP packet from your machine is wrapped inside another IP packet. This is of particular use mobile IP and IP multicast.
- IPX

  IPX protocol is used in Novel Netware systems. Including IPX support in the Linux kernel allows a Linux computer to communicate with Netware machines.
- IPv6

  IPv6, version 6 of the IP protocol, is the next generation of which is slowly being adopted. IPv6 includes support for the current IP protocol. Linux support for IPv6 is slowly developing. You can find more information at http://www.terra.net/ipv6/

- IP masquerade
  IP masquerade allows multiple computers to use a single IP address. One situation where this can be useful is when you have a single dialup connection to the Internet via an Internet Service Provider (ISP). Normally, such a dialup connection can only be used by the machine which is connected. Even if the dialup machine is on a LAN with other machines connected they cannot access the Internet. However with IP masquerading it is possible to allow all the machines on that LAN access the Internet.
- Network Address Translation
  Support for network address translation for Linux is still at an alpha stage. Network address translation is the "next version" of IP masquerade. See http://www.csn.tu-chemnitz.de/HyperNews/get/linux-ip-nat.html for more information.
- IP proxy server
  Mobile IP
  Since an IP address consists of both a network address and a host address it can normally only be used when a machine is connected to the network specified by the network address. Mobile IP allows a machine to be moved to other networks but still retain the same IP. IP encapsulation is used to send packets destined for the mobile machine to its new location. See http://anchor.cs.binghamton.edu/mobileip/ for more information.
- IP multicast
  IP multicast is used to send packets simultaneously to computers and separate IP networks. It is used for a variety of audio and video transmission. See http://www.teksouth.com/linux/multicast/ for more information.

17.2 Ethernet Basics

The following provides very brief background information on Ethernet which is a LAN protocol.

17.2.1 Ethernet addresses

Every Ethernet card has built into it a 48 bit address (called an Ethernet address or a Media Access Control (MAC) address or HW address). The high 24 bits of the address are used to assign a unique number to manufacturers of Ethernet addresses and the low 24 bits are assigned to individual Ethernet cards made by the manufacturer.

Some example Ethernet addresses, you will notice that Ethernet addresses are written using 6 tuple's of HEX numbers, are listed below

```
00:00:0C:03:79:2F
00:40:F6:60:4D:A4
```

Ethernet is a broadcast medium

Every packet, often called an Ethernet frame, of information sent on Ethernet contains a source and destination MAC address. The packet is placed on a Ethernet network and every machine, actually the Ethernet card, on the network looks at the packet. If the card recognizes the destination MAC as its own it "grabs" the packet and passes it to the Network access layer.

It is possible to configure your Ethernet card so that it grabs all packets sent on the network. This is how it is possible to "listen in" on other people on a Ethernet network.

A single Ethernet network cannot cover much more than a couple of hundred meters. However, how far depends on the type of cabling used.

17.2.2 Converting hardware addresses to Internet addresses

The network access layer, the lowest level of the TCP/IP protocol stack is responsible for converting Internet addresses into hardware addresses. This is how TCP/IP can be used over a large number of different networking hardware.

Address Resolution Protocol

The mapping of Ethernet addresses into Internet addresses is performed by the Address Resolution Protocol (ARP). ARP maintains a table that contains the translation between IP address and Ethernet address.

When the machine wants to send data to a computer on the local Ethernet network the ARP software is asked if it knows about the IP address of the machine (remember the software deals in IP addresses). If the ARP table contains the IP address the Ethernet address is returned.

If the IP address is not known a packet is broadcast to every host on the local network, the packet contains the required IP address. Every host on the network examines the packet. If the receiving host recognizes the IP address as its own, it will send a reply back that contains its Ethernet address. This response is then placed into the ARP table of the original machine (so it knows it next time).

The ARP table will only contain Ethernet addresses for machines on the local network. Delivery of information to machines not on the local network requires the intervention of routing software which is introduced later in the chapter.

arp

On a UNIX machine you can view, modify, remove the contents of the ARP table using the arp command. **arp -a** will display the entire table.

That is, we can see the arp cache, remove a hosts entry from the arp cache, etc. In a networked system when a packet arrives at router machine (often a UNIX machine) then the IP address to Ethernet address mapping is needed. This is achieved by arp protocol. These mappings are stored in arp cache such that next time another packet arrives with the same IP address then its Ethernet or physical address is calculated by carrying out a lookup operation on this arp cache. With arp command we can modify, view, delete the entries of this cache.

Some other options of arp command are Table 17.1

Table 17.1 Options with arp command.

arp –a	*Displays all entries are displayed*
arp -a hostname	*Displays entry of the given host*
arp -d hostname	*Removes the entry of the specified host*
arp -s hostname HW_addr	*Creates manually ARP entry for the host with the given hardware address (HW address has to be given in hexadecimal separated by colons)*

To see how new entries are added to the cache the next example shows the ping command. Ping is often used to test a network connection and to see if a particular machine is alive. In this case we are pinging src.doc.ic.ac.uk.

ping src.doc.ic.ac.uk

```
PING src.doc.ic.ac.uk (138.77.37.102): 56 data bytes
64 bytes from 138.77.37.102: icmp_seq=0 ttl=64 time=19.0 ms

--- pug.cqu.edu.au ping statistics ---
1 packets transmitted, 1 packets received, 0% packet loss
round-trip min/avg/max = 19.0/19.0/19.0 ms
```

Now checkup the arp cache by running arp –a command. We will not find any new entry. Now, you can try by pinging a machine in our LAN and see the arp cache content. We find an entry for this local machine.

17.2.3 SLIP, PPP

SLIP and PPP, used to connect machines via serial lines (and modems) are not broadcast media. They are simple "point-to-point" connections between two computers. This means that when information is placed on a SLIP/PPP connection only the two computers at either end of that connection can see the information. SLIP/PPP are usually used when a computer is connected to a network via a modem or a serial connection.

17.3 TCP/IP Basics

Before going any further it is necessary to introduce some of the basic concepts related to TCP/IP networks. An understanding of these concepts is essential for the next steps in connecting a Linux machine to a network. The concepts introduced in the following includes

- **Hostnames**
  Every machine (also known as a host) on the Internet has a name. This section introduces hostnames and related concepts.
- **IP addresses**
  Each network interface on the network also has a unique IP address. This section discusses IP addresses, the components of an IP address, subnets, network classes and other related issues.
- **Name resolution**
  Human beings use hostnames while the IP protocols use IP addresses. There must be a way, name resolution, to convert hostnames into IP addresses. This section looks at how this is achieved.
- **Routing**
  When network packets travel from your computer to a Web site in the United States there are normally a multitude of different paths that packet can take. The decisions about which path it takes are performed by a routing algorithm. This section briefly discusses how routing occurs.

17.3.1 Hostnames

Most computers on a TCP/IP network are given a name, usually known as a host name (a computer can be known as a host). The hostname is usually a simple name used to uniquely identify a computer within a given site. A fully qualified Internet host name, also known as a fully qualified domain name (FQDN), uses the following format

```
hostname.site.domain.country
```

- Hostname
  A name by which the computer is known. This name must be unique to the site on which the machine is located.
- Site
  A short name given to the site (company, University, government department etc) on which the machine resides.

- Domain
  Each site belongs to a specific domain. A domain is used to group sites of similar purpose together. Table 17.2 provides an example of some domain names. Strictly speaking a domain name also includes the country.
- Country
  Specifies the actual country in which the machine resides. Table 17.3 provides an example of some country names. You can see a list of the country codes at http://www.bcpl.net/~jspath/isocodes.html

Table 17.2 Example Internet domains.

Domain	Purpose
edu	Educational institution, university or school
com	Commercial company
gov	Government department
Net	Networking companies

Table 17.3 Example Country Codes.

Country code	Country
nothing or us	United States
au	Australia
uk	United Kingdom
in	India
ca	Canada
fr	France

hostname

Under Linux the hostname of a machine is set using the hostname command. Only the root user can set the hostname. Any other user can use the hostname command to view the machine's current name.

hostname
darkstar.org

To change hostname:

hostname fred

hostname
fred

Changes to the hostname performed using the hostname command will not apply after rebooting. The hostname is set during start-up from one of configuration files, /etc/sysconfig/network If we wish a change in hostname to be retained after you reboot you will have to change this file.

A fully qualified name must be unique to the entire Internet. Which implies every hostname on a site should be unique.

It is not always necessary to specify a fully qualified name; especially to refer to a machine in local LAN.

17.3.2 IP/Internet Addresses

Alpha-numeric names, like hostnames, cannot be handled efficiently by computers, at least not as efficiently as numbers. For this reason, hostnames are only used for us humans. The computers and other equipment involved in TCP/IP networks use numbers to identify hosts on the Internet. These numbers are called IP addresses. This is because it is the Internet Protocol (IP) which provides the addressing scheme.

IP addresses are currently 32 bit numbers (i.e. in IPv4); IPv6 the next generation of IP uses 128 bit address. IP addresses are usually written as four numbers separated by full stops (called dotted decimal form) e.g. 132.22.42.1. Since IP addresses are 32 bit numbers, each of the numbers in the dotted decimal form are restricted to between 0-255 (32 bits divide by 4 numbers gives 8 bits per number and 255 is the biggest number you can represent using 8 bits). This means that 257.33.33.22 is an invalid address.

Dotted Quad to Binary

The address 132.22.42.1 in dotted decimal form is actually stored on the computer as 10000100 00010110 00101010 00000001. Each of the four decimal numbers represent one byte of the final binary number

- 32 = 10000100
- 22 = 00010110
- 42 = 00101010
- 1 = 00000001

Networks and hosts

An IP address actually consists of two parts

- a network portion, and

  This is used to identify the network that the machine belongs to. Hosts on the same network will have this portion of the IP address in common. This is one of the reasons why IP masquerading is required for mobile computers (e.g. laptops). If you move a computer to a different network you must give it a different IP address which includes the network address of the new network it is connected to.
- the host portion.
- This is the part which uniquely identifies the host on the network.

The network portion of the address forms the high part of the address (the bit that appears on the left hand side of the number). **The size of the network and host portions of an IP address is specified by another 32 bit number called the netmask (also known as the subnet mask).**

To calculate which part of an IP address is the network and which the host the IP address and the subnet mask are treated as binary numbers (see diagram 15.?). Each bit of the subnet mask and the IP address are compared and

- if the bit is set in both the IP address and the subnet mask then the bit is set in the network address,
- if the bit is set in the IP address but **not** set in the subnet mask then the bit is set in the host address.

For example

IP address	138.77.37.21	10001010 01001101 00100101 00010101
netmask	255.255.255.0	11111111 11111111 11111111 00000000
network address	138.77.37.0	10001010 01001101 00100101 00000000
host address	0.0.0.21	00000000 00000000 00000000 00010101

The Internet is a network of networks

The structure of IP addresses can give you some idea of how the Internet works. It is a network of networks. We start with a collection of machines all connected via the same networking hardware, a local area network. All the machines on this local area network will have the same network address, each machine also has a unique host address.

The Internet is formed by connecting a lot of local area networks together. Usually, in a LAN one machine is called as router. Actually, all these routers are connected with some hierarchy involving MAN's, WAN's. These WAN's are connected; forming Internet. While connecting LAN's, MAN's and WAN's, we use variety of intermediate units known as repeaters, bridges, routers and gateways.

Network Classes

During the development of the TCP/IP protocol stack IP addresses were divided into classes. There are three main address classes, A, B and C. Table 17.4 summarizes the differences between the three classes. The class of an IP address can be deduced by the value of the first byte of the address.

Table 17.4 Network classes.

Class	First byte value	Netmask	Number of hosts
A	1 to 126	255.0.0.0	16 million
B	128 to 191	255.255.0.0	64,000
C	192 to 223	255.255.255.0	254
Multicast	224 - 239	240.0.0.0	

If you plan on setting up a network that is connected to the Internet the addresses for your network must be allocated to you by central controlling organization. You can't just choose any set of addresses you wish, chances are they are already taken my some other site.

If your network will not be connected to the Internet you can choose from a range of addresses which have been set aside for this purpose. These addresses are shown in Table 17.5

Table 17.5 Networks reserved for private networks.

Network class	Addresses
A	10.0.0.0 to 10.255.255.255
B	172.16.0.0 to 172.31.255.255
C	192.168.0.0 to 192.168.255.255

The addresses 127.0.0.X are special IP addresses. It refers to the local host. The local host allows software to address the local machine in exactly the same way it would address a remote machine. Usually these addresses are uses to test network SW's developed.

Assigning IP addresses in a LAN: A example from Class C Networks

Some IP addresses are reserved for specific purposes and you should not assign these addresses to a machine. Table 17.6 lists some of these addresses

Table 17.6 Reserved IP addresses.

Address	Purpose
xx.xx.xx.0	Network address
xx.xx.xx.1	Gateway address *
xx.xx.xx.255	broadcast address
127.0.0.1	loopback address

* this is not a set standard

Gateways and routers are able to distribute data from one network to another because they are actually physically connected to two or more networks through a number of network interfaces.

As mentioned earlier the network address is the IP address with a host address that is all 0's. The network address is used to identify a network. The broadcast address is the IP address with the host address set to all 1's and is used to send information to all the computers on a network, typically used for routing and error information.

Subnetting is also used in practice to devide a larger network of an organization into a set of small nets.

17.3.3 Name resolution

The process of taking a hostname and finding the IP address is called **name resolution**. This is very much needed as computers works on the basis of numbers, i.e. addresses; whereas humans finds comfort dealing with symbolic things, i.e. names.

Methods of name resolution

There are two methods that can be used to perform name resolution

- the /etc/hosts file, and
- the Domain Name Service.

/etc/hosts

One way of performing name resolution is to maintain a file that contains a list of hostnames and their equivalent IP addresses. When we want to know a machine's IP address we look up the file. If any network SW need's IP address it will check in this file. Under UNIX/Linux the file is /etc/hosts. /etc/hosts is a text file with one line per host. Each line has the format

IP_address hostname

or

IP_address hostname alias

Comments can be indicated by using the hash # symbol. Aliases are used to indicate shorter names or other names used to refer to the same host.

Problems with /etc/hosts

With over 3 million machines on the Internet it should be obvious that this is not a smart solution as the file size increases and lookup operation takes more time. Also, updating this file is not easy task..

Domain name service (DNS)

The Internet Domain Name System (DNS) was developed as a distributed database to solve this problem. Its primary goal is to allow the allocation of host names to be distributed amongst multiple naming authorities, rather than centralized at a single point.

DNS structure

The DNS is arranged as a hierarchy, both from the perspective of the structure of the names maintained within the DNS, and in terms of the delegation of naming authorities. At the top of the hierarchy is the root domain "." which is administered by the Internet Assigned Numbers Authority (IANA). Administration of the root domain gives the IANA the authority to allocate domains beneath the root.

The process of assigning a domain to an organizational entity is called delegating, and involves the administrator of a domain creating a sub-domain and assigning the authority for allocating sub-domains of the new domain the sub domain's administrative entity.

Even though the DNS supports many levels of sub-domains, delegations should only be made where there is a requirement for an organization or organizational sub-division to manage their own name space. Any sub-domain administrator must also demonstrate they have the technical competence to operate a domain name server, or arrange for another organization to do so on their behalf.

Domain Name Servers

The DNS is implemented as collection of inter-communicating name servers. At any given level of the DNS hierarchy, a name server for a domain has knowledge of all the immediate sub-domains of that domain.

For each domain there is a primary name server, which contains authoritative information regarding Internet entities within that domain. In addition Secondary name servers can be configured, which periodically download authoritative data from the primary server. Secondary name servers provide backup to the primary name server when it is not operational, and further improve the overall performance of the DNS, since the name servers of a domain that respond to queries most quickly are used in preference to any others.

/etc/resolv.conf

When performing a name resolution most UNIX machines will check their /etc/hosts first and then check with their name server. How does the machine know where its domain name server is. The answer is in the /etc/resolv.conf file.

resolv.conf is a text file with three main types of entries

- # comments

  Anything after a # is a comment and ignored.

- domain *name*

  Defines the default domain. This default domain will be appended to any hostname that does not contain a dot.

- name server *address*

  This defines the IP address of the machines domain name server. It is possible to have multiple name servers defined and they will be queried in order (useful if one goes down).

For example

The /etc/resolv.conf file from my machine is listed below.

domain cqu.edu.au

nameserver 138.77.5.6

nameserver 138.77.1.1

17.3.4 Routing

So far we've looked at names and addresses that specify the location of a host on the Internet. We now move onto routing. Routing is the act of deciding how each individual datagram (packet) finds its way through the multiple different paths to its destination.

Simple routing

For most UNIX/Linux computers the routing decisions they must make are simple. If the datagram is for a host on the local network then the data is placed on the local network and delivered to the destination host. If the destination host is on a remote network then the datagram will be forwarded to the local gateway. The local gateway will then pass it on further.

Routing tables

Routing is concerned with finding the right **network** for a datagram. Once the right network has been found the datagram can be delivered to the host.

Most hosts (and gateways) on the Internet maintain a routing table. The entries in the routing table contain the information to know where to send datagrams for a particular network.

Constructing the routing table

The routing table can be constructed in one of two ways

- constructed by the Systems Administrator, sometimes referred to as static routes,
- dynamically created by a number of different available routing protocols

The dynamic creation by routing protocols is complex and beyond the scope of this subject.

Making the connections Physically

Ifconfig

Network interfaces are configured using the ifconfig command and has the standard format for turning a device on

ifconfig *device_name IP_address* netmask *netmask* up

For example

- ifconfig eth0 138.77.37.26 netmask 255.255.255.0 up
  Configures the first Ethernet address with the IP address of 138.77.37.26 and the netmask of 255.255.255.0.
- ifconfig lo 127.0.0.1
  Configures the loopback address appropriately.
  Other parameters for the ifconfig command include

- up and down
  These parameters are used to take the device up and down (turn it on and off). ifconfig eth0 down will disable the eth0 interface and will require an ifconfig command like the first example above to turn it back on.
- -arp
  Will turn on/off the address resolution protocol for the specified interface.
- -pointtopoint *addr*
  Used to specify the IP address (*addr*) of the computer at the far end of a point to point link.

Configuring the name resolver

Once the device/interface is configured you can start using the network. However you'll only be able to use IP addresses. At this stage the networking system on your computer will not know how to resolve hostnames (convert hostnames into IP addresses).

This is where the name resolver and its associated configuration files enter the picture. In particular the three files we'll be looking at are

- /etc/resolv.conf
- Specifies where the main domain name server is located for your machine.
- /etc/hosts.conf
-

Allows you to specify how the name resolver will operate. For example, will it ask the domain name server first or look at a local file.

- /etc/hosts

A local file which specifies the IP/hostname association between common or local computers.

/etc/resolv.conf

The /etc/resolv.conf is the main configuration file for the name resolver code. Its format is quite simple. It is a text file with one keyword per line. There are three keywords typically used, they are:

- domain
  this keyword specifies the local domain name.
- search
  this keyword specifies a list of alternate domain names to search for a hostname
- nameserver
  this keyword, which may be used many times, specifies an IP address of a domain name server to query when resolving names

An example /etc/resolv.conf might look something like:

```
domain maths.wu.edu.au
search maths.wu.edu.au wu.edu.au
nameserver 192.168.10.1
nameserver 192.168.12.1
```

This example specifies that the default domain name to append to unqualified names (i.e. hostnames supplied without a domain) is maths.wu.edu.au and that if the host is not found in that domain to also try the wu.edu.au domain directly. Two name servers entry are supplied, each of which may be called upon by the name resolver code to resolve the name.

/etc/host.conf

The /etc/host.conf file is where you configure some items that govern the behavior of the name resolver code.

The format of this file is described in detail in the resolv+ man page. In nearly all circumstances the following example will work for you:

```
order hosts,bind
multi on
```

This configuration tells the name resolver to check the /etc/hosts file before attempting to query a name server and to return all valid addresses for a host found in the /etc/hosts file instead of just the first.

/etc/hosts

We have already discusses about this file in previous sections. In a well managed system the only hostnames that usually appear in this file are an entry for the loopback interface and the local hosts name such as the following.

```
# /etc/hosts
localhost loopback
192.168.0.1 this.host.name
```

Configuring routing

Routing is a huge and complex topic. It is not possible to provide a detailed introduction in the confines of this text. If you need more information you should take a look at the NET-3 HOW-TO, the Network Administrators Guide and other documentation.

Ok, so how does routing work ? Each host keeps a special list of routing rules, called a routing table. This table contains rows which typically contain at least three fields, the first is a destination address, the second is the name of the interface to which the datagram is to be routed and the third is optionally the IP address of another machine which will carry the datagram on its next step through the network.

In Linux you can see this table by using the following command:

```
# cat /proc/net/route
```

or by using either of the following commands:

```
# /sbin/route -n
# /bin/netstat -r
```

The routing process is fairly simple: an incoming datagram is received, the destination address (who it is for) is examined and compared with each entry in the table. The entry that best matches that address is selected and the datagram is forwarded to the specified interface. If the gateway field is filled then the datagram is forwarded to that host via the specified interface, otherwise the destination address is assumed to be on the network supported by the interface.

To manipulate this table a special command is used. This command takes command line arguments and converts them into kernel system calls that request the kernel to add, delete or modify entries in the routing table. The command is called `route'.

A simple example. Imagine we have an Ethernet network. We have been told it is a class-C network with an address of 192.168.1.0. You've been supplied with an IP address of 192.168.1.10 for our use and have been told that 192.168.1.1 is a router connected to the Internet.

The first step is to configure the interface as described earlier. We would use a command like:

```
# ifconfig eth0 192.168.1.10 netmask 255.255.255.0 up
```

We now need to add an entry into the routing table to tell the kernel that datagrams for all hosts with addresses that match 192.168.1.* should be sent to the Ethernet device. You would use a command similar to:

```
# route add -net 192.168.1.0 netmask 255.255.255.0 eth0
```

Note the use of the `-net' argument to tell the route program that this entry is a network route. Your other choice here is a `-host' route which is a route that is specific to one IP address.

This route will enable you to establish IP connections with all of the hosts on your Ethernet segment. But what about all of the IP hosts that aren't on your Ethernet segment ?

It would be a very difficult job to have to add routes to every possible destination network, so there is a special trick that is used to simplify this task. The trick is called the `default' route. The default route matches every possible destination, but poorly, so that if any other entry exists that matches the required address it will be used instead of the default route. The idea of the default route is simply to enable you to say "and everything else should go here". In the example I've contrived you would use an entry like:

```
# route add default gw 192.168.1.1 eth0
```

The `gw' argument tells the route command that the next argument is the IP address, or name, of a gateway or router machine which all datagrams matching this entry should be directed to for further routing.

So, your complete configuration would look like:

```
# ifconfig eth0 192.168.1.10 netmask 255.255.255.0 up
# route add -net 192.168.1.0 netmask 255.255.255.0 eth0
# route add default gw 192.168.1.1 eth0
```

These steps are actually performed automatically by the startup files on a properly configured Linux box.

Startup files

In the previous section we've looked at the individual steps used to configuring networking on a simple Linux machine. On a normal Linux machine these steps are performed automatically in the system startup files (refer back to chapter 12 for a discussion on these). While the commands introduced in the previous section are standard Linux/UNIX commands the startup and associated configuration files used by different distributions. This section briefly summarizes the startup files which are used on a Redhat 5.0 machine.

The files used include

- /etc/sysconfig/network

  A text file which defines shell variables for hostname, domain, gateway and gateway device.
- /etc/sysconfig/network-scripts

  A collection of scripts used to perform common tasks including bringing network interfaces up and down.
- /etc/rc.d/init.d/network

  A shell script which actually brings up the networking on start-up. Linked to from a number of scripts in the rcX.d directories.

17.3.5 Network "management" tools

nslookup

The nslookup command is used to query a name server and is supplied as a debugging tool. It is generally used to determine if the name server is working correctly and for querying information from remote servers. nslookup can be used from either the command line or interactively. Giving nslookup a hostname will result in it asking the current domain name server for the IP address of that machine. nslookup also has an ls command that can be used to view the entire records of the current domain name server.

For example

Nslookup

nslookup rambo

```
Server    : circus.cqu.edu.au
Address   : 138.77.5.6

Name           :  jasper.cqu.edu.au
Address   : 138.77.1.1
netstat
```

netstat

The netstat command is used to display the status of network connections to a UNIX machine. One of the functions it can be used for is to display the contents of the kernel routing table by using the -r switch.

For example

The following examples are from two machines on CQU's Rockhampton campus. The first one is from telnet jasper

netstat -rn

Kernel routing table

Destination	Gateway	Genmask	Flags	Metric	Ref	Use	Iface
138.77.37.0	0.0.0.0	255.255.255.	0	U	0	0	109130 eth0
127.0.0.0	0.0.0.0	255.0.0.0	U	0	0	9206	lo
0.0.0.0	138.77.37.1	0.0.0.0	UG	0	0	2546951	eth0

netstat -rn

Routing tables

Destination	Gateway	Flags	Refcnt	Use	Interface
127.0.0.1	127.0.0.1	UH	56	7804440	lo0
default	138.77.1.11	UG	23	1595585	ln0
138.77.32	138.77.1.11	UG	0	19621	ln0
138.77.16	138.77.1.11	UG	0	555	ln0
138.77.8	138.77.1.11	UG	0	385345	ln0
138.77.80	138.77.1.11	UG	0	0	ln0
138.77.72	138.77.1.11	UG	0	0	ln0
138.77.64	138.77.1.11	UG	0	0	ln0
138.77.41	138.77.1.11	UG	0	0	ln0

traceroute

For some reason or another, users on one machine cannot connect to another machine or if they can any information transfer between the two machines is either slow or plagued by errors. What do you do?

The traceroute command provides a way of discovering the path taken by information as it goes from one machine to another and can be used to identify where problems might be occurring. On the Internet that path may not always be the same.

traceroute knuth

traceroute to knuth.cqu.edu.au (138.77.36.20), 30 hops max, 40 byte packets
1 knuth.cqu.EDU.AU (138.77.36.20) 2 ms 2 ms 2 ms

jasper is one network away from aldur

traceroute jasper

traceroute to jasper.cqu.edu.au (138.77.1.1), 30 hops max, 40 byte packets

1 centaurus.cqu.EDU.AU (138.77.36.1) 1 ms 1 ms 1 ms

2 jasper.cqu.EDU.AU (138.77.1.1) 2 ms 1 ms 1 ms

A machine still on the CQU site but a little further away

bash$ traceroute jade

traceroute to jade.cqu.edu.au (138.77.7.2), 30 hops max, 40 byte packets

1 centaurus.cqu.EDU.AU (138.77.36.1) 1 ms 1 ms 1 ms

2 hercules.cqu.EDU.AU (138.77.5.3) 4 ms 2 ms 12 ms

3 jade.cqu.EDU.AU (138.77.7.2) 3 ms 13 ms 3 ms

17.4 Basics of Transport layer and Services

The chapter starts by giving an overview of how network services work and then moves onto describing in detail how the UNIX operating system starts network services. The chapter closes with a detailed look at some specific network services including file/print sharing, messaging (email) and the World-Wide Web.

The provision of network services like FTP, telnet, e-mail and others relies on these following components

- **network ports,**
  Network ports are the logical (that means that ports are an imaginary construct which exists only in software) connections through which the information flows into and out of a machine. A single machine can have thousands of programs all sending and receiving information via the network at the same time. The delivery of this information to the right programs is achieved through ports.
- **network servers,**
  Network servers are the programs that sit listening at pre-defined ports waiting for connections from other hosts. These servers wait for a request, perform some action and send a response back to the program that requested the action. In general network servers operate as daemons.
- **network clients**, and
  Users access network services using client programs. Example network clients include Netscape, Eudora and the ftp command on a UNIX machine. **network protocols.**

  Network protocols specify how the network clients and servers communicate. They define the small "language" which both understand.

17.4.1 Ports

All network protocols, including http ftp SMTP, use either TCP or UDP to deliver information. Every TCP or UDP header contains two 16 bit numbers that are used to identify the source port (the port through which the information was sent) and the destination port (the port through which the information must be delivered.) Similarly, the IP header also contains numbers which describe the IP addresses of the computers which are sending and receiving the current packet.

Since port numbers are 16 bit numbers, there can be approximately 64,000 (2^{16} is about 64,000) different ports. Some of these ports are used for predefined purposes. The ports 0-256 are used by the network servers for well known Internet services (e.g. telnet, FTP, SMTP). Ports in the range from 256-1024 are used for network services that were originally UNIX specific. Network client programs and other programs should use ports above 1024.

Table 17.7 lists some of the port numbers for well known services.

Table 17.7 Reserved Ports.

Port number	Purpose
20	ftp-data
21	ftp
23	telnet
25	SMTP (mail)
80	http (WWW)
119	nntp (network news)

This means that when you look at a TCP/UDP packet and see that it is addressed to port 25 then you can be sure that it is part of an email message being sent to a SMTP server. A packet destined for port 80 is likely to be a request to a Web server.

Reserved ports

So how does the computer know which ports are reserved for special services? On a UNIX computer this is specified by the file /etc/services. Each line in the services file is of the format

```
service-name port/protocol aliases
```

Where service-name is the official name for the service, port is the port number that it listens on, protocol is the transport protocol it uses and aliases is a list of alternate names.

The following is an extract from an example /etc/services file. Most /etc/services files will be the same, or at least very similar.

```
echo 7/tcp
echo 7/udp
discard 9/tcp sink null
discard 9/udp sink null
systat 11/tcp users
daytime 13/tcp
daytime 13/udp
ftp-data 20/tcp
ftp 21/tcp
telnet 23/tcp
smtp 25/tcp mail
nntp 119/tcp usenet # Network News Transfer
ntp 123/tcp # Network Time Protocol
```

We should be able to match some of the entries in the above example, or in the /etc/services file on your computer, with the entries in Table 17.1.

The **netstat** command can be used for a number of purposes including looking at all of the current active network connections. The following is an example of the output that netstat can produce (it's been edited to reduce the size).

netstat -a

```
active Internet connections (including servers)
proto Recv-Q Send-Q Local Address          Foreign Address        (State) User
root
tcp     1   7246 cq-pan.cqu.edu.au:www lore.cs.purdue.e:42468 CLOSING root
tcp     0   0 cq-pan.cqu.edu.au:www sdlab142.syd.cqu.:1449 CLOSE root
tcp     0   0 cq-pan.cqu.edu.au:www dialup102-4-9.swi:1498 FIN_WAIT2 root
tcp     0   22528 cq-pan.cqu.edu.au:www 205.216.78.103:3058 CLOSE root
tcp     1   22528 cq-pan.cqu.edu.au:www barney.poly.edu:47547 CLOSE root
tcp     0   0 cq-pan.cqu.edu.au:www eda.mdc.net:2395 CLOSE   root
tcp     0   22528 cq-pan.cqu.edu.au:www  eda.mdc.net:2397 CLOSE   root
tcp     0   0 cq-pan.cqu.edu.au:www  cphppp134.cyberne:1657 FIN_WAIT2 root
tcp     0   22528 cq-pan.cqu.edu.au:www  port3.southwind.c:1080 CLOSE root
tcp     0   9 cq-pan.cqu.edu.:telnet dinbig.cqu.edu.au:1107 ESTABLISHED root
tcp     0   0 cq-pan.cqu.edu.au:ftp  ppp2-24.INRE.ASU.:1718 FIN_WAIT2 root
```

Explanation

Table 17.8 explains each column of the output. Taking the column descriptions from the table, it is possible to make some observations

- All of the entries, but the last two, are for people accessing this machine's (cq-pan.cqu.edu.au) World-Wide Web server. You can say this because of cq-pan.cqu.edu.au:www. This tells us that the port on the local machine is the www port (port 80).
- In the second last entry, I am telneting to cq-pan from my machine at home. At that stage my machine at home was called dinbig.cqu.edu.au. The telnet client is using port 1107 on dinbig to talk to the telnet daemon.
- the last entry is someone connecting to CQ-PAN's ftp server,
- the connection for the first entry is shut down but not all the data has been sent (this is what the CLOSING state means). This entry, from a machine from Purdue University in the United States, still has 7246 bytes still to be acknowledged

Table 17.8 Columns for netstat.

Column name	Explanation
Proto	the name of the transport protocol (TCP or UDP) being used
Recv-Q	the number of bytes not copied to the receiving process
Send-Q	the number of bytes not yet acknowledged by the remote host
Local Address	the local hostname (or IP address) and port of the connection
Foreign Address	the remote hostname (or IP address) and remote port
State	the state of the connection (only used for TCP because UDP doesn't establish a connection), the values are described in the man page
User	some systems display the user that owns the local program serving the connection

17.4.2 Network servers

The /etc/services file specifies which port a particular protocol will listen on. For example SMTP (Simple Mail Transfer Protocol, the protocol used to transfer mail between different machines on a TCP/IP network) uses port 25. This means that there is a network server that listens for SMTP connections on port 25.

This begs some questions

- How do we know which program acts as the network server for which protocol?
- How is that program started?

How network servers start

There are two methods by which network servers are started

- executed as a normal program (usually in the start-up files)
  Servers started in this manner will show up in a ps list of all the current running processes. These servers are always running, waiting for a connection on the specified port. This means that the server is using up system resources (RAM etc) because it is always in existence but it also means that it is very quick to respond when requests arrive for their services.
- by the inetd daemon
  The inetd daemon listens at a number of ports and when information arrives, it starts the appropriate network server for that port. Which server, for which port, is specified in the configuration file /etc/inetd.conf.

Starting a network server via inetd is usually done when there aren't many connections for that server. If a network server is likely to get a large number of connections (a busy mail or WWW server for example) the daemon for that service should be started in the system startup files and always listen on the port.

The reason for this is overhead. Using inetd takes longer.
The /etc/inetd.conf file specifies the network servers that the inetd daemon should execute. The inetd.conf file consists of one line for each network service using the following format (Table 17.9 explains the purpose of each field).

service-name socket-type protocol flags user server_program args

Table 17.9 Fields of /etc/inetd.conf file.td

etd.conf **Field**	**Purpose**
service-name	The service name, the same as that listed in /etc/services
socket-type	The type of data delivery services used (we don't cover this). Values are generally stream for TCP, dgram for UDP and raw for direct IP
protocol	the transport protocol used, the name matches that in the /etc/protocols file
flags	how inetd is to behave with regards this service (not explained any further)
user	the username to run the server as, usually root but there are some exceptions, generally for security reasons
server_program	the full path to the program to run as the server
args	command line arguments to pass to the server program

How it works

Whenever the machine receives a request on a port (on which the inetd daemon is listening on), the inetd daemon decides which program to execute on the basis of the /etc/inetd.conf file.

17.4.3 Network clients

A network client is simply a program (whether it is text based or a GUI program) that knows how to connect to a network server, pass requests to the server and then receive replies.

By default when you use the command telnet jasper, the telnet client program will attempt to connect to port 23 of the host jasper (23 is the telnet port as listed in /etc/services).

It is possible to use the telnet client program to connect to other ports. For example the command telnet jasper 25 will connect to port 25 of the machine jasper.

17.4.4 Network protocols

Each network service generally uses its own network protocol that specifies the services it offers, how those services are requested and how they are supplied. For example, the ftp protocol defines the commands that can be used to move files from machine to machine. When you use a command line ftp client, the commands you use are part of the ftp protocol.

Request for comment (RFCs)

For protocols to be useful, both the client and server must agree on using the same protocol. If they talk different protocols then no communication can occur. The standards used on the Internet, including those for protocols, are commonly specified in documents called Request for Comments (RFCs). (Not all RFCs are standards). Someone proposing a new Internet standard will write and submit an RFC. The RFC will be distributed to the Internet community who will comment on it and may suggest changes. The standard proposed by the RFC will be adopted as a standard if the community is happy with it.

Table 17.10 RFCs for Protocols.

Protocol	RFC
FTP	959
Telnet	854
SMTP	821
DNS	1035
TCP	793
UDP	768

Table 17.10 lists some of the RFC numbers which describe particular protocols. RFCs can and often are very technical and hard to understand unless you are familiar with the area (the RFC for ftp is about 80 pages long).

Text based protocols

Some of these protocols smtp ftp nntp http are text based. They make use of simple text-based commands to perform their duty. Table 17.11 contains a list of the commands that smtp understands. smtp (simple mail transfer protocol) is used to transport mail messages across a TCP/IP network.

Table 17.11 SMTP commands.

Command	**Purpose**
HELO *hostname*	start-up and give your hostname
MAIL FROM: *sender-address*	mail is coming from this address
TO: *recipient-address*	please send it to this address
VRFY *address*	does this address actually exist (verify)
EXPN *address*	expand this address
DATA	I'm about to start giving you the body of the mail message
RSET	oops, reset the state and drop the current mail message
NOOP	do nothing
DEBUG [*level*]	set debugging level
HELP	give me some help please
QUIT	close this connection

How it works

When transferring a mail message a client (such as Eudora) will connect to the SMTP server (on port 25). The client will then carry out a conversation with the server using the commands from Table 17.11. Since these commands are just straight text you can use telnet to simulate the actions of an email client.

Doing this actually has some real use. I often use this ability to check on a mail address or to expand a mail alias. The following shows an example of how I might do this.

The text in bold is what I've typed in. The text in italics are comments I've added after the fact.

beldin:~$ **telnet localhost 25**

Trying 127.0.0.1...

Connected to localhost.

Escape character is '^]'.

220-beldin.cqu.edu.au Sendmail 8.6.12/8.6.9 ready at Wed, 1 May 1996 13:20:10 +1 000

220 ESMTP spoken here

vrfy david *check the address david*

250 David Jones <david@beldin.cqu.edu.au

vrfy joe *check the address joe*

550 joe... User unknown

vrfy postmaster *check the address postmaster*

250 <postmaster@beldin.cqu.edu.au

expn postmaster *postmaster is usually an alias, who is it really??*

250 root <postmaster@beldin.cqu.edu.au

17.5 Services on Intranet

The following is a list of the most common services that an Intranet might supply (by no means all of them). This is the list of services we'll discuss in more detail in this chapter. The list includes

- file sharing,
  The common ability to share access to applications and data files. It's much simpler to install one copy of an application on a network server than it is to install 35 copies on each individual PC.
- print sharing, and
  The ability for many different machines to share a printer. It is especially economically if the printer is an expensive, good quality printer.
- electronic mail.
  Sometimes called messaging. Electronic mail is fast becoming an essential tool for most businesses.

In the subsequent chapters we shall discuss about them independently.

17.5.1 finger command

This command is used to know the information about the user such as when he has logged into machine, when did he/she see their email, etc in addition to content of .plan (and other files) of his home directory.

Example:

finger root gave the following result.

```
Login: root                          Name: root
Directory: /root                     Shell: /bin/bash
On since Tue Feb 12 09:55 (IST) on :0 (messages off)
On since Tue Feb 12 09:59 (IST) on pts/0 from :0.0
New mail received Tue Feb 12 10:01 2002 (IST)
    Unread since Sun Feb 10 00:03 2002 (IST)
Plan:
I have class at 9.00AM
10.00AM
4.30 to 9.00PM
```

If any user wants to convey any thing to the people who fingers his account he can write in his .plan file. Best thing we can write is our schedule today. Such that, other people can see and accordingly they can start interactive sessions such as talk, chat, or calling by phone etc.

If this command is executed without any arguments then displays details of all currently logged in users (similar to who command) such as:

```
Login   Name    Tty       Idle  Login Time   Office    Office Phone
rao             pts/2           Feb 12 10:37 (localhost)
root    root    *:0             Feb 12 09:55
root    root    pts/0           Feb 12 10:33 (:0.0)
root    root    pts/1           Feb 12 10:36
```

Remote Login Services

17.5.2 rlogin

With the help of this command it is possible to login to remote machine if we happened to have legal username and password on that machine. When we do so, the current machine becomes terminal to that remote machines. After that whatever file we create it will be stored in that remote machine. When we run a command, that remote machines processor and RAM is used for running the same.

Example:

```
rlogin IPaddressormachinename -l username
```

It will prompt the password and after entering valid password we will see that remote machines prompt. For proper functioning TERM environment variable on local machine should be set appropriately such that it matches with that remote machine. Usually, rlogin is used for GUI based remote login service unlike telnet service.

17.5.3 telnet command:

```
telnet IPaddressormachinename
```

The following output appear on the screen

```
Trying 127.0.0.1...
Connected to localhost.localdomain (127.0.0.1).
Escape character is '^]'.
Red Hat Linux release 9 (Shrike)
Kernel 2.4.20-8 on an i686
login:
Login incorrect

login:
```

When we enter legal username and password then we will be logging into that remote machine and we will see its prompt. Here also the local machine becomes dumb terminal for the remote machine.

Unlike rlogin service this supports only character based remote login service.

17.5. 4 ftp command

This command is used to transfer files from one machine to another machine.

```
ftp Ipaddressormachiename
```

This command gives a prompt namingly ftp> after we enter legal user name and password of that remote machine. Once we have logged in, we can download files with command **get filename.** We can use commands such as ls, cd etc on remote machine directory while mls, mcd commands can be used on local machine. We can set transfer as ascii or binary by simply typing ascii or binary commands at ftp> prompt.

We can put files of the local directory using **put filename** command. On some ftp servers we can download files using mget and upload files using mput command.

If we execute ftp command without any argument then we will see ftp> prompt. Using **open Ipaddressormachinename** we can connect to remote machine for file transfer. By type ! symbol at the ftp> prompt we can exit from the ftp program.

There are many ftp servers are available in the internet for free download. While logging into those servers we can login with anonymous as username and our email address as password. Thus these servers are often called as anonymous servers. From these servers we can download only. If we have some SW is available and want to be available freely to others we have to contact these servers administrators who can give permission temporarily to upload our SW into their servers.

17.6 Conclusions

This chapter explores the basics of TCP/IP networks. Ethernet address, IP address, port address, network address are explained in a lucid manner and how they are used when a packet is traveling from one host to another host.

18 Compiling C and C++ Programs Under Linux

18.1 Introduction to C Compiler

The easiest case of compilation is when you have all your source code set in a single file. Lets assume there is a file named 'x.c' that we want to compile. We will do so using a commands similar to:

cc x.c (In most of the flavors of Unix's)

gcc x.c (In Gnu C compiler)

acc x.c (In Solaris)

Every compiler might show its messages (errors, warnings, etc.) differently, but in all cases, you'll get a file 'a.out' as a result, if the compilation completed successfully. Note that some older systems (e.g. SunOS) come with a C compiler that does not understand ANSI-C, but rather the older 'K&R' C style. In such a case, you'll need to use gcc (hopefully it is installed), or learn the differences between ANSI-C and K&R C (not recommended if you don't *really* have to), or move to a different system. This "a.out" file has some format which we will explain in the next chapters.

Compilation in general is split into roughly 5 stages (as shown in Figure 18.1): Preprocessing, Parsing, Translation, Assembling, and Linking

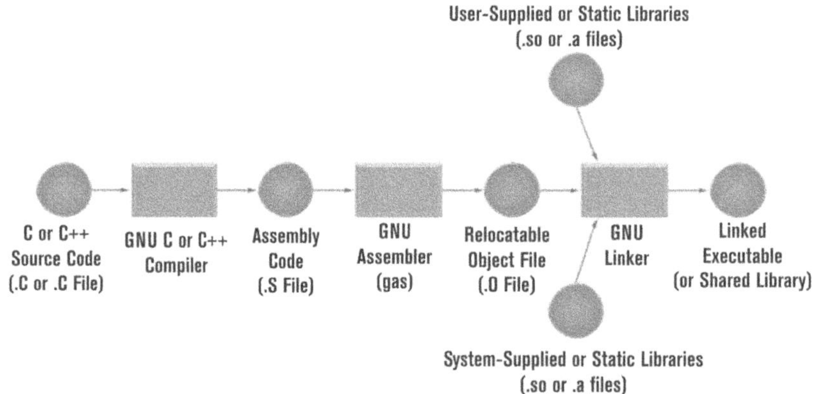

Figure 18.1 Stages in C Program Compilation.

18.1.1 Understanding Of Compilation Steps

Now that we've learned that compilation is not just a simple process, lets try to see what is the complete list of steps taken by the compiler in order to compile a C program.

1. Driver - what we invoked as "cc" or "gcc". This is actually the "engine", that drives the whole set of tools the compiler is made of. We invoke it, and it begins to invoke the other tools one by one, passing the output of each tool as an input to the next tool.

2. C Pre-Processor - normally called "cpp". It takes a C source file, and handles all the pre-processor definitions (#include files, #define macros, conditional source code inclusion with #ifdef, etc.)
3. The C Compiler - normally called "cc1". This is the actual compiler, that translates the input file into assembly language.
4. Optimizer - sometimes comes as a separate module and sometimes as the found inside the compiler module. This one handles the optimization on a representation of the code that is language-neutral. This way, you can use the same optimizer for compilers of different programming languages.
5. Assembler - sometimes called "as". This takes the assembly code generated by the compiler, and translates it into machine language code kept in object files.
6. Linker-Loader - This is the tool that takes all the object files (and C libraries), and links them together, to form one executable file, in a format the operating system supports. A Common format these days is known as "ELF". On SunOS systems, and other older systems, a format named "a.out" was used. This format defines the internal structure of the executable file - location of data segment, location of source code segment, location of debug information and so on.

If we run the following commands we get the executable files of the above programs namingly cpp (don't confuse cpp as cp plus plus!!), cc1, as and collect2.

```
gcc –print-prog-name=cpp
gcc –print-prog-name=cc1
gcc –print-prog-name=as
gcc –print-prog-name=collect2
```

The compilation is split in to many different phases; not all compiler employs exactly the same phases, and sometimes (e.g. for C++ compilers) the situation is even more complex. But the basic idea is quite similar - split the compiler into many different parts, to give the programmer more flexibility, and to allow the compiler developers to re-use as many modules as possible in different compilers for different languages (by replacing the preprocessor and compiler modules), or for different architectures (by replacing the assembly and linker-loader parts).

18.2 Detailed Analysis of Compilation Process

Suppose that you want the resulting program to be called with another name other than "a.out" then we can use the following line to compile it:

```
cc –o executable_filename  x.c
gcc –o executable_filename  x.c
```

18.2.1 Running The Resulting Program

Once we created the program, we wish to run it. This is usually done by simply typing its name at the command prompt.

```
executable_filename
```

However, this requires that the current directory be in our PATH (which is a variable telling our Unix shell where to look for programs we're trying to run). In many cases, this directory is not placed in our PATH. Thus in order to run our program we can try:

```
./executable_filename
```

This time we explicitly told our Unix shell that we want to run the program which is in the current directory. If we're lucky enough, this will suffice. However, yet one more obstacle could block our path - file permission flags.

When a file is created in the system, it is immediately given some access permission flags. These flags tell the system who should be given access to the file, and what kind of access will be given to them. Traditional Unix systems use 3 kinds of entities to which they grant (or deny) access: The user which owns the file, the group which owns the file, and everybody else. Each of these entities may be given access to read the file ('r'), write to the file ('w') and execute the file ('x').

Now, when the compiler created the program file for us, we became owners of the file. Normally, the compiler would make sure that we get all permissions to the file - read, write and execute. It might be, thought that something went wrong, and the permissions are set differently. In that case, we can set the permissions of the file properly (the owner of a file can normally change the permission flags of the file), using a command like this:

```
chmod u+rwx executable_filename
```

This means "the user ('u') should be given ('+') permissions read ('r'), write ('w') and execute ('x') to the file 'executable_filename'. Now we'll surely be able to run our program. Again, normally you'll have no problem running the file, but if you copy it to a different directory, or transfer it to a different computer over the network, it might loose its original permissions, and thus you'll need to set them properly, as shown above. Note too that you cannot just move the file to a different computer an expect it to run - it has to be a computer with a matching operating system (to understand the executable file format), and matching CPU architecture (to understand the machine-language code that the executable file contains).

Finally, the run-time environment has to match. For example, if we compiled the program on an operating system with one version of the standard C library, and we try to run it on a version with an incompatible standard C library, the program might crush, or complain that it cannot find the relevant C library. This is especially true for systems that evolve quickly (e.g. Linux with libc5 vs. Linux with libc6), so beware.

18.2.2 The C Preprocessor

The preprocessor is what handles the logic behind all the # directives in C. It runs in a single pass, and essentially is just a substitution engine [Aho].

Consider the following simple program with the definitions of a symbolic constants (also called as manifest constants) and a macro. In the following program NUM is defined and during the pre-processing stage where ever NUM is written in the program, there 3 will be replaced. In many production programs, you prefer from use a macro in place of a fixed constant such that in future if we want to change the fixed constant, we change this macro line only [Michael K Johnson]. This makes programmer life easy.

```
#define NUM 3
#define NORM(a,b)   sqrt(a*a+b*b)
int main()
{
int i;
float val;

for(i=0;i<NUM;i++)
printf("Hello  %d \n", i);

val=NORM(2,3);

return 0;
}
```

To only preprocess the C language program:

gcc –E filename.c

The following is the output after preprocessing. For the simplicity sake we did not include any header file such as "stdio.h". The bold and underlined text matter in the following text is the result after preprocessing.

```
int main()
{
int i;
float val;

for(i=0;i<3;i++)
printf("Hello  %d \n", i);

val=sqrt(2*2 +3*3);

return 0;
}
```

The **gcc -E** runs only the preprocessor stage. This places all include files into your .c file, and also translates all macros into inline C code and replaces all the occurrences of symbolic constants with their values or definitions. You can add **-o file** to redirect result of preprocessing in to a file. That is, using command like the following.

gcc –E filename.c –o outputfilename

#undef

#undef fulfills the inverse functionality of **#define**. It eliminates to the list of defined constants the one that has the name passed as a parameter to **#undef**:

```
#define MAX_WIDTH 100
char str1[MAX_WIDTH];
#undef MAX_WIDTH
#define MAX_WIDTH 200
char str2[MAX_WIDTH];
```

#ifdef, #ifndef, #if, #endif, #else and #elif

These directives allow to discard part of the code of a program if a certain condition is not fulfilled.

#ifdef allows that a section of a program is compiled only if the *defined constant* that is specified as the parameter has been defined, independently of its value. Its operation is:

```
#ifdef name
// code here
#endif
```

For example :

```
#include<stdio.h>
int main()
{
int i=0;

#ifdef DEBUG
for(i=0;i<NUM;i++)
#endif

printf("Hello  %d \n", i);


return 0;
}
```

If we compile the above program with "**gcc –D DEBUG filename.c**" and run we will find for loop is executed. We can check the same from the output of preprocessing stage with –E option.

If we compile the above program with "**gcc filename.c**" and run we will find no loop is executed. That is if DEBUG is defined that for loop is included in the program and compiled otherwise it is not included.

Similarly, execute the following program

```
#include<stdio.h>
int main()
{
int i=0;

#if DEBUG==1
for(i=0;i<NUM;i++)
#endif

printf("Hello  %d \n", i);

return 0;
}
```

If we compile the above program with "**gcc –D DEBUG=1 filename.c**" or "**gcc –D DEBUG filename.c**" and run we will find for loop is executed. We can check the same from the output of preprocessing stage with –E option.

If we compile the above program with "gcc filename.c" and run then we will find that no for loop is executed.

#ifndef serves for the opposite for **#ifdef**. The code between the **#ifndef** directive and the **#endif** directive is only compiled if the constant name that is specified has not been defined previously. For example:

```
#ifndef MAX_WIDTH
#define MAX_WIDTH 100
#endif
char str[MAX_WIDTH];
```

For example:

```
#include<stdio.h>

#ifndef N
#define N 100
#endif
```

```
int main()
{
int i=0;

for(i=0;i<N;i++)

printf("Hello  %d \n", i);


return 0;
}
```

Compile the above program with both the following commands and check how the program behaves by running the resulting executable programs.

gcc filename.c

gcc –D N=5 filename.c

In the first case, the *defined constant N* has not yet been defined it would be defined with a value of 100. Thus for loop runs 100 times. Where as in the second case, we are giving constant N value as 5 along with gcc command. Thus, it will be considered as 5 and thus for loop runs five times.

Also, the **#if**, **#else** and **#elif** (*elif = else if*) directives serve (see the above example) so that the portion of code that follows is compiled only if the specified condition is met. The condition can only serve to evaluate constant expressions. For example:

```
#if MAX_WIDTH>200
#undef MAX_WIDTH
#define MAX_WIDTH 200

#elsif MAX_WIDTH<50
#undef MAX_WIDTH
#define MAX_WIDTH 50

#else
#undef MAX_WIDTH
#define MAX_WIDTH 100
#endif

char str[MAX_WIDTH];
```

Notice how the structure of chained directives **#if**, **#elsif** and **#else** finishes with **#endif**.

These conditional compilation statements enable the programmer to control the execution of preprocessor directives, and the compilation of program code. Each of the conditional preprocessor directives evaluates a constant integer expression. Cast expressions, sizeof() expressions, and enumeration constants cannot be evaluated in preprocessor directives. The conditional preprocessor construct is much like the if selection structure.

Consider the following preprocessor code:

```
#if !defined(NULL)
#define NULL 0
#endif
```

These directives determine if NULL is defined. The expression defined(NULL) evaluates to 1 if NULL is defined; 0 otherwise. If the result is 0, !defined(NULL) evaluates to 1, and NULL is defined.

We can also use logical AND and OR operators of C language also here like the following manner.

```
#if (SIMVAL != 2 && SIMVAL != 3)
#error SIMVAL must be defined to either 2 or 3
#endif
```

#line

When we compile a program and errors happen during the compiling process, the compiler shows the error that happened preceded by the name of the file and the line within the file where it has taken place.

The **#line** directive allows us to control both things, the line numbers within the code files as well as the file name that we want to appear when an error takes place. Its form is the following one:

#line *number* **"***filename***"**

Where *number* is the new line number that will be assigned to the next code line. The line number of successive lines will be increased one by one from this. *The filename* is an optional parameter that serves to replace the file name that will be shown in case of error from this directive until another one changes it again or the end of the file is reached. For example:

```
#line 1 "assigning variable"
int a?;
```

This code will generate an error that will be shown as error in file "assigning variable", line 1.

This #line preprocessor directive causes the subsequent source code lines to be renumbered starting with the specified constant integer value. The directive

```
#line 100
```

Starts line numbering from 100 beginning with the next source code line.

The directive normally is used to help make the messages produced by syntax errors and compiler warnings more meaningful. The line numbers do not appear in the source file.

#error

This directive aborts the compilation process when it is found returning the error that is specified as the parameter:

```
#ifndef __cplusplus
#error A C++ compiler is required
#endif
```

This example aborts the compilation process if the *defined constant* **__cplusplus** is not defined.

#warning

This directive does not aborts the compilation process when it is found returning the error that is specified as the parameter:

```
#ifndef __cplusplus
#warning A C++ compiler is required
#endif
```

If the *defined constant* **__cplusplus** is not defined this example gives warning message and continues the compilation process

#include

This directive has also been used assiduously in other sections of this tutorial. When the preprocessor finds an **#include** directive it replaces it by the whole content of the specified file. There are two ways to specify a file to be included:

```
#include "file"
#include <file>
```

The only difference between both expressions is the directories in which the compiler is going to look for the file. In the first case where the file is specified between quotes, the file is looked for in the same directory that includes the file containing the directive. In case that it is not there, the compiler looks for the file in the default directories where it is configured to look for the standard header files.

If the file name is enclosed between angle-brackets **<>** the file is looked for directly where the compiler is configured to look for the standard header files.

The # And ## Operators

The # and ## preprocessor operators are available in ANSI C. The # operator causes a replacement text token to be converted to a string surrounded by double quotes as explained before.

Consider the following macro definition,

```
#define HELLO(x) printf("Hello, " #x "\n");
```

When HELLO(John) appears in a program file, it is expanded to

```
printf("Hello, " "John" "\n");
```

The string "John" replaces #x in the replacement text. Strings separated by white space are concatenated during preprocessing, so the above statement is equivalent to,

```
printf("Hello, John\n");
```

Note that the # operator **must** be used in a macro with arguments because the operand of # refers to an argument of the macro.

The ## operator concatenates two tokens. Consider the following macro definition,

```
#define CAT(p,q) p ## q
```

When CAT appears in the program, its arguments are concatenated and used to replace the macro. For example, CAT(O,K) is replaced by OK in the program. The ## operator must have two operands.

Program example:

```
#include <stdio.h>
#include <stdlib.h>
#define HELLO(x) printf("Hello, " #x "\n");
#define SHOWFUNC(x) Use ## Func ## x
int main(void)
{
//new concatenated identifier, UseFuncOne
char * SHOWFUNC(One);
char * SHOWFUNC(Two);
SHOWFUNC(One) = "New name, UseFuncOne";
SHOWFUNC(Two) = "New name, UseFuncTwo";
HELLO(Birch);
printf("SHOWFUNC(One) -> %s \n",SHOWFUNC(One));
printf("SHOWFUNC(One) -> %s \n",SHOWFUNC(Two));
system("pause");
return 0;
}
```

There are standard predefined macros as shown in Table 18.1. The identifiers for each of the predefined macros begin and end with two underscores. These identifiers and the defined identifier cannot be used in #define or #undef directive.

There are a lot more predefined macros extensions that are compilers specific, please check your compiler documentation. The standard macros are available with the same meanings regardless of the machine or operating system your compiler installed on.

```
#include<stdio.h>
int main()
{
printf("%d %s %s %s %s\n", __LINE__, __DATE__, __TIME__, __FILE__);

}
```

Table 18.1 The Predefined Macros.

Symbolic Constant	**Explanation**
__DATE__	The date the source file is compiled (a string of the form "mmm dd yyyy" such as "Jan 19 1999").
__LINE__	The line number of the current source code line (an integer constant).
__FILE__	The presumed names of the source file (a string).
__TIME__	The time the source file is compiled (a string literal of the form :hh:mm:ss).
__STDC__	The integer constant 1. This is intended to indicate that the implementation is ANSI C compliant.

#pragma

This directive is used to specify diverse options to the compiler. These options are specific for the platform and the compiler you use. Consult the manual or the reference of your compiler for more information on the possible parameters that you can define with **#pragma**.

If we use -save-temps option with gcc compiler, it saves the temporary files which it creates while machine language file is created.

For example:

gcc –save-temps a.c

The above command creates files "a.i", "a.s", "a.o" and "a.out" (in the order). That is "a.i" is created after preprocessing and is text file. The file "a.s" is created by assembler from the file "a.i". The file "a.o" is object file created from "a.s" and finally "a.out" is created after linking.

The –M option displays dependencies among the files needed for make command. For example, if we have a file "a.h" which another file "b.h" and "a.h" is included in "a.c" and if we execute the following command

gcc -M a.c

We get the following output.

a.o: a.c /usr/include/stdio.h <other system defined header files> a.h b.h

This knowledge is needed from create make files which we define in the forthcoming chapters.

Similarly, -H option with gcc produce output how the files are included during preprocessing stage. That first which file is included and then which file is included, etc. Try the following command.

gcc –H a.c

Also, try both the options and observe the output.

gcc –M -H a.c

18.2.3 The Assembler

Consider the following program.

```
#include<stdio.h>
int main()
{
int i=3;
printf("Hello  %d \n", i*2);

return 0;
}
```

Assembly code generated by gcc.

```
    .file     "b.c"
    .section .rodata
.LC0:
    .string  "Hello  %d \n"
    .text
.globl main
    .type    main,@function
main:
    pushl    %ebp
    movl     %esp, %ebp
    subl     $8, %esp
    andl     $-16, %esp
    movl     $0, %eax
    subl     %eax, %esp
    movl     $3, -4(%ebp)
    subl     $8, %esp
    movl     -4(%ebp), %eax
    sall     $1, %eax
    pushl    %eax
```

```
        pushl   $.LC0
        call    printf
        addl    $16, %esp
        movl    $0, %eax
        leave
        ret
.Lfe1:
        .size   main,.Lfe1-main
        .ident  "GCC: (GNU) 3.2.2 20030222 (Red Hat Linux 3.2.2-5)"
```

The program gcc itself is actually just a front end that executes various other programs corresponding to each stage in the compilation process [Ronald F Gulmette]. To get it to print out the commands it executes at each step, use **gcc -v**

gcc -S

gcc -S will take .c files as input and output .s assembly files in AT&T syntax. If you wish to have Intel syntax, add the option -masm=intel. To gain some association between variables and stack usage, use add -fverbose-asm to the flags [PatrickAlken].

In addition, gcc can be called with various optimization options that can do interesting things to the assembly code output. There are between 4 and 7 general optimization classes that can be specified with a -ON, where 0 <= N <= 6. 0 is no optimization (default), and 6 is usually maximum, although often no optimizations are done past 4, depending on architecture and gcc version.

There are also several fine-grained assembly options that are specified with the -f flag. The most interesting are -funroll-loops, -finline-functions, and -fomit-frame-pointer. Loop unrolling means to expand a loop so that there are n copies of the code for n iterations of the loop (i.e. no jmp statements to the top of the loop). On modern processors, this optimization is negligible. Inlining functions means to effectively convert all functions in a file to macros, and place copies of their code directly in line in the calling function (like the C++ inline keyword). This only applies for functions called in the same C file as their definition. It is also a relatively small optimization. Omitting the frame pointer (aka the base pointer) frees up an extra register for use in your program. If you have more than 4 heavily used local variables, this may be rather large advantage, otherwise it is just a nuisance (and makes debugging much more difficult).

18.2.4 Creating Object Files but not linked files

If we need to create only object files from the C or C++ source files –c option can be used. Usually this option is used with individual C files to create their object files; further, these object files can be used in creating libraries (explained in next chapters) and SW system.

gcc –c filename.c

We will get file with the name "filename.o".

Let's suppose we have files `a.c', `b.c' and `c.c'. We write:

gcc -c a.c b.c c.c

This creates files `a.o', `b.o' and `c.o'. Next we link them into one file called `myprog'.

gcc -o myprog a.o b.o c.o

18.2. 5 Creating Debug-Ready Code

Normally, when we write a program, we want to be able to debug it - that is, test it using a debugger that allows running it step by step, setting a break point before a given command is executed, looking at contents of variables during program execution, and so on. In order for the debugger to be able to relate between the executable program and the original source code, we need to tell the compiler to insert information to the resulting executable program that'll help the debugger. This information is called "debug information". In order to add that to our program, lets compile it differently:

```
gcc -g file.c -o executable_filename
```

The '-g' flag tells the compiler to use debug info, and is recognized by mostly any compiler out there. You will note that the resulting file is much larger than that created without usage of the '-g' flag. The difference in size is due to the debug information. We may still remove this debug information using the strip command, like this:

```
strip executable_filename
```

You'll note that the size of the file now is even smaller than if we didn't use the '-g' flag in the first place. This is because even a program compiled without the '-g' flag contains some symbol information (function names, for instance), that the strip command removes. You may read the subsequent sections to know more about strip command.

18.2.6 Creating Optimized Code

After we created a program and debugged it properly, we normally want it to compile into an efficient code, and the resulting file to be as small as possible. The compiler can help us by optimizing the code, either for speed (to run faster), or for space (to occupy a smaller space), or some combination of the two. The basic way to create an optimized program would be like this:

```
gcc -O file.c -o  executable_filename
```

The '-O' flag tells the compiler to optimize the code. This also means the compilation will take longer, as the compiler tries to apply various optimization algorithms to the code. This optimization is supposed to be conservative, in that it ensures us the code will still perform the same functionality as it did when compiled without optimization (well, unless there are bugs in our compiler). Usually can define an optimization level by adding a number to the '-O' flag. The higher the number - the better optimized the resulting program will be, and the slower the compiler will complete the compilation. One should note that because optimization alters the code in various ways, as we increase the optimization level of the code, the chances are higher that an improper optimization will actually alter our code, as some of them tend to be non-conservative, or are simply rather complex, and contain bugs. For example, for a long time it was known that using a compilation level higher than 2 (or was it higher than 3?) with gcc results bugs in the executable program. After being warned, if we still want to use a different optimization level (lets say 4), we can do it this way:

```
gcc -O4 single_compile.c -o single_compile
```

And we're done with it. If you'll read your compiler's manual page, you'll soon notice that it supports an almost infinite number of command line options dealing with optimization. Using them properly requires thorough understanding of compilation theory and source code optimization theory, or you might damage your resulting code. A good compilation theory course (preferably based on "the Dragon Book" by Aho, Sethi and Ulman) could do you good.

Also, some other options such as –floop-optimize, -finline-functions, or f-no-inline-functions etc can be used depending upon the requirement.

18.2.7 Getting Extra Compiler Warnings

Normally the compiler only generates error messages about erroneous code that does not comply with the C standard, and warnings about things that usually tend to cause errors during runtime. However, we can usually instruct the compiler to give us even more warnings, which is useful to improve the quality of our source code, and to expose bugs that will really bug us later. With gcc, this is done using the '-W' flag. For example, to let the compiler to use all types of warnings it is familiar with; we'll use a command line like:

```
cc -Wall filename.c –o filename
```

This will first annoy us - we'll get all sorts of warnings that might seem irrelevant. However, it is better to eliminate the warnings than to eliminate the usage of this flag. Usually, this option will save us more time than it will cause us to waste, and if used consistently; we will get used to coding proper code without thinking too much about it. One should also note that some code that works on some architecture with one compiler might break if we use a different compiler, or a different system, to compile the code on. When developing on the first system, we'll never see these bugs, but when moving the code to a different platform, the bug will suddenly appear. Also, in many cases we eventually will want to move the code to a new system, even if we had no such intentions initially.

Note that sometimes '-Wall' will give you too many errors, and then you could try to use some less verbose warning level. Read the compiler's manual to learn about the various '-W' options, and use those that would give you the greatest benefit. Initially they might sound too strange to make any sense, but if you are (or when you will become) a more experienced programmer, you will learn which could be of good use to you.

18.2.8 Linking Libraries

Whenever we use library functions other than standard libc functions, we have to include appropriate header file and at the same time during compilation we have to use –l option to inform the compiler that it has to link with the specified library. For example, if we use any mathematical functions such as sqrt(), pow(), log10() etc in our program aa.c then we have to compile the same with –lm option. That is:

```
gcc –o aa aa.c –lm
```

In the above command, -lm informs the gcc that it has to search for a library file " libm.so.*" in standard directories. Similarly, if we use any X windows library functions we may have to give –lx11 or –lxt along the command line with gcc command which makes it to search for library files "libx11.so.* " and "libxt.so.*" in standard directories.

If we want to instruct the gcc that it has to search for some other directories for the required library files, we have to use –L option with it. In the chapter on "Libraries" we have described about this in detail.

It is also common that functions are developed as separate files and use them and create final executable file. Whether we are using the standard library function or the one's developed by us the compiler toolchain (the ones explained in Figure 18.1) has to be able to build the executable according to specifications that the kernel understands and expects.

The part of the toolchain that makes sure that your program meets the kernel's expectations is the linker, ld. Actually, the linker performs several functions that are crucial to the process of building a working executable, and so it's worth taking a deeper look at this little-known portion of the compiler toolchain.

What the Linker Does[1]

Any time you run an executable, the kernel must create a new virtual address space for the process to run in and then load (or copy) the executable into that newly created space.

As we discussed earlier each process is given its own virtual address space, which is partitioned into identical large sections (as depicted in Figure 18.5 such as text, data, stack, and heap). The kernel expects that the start of these large sections of a process will always be located at the same virtual address.

In order for that to be possible, every program must be set up according to the specifications that the kernel expects at the time that it's compiled, and that's one of the linker's jobs. The linker and the kernel share an understanding of how the virtual address space should be laid out, and the linker knows how to put all the pieces of a program that you're compiling into the proper sections of the virtual address space. It also adjusts things so that all of the different addresses that are used by the program point where they should. (We'll talk more about this in minute.)

One section of the virtual address space contains the actual machine code instructions that make up the program -- the section labeled "Other Program Data," which contains the code (or text) segment. Let's see how the linker builds this part of the executable.

Object Files

As we discussed earlier, after the compiler (gcc) and the assembler (as) finish their respective jobs, they hand off a set of relocatable object modules to the linker, which must then make a functioning executable out of them.

You might be wondering what "relocatable" means in this particular context. In this case, it doesn't mean "may be relocated," but rather "must be relocated." The linker builds the code segment by placing the code from each object module -- one after another -- in the code segment portion of the virtual address space as though it were placing different sized books in a bookshelf.

When the assembler builds each object module, there's absolutely no way that it can know exactly where that module will reside in the virtual address space, so it doesn't bother to try to figure it out. Instead, it lets the linker adjust the addresses in every module. This adjustment process is known as "relocation" (and this is where the term "relocatable object module" comes from).

Disassembling Object Files

In order to appreciate what the linker has to do in order to make all of this work, let's take a closer look at an object file and see just what it contains. Since they contain assembly code that's been run through the assembler, we can "disassemble" the object file in order to recover the original assembly code.

---

[1] Benjamin Chelf,chelf@codesourcery.com.

Listing of the three files: a.c, b.c, and main.c are as follows..

File a.c

```
int a ()
{
  int i = 0;
i++;
 foo:
i--;
  goto foo;
}
```

File b.c

```
int b()
{
 b();
}
```

File main.c

```
main()
{
a();
b();
}
```

Compile these functions separately. That is,

```
gcc -c a.c
gcc -c b.c
gcc -c main.c
```

Once they've been compiled into the object modules a.o, b.o, and main.o, we can run the command objdump -d on each of them in order to see what their assembly code looks like (see Figure 18.2).

```
a.o:    file format elf32-i386
00000000 <a>:
   0:   push   %ebp
   1:   mov    %esp,%ebp
   3:   sub    $0x4,%esp
   6:   movl   $0x0,0xfffffffc(%ebp)
   d:   lea    0xfffffffc(%ebp),%eax
  10:   incl   (%eax)
  12:   lea    0xfffffffc(%ebp),%eax
  15:   decl   (%eax)
  17:   jmp    12 <a+0x12>

b.o:    file format elf32-i386
00000000 <b>:
   0:   push   %ebp
   1:   mov    %esp,%ebp
   3:   sub    $0x8,%esp
   6:   call   7 <b+0x7>
   b:   mov    %ebp,%esp
   d:   pop    %ebp
   e:   ret

main.o: file format elf32-i386
00000000 <main>:
   0:   push   %ebp
   1:   mov    %esp,%ebp
   3:   sub    $0x8,%esp
   6:   call   7 <main+0x7>
   b:   call   c <main+0xc>
  10:   mov    %ebp,%esp
  12:   pop    %ebp
  13:   ret
```

Figure 18.2 Disassembly for a.o, b.o, and main.o

In each listing, the first column starts at 0 and increases. This is the location (or address) of the assembly language instruction which is listed in the subsequent columns. The assembler always starts building an object module at address 0. The linker must relocate all of these instructions to their new virtual addresses.

There are two other areas of importance in the address to the linker: the jumps (or branches) made by the code, and calls to functions.

Relative Jumps

In the assembly code for a.o, notice that the instruction at address 17 reads "jmp 12 <a+0x12>" (and corresponds to the goto in a.c). Indicating that the program should jump to the instruction at address 12 (which is "lea 0x fffffffc(%ebp),%eax").

However, the destination address 12 was specified as being relative to the start of the a() function. That's what the "<a+0x12>" means: jump to the instruction that's 12 bytes after the start of the a() function. This means that no matter where the a() function is placed in the virtual address space, the jump always knows where to go. This is called a relative jump, and nearly every compiler creates code that uses them.

The use of relative jumps is one characteristic of what's known as "position-independent code" (PIC). In addition to being relocatable, modules compiled in PIC mode can be turned into shared libraries, which can also be used simultaneously by multiple processes, reducing the memory use of the entire system. We'll talk more about shared libraries in next month's column.

Because the compiler generated the relative jump, the linker only needs to relocate the jump instruction to its new place in the virtual address space. The actual instruction itself doesn't need to be changed. However, the linker does need to change an instruction whenever functions are being called.

Calling Functions in Other Modules

Let's look at disassembly for b.o, specifically the instruction at address 6: "call 7 <b+0x7>". This means we should call a function. However, it looks like the call is to a function at address 7, which is right in the middle of an instruction. What's going on here?

It turns out that 7 is not an actual address, but rather an offset or index into a table. As b.c is compiled, a table of functions that are called from within b.c is created. This table contains "relocation records" and can be listed by running "objdump -x" on b.o.

The relocation records for b.o and main.o are shown in Figure 18.3 (note that they have been slightly edited because of space constraints). You can see that the value of the offset for "a" is 7 , which corresponds to the call to the function a() in b.c.

```
b.o:
RELOCATION RECORDS FOR [.text]:
OFFSET   VALUE
00000007 a

main.o:
RELOCATION RECORDS FOR [.text]:
OFFSET   VALUE
00000007 a
0000000c b
```

Figure 18.3 Relocation Records for b.o and main.o

When the linker processes b.o, it takes a look at the relocation records and sees if the function a() is present in any of the other object modules (or system libraries). If the relocation record were not found, an "unsatisfied reference" error would be generated.

However, as the function a() does exist (in a.o), the call instruction is then rewritten -- or patched -- in order to be able to use the virtual address of the a() function within a.o.

We can examine the two call instructions in main.o and how that generates two relocation records (to the functions a() and b()).

The Finished Product

Let's take a look at what the three modules look like once the linker has finished its task. Figure 18.4 contains a dump of the final executable (obtained by running "objdump -d" on the executable).

```
08048430 <a>:
 8048430:  push  %ebp
 8048431:  mov   %esp,%ebp
 8048433:  sub   $0x4,%esp
 8048436:  movl  $0x0,0xfffffffc(%ebp)
 804843d:  lea   0xfffffffc(%ebp),%eax
 8048440:  incl  (%eax)
 8048442:  lea   0xfffffffc(%ebp),%eax
 8048445:  decl  (%eax)
 8048447:  jmp   8048442 <a+0x12>

...

08048450 <b>:
 8048450:  push  %ebp
 8048451:  mov   %esp,%ebp
 8048453:  sub   $0x8,%esp
 8048456:  call  8048430 <a>
 804845b:  mov   %ebp,%esp
 804845d:  pop   %ebp

...

08048460 <main>:
 8048460:  push  %ebp
 8048461:  mov   %esp,%ebp
 8048463:  sub   $0x8,%esp
 8048466:  call  8048430 <a>
 804846b:  call  8048450 <b>
 8048470:  mov   %ebp,%esp
 8048472:  pop   %ebp
```

Figure 18.4 How a(), b(), and main() Appear in the Final Executable.

Also note that the jmp instruction at 0x 8048447 in the a() function is the same as it was in the a.o file. Although the "12" has been replaced in the output with the correct virtual address, it's still really "<a+0x12>". The call instructions to a() and b() have also had the correct addresses inserted.

18.2.9 Monitoring Compilation Times

It is possible with -time option to know the actual CPU time taken by preprocessor, cc1, and linker etc. The -Q option gives detail information about the compilation.

```
gcc -time b1.c a.c
# cc1 0.02 0.01
# as 0.00 0.00
# cc1 0.01 0.01
# as 0.00 0.00
# collect2 0.02 0.01

gcc -Q b1.c a.c

main
Execution times (seconds)
 life analysis      : 0.01 (33%) usr  0.00 ( 0%) sys  0.01 (14%) wall
 preprocessing      : 0.01 (33%) usr  0.01 (100%) sys  0.00 ( 0%) wall
 parser             : 0.00 ( 0%) usr  0.00 ( 0%) sys  0.03 (43%) wall
 final              : 0.00 ( 0%) usr  0.00 ( 0%) sys  0.01 (14%) wall
 TOTAL              : 0.03            0.01            0.07
 LCM

Execution times (seconds)
 parser             : 0.00 ( 0%) usr  0.00 ( 0%) sys  0.01 (33%) wall
 global alloc       : 0.01 (100%) usr 0.00 ( 0%) sys  0.01 (33%) wall
 TOTAL              : 0.01            0.00            0.03
```

Architecture Specific Optimizations

Some of the features of compiler are very specific to computer architecture. It is wise to specify the architecture type along the command line to gcc command such that the resultant executable file is created which exploits the available architectural features of the processor. For this we use option -march. For example:

```
gcc  -march=pentium4 a.c
gcc -march=athlon-xp  a.c
gcc  -march=i386   a.c
gcc  -march=i686   a.c
```

18.2.10 Specifying Include Directories Along The Command Line

With the help of -I option we can specify a set of directory names along with gcc command to search for include files (header files). Directories named by -I are searched before the standard system include directories. It is dangerous to specify a standard system include directory with -I option.

Example :

```
gcc –o aa  aa.c –I /home/venkat/lib
```

To know which directories are searched by the gcc from find include files, run the following command.

```
gcc –print-search-dirs
```

Output is as follows:

install: /usr/lib/gcc-lib/i386-redhat-linux/3.2.2/

programs: =/usr/lib/gcc-lib/i386-redhat-linux/3.2.2/:/usr/lib/gcc-lib/i386-redhat-linux/3.2.2/:/usr/lib/gcc-lib/i386-redhat-linux/:/usr/lib/gcc/i386-redhat-linux/3.2.2/:/usr/lib/gcc/i386-redhat-linux/:/usr/lib/gcc-lib/i386-redhat-linux/3.2.2/../../../../i386-redhat-linux/bin/i386-redhat-linux/3.2.2/:/usr/lib/gcc-lib/i386-redhat-linux/3.2.2/../../../../i386-redhat-linux/bin/

libraries: =/usr/lib/gcc-lib/i386-redhat-linux/3.2.2/:/usr/lib/gcc/i386-redhat-linux/3.2.2/:/usr/lib/gcc-lib/i386-redhat-linux/3.2.2/../../../../i386-redhat-linux/lib/i386-redhat-linux/3.2.2/:/usr/lib/gcc-lib/i386-redhat-linux/3.2.2/../../../../i386-redhat-linux/lib/:/usr/lib/gcc-lib/i386-redhat-linux/3.2.2/../../../i386-redhat-linux/3.2.2/:/usr/lib/gcc-lib/i386-redhat-linux/3.2.2/../../../:/lib/i386-redhat-linux/3.2.2/:/lib/:/usr/lib/i386-redhat-linux/3.2.2/:/usr/lib/

18.2.11 Size Command

The size program prints out the size in bytes of each of the text, data, and BSS sections, along with the total size in decimal and hexadecimal.

```
size a.out
text  data   bss   dec   hex filename
1458   276     8  1742   6ce a.out
```

An executable file contains code, data and BSS (block started by symbol). However, when a program is loaded and a process is created then it will have five conceptually different areas of memory allocated to it (More details can be discussed in next chapters):

Code

Also referred as the *text segment (*The respective portion in the executable file is called as the *text section)*, this is the area in which the executable instructions reside. Linux and Unix arrange things so that multiple running instances of the same program share their code if possible; only one copy of the instructions for the same program resides in memory at any time.

Initialized data

Statically allocated and global data that are initialized with nonzero values live in the *data segment*. Each process running the same program has its own data segment. The portion of the executable file containing the data segment is the *data section*.

Zero-initialized data

Global and statically allocated data that are initialized to zero by default are kept in what is colloquially called the *BSS* area of the process. Each process running the same program has its own BSS area. When running, the BSS data are placed in the data segment. In the executable file, they are stored in the *BSS section*.

In order to support above statements, the following programs are compiled and on their executable file's size command is executed.

```
#include <stdio.h>
main()
{
static int a[2048]={9,9,0,0};
}
```

Result of the size of on the executable file of the above program.

```
text    data    bss    dec     hex  filename
 702    8464      4   9170    23d2  a.out
```

```
#include <stdio.h>
int a[2048]={9,9,0,0};
main()
{
}
```

Result of the size of on the executable file of the above program.

```
text    data    bss    dec     hex  filename
 702    8464      4   9170    23d2  a.out
```

The above two programs results suggests that both initialized static and global variables occupies data segment.

```
#include <stdio.h>
int a[2048];
main()
{
}
```

Result of the size of on the executable file of the above program.

```
text    data   bss    dec    hex   filename
702     252    8224   9178   23da  a.out
```

```
#include <stdio.h>
main()
{
static int a[2048];
}
```

Result of the size of on the executable file of the above program.

```
text    data   bss    dec    hex   filename
702     252    8224   9178   23da  a.out
```

The above two programs results suggests that both un initialized static and global variables occupies BSS segment.

```
#include <stdio.h>
main()
{
int a[2048];

}
```

Result of the size of on the executable file of the above program.(same results will be observed if the array is initialized to values)

```
text    data   bss    dec    hex   filename
706     252    4      962    3c2   a.out
```

The above program's results suggests that the automatic arrays will not occupy either data or BSS segments.

Heap

The *heap* is where dynamic memory (obtained by malloc() and friends) comes from. As memory is allocated on the heap, the process's address space grows. It is also typical for the heap to start immediately after the BSS area of the data segment.

Stack

The *stack segment* is where local variables are allocated. Local variables are all variables declared inside the opening left brace of a function body (or other left brace) that aren't defined as static. Also stack is used for storing function parameters, as well as for "invisible" bookkeeping information generated by the compiler, for function return value and for storing return address representing the return from a function to its caller. Variables stored on the stack "disappear" when the function containing them returns; the space on the stack is reused for subsequent function calls.

When a program is running, the initialized data, BSS, and heap areas are usually placed into a single contiguous area: the data segment. The stack and code segments are separate from the data segment.

18.2.12 The strip command

This command discards all symbols from object files. It modifies the object files themselves instead of writing the modified copies with different names. It can work on archive files also. This may reduce the executable file size substantially with simple programs. Of course, after executing strip command the resulting executable file can be executed without any difficulty.

strip a.out

If we want the resulting file to be written in another file with -o option.

```
strip a.out -o a        #here file "a" is executable file after stripping
strip -s a.out -o a     # removes all symbols from executable file
strip -g a.out -o a     # removes debugging information from the executable file
```

Checkup the size of the executable file (using ls -l command) after and before the strip command to see the file size change.

The strip program removes the symbols such as the program's variables and function names from the object (executable) file. (The symbols are not loaded into memory when the program runs.) This can save significant disk space for a large program, which make it impossible to debug a core dump if it occur. (On modern systems this isn't worth the trouble; don't use strip.) Even after removing the symbols, the file is still larger than what gets loaded into memory since the object file format maintains additional data about the program, such as what shared libraries it may use, if any.

18.2.13 The as command

It is also possible to first create an assembly code (from C source), and then object code and then finally executable code.

```
gcc -S file.c           #creates file.s
as  file.s -o file.o    # object file aa.o is created
gcc file.o              # executable file a.out is created
```

By simply typing a.out at the command prompt we can execute the program.

It is also possible to add some assembly programs if needed to the generated assembly program (Next chapter's talks about this in detail).

18.2.14 The ldd command

This command prints the shared libraries required by each of the programs given along the command line. Also, if we specify the shared library name along the command line it displays what other shared libraries it uses.

For example

ldd /usr/lib/lynx gives the following output

```
libncurses.so.5 => /usr/lib/libncurses.so.5 (0x40033000)
libssl.so.4 => /lib/libssl.so.4 (0x40072000)
libcrypto.so.4 => /lib/libcrypto.so.4 (0x400a7000)
libc.so.6 => /lib/tls/libc.so.6 (0x42000000)
libz.so.1 => /usr/lib/libz.so.1 (0x40198000)
libresolv.so.2 => /lib/libresolv.so.2 (0x401a6000)
libgssapi_krb5.so.2 => /usr/kerberos/lib/libgssapi_krb5.so.2 (0x401b9000)
libkrb5.so.3 => /usr/kerberos/lib/libkrb5.so.3 (0x401cc000)
libk5crypto.so.3 => /usr/kerberos/lib/libk5crypto.so.3 (0x4022a000)
libcom_err.so.3 => /usr/kerberos/lib/libcom_err.so.3 (0x4023a000)
libdl.so.2 => /lib/libdl.so.2 (0x4023c000)
/lib/ld-linux.so.2 => /lib/ld-linux.so.2 (0x40000000)
```

ldd /usr/lib/libncurses.so.5 gives the following output

```
libc.so.6 => /lib/tls/libc.so.6 (0x42000000)
/lib/ld-linux.so.2 => /lib/ld-linux.so.2 (0x40000000)
```

18.2.15 Creating Dynamic Executable and Static Executable

By default, gcc creates dynamic executable files. Usually, the resulting file size will be smaller than the statically linked executable file.

gcc aa.c

ls –l a.out command displays the size as:

```
-rwxr-xr-x 1 root     root     11531 Nov 30 01:32    a.out
```

gcc -static aa.c

ls –l a.out command displays the size as:

```
-rwxr-xr-x 1 root     root     423439 Nov 30 01:34   a.out
```

From check whether the executable file is statically linked or dynamically linked, we can use:

file objectfilename

For example:

```
gcc aa.c
file a.out
```

The above command gives the following results.

a.out: ELF 32-bit LSB executable, Intel 80386, version 1 (SYSV), for GNU/Linux 2.2.5, dynamically linked (uses shared libs), not stripped

```
gcc -static aa.c
file a.out
```

The above command gives the following results.

a.out: ELF 32-bit LSB executable, Intel 80386, version 1 (SYSV), for GNU/Linux 2.2.5, statically linked, not stripped

The above commands can work on stripped executable files also.

18.2.16 Indent Command

With the help of this command, we can change the appearance of a C program by inserting or deleting white spaces.

Example

```
indent   C_source_filename
```

18.2.17 splint command

With the help of this command we can check C programs for security vulnerabilities, common programming mistakes., certain language constructs that may cause portability problems, syntax and data type errors. In fact, this identifies syntactical errors better than the compiler and produces errors in better human understandable form.

```
#include <stdio.h>
int main ()
{
int a,*x;
a=1.656;
x=1009;
scanf("%d",a);
x=(char *)malloc(10);
free(x);
printf("%d", *x);
return 0;
}
```

Result of splint command on the above file:

```
aa.c: (in function main)
aa.c:5:1: Assignment of double to int: a = 1.656
  To allow all numeric types to match, use +relaxtypes.
aa.c:6:1: Assignment of int to int *: x = 1009
  Types are incompatible. (Use -type to inhibit warning)
aa.c:7:12: Format argument 1 to scanf (%d) expects int * gets int: a
  Type of parameter is not consistent with corresponding code in format string.
  (Use -formattype to inhibit warning)
   aa.c:7:9: Corresponding format code
aa.c:7:1: Return value (type int) ignored: scanf("%d", a)
  Result returned by function call is not used. If this is intended, can cast result
to (void) to eliminate message. (Use -retvalint to inhibit warning)
aa.c:8:1: Assignment of char * to int *: x = (char *)malloc(10)
  To make char and int types equivalent, use +charint.
aa.c:10:15: Variable x used after being released
  Memory is used after it has been released (either by passing as an only param
or assigning to an only global). (Use -usereleased to inhibit warning)
   aa.c:9:6: Storage x released
aa.c:10:15: Dereference of possibly null pointer x: *x
  A possibly null pointer is dereferenced. Value is either the result of a function
which may return null (in which case, code should check it is not null), or a
global, parameter or structure field declared with the null qualifier. (Use -
nullderef to inhibit warning)
   aa.c:8:3: Storage x may become null
```

Now run splint command on the following program.

```
#include<stdio.h>
void ff()
{
int *p=(int *) malloc(10);
}
int main()
{
char *p="rama";
free(p);
printf("%s\n", p);
}
```

Output of splint.

```
nul.c: (in function ff)
nul.c:5:2: Fresh storage p not released before return
  A memory leak has been detected. Storage allocated locally is not released
  before the last reference to it is lost. (Use -mustfreefresh to inhibit
  warning)
   nul.c:4:27: Fresh storage p created
nul.c:4:6: Variable p declared but not used
  A variable is declared but never used. Use /*@unused@*/ in front of
  declaration to suppress message. (Use -varuse to inhibit warning)
nul.c: (in function main)
nul.c:9:6: Function call may modify observer p: p
  Storage declared with observer is possibly modified. Observer storage may not
  be modified. (Use -modobserver to inhibit warning)
   nul.c:8:9: Storage p becomes observer
nul.c:9:6: Observer storage p passed as only param: free (p)
  Observer storage is transferred to a non-observer reference. (Use
  -observertrans to inhibit warning)
   nul.c:8:9: Storage p becomes observer
nul.c:10:16: Variable p used after being released
  Memory is used after it has been released (either by passing as an only param
  or assigning to an only global). (Use -usereleased to inhibit warning)
   nul.c:9:6: Storage p released
nul.c:11:2: Path with no return in function declared to return int
  There is a path through a function declared to return a value on which there
  is no return statement. This means the execution may fall through without
  returning a meaningful result to the caller. (Use -noret to inhibit warning)
```

18.2.18 Use of cc1 command

We can execute cc1 command directly. However, it needs "a.i" file, i.e. the file after preprocessing. It gives statistics such as the following.

```
/usr/lib/gcc-lib/i386-redhat-linux/cc1  a.i
```

Output

```
main
          Execution times (seconds)
           preprocessing   :  0.01 ( 6%) usr   0.00 ( 0%) sys   0.01 ( 6%) wall
           parser          :  0.01 ( 6%) usr   0.00 ( 0%) sys   0.01 ( 6%) wall
           flow analysis   :  0.01 ( 6%) usr   0.00 ( 0%) sys   0.01 ( 6%) wall
           mode switching  :  0.01 ( 6%) usr   0.00 ( 0%) sys   0.01 ( 6%) wall
           global alloc    :  0.01 ( 6%) usr   0.00 ( 0%) sys   0.01 ( 6%) wall
           reg stack       :  0.01 ( 6%) usr   0.00 ( 0%) sys   0.01 ( 6%) wall
           rest of         :  0.01 ( 6%) usr   0.00 ( 0%) sys   0.01 ( 6%) wall
           compilation
           TOTAL           :  0.16             0.01             0.17
```

18.3 Functions with Variable Number of Arguments

Most of the young C programmers wonders how it became possible for C standard library developers to write functions such as printf(), scanf() to take variable number of arguments. Also, it is often desirable to implement a function where the number of arguments is not known, or is not constant, when the function is written.

```
int f(int, ... ) {
        .     .
        .
}
```

In order to achieve this, the functions declared in the <stdarg.h> header file must be included. This introduces a new type, called a va_list, and three functions that operate on objects of this type, called va_start, va_arg, and va_end.

Before manipulating variable argument list, va_start must be called whose prototype is:

```
void va_start(valist ap, parmN);
```

The va_start macro initializes ap for subsequent use by the functions va_arg and va_end. The second argument to va_start, parmN is the identifier naming the rightmost parameter in the variable parameter list in the function definition (the one just before the , ...). The identifier parmN must not be declared with register storage class or as a function or array type.

The arguments supplied can be accessed by calling va_arg() macro repeatedly. This is peculiar because the type returned is determined by an argument to the macro. Note that this is impossible to implement as a true function, only as a macro. It is defined as

```
type va_arg(va_list ap, type);
```

Each call to this macro will extract the next argument from the argument list as a value of the specified type (If the next argument is not of the specified type, the behavior is undefined). Take care here to avoid problems which could be caused by arithmetic conversions. Use of char or short as the second argument to va_arg is invariably an error: these types always promote up to one of signed int or unsigned int, and float converts to double. Note that it is implementation defined whether objects declared to have the types char, unsigned char, unsigned short and unsigned bitfields will promote to unsigned int, rather complicating the use of va_arg. This may be an area where some unexpected subtleties arise; only time will tell.

The behavior is also undefined if va_arg is called when there were no further arguments.

When all the arguments have been processed, the va_end function should be called. This will prevent the va_list supplied from being used any further. If va_end is not used, the behavior is undefined.

The entire argument list can be re-traversed by calling va_start again, after calling va_end. The va_end function is declared as

```
void va_end(va list ap);
```

The following example shows the use of va_start, va_arg, and va_end to implement a function that returns the average of its integer arguments.

```
#include <stdlib.h>
#include <stdarg.h>
#include <stdio.h>

int AVG(int nargs, ...){
      register int i;
      int avg;
      va_list ap;

      va_start(ap, nargs);
   avg=0;
      for(i = 1; i <= nargs; i++)
            avg+= va_arg(ap, int);

      va_end(ap);
      return (avg/nargs);
}

void f(void) {
      printf("%d\n",AVG(3, 33,44,55));
}


main(){
      f();
      exit(0);
}
```

18.4 Compiling A Multi-Source "C" Programs

We have learned how to compile a single-source program properly (hopefully by now you played a little with the compiler and tried out a few examples of your own). Yet, sooner or later you'll see that having all the source in a single file is rather limiting, for several reasons:

- As the file grows, compilation time tends to grow, and for each little change, the whole program has to be re-compiled.
- It is very hard, if not impossible, that several people will work on the same project together in this manner.
- Managing your code becomes harder. Backing out erroneous changes becomes nearly impossible.
- Also, developing programs as a single file limits code sharing or reusing.

The solution to this would be to split the source code into multiple files, each containing a set of closely-related functions (or, in C++, all the source code for a single class).

There are two possible ways to compile a multi-source C program. The first is to use a single command line to compile all the files. Suppose that we have a program whose source is found in files "main.c", "a.c" and "b.c". We could compile it this way:

```
gcc main.c a.c b.c -o hello_world
```

This will cause the compiler to compile each of the given files separately, and then link them all together to one executable file named "hello_world". Two comments about this program:

1. If we define a function (or a variable) in one file, and try to access them from a second file, we need to declare them as external symbols in that second file. This is done using the C "extern" keyword.
2. The order of presenting the source files on the command line may be altered. The compiler (actually, the linker) will know how to take the relevant code from each file into the final program, even if the first source file tries to use a function defined in the second or third source file.

The problem with this way of compilation is that even if we only make a change in one of the source files, all of them will be re-compiled when we run the compiler again. In order to overcome this limitation, we could divide the compilation process into two phases - compiling, and linking. Let us first see how this is done, and then we will explain.

```
cc -c main.cc
cc -c a.c
cc -c b.c
cc main.o a.o b.o -o hello_world
```

The first 3 commands have each taken one source file, and compiled it into "object file", (as explained above) with the same names, but with a ".o" suffix. It is the "-c" flag that tells the compiler only to create an object file, and not to generate a final executable file just yet. The object file contains the code for the source file in machine language, but with some unresolved symbols. For example, the "main.o" file refers to a symbol named "func_a", which is a function defined in file "a.c". Surely we cannot run the code like that. Thus, after creating the 3 object files, we use the 4th command to link the 3 object files into one program. The linker (which is invoked by the compiler now) takes all the symbols from the 3 object files, and links them together - it makes sure that when "func_a" is invoked from the code in object file "main.o", the function code in object file "a.o" gets executed. Further more, the linker also links the standard C library into the program, in this case, to resolve the "printf" symbol properly.

To see why this complexity actually helps us, we should note that normally the link phase is much faster than the compilation phase. This is especially true when doing optimizations, since that step is done before linking. Now, lets assume we change the source file "a.c", and we want to re-compile the program. We'll only need now two commands:

```
cc -c a.c
cc main.o a.o b.o -o hello_world
```

In our small example, it's hard to notice the speed-up, but in a case of having few tens of files each containing a few hundred lines of source-code, the time saving is significant; not to mention even larger projects.

18.5 How main() is executed on Linux[2]

In the previous sections, we have explained how from compile C language programs in addition to other tools usage. In the following paragraphs, we try from answer the question how does Linux execute main()? On Linux, our C main() function is executed by the cooperative work of GCC, libc and Linux's binary loader. Preferably read chapter on "Assembly Programming under Linux" also. We will use the following simple C program ("simple.c") to illustrate how it works.

```
int main()
{
  return(0);
}
```

```
gcc -o simple simple.c
```

To see what's in the executable, let's use a tool "objdump". More about this command will be discussed in the next chapters.

```
objdump -f simple
simple:     file format elf32-i386
architecture: i386, flags 0x00000112:
EXEC_P, HAS_SYMS, D_PAGED
start address 0x080482d0
```

From the output we can understand that the file is "ELF32" format and the start address is "0x080482d0".

ELF is acronym for Executable and Linking Format. It's one of the several object and executable file formats used on Unix systems. For our discussion, the interesting thing about ELF is its header format. Every ELF executable has ELF header, which is the following. More details about ELF is given in a separate chapter.

```
typedef struct
{
unsigned char       e_ident[EI_NIDENT]; /* Magic number and other info */
```

[2] http://www.linuxgazette.com/ Copyright © 2002, Hyouck "Hawk" Kim. This material may be distributed only subject to the terms and conditions set forth in the Open Publication License, v1.0 or later (the latest version is available at http://www.opencontent.org/openpub/).

```
Elf32_Half e_type;             /* Object file type */
Elf32_Half e_machine;          /* Architecture */
Elf32_Word          e_version;          /* Object file version */
Elf32_Addr e_entry;            /* Entry point virtual address */
Elf32_Off  e_phoff;            * Program header table file offset */
Elf32_Off  e_shoff;           /* Section header table file offset */
Elf32_Word          e_flags;           /* Processor-specific flags */
Elf32_Half e_ehsize;         /* ELF header size in bytes */
Elf32_Half e_phentsize;      /* Program header table entry size */
Elf32_Half e_phnum;          /* Program header table entry count */
Elf32_Half e_shentsize;      /* Section header table entry size */
Elf32_Half e_shnum;          /* Section header table entry count */
Elf32_Half e_shstrndx;       /* Section header string table index */
} Elf32_Ehdr;
```

In the above structure, there is "e_entry" field, which is starting address of an executable.

What's starting address "0x080482d0"?

For this question, let's disassemble the machine language file "simple". There are several tools to disassemble an executable. We will use objdump for this purpose also.

```
objdump --disassemble simple
```

The output is a little bit long, so we will not show entire output from objdump. Our intention is see what's at address 0x080482d0. Here is the output.

```
080482d0 <_start>:
80482d0:    31 ed              xor    %ebp,%ebp
80482d2:    5e                 pop    %esi
80482d3:    89 e1              mov    %esp,%ecx
80482d5:    83 e4 f0           and    $0xfffffff0,%esp
80482d8:    50                 push   %eax
80482d9:    54                 push   %esp
80482da:    52                 push   %edx
80482db:    68 20 84 04 08     push   $0x8048420
80482e0:    68 74 82 04 08     push   $0x8048274
80482e5:    51                 push   %ecx
80482e6:    56                 push   %esi
80482e7:    68 d0 83 04 08     push   $0x80483d0
80482ec:    e8 cb ff ff ff     call   80482bc <_init+0x48>
80482f1:    f4                 hlt
80482f2:    89 f6              mov    %esi,%esi
```

Those people who knows assembly language can understand that the executable file contains some kind of starting routine called "_start" at the starting address. It clears a register, push some values into stack and call a function. According to this instruction, the stack frame should look like this.

```
Stack Top -------------------
          0x80483d0
          -------------------
          esi
          -------------------
          ecx
          -------------------
          0x8048274
          -------------------
          0x8048420
          -------------------
          edx
          -------------------
          esp
          -------------------
          eax
          -------------------
```

If you look at disassembled output from objdump carefully, you can that the addresses pushed into stack are addresses of functions. To summarize:

0x80483d0 : This is the address of our main() function.

0x8048274 : _init function.

0x8048420 : _fini function _init and _fini is initialization/finalization functions of GCC.

Let us look for address 80482bc from the disassembly output.

```
80482bc:   ff 25 48 95 04 08        jmp    *0x8049548
```

Here *0x8049548 is a pointer operation.

It just jumps to an address stored at address 0x8049548.

As we know that this object file "simple" is dynamically linked, the address may be filled during run time. As explained earlier, If you issue the command "ldd simple" we get the following result.

```
libc.so.6 => /lib/i686/libc.so.6 (0x42000000)
/lib/ld-linux.so.2 => /lib/ld-linux.so.2 (0x40000000)
```

You can see all the libraries dynamically linked with simple. And all the dynamically linked data and functions have "dynamic relocation entry" in executable file i.e. in ELF records.

We can see all dynamic link entries with objdump command.

```
objdump -R simple
simple:     file format elf32-i386
DYNAMIC RELOCATION RECORDS
OFFSET   TYPE              VALUE
0804954c R_386_GLOB_DAT    __gmon_start__
08049540 R_386_JUMP_SLOT   __register_frame_info
08049544 R_386_JUMP_SLOT   __deregister_frame_info
08049548 R_386_JUMP_SLOT   __libc_start_main
```

Here address 0x8049548 is called "jump slot", which perfectly makes sense. And according to the table, actually we want to call __libc_start_main.

The __libc_start_main is a function in libc.so.6. If you look for __libc_start_main in glibc source code, the prototype looks like this.

```
extern int BP_SYM (__libc_start_main)(int *main)(int, char **, char**),
int argc,
char *__unbounded *__unbounded ubp_av,
void (*init) (void),
void (*fini) (void),
void (*rtld_fini) (void),
void *__unbounded stack_end)
__attribute__ ((noreturn));
```

And all the assembly instructions do is set up argument stack and call __libc_start_main.

What this function does is setup/initialize some data structures/environments and call our main().

Let's look at the stack frame with this function prototype.

```
Stack Top   -------------------
               0x80483d0                  main
            -------------------
               esi                        argc
            -------------------
               ecx                        argv
            -------------------
               0x8048274                  _init
            -------------------
               0x8048420                  _fini
            -------------------
               edx                        _rtlf_fini
            -------------------
               esp                        stack_end
            -------------------
               eax                        this is 0
            -------------------
```

According to this stack frame, esi, ecx, edx, esp, eax registers should be filled with appropriate values before __libc_start_main() is executed. And clearly this registers are not set by the startup assembly instructions shown before. Instead kernel involves in between.

Really, when we execute a program by entering a name at the shell prompt, this is what happens on Linux machine.

1. The shell calls the kernel system call "execve" with argc/argv.
2. The kernel system call handler gets control and start handling the system call. In kernel code, the handler is "sys_execve". On x86, the user-mode application passes all required parameters to kernel with the following registers.
   - ebx : pointer to program name string
   - ecx : argv array pointer
   - edx : environment variable array pointer.
3. The generic execve kernel system call handler, which is do_execve, is called. What it does is set up a data structure and copy some data from user space to kernel space and finally calls search_binary_handler(). Linux can support more than one executable file format such as a.out and ELF at the same time. For this functionality, there is a data structure "struct linux_binfmt", which has a function pointer for each binary format loader. And search_binary_handler() just looks up an appropriate handler and calls it. In our case, load_elf_binary() is the handler. Here is the bottom line of the function. It first sets up kernel data structures for file operation to read the ELF executable image in. Then it sets up a kernel data structure: code size, data segment start, stack segment start, etc. And it allocates user mode pages for this process and copies the argv and environment variables to those allocated page addresses. Finally, argc, the argv pointer, and the environment variable array pointer are pushed to user mode stack by create_elf_tables(), and start_thread() starts the process execution rolling.

Layout of segment created can be represented with *Figure 18.5* Yellow parts represent correspondent program sections. Shared libraries are not shown here; their layout duplicates layout of program.

code	.text section
data	.data section
bss	.bss section
... ...	free space
stack	stack (described later)
arguments	program arguments
environment	program environment
program name	filename of program (duplicated in arguments section)
Null (dword)	final dword of zero

Figure 18.5 Segment layout of an ELF binary.

Stack layout

Initial stack layout is very important, because it provides access to command line and environment of a program. Here is a picture (Figure 18.6) of what is on the stack when program is launched:

argc	[dword] argument counter (integer)
argv[0]	[dword] program name (pointer)
argv[1] **...** **argv[argc-1]**	[dword] program args (pointers)
NULL	[dword] end of args (integer)
env[0] **env[1]** **...** **env[n]**	[dword] environment variables (pointers)
NULL	[dword] end of environment (integer)

Figure 18.6 Stack layout of an ELF binary.

By the time, when the _start assembly instruction gets control of execution, the stack frame contain

To Summarize

1. GCC build your program with crtbegin.o/crtend.o/gcrt1.o And the other default libraries are dynamically linked by default. Starting address of the executable is set to that of _start.
2. Kernel loads the executable and setup text/data/bss/stack, especially, kernel allocate page(s) for arguments and environment variables and pushes all necessary information on stack.
3. Control is passed to _start. _start gets all information from stack setup by kernel, sets up argument stack for __libc_start_main, and calls it.
4. The __libc_start_main initializes necessary stuffs, especially C library(such as malloc) and environment and calls our main.
5. Our main is called with main(argv, argv) Actually, here one interesting point is the signature of main. The __libc_start_main thinks main's signature as main(int, char **, char **).

The same procedure can be explained in Figure 18.7 along with the names of the functions.

Function	Kernel file	Comments
shell	...	on user side one types in program name and strikes enter
execve()	...	shell calls libc function
sys_execve()	...	libc calls kernel...
sys_execve()	arch/i386/kernel/process.c	arrive to kernel side
do_execve()	fs/exec.c	open file and do some preparation
search_binary_handler()	fs/exec.c	find out type of executable
load_elf_binary()	fs/binfmt_elf.c	load ELF (and needed libraries) and create user segment
start_thread()	include/asm-i386/processor.h	and finally pass control to program code

Figure 18.7 Startup process of an ELF binary[3].

18.6 Compiling A Single-Source "C++" Program

Now that we saw how to compile C programs, the transition to C++ programs is rather simple. All we need to do is use a C++ compiler, in place of the C compiler we used so far. So, if our program source is in a file named 'executable filename.cc' ('cc' to denote C++ code. Some programmers prefer a suffix of 'C' for C++ code), we will use a command such as the following:

g++ file.cc -o executable_filename

Or on some systems you'll use "CC" instead of "g++" (for example, with Sun's compiler for Solaris), or "aCC" (HP's compiler), and so on. You would note that with C++ compilers there is less uniformity regarding command line options, partially because until recently the language was evolving and had no agreed standard. But still, at least with g++, you will use "-g" for debug information in the code, and "-O" for optimization.

18.7 Combining C and C++ programs

While developing practical SW systems, we may encounter the need for mixed language programming. That is, we may be required to use some C programs and some other C++ programs while building the SW system. This can be achieved in many ways. In the chapter on Assembly Language, we will discuss about how to mix assembly within C program.

In the case of C and C++ mixed programming, we can compile C programs using gcc compiler and create object files and using g++ compiler we can compile C++ programs and create object files. All the object files can be used to create final executable file.

---

[3] source for figures 2,3 and 4 is linuxassembly.com

For example, consider the following C function in a file a.c. We can use the same in C++ program (g1.C) by specifying that "a.c" file is external file and contains C code as shown in the program "g1.C".

```
File a.c:

int LCM(int x, int y)
{
 int a=x<y?y:x;

while(a<=(x*y))
{
 if( (a%x==0)&&(a%y==0)) return a;

a++;
}

}

File g1.C

#include<iostream.h>
extern "C" {
#include "a.c"
}

int main()
{

int x,y;

cout<<"Enter Two Integers"<<endl;

cin>>x>>y;

cout<<"LCM="<<LCM(x,y)<<endl;

}
```

To compile and run this C++ program, we can enter the following commands.

```
g++ -o g1 g1.C
./g1
```

Note : Please note that we can directly use the C file which is having a function code as there is no difference exists between functions of C and C++. That is, we can as well modify the g1.C to have the following code.

```
#include<iostream.h>

int LCM(int,int);
int main()
{

int x,y;

cout<<"Enter Two Integers"<<endl;

cin>>x>>y;

cout<<"LCM="<<LCM(x,y)<<endl;

}
```

To compile and run the g1.C, execute the following commands.

```
g++ -o g11 g1.C a.c
./g11
```

In the following example, we have explained how a C function (the one defined in the above a.c file) can be used in C++ and specifically from a member function of a class. A header file "a.h" is used in C++ program "RAT.C". This header file contains preprocessor directives to indicate the C++ compiler that LCM is an external "C" function . Compile "RAT.C" to object file. Then both the object files are linked to get the finally executable file (Note: this "RAT.C" defines a class to represent rational number and over loads + operator between rational number type of objects).

File a.h

```
#ifdef __cplusplus
extern "C" {
#endif
extern int LCM(int, int);
#ifdef __cplusplus
}
#endif
```

File RAT.C

```
#include<iostream.h>
```

```
#include "a.h"

class RAT
{
int p,q;

public:
void INP()
{
cin>>p>>q;
TRIM();
}
void OUT()
{
cout <<p<<"/"<<q<<endl;
}

RAT operator+(RAT X)
{
 RAT T;
 int lcm=LCM(q,X.q);
 T.p=p*lcm/q+X.p*lcm/X.q;
 T.q=lcm;
T.TRIM();
return T;
}
void TRIM()
{
 int a=p>q?q:p;

/* Finding GCF */
while(a)
{
 if( (p%a==0)&&(q%a==0)) break;

a--;
}
/* Divide both numerator and denominator with GCF*/

p=p/a; q=q/a;


}
};
```

```
int main()
{
RAT A,B,C;
A.INP();
B.INP();
C=A+B;
C.OUT();
}
```

To compile and Test

```
gcc –c a.c
g++ -c RAT.C
g++ RAT.o a.o

./a.out
1 2
2 3
7/6
```

Similarly, if we want a C++ function to be used in a C program, first we have to mention that C++ function is having external linkage for C language.

An example C++ file

```
extern "C" int abs(int x)
{
 return (x<0?-x:x);
}
```

Header file "y.h"

```
#ifdef __cplusplus
extern "C"
#endif
int abs(int x);
```

C file "z.c"

```
#include<stdio.h>
#include "y.h"
int main()
{
 int p=-19;

printf("%d\n", abs(p) );
}
```

To create executable file, continue the following manner.

```
gcc –c z.c
g++ -c y.C
g++ -o aa z.o y.o
./aa
```

You can declare at most one function of an overloaded set as extern "C" because only one C function can have a given name. If you need to access overloaded functions from C, you can write C++ wrapper functions with different names as the following example demonstrates.

File having C++ overloaded functions (yy.C)

```
 int abs(int x)
{
 return (x<0?-x:x);
}
 float abs(float x)
{
 return (x<0?-x:x);
}
 double abs(double x)
{
 return (x<0?-x:x);
}

extern "C" int abs_int(int x){ return abs(x); }
extern "C" float abs_float(float x){ return abs(x); }
extern "C" double abs_double(double x){ return abs(x); }
```

Header file "yy.h" contains

```
#ifdef __cplusplus
extern "C"
#endif
int abs_int(int x);
double abs_float(float x);
float abs_double(double x);
```

The c program which calls the functions in C++ program contains the following.

```
#include<stdio.h>
#include "yy.h"
int main()
{
 int p=-19;
float x=1.212;
double y=-1.222222;

printf("%d %f %lf\n", abs_int(p), abs_float(x), abs_double(y) );
}
```

To create executable file, continue the following manner.

```
gcc –c zz.c
g++ -c yy.C
g++ -o aaa zz.o yy.o
./aaa
```

We may also need wrapper functions to call template functions because template functions cannot be declared as extern "C": The above "yy.C" C++ program can be changed as follows to achieve this.

```
template<class A>
 A abs(A x)
{
 return (x<0?-x:x);
}

extern "C" int abs_int(int x){ return abs(x); }
extern "C" float abs_float(float x){ return abs(x); }
extern "C" double abs_double(double x){ return abs(x); }
```

As usual, compile this C++ program separately and C program separately and link using g++.

The following examples, explains how to pass C++ class type of objects/addresses to C functions.

The following header file "RAT.h" has to be included in both C and C++ programs. In C++ program if this header is included, class RAT will be defined and at the same time function f() will declared as external. Similarly, if this header file is included in a C program, then class RAT will not get defined. Rather, an incomplete declaration of structure with the same name RAT gets defined. In addition, declarations of the functions f(), XYZ() are included.

We did write extern "C" functions in C++ that access class RAT objects and call them from C code. This became possible as unlike C++, C will not distinguish pointers whether they are of class RAT type or struct RAT type. Thus, it became possible to send class RAT type of object to C function. However, this is not a good programming practice though.

```
#ifndef RAT_H
 #define RAT_H

 #ifdef __cplusplus

class RAT
{
 int p,q;
public:
void INP(){ cin>>p>>q;}
void OUT(){ cout<<p<<"\t"<<q<<endl;}
};


 #else
  typedef
    struct RAT
      RAT;
 #endif

 #ifdef __cplusplus
 extern "C" {
 #endif

 #if defined(__STDC__) || defined(__cplusplus)
  extern void f(RAT *);
  extern void XYZ(RAT *);
 #else
  extern void f();        /* K&R style */
```

```
 extern void XYZ();
#endif

#ifdef __cplusplus
}
#endif

#endif /*RAT_H*/
```

The C++ program file (pp.C)

```
#include<iostream.h>
#include "RAT.h"

void XYZ(RAT *P)
{
P->INP();
P->OUT();
}

int main()
{
 RAT A;
f(&A);
}
```

The C program file (pq.c)

```
#include "RAT.h"
void f( RAT *A)
{
 XYZ(A);
}
```

To compile and run the program, do execute the following commands.

```
g++ -c pp.C
gcc –c pq.c
g++ -o pp  pp.o pq.o
./pp
```

18.8 Better C coding practice

There are many rules, practices and suggestions exists for C coding. Better coding practices will help in improving readability, understandability of the code developed.

For example, some people recommend creating abstract data types of the form:

```
typedef struct T *T;
```

Then values of the abstract type can be declared as:

```
T t;
```

making t look like an object in its own right. However this obscures the fact that t is a reference to an object, rather than an object itself. This also prevents passing t by value rather than by reference.

Thus in the following paragraphs we shall explore better coding practices.

Comments

Comments can add immensely to the readability of a program, but used heavily or poorly placed they can render good code completely incomprehensible. It is far better to err on the side of too few comments rather than too many - at least then people can find the code! Also, if your code needs a comment to be understood, then you should look for ways to rewrite the code to be clearer. And comments that aren't there won't get out of date. (An inaccurate or misleading comment hurts more than a good comment helps! Be sure that your comments stay right.)

Good places to put comments are:

- a broad overview at the beginning of a module
- data structure definitions
- global variable definition
- at the beginning of a function
- tricky steps within a function

If you do something weird, a comment to explain why can save future generations from wondering what drug you were on and where to get it. If you do something clever, brag about it. Not only will this inflate your ego, but it will also subtly tip off others as to where to look first for bugs. Finally, avoid fancy layout or decoration.

```
/* single line comments look like this */

/*
* Important single line comments look like multi-line comments.
*/

/*
 * Multi line comments look like this.  Put the opening and closing
 * comment sequences on lines by themselves.  Use complete sentences
* with proper English grammar, capitalization, and punctuation.
*/

/* but you don't need to punctuate or capitalize one-liners */
```

The opening / of all comments should be indented to the same level as the code to which it applies, for example:

```
if (fubar()) {

    ...
}
```

If you put a comment on the same line as code, set it off from the code with a few tabs. Don't continue such a comment across multiple lines. For example:

```
printf("hi\n");          /* hello revisited */
```

In fact, try to avoid such comments altogether - if it`s not important enough to warrant a complete sentence, does it really need to be said?

The size of the comment should be proportional to the size of the code that it refers to. Consequently, properties of code that can fit within a single 24-line screen should not be commented unless they are not obvious. By contrast, even obvious global properties and invariants may need to be made explicit. This doesn't have to be through comments, though. The assert() macro is an excellent ``executable comment''.

Line Breaking

Lines should be limited to 80 characters in width, so as to fit into standard terminal displays without wrapping. How you choose to break your lines and indent the subsequent continued lines is left up to you. One method that you might like to use is to attempt to break lines before operators (particularly the logical boolean operators if the statement contains them) and half-indent the subsequent line by an additional two spaces. Whichever way you choose, please try to be consistent.

Whitespace

Whitespace should be used to form the statement into as close an approximation to english as possible. This means that whitespace should be used between binary operators and operands, between conditionals and their conditions ('if' is not a function), and after commas used to seperate parameters. Note that whitespace between function names and parameters is discouraged, as the function call is considered an indivisible unit. This rule can be bent in the interests of shorter lines, as long as the ultimate aim of keeping a line readable is kept in mind.

While the authors will not attempt to perscribe use of empty lines in code, typically empty lines should be used to seperate logical sections (like paragraphs in english text). It is possible to overuse empty lines to make less code fit on a screen, hence making code more difficult to read.

Brace Placement

Opening braces should be on the same line as the conditional or declarative statement that the brace is a part of. Closing braces should be on a line by themselves. This style was adopted to try and keep code length to a minimum, while retaining reasonable readability. The authors realise that not everyone agrees with this position, but we don't care :o). Seriously, there is probably no objective reasoning to prefer this to a brace-on-next-line style, so we chose the one we're most comfortable with.

Another issue in brace placement is whether to brace single statements in a conditional. While the authors recommend bracing all statements in conditionals, as it makes adding more statements to it later easier and less error-prone, they see this as somewhat less important than other issues

Source File Organization

Use the following organization for source files:

includes of system headers

includes of local headers

type and constant definitions

global variables

functions

A reasonable variation might be to have several repetitions of the last three sections.

Within each section, order your functions in a ``bottom up'' manner - defining functions before their use. The benefit of avoiding redundant (hence error-prone) forward declarations outweighs the minor irritation of having to jump to the bottom of the file to find the main functions.

In header files, use the following organization:

type and constant definitions

external object declarations

external function declarations

Again, several repetitions of the above sequence might be reasonable. Every object and function declaration must be preceded by the keyword extern.

Also, avoid having nested includes.

Declarations and Types

Avoid exporting names outside of individual C source files; i.e., declare as static every function and global variable that you possibly can.

When declaring a global function or variable in a header file, use an explicit extern. For functions, provide a full ANSI C prototype. For example:

```
extern int errno;
extern void free(void *);
```

Do not use parameter names in function prototypes - you are increasing the risk of a name collision with a previously-defined macro, e.g.:

```
#define fileptr stdin
...
extern int foo(FILE *fileptr);
```

Instead, doc ument parameter names only as necessary using comments:

```
extern void veccopy(double * /*dst*/, double * /*src*/, size_t);
```

Why the extern? It is OK to *declare* an object any number of times, but in all the source files there can be only one definition. The extern says ``This is only a declaration.'' (A definition is something that actually allocates and initializes storage for the object.)

Header files should *never* contain object definitions, only type definitions and object declarations. This is why we require extern to appear everywhere except on the real definition.

In function prototypes, try not to use const. Although the ANSI standard makes some unavoidable requirements in the standard library, we don't need to widen the problem any further. What we are trying to avoid here is a phenomenon known as ``const poisoning'', where the appearance of const in some prototype forces you to go through your code and add const all over the place.

Don't rely on C's implicit int typing; i.e., don't say:

```
extern foo;
say:
extern int foo;
```

Similarly, don't declare a function with implicit return type. If it returns a meaningful integer value, declare it int. If it returns no meaningful value, declare it void. (By the way, the C standard requires you to declare main() as returning int.)

Provide typedefs for all struct and union types, and put them before the type declarations. Creating the typedef eliminates the clutter of extra struct and union keywords, and makes your structures look like first-class types in the language. Putting the typedefs before the type declarations allows them to be used when declaring circular types. It is also nice to have a list of all new reserved words up front.

```
typedef struct Foo Foo;
typedef struct Bar Bar;

struct Foo {
    Bar *bar;
};

struct Bar {
    Foo *foo;
};
```

This give a particularly nice scheme of exporting opaque objects in header files.

```
In header.h:
typedef struct Foo Foo;
In source.c:

#include "header.h"

struct Foo { .. };
```

Then a client of header.h can declare a

```
Foo *x;
```

but cannot get at the contents of a Foo. In addition, the user cannot declare a plain (non pointer) Foo, and so is forced to go through whatever allocation routines you provide. We strongly encourage this modularity technique.

If an enum is intended to be declared by the user (as opposed to just being used as names for integer values), give it a typedef too. Note that the typedef has to come **after** the enum declaration.

Don't mix any declarations in with type definitions; i.e., don't say:

```
struct foo {
    int x;
} object;

Also don't say:
typedef struct {
    int x;
} type;
```

Declare each field of a structure on a line by itself. Think about the order of the fields. Try to keep related fields grouped. Within groups of related fields, pick some uniform scheme for organizing them, for example alphabetically or by frequency of use. When all other considerations are equal, place larger fields first, as C's alignment rules may then permit the compiler to save space by not introducing "holes" in the structure layout.

Use of the Preprocessor

For constants, consider using :

```
enum { Red = 0xF00, Blue = 0x0F0, Green = 0x00F };
static const float pi = 3.14159265358;
```

instead of #defines, which are rarely visible in debuggers.

Macros should avoid side effects. If possible, mention each argument exactly once. Fully parenthesize all arguments. When the macro is an expression, parenthesize the whole macro body. If the macro is the inline expansion of some function, the name of the macro should be the same as that of the function, except fully capitalized. When continuing a macro across multiple lines with backslashes, line up the backslashes way over on the right edge of the screen to keep them from cluttering up the code.

```
#define OBNOXIOUS(X)                              \
    (save = (X),                        \
     dosomethingwith(X),                \
     (X) = save)
```

Try to write macros so that they are syntactically expressions. C's comma and conditional operators are particularly valuable for this. If you absolutely cannot write the macro as an expression, enclose the macro body in do { ... } while (0). This way the expanded macro plus a trailing semicolon becomes a syntactic statement.

If you think you need to use #ifdef, consider restricting the dependent code to a single module. For instance, if you need to have different code for Unix and MS_DOS, instead of having #ifdef UNIX and #ifdef dos everywhere, try to have files unix.c and dos.c with identical interfaces. If you can't avoid them, make sure to document the end of the conditional code:

```
#ifdef FUBAR
    some code
#else
    other code
#endif /* FUBAR */
```

Some sanctioned uses of the preprocessor are :

- Commenting out code: Use #if 0.
- Using GNU C extensions: Surround with #ifdef __GNUC__.
- Testing numerical limits: Feel free to conditionalize on the constants in the standard headers <float.h> and <limits.h>.

If you use an #if to test whether some condition holds that you know how to handle, but are too lazy to provide code for the alternative, protect it with #error, like this:

```
#include <limits.h>

#if INT_MAX > UCHAR_MAX
enum { Foo = UCHAR_MAX + 1, Bar, Baz, Barf };
#else
#error "need int wider than char"
#endif
```

Naming Conventions

Names should be meaningful in the **application** domain, not the **implementation** domain. This makes your code clearer to a reader who is familiar with the problem you're trying to solve, but is not familiar with your particular way of solving it. Also, you may want the implementation to change some day. Note that well-structured code is layered internally, so your implementation domain is also the application domain for lower levels.

Names should be chosen to make sense when your program is read. Thus, all names should be parts of speech which will make sense when used with the language's syntactic keywords. Variables should be noun clauses. Boolean variables should be named for the meaning of their "true" value. Procedures (functions called for their side-effects) should be named for what they do, not how they do it. Function names should reflect what they *return*, and boolean-valued functions of an object should be named for the property their true value implies about the object. Functions are used in expressions, often in things like if's, so they need to read appropriately. For instance,

```
if (checksize(s))
```

is unhelpful because we can't deduce whether checksize returns true on error or non-error; instead

```
if (validsize(s))
```

makes the point clear and makes a future mistake in using the routine less likely.

Longer names contain more information than short names, but extract a price in readability. Compare the following examples:

```
for (elementindex = 0; elementindex < DIMENSION; ++elementindex)
printf("%d\n", element[elementindex]);

for (i = 0; i < DIMENSION; ++i)
printf("%d\n", element[i]);
```

In the first example, you have to read more text before you can recognize the for-loop idiom, and then you have to do still more hard work to parse the loop body. Since clarity is our goal, a name should contain only the information that it has to.

Carrying information in a name is unnecessary if the declaration and use of that name is constrained within a small scope. Local variables are usually being used to hold intermediate values or control information for some computation, and as such have little importance in themselves. For example, for array indices names like i, j, and k are not just acceptable, they are desirable.

Similarly, a global variable named x would be just as inappropriate as a local variable named elementindex. By definition, a global variable is used in more than one function or module (otherwise it would be static or local), so all of it's uses will not be visible at once. The name has to explain the use of the variable on its own. Nevertheless there is still a readability penalty for long names: casefold is better than case_fold_flag_set_by_main.

In short, follow to make variable name size proportional to scope:

length(name(variable)) ~ log(countlines(scope(variable)))

Use some consistent scheme for naming related variables. If the top of memory is called physlim, should the bottom be membase? Consider the suffix -max to denote an inclusive limit, and -lim to denote an exclusive limit.

Don't take this too far, though. Avoid ``Hungarian''-style naming conventions which encode type information in variable names. They may be systematic, but they'll screw you if you ever need to change the type of a variable. If the variable has a small scope, the type will be visible in the declaration, so the annotation is useless clutter. If the variable has a large scope, the code should modular against a change in the variable's type. In general, I think any deterministic algorithm for producing variable names will have the same effect.

Nevertheless, if the type name is a good **application-domain** description of the variable, then use it, or a suitable abbreviation. For instance, when implementing an ADT I would write:

```
/*
 * Execute registered callback and close socket.
 */
void
chan_close(Chan *chan)    /* No better name for parameter than "chan" */
{
(*chan->deactivate)(chan->arg);
(void) close(chan->fd);
}
```

but when using the ADT I would write:

```
  /*
* Log a message when the watched-for event happens.
*/
struct Monitor {
int (*trigger)(void *region);
  void *region;
  char *message;
  Chan *log;          /* describes how Chan is used */
};
```

There are weaknesses in C for large-scale programming - there is only a single, flat name scope level greater than the module level. Therefore, libraries whose implementations have more than one module can't guard their inter-module linkage from conflicting with any other global identifiers. The best solution to this problem is to give each library a short prefix that it prepends to all global identifiers.

Abbreviations or acronyms can shorten things up, but may not offer compelling savings over short full words. When a name has to consist of several words (and it often doesn't), separate words by underscores, not by BiCapitalization. It will look better to English-readers (the underscore is the space-which-is-not-a-space). Capitalization is reserved for distinguishing syntactic namespaces.

C has a variety of separately maintained namespaces, and distinguishing the names by capitalization improves the odds of C's namespaces and scoping protecting you from collisions while allowing you to use the same word across different spaces. C provides separate namespaces for:

Preprocessor Symbols

Since macros can be dangerous, follow tradition fully capitalize them, otherwise following the conventions for function or variable names.

```
#define NUSERTASKS 8
#define ISNORMAL(S) ((S)->state == Normal)
```

Any fully capitalized names can be regarded as fair game for #ifdef, although perhaps not for #if.

Labels

Limited to function scope, so give it a short name, lowercase. Give meaningful name such that the corresponding goto statement can be read aloud, and name it for **why** you go there, not what you do when you get there. For instance,

```
goto bounds_error;
```

is more helpful than

```
goto restore_pointer;
```

Structure, Union, or Enumeration Tags

Having these as separate namespaces creates an artificial distinction between structure, union, and enumeration types and ordinary scalar types. i.e. you can't simplify a struct type to a scalar type by replacing

```
struct Foo { long bar; };
```

with

```
typedef long Foo;
```

since you still have the "struct" keyword everywhere, even when the contents are not being examined. The useless "struct" keywords also clutter up the code. Therefore we advocate creating a typedef mirror of all struct tags:

```
typedef struct Foo Foo;
```

Capitalize the tag name to match the typedef name.

Structure or Union Members

Each structure or union has a separate name space for its members, so there is no need to add a distinguishing prefix. When used in expressions they will follow a variable name, so make them lowercase to make the code look nice. If the type of a member is an ADT, the name of the type is often a good choice for the name of the variable (but in lowercase). You do **not** prefix the member names, as in:

```
struct timeval { unsigned long tv_sec; long tv_usec; };
```

for they are already in a unique namespace.

Ordinary Identifiers

all other ordinary identifiers (declared in ordinary declarators, or as enumerations constants).

Typedef Names

Capitalized, with no _t suffix or other cutesy thing to say ``I'm a type'' - we can see that from it's position in the declaration! (Besides, all names ending with _t are reserved by POSIX.) The capitalization is needed to distinguish type names from variable names - often both want to use the same application-level word.

Enumeration Constants

Capitalize. If absolutely necessary, consider a prefix.

```
enum Fruit { Apples, Oranges, Kumquats };
```

Function Names

Lowercase. If they are static (and most should be), make the name short and sweet. If they are externally-visibly, try to give then a prefix unique to the module or library.

Function Parameters

Since they will be used as variables in the function body, use the conventions for variables.

Variables

Lowercase.

Lastly, develop some standard idioms to make names automatic. For instance:

```
int i, j, k;   /* generic indices */
char *s, *t;           /* string pointers */
char *buf; /* character array */
double x, y, z;       /* generic floating-point */
size_t n, m, size;   /* results of sizeof or arguments to malloc */
Foo foo, *pfoo, **ppfoo;    /* sometimes a little hint helps */
```

Indentation and Layout

Try to stay inside the mythical 79 column limit. If you can't, look for a tasteful place to break the line (there are some ideas below). Avoid ideas that would lead to indenting that doesn't align on a tab stop. If worst comes to worst, grit your teeth and tolerate the long line.

Use real tab characters for indenting. Tabs are always 8 spaces. This policy has the following advantages :

- It doesn't require a fancy editor; not everyone uses emacs.
- It is easy to write miscellaneous program text processing tools that count leading tabs.
- It encourages you to break deeply nested code into functions.

If you use short names and write simple code, your horizontal space goes a long way even with tab indenting.

Use the One True Brace Style (1TBS) as seen in K&R. The following quotation from Henry Spencer's *Ten Commandments for C Programmers* says it better than I can:

Thou shalt make thy program's purpose and structure clear to thy fellow man by using the One True Brace Style, even if thou likest it not, for thy creativity is better used in solving problems than in creating beautiful new impediments to understanding.

- The Eighth Commandment

The rationale behind this brace style, straight from the horse's (Dennis') mouth, is that the braces are just line noise to make the compiler happy, and so don't deserve to be specially set apart. (The GNU style is a particularly bad offender in this regard!) Also, the 1TBS conserves vertical space, which is important for those of us working on 24 line displays. (It also helps avoid excessive eye movement on big displays.)

Purists point out that 1TBS is inconsistent since it has one style for statements and another for functions. That's okay since functions are special anyway (you can't nest them). It's also good to know that with most editors you can get to the top of the current function by searching backward for the regexp ^{.

Avoid unnecessary curly braces, but if one branch of an if is braced, then the other should be too, even if it is only a single line. If an inner nested block is braced, then the outer blocks should be too.

Some examples:

```
if (foo == 7) {
    bar();
} else if (foo == 9) {
    barf();
    bletch();
} else {
    boondoggle();
    frobnicate();
}

do {
    for (i = 0; i < n; ++i)
            a[i] = 0;
    plugh();
    xyzzy();
} while (!blurf());
```

In switch statements, be sure every case ends with either a break, continue, return, or /* fall through */ comment. Especially don't forget to put a break on the last case of a switch statement. If you do, I promise someone will forget to add one someday when adding new cases.

```
switch (phase) {
case New:
    printf("don't do any coding tonight\n");
    break;
case Full:
    printf("beware lycanthropes\n");
    break;
case Waxing:
case Waning:
    printf("the heavens are neutral\n");
    break;
default:
    /*
     * Include occasional sanity checks in your code.
     */
    fprintf(stderr, "and here you thought this couldn't happen!\n");
    abort();
}
```

This last example also illustrates how to handle labels, including case labels and goto labels: put each label on a line by itself, and outdent it by a tab stop. However, if outdenting a label would take it all the way out to the left edge of the screen, insert a leading space.

Use goto sparingly. Two harmless places to use it are to break out of a multilevel loop, or to jump to common function exit code. (Often these are the same places.)

Lay out your functions like this:

```
/*
 * Optional comment describing the function.
 */
type
name(args)
{
    declarations

    code
}
```

It is important that the name of the function be in the first column of text with no indentation. Some text processing utilities (e.g. etags) rely on this to find function definitions. Even if you don't use such tools, it's extremely helpful to know that the regular expression ^*name* matches the single definition of the function.

Note that we will *not* be using old-style function definitions where the args are declared outside the parameter list. Include a blank line between the local variable declarations and the code. Also feel free to include other blank lines, particularly to separate major blocks of code.

Multiple declarations can go on one line, but if the line gets too long don't try to continue it in some fancy way, just start a new declaration on the next line. Avoid declarations in all but the most complex inner blocks. Avoid initializations of automatic variable in declarations, since they can be mildly disconcerting when stepping through code with a debugger. Don't declare external objects inside functions, declare them at file scope. Finally, don't try to go into denial over C's ``declaration by example'' syntax. Say:

```
char *p;
not:
char* p;
```

In the long run, such fights with the language will only cause you grief. (One of the reason's Stroustrup's original C++ book was practically unreadable was because he was constantly fighting with C.)

Use spaces around keywords. Use spaces around binary operators, except . and ->, for they are morally equivalent to array subscripts, and the ``punctuation'' operator ','. Don't use spaces around unary operators, except sizeof and casts. Example:

```
x = -y + z + sizeof (Foo) + bar();
```

Note that function call is a unary operator, so don't use a space between a function name and the opening parenthesis of the arguments. The reason for making an exception for sizeof is that it is a syntactic keyword, not a function. These rules lead to:

```
if (something)
for syntactic keywords, and
foo(something)
for functions. Don't parenthesize things unnecessarily; say
return 7;
not
return (7);
and especially not
return(7);
```

Remember, return is the exact antonym of function call! The parsing precedence of the bitwise operations (&, |, ^, ~) can be surprising. Always use full parentheses around these operators.

Some C style guides take this a bit too far, though. One author went as far as to suggest that C programmers should rely on * and / bind more tightly than + and -, and parenthesize the rest. This is a good way to write Lisp code, but it makes C look ugly. A C programmer should be able to recognize its idioms and be able to parse code like:

```
while (*s++ = *t++)
    ;
```

If an expression gets too long to fit in a line, break it next to a binary operator. Put the operator at the beginning of the next line to emphasize that it is continued from the previous line. Don't add additional indenting to the continued line. This strategy leads to particularly nice results when breaking up complicated conditional expressions:

```
if (x == 2 || x == 3 || x == 5 || x == 7
|| x == 11 || x == 13 || x == 17 || x == 19)
    printf("x is a small prime\n");
```

This example also illustrates why you shouldn't add additional indenting when continuing a line - in this case, it could get confused with the condition body. Avoid breakpoints that will give the reader false notions about operator precedence, like this:

```
if (x == 2 || x > 10
&& x < 12 || x == 19)
```

If you're breaking an expression across more than two lines, try to use the same kind of breakpoint for each line. Finally, if you're getting into really long expressions, your code is probably in need of a rewrite.

Avoid sloppiness. Decide what your style is and follow it precisely. I often see code like this:

```
struct foo
{
    int baz ;
    int  barf;
    char * x, *y;
};
```

All those random extra spaces make me wonder if the programmer was even paying attention!

The indent utility can automatically check most of these indentation conventions. The style given here corresponds to the indent options

```
-bap -bad -nbc -bs -ci0 -di1 -i8
```

which can be specified in a file named indent.pro in your home directory. Note that indent tends to mess up typedef-defined identifiers unless they are explicitly given on the command line.

Expressions and Statements

In C, assignments are expressions, not statements. This allows multiple assignment

```
a = b = c = 1;
```

and assignment within expressions

```
if (!(bp = malloc(sizeof (Buffer)))) {
    perror("malloc");
    abort();
}
```

This capability can sometimes allow concise code, but at other times it can obscure important procedure calls and updates to variables. Use good judgement.

The C language lacks a true boolean type, therefore its logic operations (! == > < >= <=) and tests (in the conditional operator ?: and the if, while, do, and for statements) have some interesting semantics. Every boolean test is an implicit comparison against zero (0). However, zero is not a simple concept. It represents:

- the integer zero for all integral types
- the floating point 0.0 (positive or negative)
- the nul character
- the null pointer

In order to make your intentions clear, explicitly show the comparison with zero for all scalars, floating-point numbers, and characters. This gives us the tests

```
(i == 0)        (x != 0.0)        (c == '\0')
instead of
(i)     (!x)              (c)
```

An exception is made for pointers, since 0 is the only language-level representation for the null pointer. (The symbol NULL is *not* part of the core language - you have to include a special header file to get it defined.) In short, pretend that C has an actual boolean type which is returned by the logical operators and expected by the test constructs, and pretend that the null pointer is a synonym for false.

Write infinite loops as:

```
for (;;)
    ...
not
while (1)
    ...
```

The former is idiomatic among C programmers, and is more visually distinctive.

Feel free to use a for loop where some of the parts are empty. The purpose of for is to centralize all loop control code in one place. If you're thinking ``for each of these things, we have to do something,'' use a for loop. If a for statement gets too long to fit in a line, turn it into a while. If your loop control is that complicated, it probably isn't what for is for (pun intended).

Never return from the function main(), explicitly use exit(). They are no longer equivalent - there is an important distinction when using the atexit() feature with objects declared locally to main(). Don't worry about the details, just use this fact to program consistently. This does spoil the potential for calling main() recursively, which is usually a silly thing to do.

Functions

Functions should be short and sweet. If a function won't fit on a single screen, it's probably too long. Don't be afraid to break functions down into smaller helper functions. If they are static to the module an optimizing compiler can inline them again, if necessary. Helper functions can also be reused by other functions.

However, sometimes it is hard to break things down. Since functions don't nest, variables have to be communicated through function arguments or global variables. Don't create huge interfaces to enable a decomposition that is just not meant to be.

Further Reading

There is a wonderful Web page on Programming in C which features such goodies as Rob Pike's Notes on Programming in C, Henry Spencer's The Ten Commandments for C Programmers, and the ANSI C Rationale. These are all required reading.

18.9 Conclusions

This chapter explains about the compiling C program's in Linux/Unix environment. The compilation stages and their objectives are explained in a step by step fashion. Also, multi file programming is also explained. At the end, how a "c++" program can be compiled under Linux/Unix is also explained. Also, how C, C++, programs can be mixed also explained in a step by step fashion. Moreover, how actually main() is initiated and how Linux OS coordinates the same is a special dealing in this chapter.

19 GNU Debugger

19.1 Introduction

GNU Debugger mainly concerned with debugging of program's of some languages run on Linux operating system. This debugger consists of gdb command and commands that run with gdb shell. The gdb command concerns with what is to be debugged and shell commands with how it is to be debugged.

19.1.1 Bugs And Debugging

A bug is an error. Debugging means detecting the bugs. Bugs occur at specification or design or coding times. If a program is incorrectly specified, inevitably fail to perform as required. Bugs that occur at design time lead to incorrect results. Bugs that occur at coding time are detected and removing using many methods. These methods include debuggers and some system defined functions and displaying of messages at runtime.

Normally, We debug program's by including printf statements in the code as and when require. Apart from this, there are three types of debugging is carried out.

- First, we can do debugging using constants defined by # define.
- Second, debugging can be done by system defined macros. Macros and their description is as follows :

Macro	Description
LINE	A decimal constant representing the current line number.
FILE	A string representing the current file name.
DATE	A string of the form "Mmm:dd:yyyy", the current date.
TIME	A string of the form "hh:mm:ss", the current time.

- Third is the debuggers provided and used with Linux. They are gdb, sdb and dbx. There are front ends for gdb (such as xxgdb, tgdb, ddd)which makes it more user friendly.

19.2 Debugging Using gdb

GDB, a short name of gnu debugger is a free software protected by GNU General Public License (GPL). GDB allows user to see what is happening when a program is getting executed.

GDB can do the following things.

- Start your program, specifying anything that might affect its behavior.
- Make your program stop on specified conditions.
- Examine what has happened, when your program has stopped.
- Change things in your program, so that you can experiment with correcting effects of one bug and learn about others.

GDB can be also used to debug Fortran programs if Fortran compiler is loaded. GDB is invoked with a shell command gdb. Once started, it reads commands from the terminal until we press quit command.

We can run gdb command without options. But in general we run it as follows.

gdb program

Here program is the name of the executable file to be debugged.

In order to run a file using gdb, the program must be compiled with –g option. This option makes debugging information attached to original executable file. If we want to know more details about gdb, we can run the same with -help option as shown below.

```
gdb -help
```

This command displays the following output.

This is the GNU debugger. Usage:

```
gdb [options] [executable-file [core-file or process-id]]
gdb [options] --args executable-file [inferior-arguments ...]
```

Options:

--args	Arguments after executable-file are passed to inferior
--[no]async	Enable (disable) asynchronous version of CLI
-b BAUDRATE	Set serial port baud rate used for remote debugging.
--batch	Exit after processing options.
--cd=DIR	Change current directory to DIR.
--command=FILE	Execute GDB commands from FILE.
--core=COREFILE	Analyze the core dump COREFILE.
--pid=PID	Attach to running process PID.
--dbx	DBX compatibility mode.
--directory=DIR	Search for source files in DIR.
--epoch	Output information used by epoch emacs-GDB interface.
--exec=EXECFILE	Use EXECFILE as the executable.

```
--fullname        Output information used by emacs-GDB interface.

--help            Print this message.

--interpreter=INTERP

                  Select a specific interpreter / user interface

--interpreter=INTERP

                  Select a specific interpreter / user interface

--mapped          Use mapped symbol files if supported on this system.

--nw              Do not use a window interface.

--nx              Do not read .gdbinit file.

--quiet           Do not print version number on startup.

--readnow         Fully read symbol files on first access.

--se=FILE         Use FILE as symbol file and executable file.

--symbols=SYMFILE  Read symbols from SYMFILE.

--tty=TTY         Use TTY for input/output by the program being debugged.

--version         Print version information and then exit.

-w                Use a window interface.

--write           Set writing into executable and core files.

--xdb             XDB compatibility mode.
```

Example 1

Let us consider a simple program (ex1.c) and see how we can debug using gdb.

```
#include<stdio.h>
int main()
```

```
{
 printf("Hello How are you?\n");
return 23;
}
```

First compile the same using -g option. That is, execute the following command.

gc c -g ex1.c

In order to debug the resultant executable file, execute the following command which gives many details before displaying gdb prompt (i.e. (gdb))

```
gcc a.out
GNU gdb Red Hat Linux (5.3post-0.20021129.18rh)

Copyright 2003 Free Software Foundation, Inc.
GDB is free software, covered by the GNU General Public License, and you are
welcome to change it and/or distribute copies of it under certain conditions.
Type "show copying" to see the conditions.
There is absolutely no warranty for GDB. Type "show warranty" for details.
This GDB was configured as "i386-redhat-linux-gnu"...
(gdb) r

Starting program: /root/nav/a.out
Hello How are You?
Program exited with code 023.
(gdb) q
```

If we want to start gdb and do not interested to see all those messages then we can start gdb with **-q option** such as:

```
gdb -q a.out

(gdb) r

Starting program: /root/a.out

Hello How are You?

Program exited with code 023.

(gdb) q
```

19.2.1 Commands which can be used at gdb prompt

Break :

Break command is used to set a breakpoint at any line of a file or any function.

Synopsis :

Break [file :] function

Here file is name of file and function is the name of function where breakpoint is needed. If we want a break point at a line. The execution stops just before that instruction. If we give a break point for a function, the execution stops at the first statement of function.

Run : Run command is used to run the program being debugged. If we type this command while program is being debugged then we are asked if we want to do it from the beginning.

Synopsis :

Run [arglist]

Arglist is the list of command line arguments. It is optional. The short form of run is 'r'

Back Trace :

Back trace command is used for displaying program stack. This display the runtime stack of program.

Synopsis :

bt :

This command enables us to know the functions and their information that are currently active. bt is short form of back t race.

Print :

Print command is used to display the values of variables and expressions at the moment of program.

Synopsis:

Print Expr:

Expression might be a single variable or an expression in general. If we give name of variable proceeded by '&' symbol for expr then the address where the value is stored displayed. The short form of print is p.

Continue:

Continue command continues the execution of a program from a break point until the next break pointy or end of the program.

Synopsis:

Continue:

Continue helps in flow of program from break point to break point enabling the programmers detect the points where bug is present. Short form of continue is C.

Next :

Next command is used to executed the next line of program being debugged. It step-over any function calls in the line.

Synopsis :

Next :

This command steps over any function calls in the line it treats the line with function call as a single instruction. Short form is in.

Step :

Step command is same as next except that it steps into any function that occurs in the line.

Synopsis:

Step command is same as next except that it steps into any function that occurs in the line.

Synopsis:

Step:

This command helps in tracking even the functions that occur in the line thus making the process of debugging a file much more clearer than with next.

Edit:

Edit helps in finding the line of program where execution was stopped.

Synopsis:

Edit [file :] function

List:

List command types the text of program in the vicinity where it is presently stopped. Function is name of function and file is name of file.

Help:

Help command shows information about command name.

```
Help [name]
```

Here name of command is optional. If it is not given, then the information about gdb commands is displayed.

Quit:

This is used for exiting from gdb.

Synopsis:

```
Quit
```

Short from of quite is q.

Example 2

Consider another example (ex2.c) which takes command line arguments.

```
#include<stdio.h>
int main(int N, char *a[])
{
  int i;
 for(i=0;i<N;i++)
 printf("a[i]\n");
return 23;
}
```

Compile the above program with -g option and then start gdb. That is :

gcc -g ex2.c

gdb -q a.out

(gdb)**r Ram Rao 123**

Starting program: /root/a.out Ram Rao 123

/root/a.out

Ram

Rao

123

Program exited with code 04

(gdb)**q**

If we want, we can write all the commands which we want to give to gdb in a file and then ask gdb to use them while debugging our program. For example, let the file "abc" contains the following gdb commands.

```
break 2
break 3
r Ram Rao 123
next
next
next
next
next
next
next
next
next
next
q
```

Now, start gdb as follows:

```
gdb -q a.out -x abc
```

Example 3

Some other gdb commands are explained using the following example. In the following output of a gdb session, you can see (bold underlined ones) how gdb commands can be used while debugging a program.

Line No. Program Text

```
# include <stdioh>
int isprime (int x)
{
int i;
for (i=2; i <=x/2; i++)
if (x % i = = 0)
return 0;
return 1;
}
int main ( )
{
int I, x;
for (I=1; I< = 3; I ++)
{
printf ("Enter a number")
scanf ("%d",&x);
if (! isprime (x) )
printf ("not a prime number\n")
else
printf (" a prime number")
}
return 0;
}
```

Now the commands are executed for this program gdbex.c at the command prompt.

```
gcc -g gdbex.c

gdb -q a.out

(gdb) r
```

Starting program: /root/a.out.

Enter a number **23**

It is a prime number.

Enter a number **44**

Not a prime number

Enter a number **31**

A prime number

Program is exited with code 060

Here the program is executed until end as it has no break points.

Now we keep breakpoints

(gdb) **break 18**

Breakpoint 1 at OX80483 Fe: file gdbex.c line 18.

Here a breakpoint at; line 18 is created with number 1.

Now turn the program.

(gdb) r

Starting program: /root/a-out

Enter a number **23**

It is a prime

Enter a number **44**

Break point/main ( ) at gdbex.c: 18

18 printf ("not a prime")'

Here it is observed that execution of program stopped at line 18.

We can print the values of variable currently as follows:

(gdb) **print x**

$ 1 = 44

(gdb) **print &x**

$ 2 = (int *) OXFFF ecb 4

Here address of x is displayed

(gdb) print I

$ 3 = 2

(gdb) **print &I**

$ 4 = (int *)) OXbFFF ecbo

In for requires a special mention.

Info command gives information of files when it is being debugged. The information consists of addresses, registers, args, breakpoints, catch points, files functions, local variables, macros, memory and procedures

(gdb) **info locals**

x = 44

i = 2

The above gave information about local variables in the program.

```
(gdb) info registers
eax       0X0         0
ecx       0X0         0
edx       0X0         0
ebx       0X42130a14  1708544020
esp       0XFFFecbo   0XbFFFecb0
ebp       0XbFFFecb8  0XbFFFecb8
esi       0X40015360  1073828704
edc       0X80484sc   134513756
eip       0X80483fe   0X80483fe
e flags   0X243  582
es  0X236  35
ss  0X2b   43
es  Ox2b   43
es  0X2b   43
Fs  0X0    0
Gs  0X33   51
```

The above gave information about values of registers.

(gdb) **info args**
no arguments
this is regarding command line arguments
(gdb) **info functions**
All defined Functions
File gdbex .c
int isprime (int)
Non-debugging symbols
0X08048254 – init
0X0804827C – scanf
the above gave info about functions
(gdb) **info breakpoints**
Num Type Disp Enb AddressWhat
1 breakpoint la y 0X080483Fe in main at gdbex.C;8
breakpoint already hit 1 time.
The above gave information about breakpoints currently active.
(gdb) **info files**
This gives information about files are follows:
Name of targets and file being debugged.
Unix child process.
Using the running image of child process 2077.............

```
Local  execfile
          '/root/a-out', fitype  ELF32-i386
          entry point; 0X80482ac.
          ..........
          ..........
       (gdb) info proc
       process 2077
       cmdline = a.out
       cmd = /root
       exe = /a.out.
       (gdb) list
       13 for (I = 1, I <=3, I + +)
       14 {
       15 printf ("Enter a number");
       16 scanf ("%d", &x)
       17 if (!isprime (x))
       18 printf ("not a prime number");
       19 else
       21 }
       22 }
       Back tracing at this stage is as follows:
       (gdb) bt
       # 0 main (  ) at gdbex. C: 18
       # 1.0X4215574 in_libc_start_main (  )
          from lib/tls/.libc. so.6
       (gdb) break 5
       break point 2 at 0X8048362: File of gdbex.c lines
       (gdb) c
       continuing
       not a prime number
       enter a number 7
       'breakpoint 2, isprime(x=7) at gdbex.c:5
       5 For (i=2; i<=x/2; i ++)
       (gdb) info locals
       i = 1108544020
         contains garbage as it is not get initialized
       (gdb) step
       6 if (x % ==0)
       (gdb) info locals
       i = 2
       i is initialized.
       (gdb) c
```

continuing
is a prime number
program exited with code 0260
This ends the program
(gdb) **delete 1**
(gdb) **delete**
Delete all breakpoints? 1 y or n 2 y
The first deletes a specific
Breakpoint named 1 and second deletes all breakpoints.
(gdb) **break 16**
breakpoint 3 at 0X80483 ds: file gdbex.c, line 10.
(gdb) **step 2**
isprime (x = 23) at gdbex.c:5
5 For (i =, i<=x/2, i ++)
this step made 2 steps forward (one into the function is prime)
(gdb) **c**
continuing
it is prime
break point 3, main ( ) at gdbex.c: 16
16 scan F ("%d", & x);
(gdb) **step**
enter a number 56
17 (Fcl, isprime (x))
(gdb) **next**
18 printf ("not a prime");
her it is observed that next stepper over function is prime in line 17.
(gdb) **c**
enter a number 33
not a prime
program exited with code. 060.
(gdb) **break isprime**
break point 1 at 0X6; File gdbex.c, line 5
(gdb) **r**
starting program: /root/a.out
enter a number 54
breakpoint 1, is prime (x=54) at gdbex.c.5
5 for (i =2; i <=x/2; i ++)
here break point is given for a function
(gdb) **break main**
breakpoint 2 at 0X8048369: File gdbex.c, line 13
(gdb) **r**
starting program: /root/a.out
breakpoint 2 main ( ) at gdbex.c:13
13 For (i =1; i <=3; i ++)

```
(gb) break 5
breakpoint 5, at 0X8048362: File gdbex.c Line 5.
(gdb) delete
delete all breakpoints/y orn) y
(gdb) break 5
breakpoint 1, at 0X8048362: File gdbex.c, line 5
(gdb) r
starting program: /root/a.out
enter a number 34
breakpoint, is prime (x=34) at gdbex.c:5
for (i =2; i <=x/2; i ++)
(gdb) bt
# 0 is prime (x=34) at gdbex..c: 5
# 1 0X0804887 in main ( ) at gdbex.c:17
#2 42015574 in lib_start_main ( )
From /lib/tls/libc.so.6.
```

Example 4

The following program is also taken to explain about how gdb can be used for debugging programs. The example gdb-example.c, is listed below. It is a simple, yet buggy program that we will run under gdb.

```
#include "stdio.h"

void
print_scrambled(char *message)
{
 int i = 3;
 do {
  printf("%c", (*message)+i);
 } while (*++message);
 printf("\n");
}

int
main()
{
 char * bad_message = NULL;
 char * good_message = "Hello, world.";

 print_scrambled(good_message);
 print_scrambled(bad_message);
}
```

```
gcc -g gdb-example.c -o gdb-example
```

The backtrace command produces a list of the function calls, which is known as either a backtrace or a stack trace.

Reading backtraces is fairly straightforward. The data associated with each function call in the list is known as a stack frame. The outermost frame is the initial function that your program started in, and is printed at the bottom of the list. Each frame is given a number (0, 1, 2, etc.). Following the frame number is an associated memory address, which is almost entirely useless and which you can ignore. Then each frame contains the name of the function that was called, its arguments, the name of the file where the function appears, and line number. So, the stack trace for our program says that at line 20 of gdb-example.c in function main, the print_scrambled function was called--and that the program got to line eight of gdb-example.c inside the print_scrambled function.

Getting more information

Getting a backtrace may provide enough information, but it is sometimes helpful to get more information, such as the values of arguments or local variables. Another convenience provided by gdb is listing a small segment of the code around where the program is currently stopped so you can see which statements have been executed and which ones are about to be. The following gdb session demonstrates how to do these things as well as how to switch to previous stack frames using the up command.

```
gdb -q gdb-example
```

This GDB was configured as "i386-redhat-linux-gnu"...Using host libthread_db library "/lib/tls/libthread_db.so.1".

```
(gdb) run

Starting program: /home/newren/examples/gdb-example
Program received signal SIGSEGV, Segmentation fault.
0x0804835b in print_scrambled (message=0x0) at gdb-example.c:8
8         printf("%c", (*message)+i);
(gdb) backtrace
#0  0x0804835b in print_scrambled (message=0x0) at gdb-example.c:8
#1  0x080483c3 in main () at gdb-example.c:20
(gdb) list
3       void
4       print_scrambled(char *message)
5       {
6         int i = 3;
7         do {
8           printf("%c", (*message)+i);
9         } while (*++message);
10        printf("\n");
11      }
12
```

```
(gdb) info locals
i = 3
(gdb) info args
message = 0x0
(gdb) up
#1  0x080483c3 in main () at gdb-example.c:20
20        print_scrambled(bad_message);
(gdb) list
15      {
16        char * bad_message = NULL;
17        char * good_message = "Hello, world.";
18
19        print_scrambled(good_message);
20        print_scrambled(bad_message);
21      }
(gdb) info locals
bad_message = 0x0
good_message = 0x80484a1 "Hello, world."
(gdb) info args
No arguments.
(gdb) quit
The program is running.  Exit anyway? (y or n) y
```

From the gdb output, it is fairly clear that the list, info locals, and info args commands get information about the currently selected stack frame. Besides using the up command to go choose a previous frame, you can also use the down command to choose a later one or use the frame command (with a numeric argument) to choose which stack frame to switch to.

Walking through the program

gdb can also allow you to walk through the program while it is running so that you can trace its steps carefully. The following gdb session illustrates this, using the break, print, next, and step commands.

Example 5

```
gdb -q gdb-example
```

This GDB was configured as "i386-redhat-linux-gnu"...Using host libthread_db library "/lib/tls/libthread_db.so.1".

```
(gdb) break main
```

Breakpoint 1 at 0x804839c: file gdb-example.c, line 16.

```
(gdb) run
```

```
Starting program: /home/newren/examples/gdb-example
Breakpoint 1, main () at gdb-example.c:16
16      char * bad_message = NULL;
(gdb) print bad_message
$1 = 0x8048410 "U\211%G%@VS"
(gdb) next
17      char * good_message = "Hello, world.";
(gdb) print bad_message
$2 = 0x0
(gdb) next
19      print_scrambled(good_message);
(gdb) next
Khoor/#zruog$
20      print_scrambled(bad_message);
(gdb) step
print_scrambled (message=0x0) at gdb-example.c:6
6       int i = 3;
(gdb) step
8         printf("%c", (*message)+i);
(gdb) step
Program received signal SIGSEGV, Segmentation fault.
0x0804835b in print_scrambled (message=0x0) at gdb-example.c:8
8         printf("%c", (*message)+i);
(gdb) print (*message)+i
Cannot access memory at address 0x0
(gdb) quit
The program is running.  Exit anyway? (y or n) y
```

The break command sets a breakpoint--a location in the program where gdb should stop when it gets to there. Breakpoints can be set at the beginning of a function or at specific lines in program file. There are many things that can be done with breakpoints, such as making them conditional or temporary. In this example, a common and simple usage case was shown that had gdb stop at the beginning of the main function.

The next and step commands were used to make gdb move forward in the program. For statements that do not involve functions, the next and step commands are identical and merely make gdb execute one statement. For statements that involve a function, however, the two commands are different. next tells gdb to execute the entire function, while step tells gdb to move inside the function.

The print command displays the value of variables or expressions. In the example, the bad_message variable was shown both before and after it was initialized. Later in the example, gdb responded that it could not display the expression (*message)+i because a pointer (the message variable) had a NULL (meaning invalid) value. In fact, this is the bug in this program--print_scrambled does not check to see whether its argument contains a valid value.

More on setting breakpoints

Example 6

Finally, as mentioned above, gdb has a variety of ways to set breakpoints. The example below demonstrates setting breakpoints at a specific line number and in a function in a library used by the program.

```
gdb -q gdb-example
This GDB was configured as "i386-redhat-linux-gnu"...Using host libthread_db
library "/lib/tls/libthread_db.so.1".
(gdb) break gdb-example.c:19
Breakpoint 1 at 0x80483d2: file gdb-example.c, line 19.
(gdb) break printf
Function "printf" not defined.
Make breakpoint pending on future shared library load? (y or [n]) y

Breakpoint 2 (printf) pending.
(gdb) run
Starting program: /data/home/newren/floss-development/developing-with-
gnome/examples/debugging/gdb/gdb-example
Breakpoint 1, main () at gdb-example.c:19
19      print_scrambled(good_message);
(gdb) where
#0  main () at gdb-example.c:19
(gdb) cont
Continuing.

Breakpoint 3, 0x004692a6 in printf () from /lib/tls/libc.so.6
(gdb) where
#0  0x004692a6 in printf () from /lib/tls/libc.so.6
#1  0x08048394 in print_scrambled (message=0x80484c9 "Hello, world.")
   at gdb-example.c:8
#2  0x080483dd in main () at gdb-example.c:19
(gdb) cont
Continuing.

Breakpoint 3, 0x004692a6 in printf () from /lib/tls/libc.so.6
(gdb) where
#0  0x004692a6 in printf () from /lib/tls/libc.so.6
#1  0x08048394 in print_scrambled (message=0x80484ca "ello, world.")
   at gdb-example.c:8
#2  0x080483dd in main () at gdb-example.c:19
(gdb) delete 3
(gdb) cont
Continuing.
Khoor/#zruog1
```

```
Program received signal SIGSEGV, Segmentation fault.
0x08048383 in print_scrambled (message=0x0) at gdb-example.c:8
8         printf("%c", (*message)+i);
(gdb) quit
The program is running.  Exit anyway? (y or n) y
```

The cont command (shorthand form of "continue") just instructs gdb to continue running until it either hits another breakpoint or the program ends. There where command is identical to the backtrace command (it is merely an alias). The delete command removes a breakpoint, given the number of the breakpoint (the command "info breakpoints" can come in handy in connection with delete).

Segment Violations

What is a segmentation fault?

Segmentation fault is when your program attempts to use memory locations that have not been reserved for the program. Memory locations are reserved for the program by using malloc in C, and new in C++.

The following common mistakes that lead to segmentation faults

- dereferencing NULL
- dereferencing an uninitialized pointer
- dereferencing a pointer that has been freed (or deleted, in C++) or that has gone out of scope (in the case of arrays declared in functions)
- writing off the end of an array.
- a recursive function that uses all of the stack space. On some systems, this will cause a "stack overflow" report, and on others, it will merely appear as another type of segmentation fault.

The strategy for debugging all of these problems is the same: load the core file into GDB, do a backtrace, move into the scope of your code, and list the lines of code that caused the segmentation fault.

Example 7

For instance, running on a Linux system, here's an example session with the file example.c.

```
#include<stdio.h>
      void foo()
      {
         char *x = 0;
         *x = 3;
      }

      int main()
      {
         foo();
        return 0;
       }
gcc -g –o example example.c
./example
```

The above program if executed gives segment violation as it is trying to store 3 at address 0. Some times, core dumped message also appears and a file named core with extension as process's PID is seen in the current working directory. If in your configuration file such as /etc/profile core file size is mentioned as zero ten core file will not be created. Thus, if you want to create core file for analyzing your program crash then you can run the following command at shell prompt and then run your program, say example.

```
ulimit  -S –c 100000
./example
```

Now to debug your program along with core file(refer also bug-buddy[4]), run the following command.

```
gdb -q  example  corefilename
```

This just loads the program called example along with the core file which contains all the information needed by GDB to reconstruct the state of execution when the invalid operation caused a segmentation fault.

Once we've loaded up gdb, we get the following:

Program terminated with signal 11, Segmentation fault.

Some information about loading symbols

```
#0  0x0804838c in foo() () at t.cpp:4
4          *x = 3;
```

So, execution stopped inside the function called foo() on line 4, which happened to be the assignment of the number 3 to the location pointed to by x.

Simply printing the value of the pointer can often lead to the solution. In this case:

```
(gdb) print x
$1 = 0x0
```

Printing out x reveals that it points to memory address 0x0 (the 0x indicates that the value following it is in hexadecimal, traditional for printing memory addresses). The address 0x0 is invalid -- in fact, it's NULL. If you dereference a pointer that stores the location 0x0 then you'll definitely get a segmentation fault, just as we did.

If we'd gotten something more complicated, such as execution crashing inside a system call or library function (perhaps because we passed an uninitialized pointer to fgets), we'd need to figure out where we called the library function and what might have happened to cause a segment fault within it. Here's an example from another debugging session:

---

[4] A command bug-buddy is available in Fedora releases which can be used for bug reporting graphically.

Example 8

```
#include<stdio.h>
#include<string.h>
     void foo()
     {
        char *x = 0;
        strcpy(x,"Hello");
     }

     int main()
     {
        foo();
       return 0;
      }
```

```
gcc -g –o example1 example1.c
./example
```

```
#0  0x40194f93 in strcpy () from /lib/tls/libc.so.6
(gdb)
```

This time, the segment fault occurred because of something inside strcpy. Does this mean the library function did something wrong? Nope! It means that we probably passed a bad value to the function. To debug this, we need to see what we passed into strcpy.

So let's see what function call we made that led to the segment fault.

```
(gdb) backtrace
#0  0x40194f93 in strcpy () from /lib/tls/libc.so.6
#1  0x080483c9 in foo() () at t.cpp:6
#2  0x080483e3 in main () at t.cpp:11
(gdb)
```

Backtrace lists the function calls that had been made at the time the program crashed. Each function is directly above the function that called it. So foo was called by main in this case. The numbers on the side (#0, #1, #2) also indicate the order of calls, from most recent to longest ago.

To move from viewing the state within each function (encapsulated in the idea of a stack frame), we can use the up and down commands. Right now, we know we're in the strcat stack frame, which contains all of the local variables of strcat, because it's the top function on the stack. We want to move "up" (toward the higher numbers); this is the opposite of how the stack is printed.

```
(gdb) up
#1  0x080483c9 in foo() () at t.cpp:6
6         strcpy(x, "Hello");
(gdb)
```

This helps a little -- we know that we have a variable called x and a constant string. We should probably lookup the strcat function at this point to make sure that we got the order of arguments correct. Since we did, the problem must be with x.

```
(gdb) print x
$1 = 0x0
```

There it is again: a NULL pointer. The strcpy function must be dereferencing a NULL pointer that we gave it, and even though it's a library function, it doesn't do anything magical.

Example 9

The following example also gives segment violation because of the above reasons.

```
#include <stdio.h>

 int main (int argc, char **argv)
 {
   int i;

   printf ("Hello, world!\n");

   /* print first characters of command-line arguments */
   for (i=0; i<=argc; i++) {
     printf ("%c", argv[i][0]);
   }
   printf ("\n");

   return 0;
 }
```

```
./a.out rao rama
Hello, world!
```

```
Segmentation fault (core dumped)
ls -l core.*
-rw------- 1 root root 1818624 Apr 29 12:04 core.4969

gdb -q a.out core.4969

Using host libthread_db library "/lib/tls/libthread_db.so.1".
Core was generated by `./a.out rao rama'.
Program terminated with signal 11, Segmentation fault.
Reading symbols from /lib/tls/libc.so.6...done.
Loaded symbols for /lib/tls/libc.so.6
Reading symbols from /lib/ld-linux.so.2...done.
Loaded symbols for /lib/ld-linux.so.2
#0  0x080483b6 in main (argc=3,
   argv=0xfee4f394) at a4.c:11
11              printf ("%c", argv[i][0]);
(gdb) print i
$1 = 3
(gdb) print argv[i]
$2 = 0x0
 (gdb) q
```

As we did not give third argument along the command line, when i value is 3 the argv[i] is observed to be zero. Thus we are getting segment violation.

Another common mistake is not checking the return from malloc to make sure that the system isn't out of memory. In addition, another common mistake is to assume that a function that calls malloc doesn't return NULL even though it returns the result of malloc. Note that in C++, when you call new, it will throw an exception, bad_alloc, if sufficient memory cannot be allocated. Your code should be prepared to handle this situation cleanly, and if you choose to catch the exception and return NULL inside a function that ordinarily returns a new'ed pointer, this advice still holds.

```
char *create_memory()
{
   char *x = malloc(10);
   if(x == NULL)
   {
      return NULL;
   }
   strcpy(x, "a string");
   return x;
}

void use_memory()
{
   char *new_memory = create_memory();
   new_memory[0] = 'A'; /* make it a capital letter */
}
```

We did a good thing by checking to make sure that malloc succeeds before using the memory in create_memory, but we don't check to make sure that create_memory returns a valid pointer!. This is a bug that won't catch you until you're running your code on a real system unless you explicitly test your code in low memory situations.

Dereferencing an Uninitialized Pointer

Figuring out whether or not a pointer has been initialized is a bit harder than figuring out whether a pointer is NULL. The best way to avoid using an uninitialized pointer is to set your pointers to NULL when you declare them (or immediately initialize them). That way, if you do use a pointer that hasn't had memory allocated for it, you will immediately be able to tell.

If you don't set your pointers to NULL when you declare them, then you'll have a much harder time of it (remember that non-static variables aren't automatically initialized to anything in C or C++). You might need to figure out if 0x4025e800 is valid memory. One way you can get a sense of this in GDB is by printing out the addresses stored in other pointers you've allocated. If they're fairly close together, you've probably correctly allocated memory. Of course, there's no guarantee that this rule of thumb will hold on all systems.

In some cases, your debugger can tell you that an address is invalid based on the value stored in the pointer. For instance, in the following example, GDB indicates that the char* x, which I set to point to the memory address "30", is not accessible.

```
(gdb) print x
$1 = 0x1e <out of bounds>
(gdb) print *x
Cannot access memory at address 0x1e
```

Generally, though, the best way to handle such a situation is just to avoid having to rely on memory's being close together or obviously invalid. Set your variables to NULL from the beginning.

Dereferencing Free'd Memory

This is another tricky bug to find because you're working with memory addresses that look valid. The best way to handle such a situation is again preventative: set your pointer to point to NULL as soon as you've freed it. That way, if you do try to use it later, then you'll have another "dereferencing NULL" bug, which should be much easier to track.

Another form of this bug is the problem of dealing with memory that has gone out of scope. If you declare a local array such as

```
char *return_buffer()
{
   char x[10];
   strncpy(x, "a string", sizeof(x));
   return x;
}
```

then the array, x, will no longer be valid once the function returns. This is a really tricky bug to find because once again the memory address will look valid when you print it out in GDB. In fact, your code might even work sometimes (or just display weird behavior by printing whatever happens to be on the stack in the location that used to be the memory of the array x). Generally, the way you'll know if you have this kind of bug is that you'll get garbage when you print out the variable even though you know that it's initialized. Watch out for the pointers returned from functions. If that pointer is causing you trouble, check the function and look for whether the pointer is pointing to a local variable in the function. Note that it is perfectly fine to return a pointer to memory allocated in the function using new or malloc, but not to return a pointer to a statically declared array (e.g., char x[10]).

Writing off the end of the array

Generally, if you're writing off the bounds of an array, then the line that caused the segment fault in the first place should be an array access. (There are a few times when this won't actually be the case -- notably, if the fact that you wrote off an array causes the stack to be smashed -- basically, overwriting the pointer that stores where to return after the function completes.)

Of course, sometimes, you won't actually cause a segment fault writing off the end of the array. Instead, you might just notice that some of your variable values are changing periodically and unexpectedly. This is a tough bug to crack; one option is to set up your debugger to watch a variable for changes and run your program until the variable's value changes. Your debugger will break on that instruction, and you can poke around to figure out if that behavior is unexpected.

```
(gdb) watch [variable name]
Hardware watchpoint 1: [variable name]
(gdb) continue
...
Hardware watchpoint 1: [variable name]

Old value = [value1]
New value = [value2]
```

This approach can get tricky when you're dealing with a lot of dynamically allocated memory and it's not entirely clear what you should watch. To simplify things, use simple test cases, keep working with the same inputs, and turn off randomized seeds if you're using random numbers!

Stack Overflows

A stack overflow isn't the same type of pointer-related problem as the others. In this case, you don't need to have a single explicit pointer in your program; you just need a recursive function without a base case. Nevertheless, this is a tutorial about segmentation faults, and on some systems, a stack overflow will be reported as a segmentation fault. (This makes sense because running out of memory on the stack will violate memory segmentation.)

To diagnose a stack overflow in GDB, typically you just need to do a backtrace:

Explanation of Normal Recursion and Tail recursion in GDB Way

In this section, we would like to demonstrate the conceptual difference between normal recursion (also called as straight or self recursion) and tail recursion. For this purpose, we have used two versions of the functions to calculate factorial value of an integer. See, programs fact1.c and fact2.c.

As we have mentioned earlier that whenever we call a function a activation record (or stack frame) is created and memory for arguments and local variables of that function are allocated in it. The memory needed for this is used from stack part of the program.

This is true even with recursive functions. That is, for each function call of a recursive function also a stack frame is created in the direct recursion. Where as in the case of tail recursive realizations of recursive functions one stack frame is used for all recursive calls. Thus, stack utilization will be better. However, in some compilers this will not become practical unless we enable optimization flags during compilations.

In order to explain these concepts, fact1.c is compiled with –g and debugged with gdb. Similarly, fact2.c (tail recursive version) is also compiled with –g option and debugged with gdb. In addition, fact2.c is compiled with –g and –O6 options and debugged with gdb. We have specified break point after line 6 and input is given as 4 in all experiments. In each experiment, we have asked gdb to print stack frame details using bt command. You can find that no of stack frames with third experiment are always less. Also, you can find from the following experiment how during rewinding stage of recursive function calls number of stack frames reduces. The following output is captured using "script" facility of the Linux system.

You can also recompile fact1.c with –g and –O6 and debug and carry the same experiment. You may find that same number of stack frames is used here also. This supports that writing a function a tail recursive fashion is important and also the compiler has identify the same during optimizations.

Example 10

```
cat fact1.c
 #include <stdio.h>
  int fact(int n)
      {
      if(n==0) return 1;
      else
      return (n * fact(n-1) );
      }

  int main ()
  {
      int N;
      printf("Enter a Integer\n");
      scanf("%d", &N);

      printf("Factorial Value=%d\n", fact(N) );
      return 0;
  }
```

gcc -g fact1.c

gdb -q a.out

```
Using host libthread_db library "/lib/tls/libthread_db.so.1".
(gdb) break 6
Breakpoint 1 at 0x80483b1: file fact1.c, line 6.(gdb) r
Starting program: /root/gdb/a.out
Enter a Integer
4

Breakpoint 1, fact (n=4) at fact1.c:6
6           return (n * fact(n-1) );
(gdb) n
```

```
Breakpoint 1, fact (n=3) at fact1.c:6
6           return (n * fact(n-1) );
(gdb) n

Breakpoint 1, fact (n=2) at fact1.c:6
6           return (n * fact(n-1) );
(gdb) n

Breakpoint 1, fact (n=1) at fact1.c:6
6           return (n * fact(n-1) );
(gdb) bt
#0  fact (n=1) at fact1.c:6
#1  0x080483be in fact (n=2) at fact1.c:6
#2  0x080483be in fact (n=3) at fact1.c:6
#3  0x080483be in fact (n=4) at fact1.c:6
#4  0x08048418 in main () at fact1.c:15
(gdb) n
7           }
(gdb) bt
#0  fact (n=1) at fact1.c:7
#1  0x080483be in fact (n=2) at fact1.c:6
#2  0x080483be in fact (n=3) at fact1.c:6
#3  0x080483be in fact (n=4) at fact1.c:6
#4  0x08048418 in main () at fact1.c:15
(gdb) n
7           }
(gdb) bt
#0  fact (n=2) at fact1.c:7
#1  0x080483be in fact (n=3) at fact1.c:6
#2  0x080483be in fact (n=4) at fact1.c:6
#3  0x08048418 in main () at fact1.c:15
(gdb) n
7           }
(gdb) bt
#0  fact (n=3) at fact1.c:7
#1  0x080483be in fact (n=4) at fact1.c:6
#2  0x08048418 in main () at fact1.c:15
(gdb) n
7           }
(gdb) bt
#0  fact (n=4) at fact1.c:7
```

```
#1  0x08048418 in main () at fact1.c:15
(gdb) n
Factorial Value=24
main () at fact1.c:16
16              return 0;
(gdb) bt
#0  main () at fact1.c:16
(gdb) n
17          }
(gdb) n
0x004fbe33 in __libc_start_main ()
  from /lib/tls/libc.so.6
(gdb) n
Single stepping until exit from function __libc_start_main,
which has no line number information.

Program exited normally.
(gdb) q
```

Example 11

```
cat fact2.c

  #include <stdio.h>
  int fact(int n, int a)
      {
      if(n==0) return a;
      else
      return (fact(n-1,a*n) );
      }

   int main ()
   {
      int N;
      printf("Enter a Integer\n");
      scanf("%d", &N);

      printf("Factorial Value=%d\n", fact(N,1) );
      return 0;
            }
```

gcc -g fact2.c

```
gdb -q a.out
Using host libthread_db library "/lib/tls/libthread_db.so.1".
(gdb) break 6
Breakpoint 1 at 0x80483b0: file fact2.c, line 6.(gdb) r
Starting program: /root/gdb/a.out
Enter a Integer
4

Breakpoint 1, fact (n=4, a=1) at fact2.c:6
6           return (fact(n-1,a*n) );
(gdb) n

Breakpoint 1, fact (n=3, a=4) at fact2.c:6
6           return (fact(n-1,a*n) );
(gdb) n

Breakpoint 1, fact (n=2, a=12) at fact2.c:6
6           return (fact(n-1,a*n) );
(gdb) n

Breakpoint 1, fact (n=1, a=24) at fact2.c:6
6           return (fact(n-1,a*n) );
(gdb) bt
#0  fact (n=1, a=24) at fact2.c:6
#1  0x080483c5 in fact (n=2, a=12) at fact2.c:6
#2  0x080483c5 in fact (n=3, a=4) at fact2.c:6
#3  0x080483c5 in fact (n=4, a=1) at fact2.c:6
#4  0x0804841d in main () at fact2.c:15
(gdb) n
7           }
(gdb) bt
#0  fact (n=1, a=24) at fact2.c:7
#1  0x080483c5 in fact (n=2, a=12) at fact2.c:6
#2  0x080483c5 in fact (n=3, a=4) at fact2.c:6
#3  0x080483c5 in fact (n=4, a=1) at fact2.c:6
#4  0x0804841d in main () at fact2.c:15
(gdb) n
7           }
(gdb) bt
```

```
#0  fact (n=2, a=12) at fact2.c:7
#1  0x080483c5 in fact (n=3, a=4) at fact2.c:6
#2  0x080483c5 in fact (n=4, a=1) at fact2.c:6
#3  0x0804841d in main () at fact2.c:15
(gdb) n
7           }
(gdb) bt
#0  fact (n=3, a=4) at fact2.c:7
#1  0x080483c5 in fact (n=4, a=1) at fact2.c:6
#2  0x0804841d in main () at fact2.c:15
(gdb) n
7           }
(gdb) bt
#0  fact (n=4, a=1) at fact2.c:7
#1  0x0804841d in main () at fact2.c:15
(gdb) n
Factorial Value=24
main () at fact2.c:16
16          return 0;
(gdb) bt
#0  main () at fact2.c:16
(gdb) n
17        }
(gdb) n
0x004fbe33 in __libc_start_main ()
  from /lib/tls/libc.so.6
(gdb) n
Single stepping until exit from function __libc_start_main,
which has no line number information.

Program exited normally.
(gdb) q
```

gcc -g -O6 fact2.c

gdb -q a.out

```
Using host libthread_db library "/lib/tls/libthread_db.so.1".
(gdb) break 6
Breakpoint 1 at 0x80483dc: file fact2.c, line 6.(gdb) r
Starting program: /root/gdb/a.out
Enter a Integer
```

```
4

Breakpoint 1, fact (n=3, a=4) at fact2.c:6
6            return (fact(n-1,a*n) );
(gdb) n
4            if(n==0) return a;
(gdb) n

Breakpoint 1, fact (n=2, a=12) at fact2.c:6
6            return (fact(n-1,a*n) );
(gdb) n
4            if(n==0) return a;
(gdb) bt
#0  fact (n=1, a=24) at fact2.c:4
#1  0x08048438 in main () at fact2.c:4
(gdb) n

Breakpoint 1, fact (n=1, a=24) at fact2.c:6
6            return (fact(n-1,a*n) );
(gdb) bt
#0  fact (n=1, a=24) at fact2.c:6
#1  0x08048438 in main () at fact2.c:4
(gdb) n
4            if(n==0) return a;
(gdb) bt
#0  fact (n=0, a=24) at fact2.c:4
#1  0x08048438 in main () at fact2.c:4
(gdb) n
7            }
(gdb) bt
#0  fact (n=0, a=24) at fact2.c:7
#1  0x08048438 in main () at fact2.c:4
(gdb) n
main () at fact2.c:3
3            {
(gdb) bt
#0  main () at fact2.c:3
(gdb) n
4            if(n==0) return a;
(gdb) n
3            {
```

```
(gdb) n
Factorial Value=24
17        }
(gdb) n
0x004fbe33 in __libc_start_main ()
  from /lib/tls/libc.so.6
(gdb) n
Single stepping until exit from function __libc_start_main,
which has no line number information.

Program exited normally.
(gdb) q
exit
```

Attaching To an Already Running Process

We want to debug a program that cannot be launched from the command line. This may be because the program is launched from some system daemon (such as a CGI program on the web). Or perhaps the program takes very long time to run its initialization code, and starting it with a debugger attached to it will cause this startup time to be much longer. There are also other reasons, but hopefully you got the point. In order to do that, we will launch the debugger in this way:

```
gdb debug_me 9561
```

Here we assume that "debug_me" is the name of the program executed, and that 9561 is the process id (PID) of the process we want to debug.

What happens is that gdb first tries looking for a "core" file named "9561" (we'll see what core files are in the next section), and when it won't find it, it'll assume the supplied number is a process ID, and try to attach to it. If there process executes exactly the same program whose path we gave to gdb (not a copy of the file. it must be the exact same file that the process runs), it'll attach to the program, pause its execution, and will let us continue debugging it as if we started the program from inside the debugger. Doing a "where" right when we get gdb's prompt will show us the stack trace of the process, and we can continue from there. Once we exit the debugger, It will detach itself from the process, and the process will continue execution from where we left it.

In order to demonstrate this, we are using the following program which displays natural numbers from 0 onwards such that one will be printed for every 5 seconds.

Example 12

File a7.c

```
#include<stdio.h>
int N=0;
void f()
{
printf("%d\n",N++);
```

```
}

void ff()
{
f();
sleep(5);
}

int main()
{
while(1)
ff();
return 0;
}


gcc -g a7.c
./a.out &
[1] 5167
0

 gdb –q  a.out 5167
1
2
Using host libthread_db library "/lib/tls/libthread_db.so.1".
Attaching to program: /root/gdb/a.out, process 5167
Reading symbols from /lib/tls/libc.so.6...done.
Loaded symbols for /lib/tls/libc.so.6
Reading symbols from /lib/ld-linux.so.2...done.
Loaded symbols for /lib/ld-linux.so.2
0x004ca7a2 in _dl_sysinfo_int80 ()
  from /lib/ld-linux.so.2
(gdb) r
The program being debugged has been started already.
Start it from the beginning? (y or n) n
Program not restarted.
(gdb) bt
#0  0x004ca7a2 in _dl_sysinfo_int80 ()
  from /lib/ld-linux.so.2
#1  0x00570110 in __nanosleep_nocancel ()
  from /lib/tls/libc.so.6
```

```
#2  0x0056ff33 in sleep ()
  from /lib/tls/libc.so.6
#3  0x080483d5 in ff () at a7.c:11
#4  0x080483fb in main () at a7.c:17
(gdb) n
Single stepping until exit from function _dl_sysinfo_int80,
which has no line number information.
0x00570110 in __nanosleep_nocancel ()
  from /lib/tls/libc.so.6
(gdb) n
Single stepping until exit from function __nanosleep_nocancel,
which has no line number information.
0x0056ff33 in sleep () from /lib/tls/libc.so.6
(gdb) n
Single stepping until exit from function sleep,
which has no line number information.
ff () at a7.c:12
12      }
(gdb) n
0x080483fb in main () at a7.c:17
17      ff();
(gdb) n
3
4
5
6
7
q
8
9
10
(press ^C)
Program received signal SIGINT, Interrupt.
0x004ca7a2 in _dl_sysinfo_int80 ()
  from /lib/ld-linux.so.2
(gdb) q
The program is running.  Quit anyway (and detach it)? (y or n) y
Detaching from program: /root/gdb/a.out, process 5167
11
12
13
```

Now run ps command.

```
 PID TTY          TIME CMD
 5145 pts/3    00:00:00 bash
 5167 pts/3    00:00:00 a.out
 5171 pts/3    00:00:00 ps
14
15
16
```

19.3 Conclusions

This chapter explores the use of gdb command for debugging C programs under Linux. It explains how to mark break points to find out run time errors in a C program. Also, it explains how core file can be used while debugging a crashed program.

20 Make

20.1 Introduction

Make is most commonly used in Linux/Unix for automating SW system compiling and development. Compiling a program made of one source file is easy compared to the ones which is made of many sources. It is not uncommon a SW system to have multiple source files; and a function in one source file may be calling another function in another file. Thus, when a program (file) is modified or rebuilt, make helps in saving the memory space and reducing SW compilation time by re-compiling only those files which depends on the modified file.

As mentioned above, the purpose of make utility is to determine automatically which pieces of a large program need to be recompiled, and issue the commands to recompile them. This is done based on time stamps of the files in SW system and the specification file (also called as makefile) which contains dependencies among the source files. We can use make with any programming language whose compiler can be run with a shell command. Make is not limited to programs. We can use it to describe any task where some files must be updated automatically from others whenever the other one changes.

The make command has a lot of built in knowledge such as how a object file is to be created from a C/C++ source, how a C file to be generated from lex/yacc specification files, etc.,. However, we must provide a file that tells make how your application is constructed and this file is called the make file whose name can be makefile or Makefile (or any other thing).

The make file most often resides in the same directory as the other source files for the project. We can have many different make files on the same machine at any one time for different SW systems. The combination of the make command and a make file provides a very powerful tool for SW managing projects.

20.2 SYNTAX OF MAKEFILES

A makefile consists of a set of dependencies and rules. A dependency has a target (a file to be created) and a set of source files upon which it is dependent. The rules describe how to create the target from the dependent file.

The make file is read by the make command, which determines the target file or files on which make command to be executed and then compares the dates and times of the source files to decide which rules need to be invoked to construct the target. Also, the make command uses the makefile to determine the order in which the targets have to be made and the correct sequence of rules to invoke.

20.2.1 Options and parameters to make:

Example 1

For example consider the following files:

```
File a.c

void f()
{
printf("Hello\n");
}
```

File b.c

```
void ff()
{
printf("How are you?\n");
}
```

File a.h

```
void f();
void ff();
```

File main.c

```
#include<stdio.h>
#include"a.h"

int main()
{

f();
ff();

return 0;
}
```

For the above examples, the following file "makefile" is written which indicates the dependencies among the files.

```
myapp: main.o. a.o b.o
          gcc -o myapp main.o  a.o  b.o
main o: main.c.  a.h
    gcc -c  main.c
a.o: a. c
    gcc  -c a.c
b.o: b.c
    gcc  -c b.c
```

20.2.2 Dependencies

In the above example, the main.o is affected by changes to main.c and a.h, and it needs to be recreated by recompiling man.c if either of the two files changes.

Similarly, the final target file (executable) "myapp" depends on main.o, a.o and b.o; which in turn have their dependencies mentioned above.

In a makefile, we rite these rules by writing the name of the target, a colon, spaces or tabs and then a space or tab separated list of files that are used to create the target file. The dependency list for our example is

```
myapp: main o  a.o b.o
main.o: main.c   a.h
a.o: a.c
b.o: b.c
```

We can see quite easily that, if b.c changes, then we need to recompile b.o and also we need to rebuild myapp.

20.2.3 Rules

The second part of the makefile specifies the rules that describe how to create a target. In our example, what command should be used after the make command has determined that a.o needs rebuilding.

A very strange and unfortunate syntax of makefile's: the difference between a space and tab. All rules must be on line that start with a tab; a space won't do.

Run the make command by typing simply make at the command prompt. We will get the following messages on the screen.

```
gcc –c main.c
gcc –c a.c
gcc –c b
gcc –o myapp main.o a.o b.o
```

Now, you can run the program "myapp" by simply typing the following at command prompt.

```
./myapp
```

We can invoke the make command with the –f option along with make file name if it is different from default make file name's such as makefile or Makefile.

If we invoke the above example in a directory containing no source code files, we get this make error message.

```
make: * * * no rule to make target 'main.c', needed by 'main.o' stop.
```

Also, the above makefile can be modified as shown below as make command can employ it's own target generation rules.

```
myapp: main.o. a.o b.o
gcc  –o myapp main.o  a.o  b.o
main o: main.c.   a.h
a.o: a. c
b.o: b.c
```

Run the above makefile (modified) by typing make command at the command prompt. We get the following messages on the screen.

```
cc –o a.o a.c
cc –o b.o b.c
cc –o main main.c
gcc –o myapp main.o a.o b.o
```

Further, we can modify the makefile to have the following lines only (Test it) as make command has inherent mechanism to know how a.o and b.o can be generated, i.e. it assumes that a.o can be generated from a.c and b.o from b.c. Thus, it uses it's default object file creation command "cc –o".

```
myapp: main.o. a.o b.o
          gcc  –o myapp main.o  a.o  b.o
main o: main.c.   a.h
```

For example, if a.c file is modified then when we run make command, we find the following messages indicating that a.o is recreated and myapp also recreated.

```
gcc –c a.c
gcc –o myapp main.o a.o b.o
```

In order to simulate the above without really changing a.c file, we can run "touch a.c" command followed by make. As a.c file time stamp is changing, the program "myapp" is recreated.

Also, we can ask make to create the required target only. For example, the following commands are acceptable.

```
make myapp                    //to create myapp  program
make a.o                      //to create object file a.o
make main.o                   //to create  object file main.o
```

20.2.4 Options to be used with make command

-C Dir

Change to directory dir before reading the makefile's or doing anything else. If multiple -c options are specified. Each is interpreted relative to the previous one. –c/ -c etc is equivalent - c/etc.

For example let us take the above mentioned example whose files are in x directory and also in y directory . Suppose that if the object files of x were removed then when we give a command

```
make –C y –f mkfile
make –c dkp – f mkfil
```

The files in the DPK directory will be taken and thus we get an output as

make : Entering directory '/home/ ravi / dpk'
make :'myapp' is upto date
make : Leaving directory 'home/ravi/dpk'

-d

print debugging information in addition to normal processing. The debugging information says which files are being considered for remaking which file-times are being compared and with what results, which files actually need to be remade, which implicit rules are considered and which are applied .... every-thing.

Example: make -d -f makefile

- e

Give variables taken from the environment precedence over variables from makefile's.

make -e -f makefile
make : 'myapp' is upto date

-f file

Use file as a makefile
For using the –f option we must first create makefile's with the required rules.

- i

Ignore all errors in commands executed to remake files
make -i -f makefile
myapp is upto date

-I dir

Specifies a directory dir to search for included make files. If several – I options are used to specify several directories. The directories are searched in the order specified.

Unlike the arguments to other flags of make, directories given with –I flags may come directly after the flag : Idir is allowed , as well as –I dir. This syntax is allowed for compatibility with the (pre processors flag of gcc).

-**j** jobs

Specifies the number of job (commands) to run simultaneously.

-k

Continues as much as possible often an error. While the target that failed, and those that depend on it. Can not be remade, the other dependencies of these targets can be processed all the same.

Let us consider the file b.c is modified as follows. Note that semicolon is missing with the printf() function.

```
void ff ( )
{
    printf ("How are you?")
}
```

```
make –k –f makefile
```

```
cc -c 3.c
b.c: 4: parse error at end of input
make: * * * [b.0] error 1
make: Target 'myapp' not remade because of errors.
```

As the error we made is not ignorable the makefile is now updated.

- n

This options prints the commands that would be executed (but are not executed really) them.

```
make –n -f makefile
gcc -c -o a.o a.c
gcc -c b.c -o b.o
```

Do not remake the file, even if it is older then its dependencies, and do not remake anything on account of changes in file. Initially the file is treated as very old and its rules are ignored.

-p

print the database (rules and variables values) that results from reading the make files; I then execute as usual or as otherwise specified. This also prints the version information given by the –v switch.

```
make -p -f makefile
```

- q

"Question mode" Do not run any commands, or print anything; just return an exit status that is zero if the specified target already exists (up to date). Non zero otherwise.

-r

eliminate use of the built-in implicit rules. Also clear out the default list of suffix rules.

-s

silent operation do not print the commands as they are executed.

```
make  –s  – f makefile
```

- **S** (capital)

cancel the effect of the – k option. This is never necessary except in a recursive make where – k might be inherited from the top-level make via MAKE FLAGS or if you set – k in MAKEFLAGS in the env.

```
make –s    -f makefile
make: myap is upto date.
```

- **t**

Touch files (mark them up to date without really charging them) instead of running their commands this is used to pretend that the commands were done, in order to fool future invocations of make.

- v

Print the version of the make program plus a copyright, a list of authors and a notice that

```
make –v
```

GNU make version 3.791 by Richard Stalman and Roland McGrath

Built for 1686-pc-linux – gnu

Copyright © 1988. 89, 90, 91, 92, 93, 94, 95 , 96, 97, 98, 99, 2000

Free software foundation, Inc.

This is free software, see the source for copying conditions.

There is no warranty: not even for MERCHANTABILITY or FITNESS FOR A PARTICULAR PURPOSE.

-w

print a message containing the working directory before and often other processing. This may be useful for tracking down errors from complicated rest of recursive make commands.

```
make   –w  –f makefile
make: Entering directory '/home/ravi/dpk'
make. makefile: No such file or directory
make: * * * NO rule to make target 'mkfile'. Stop.
Make. Leaving directory '/home/ravi/dpk'
```

- **W** (capital)

```
- w file
```

Pretend that the target file has just been modified. When used with the –n flag. This chows you what would happen if you were to modify that file, without – n. It is almost the same as running a touch command on the given file before running make. Except that the modification time is changed only in the imagination of make.

```
make –w -f makefile

make. Nothing to be done for makefile
```

Whatever we have explained till now explains only a fraction of what make can do really. Make has extensive set of facilities and structure with the help of which we can write efficient, re-usable make scripts quickly.

A typical makefile may contain lines of the following types:

- Variable Definitions - these lines define values for variables. For example:

```
CFLAGS = -O6 –g -Wall
SRCS = main.c file1.c file2.c
CC = gcc
```

- Dependency Rules - these lines define under what conditions a given file (or a type of file) needs to be re-compiled, and how to compile it. For example:

```
main.o: main.c
        gcc -g -Wall -c main.c
```

Note that each line in the commands list must begin with a TAB character. "make" is quite picky about the makefile's syntax.

- Comments - Any line beginning with a "#" sign, or any line that contains only white-space.

For example, our example makefile can be modified as a structured one as:

```
CFLAGS    =  -g   -O6  -Wall                    // these options use is discussed
earlier
SRCS              =  main.c  a.c  b.c
CC        =  gcc

myapp:a.o b.o m.o
   gcc –o myapp m.o a.o b.o
main.o:main.c a.h

clean: /bin/rm -f  main.o a.o b.o
```

The above program can be invoked as usual to create myapp. We can execute "make clean" to remove all object files created during the process of make file's execution.

When make is invoked, it first evaluates all variable assignments, from top to bottom, and when it encounters a rule "A" whose target matches the given target (or the first rule, if no target was supplied), it tries to evaluate this rule. First, it tries to recursively handle the dependencies that appear in the rule. If a given dependency has no matching rule, but there is a file in the disk with this name, the dependency is assumed to be up-to-date. After all the dependencies were checked, and any of them required handling, or refers to a file newer than the target, the command list for rule "A" is executed, one command at a time.

When we try to compile the same source code with different compilers, or on different platforms, we write makefile's with little more flexible manner. Lets see the same makefile, but this time with the introduction of variables:

```
# use "gcc" to compile source files.
CC = gcc

# the linker is also "gcc". It might be something else with other compilers.
LD = gcc

# Compiler flags go here.
CFLAGS = -g  O6  -Wall

LDFLAGS =

# use this command to erase files.
RM = /bin/rm -f

# list of generated object files.
OBJS = main.o file1.o file2.o

# program executable file name.
PROG = myapp

# top-level rule, to compile everything.

all: $(PROG)

# rule to link the program
$(PROG): $(OBJS)
	$(LD) $(LDFLAGS) $(OBJS) -o $(PROG)

# rule for file "main.o".
main.o: main.c a.h
	$(CC) $(CFLAGS) -c main.c
```

```
# rule for file "a.o".
a.o: a.c
        $(CC) $(CFLAGS) -c a.c

# rule for file "b.o".
b.o: b.c
      $(CC) $(CFLAGS) -c b.c

# rule for cleaning re-compilable files.
clean:
      $(RM) $(PROG) $(OBJS)
```

To use one rule for all source files as all can be compiled in the same way, we may follow the following approach.

```
# linking rule
$(PROG): $(OBJS)
      $(LD) $(LDFLAGS) $(OBJS) -o $(PROG)

# now comes a meta-rule for compiling any "C" source file.
%.o: %.c
      $(CC) $(CFLAGS) -c $<
```

Here, meta-rule indicates the following:

1. The "%" character is a wildcard, that matches any part of a file's name. If we mention "%" several times in a rule, they all must match the same value, for a given rule invocation. Thus, our rule here means "A file with a '.o' suffix is dependent on a file with the same name, but a '.c' suffix".
2. The "$<" string refers to the dependency list that was matched by the rule (in our case - the full name of the source file). There are other similar strings, such as "$@" which refers to the full target name, or "$*", that refers the part that was matched by the "%" character.

Main crunch in writing make files is identifying dependencies. It is advised that programmers interested in this issue read about the compiler's "-M" flag (discussed in previous chapter on compiling), and read the manual page of "makedepend" carefully.

20.3 Automake, autoconf

Aside from using the previously described methods there is a way to pay less attention to the Makefiles and build rules and concentrate on code you write. This is possible with the magic suite named autoconf/automake. It's really an amazing beast doing all of filthy work for you. Apart from taking care of Makefiles with all dependencies and other stuff for your projects, it has a mechanism to detect your system specific parameters before the compilation and building steps are performed. Start with writing the Makefile.am to define what exactly you want to build.

bin_PROGRAMS = hello hello_SOURCES = hello.c sayhi.c misc.c ui.c AUTOMAKE_OPTIONS = foreign

The last line tells automake it's not the GNU package, e.g. it does not contain standard files named NEWS, README, AUTHORS and ChangeLog that are necessary if you want your package to be GNU compliant.

After you have Makefile.am in the project directory, there is another input file for the suite named configure.in. It's responsible for the system specific parameters checking I mentioned before. The minimalist configure.in is below.

AC_INIT(hello.c) # Initializes the configure script. On start it will check for the # main source file specified here first.

AM_INIT_AUTOMAKE(hello, 1.0) # Tells automake we have project named "hello" version 1.0

AC_PROG_CC # Adds a check for C compiler

AC_OUTPUT(Makefile) # The output file is Makefile. All the build stuff will be put there

Now you are done with the autoconf/automake input specification. Run the following programs now in the order given.

aclocal autoconf automake -a -c

This will finally create the configure script, Makefile.in and add some default documentation to your project. Now it's finally ready to compile, debug and even to distribute.

Everyone who wants to build your program on his or her Linux computer needs to run ./configure make

We run ./configure so Makefile is created from Makefile.in. This is how the autoconf/automake is organized. It generates Makefile.in from your Makefile.am. Then Makefile.in is processed by ./configure script so all the system specific things would be considered and included into the final Makefile. It will also have a default install and uninstall targets which are extremely useful for your program users.

20.4 Conclusions

This chapter explains make utility that is used for SW development. Simple and lucid examples are given such that a new entrant can understand and use make for real time SW development.

21 Revision Control System

21.1 Introduction

Software development is an incremental process involving updating of source files and testing their functionality and reverting back to previous version of the same if not behaving as expected by us. Thus, we may often find need to have the content of file(s) of a specified date and time. Revision control system's (RCS) will come to rescue us for this type of situations. RCS stores the differences of versions of a file. Files can be restored without regard to the system manager. RCS software maintains two fundamental commands " ci "(check in) –to check in the file and " co "(check out) – to check out the file.

RCS is a file management tool designed to aid development of text files (programs, documents, almost any printable file) under UNIX. RCS meets an important need in managing large projects. It allows to automate many of the tasks involved in co-ordinating a team of people who are editing and using files. These tasks include maintaining all versions of a file in a recoverable form, preventing several people from modifying the same code simultaneously, helping people to merge two different development tracks into a single version, ensuring that a single program is not undergoing multiple simultaneous versions and maintaining logs for versions and other changes.

By using RCS, we can restore files without regard with the system manager. RCS won't protect from disk crash, but they can protect from many cases of accidental file deletion (or) corruption. This tool is developed to manage multiperson development projects, ensuring that only one person has write access to a file at one time and making it possible to go back to any previous versions of a file. They are handy for any user who has important files that change frequently.

21.1.1 Creation of a file under RCS management

- Create a subdirectory called RCS in the directory where you keep the code (or) other text files you want to protect.
- It is not essential, but a good idea to add the characters id somewhere in the file you want to place under RCS. Out this in a comment filed i.e. use /*id*/ in a C program and # id in a shell script.
- Place the file under revision control. This is done by typing :

  # ci filename

  and to retrieve the file, use the following command:

  # co filename
- Basic Operations

The two fundamental commands for using RCS are ci and co. These command ci – "check in" and co- "checkout" are the one's that RCS software maintains.

RCS creates a separate RCS file for every file under its management. This file stores a description of the file, the entire change log, the current version of the file, list of users who are allowed to access the file, the file's date and time and list of changes that lets RCS reproduce any obsolete version of the file at will. On many system, by default, RCS is in the strict-access mode. This mode has two important features :

- No one is allowed to check in a file without locking it first.
- No one can modify a file unless that user (person) checked it out locked.

The first version of a file under RCS control is given number 1.1 Succeeding versions that descend linearly this file are numbered 1.2, 1.3 etc.

RCS gives the first "branch" beginning at version 1.3, the number 1.3.1. It numbers the second branch beginning at this point 1.3.2 etc. The first version along the first branch is 1.3.1.1 and the second is 1.3.1.2 etc.

The tool "rcsmerge' exists to help you merge versions from different branches of development and the tool "rcsdiff" is used to find out the differences between the two files and to create a new version that incorporates the modifications to both files.

RCS stores the differences between version of a file.

NAME

rcs – change RCS file attributes

SYNOPSIS

rcs options file ....

DESCRIPTION

rcs creates new RCS files (or) changes attributes of existing ones. An RCS file contains multiple revisions of text, an access list, a change log, descriptive text, and some control attributes. Pathnames matching an RCS suffix denote RCS files, all other denote working files.

OPTIONS

-i :create and initialise a new RCS file, but do not deposit any revision. If the RCS file has no path prefix, try to place it first into the subdirectory./RCS and then into the current directory. If the RCS file already exists, print an error message.

For example with the following commands a.c file is created and the same is deposited to rcs system.

touch a.c.

rcs –i a.c

RCS file : a.c,v

Enter description, terminated with a single :'(or)
end of file.

Note : This is NOT the log message !

>> This is a rcs file of a.c.

>>.

Check the content of the file created by running vi command on it.

vi a.c,v

Head ;
Access;

```
Symbols;
Locks, strict;
Comment @ * @;
Desc
@ this is a rcs file of a.c.
@
```

-a logins : Append the login names appearing in the comma-separated list logins to the access list of the RCS file.

For example to give access to priya, we can run the following command.s

rcs –apriya a.c

```
RCS file : a.c,v
done
```

Now check the content of file a.c,v by running vi command on it and we can see that the user name is seen in the Access list.

vi a.c,v

```
Head ;
Access;
    priya
Symbols;
Locks, strict;
Comment @ * @;
Desc
@ this is a rcs file of a.c.
@
```

-A oldfile : Append the access list of old file to the access list of the RCS file.

For example create another file, say b.c and run the following command to access list.

rcs –i b.c

```
    RCS file : b.c,v
    Enter description, terminated with a single '.'(or)
end of file.

Note : This is NOT the log message !
>> temporary file
>>.
done
```

Now we can assign access to user dolly for this file "b.c".

rcs - adolly b.c

RCS file : b.c,v
done

Now when we run the following command then user names who has permissions for b.c will be added to a.c file.

rcs -Ab.c. a.c

RCS file : a.c,v
done

Now, see the content of file a.c,v.

```
vi a.c,v
    head ;
    access;
        priya;
        dolly;
    symbols;
    locks, strict;
    comment @ * @;
    desc
    @ this is a rcs file of a.c.
    @
```

- e [logins] : Erase the login names appearing in the comma-separated list logins from the access list of the RCS file. If logins are omitted, erase the access list.

Now to remove dolly from access list of a file we can use –e option as below.

rcs - edolly a.c

RCS file : a.c,v
done

```
vi a.c,v
    head ;
    access;
        priya;
    symbols;
    locks, strict;
```

```
comment @ * @;
desc
@ this is a rcs file of a.c.
@
```

- b [rev] : set the default branch to rev. If rev is omitted, eh default branch is reset to the highest branch on the trunk. If rev begins with a period, then the default branch is prepended to it. If rev is a branch number followed by a period, then the latest revision on that branch is used.

The following command sets the 1.1 as the revision of the file a.c.

rcs -b1.1 a.c

```
RCS file : a.c,v
done
```

Run vi command to check the same in the revision file.

vi a.c,v

```
head  1.1 ;
branch 1.1.1;
access;
    priya;
symbols;
locks, strict;
comment @ * @;
desc
@ this is a rcs file of a.c.
@
```

- C string : Set the comment leader to string. An res –i without –c guesses the comment leader from the suffix of the working file name.

res -cDIE a.c

```
Res file: a.c, V
Done
```

Now, check the a.c,v file output by opening the same using vi command.

vi a.c,V

=> the string "DIE" overwrites over the comment string.

Comment @ DIE @

- l [rev] : Look the revision with number rev. If a branch is given, lock the latest revision on that branch. If rev is omitted, lock the latest revision on the default branch locking prevents overlapping changes.

The following command lock the file with the given revision.

rcs -l1.1 a.c

RCS file: RCS/a.c,V
1.1 locked
done

vi a.c,v

=> The 'lock' file is modified as
lock
root 1.1; strict;

- Rev : msg : Replace revision rev's with log message.

rcs –m1.1: FORV al.c

RCS file: a.c, v
Done

vi a1.c,v

Also, we can create a RCS file using ci command. For example,

touch a1.c
ci a1.c

RCS/a.c, v a.c
Enter description, terminated with single'.' (or) end of file.
> > This is a1 file
> > initial revision 1.1
done

vi a1.c,v
head;l
access;
symbols;
locks, strict;
comment @ * @;
1.1
data 2004.08.07.02..10.16; author root;
State Exp;

Branches ;
Next;
Desc
@ this is a1 file
@
1.1
log
@ initial revision
@

vi a1.c,v
=> The log message is modified as 'FOR U',
    log
    @ FOR U
    @

- n name [: [rev]] : Associate the symbolic name with the branch (or) revision rev. Delete the symbolic name, if both: and rev are omitted, print an error message if name is already associated with another No. A rcs –n name: RCS/A associates name with the current latest revision of all the named RCS files.

For example,

rcs -nAng:1.1 a1.c
    RCS file: a1.c,v
    Done

vi a1.c,v

The symbol field is modified as
    Symbols
        Ang: 1.1 ;

- N name [: [rev]]: act like -n, except override any previous assignment of name.

rcs -Ngel:1.1 a1.c
    RCS file: a1.c,v
    Done

vi a1.c, v
=> the symbol field is modified as
    symbols
        gel: 1.1;

-O range : Delete the revision given by range. A range consisting of a single revision no. means that revision. A range consisting of a branch no. means the latest revision on that branch. A range of the form rev1: rev2 means revisions rev1 to rev2 on the same branch: rev means from the beginning of the branch containing rev upto and including rev and rev: means from revision rev to the end of the branch containing rev.

To create new revision 1.2 and 1.3 of a1.c,v file

co -l a1.c

RCS/a1.c,v a1.c

Revision 1.1 (locked)

Done

vi a1.c

=> Update the a1.c file

ci a1.c

RCS/a1.c,v a1.c

New revision 1.2; previous : 1.1

Done

co -l a1.c

RCS/a1.c,v a1.c

Revision 1.2 (locked)

Done

vi a1.c

=> Update the a1.c file

RCS/a1.c,v a1.c

New revision 1.3; previous: 1.2

Done

To delete revisions from a file (say revisions 1.2 and 1.3) run the following command with –o option.

rcs -o1.2:1.3 a1.c

RCS file: a1.c,

Deleting revision: 1.3

Deleting revision: 1.2

Done

vi a1.c,v

head 1.1;

access ;

|

|

@

-q: Run quietly, do not print diagnostics

- : Run interactively, even if the standard input is not a terminal.

-

- s State (:[rev]: Set the state attribute of the revision rev to state. If rev is a branch no., assume the latest revision on that branch. If rev is omitted, assume the latest revision on the default branch. A useful set of states is Exp. (experimental) stab (stable) and Rel (released). By default ci(1) sets the state of a revision to Exp.

rcs -sExp:1.1 a1.c

RCS file: a1.c,v

Done

vi a1,c,v

The state file is modified as

Date - - - - - - - state Exp;

rcs -sstab: 1.1 a1.c

RCS file: a1. c,v

Done

vi a.c,v ,,_

The state field is modified as

Date - - - - - - - - - - -state stab;

- t [file] : Write descriptive text from the contents of the named file into the RCS file, deleting the existing text. If the file is omitted obtain the text from standard input, terminated by end-of-file (or) by a line containing. By itself.

vi D.C

This is Linux world

rcs -tD.C a1.c

RCS file: a1.c, v

Done

vi a1.c, v

head 1.1:

|

|

|

desc

@ this is Linux word

@

-t – string : Write descriptive text from the string into the RCS file, deleting the existing text.

rcs -t"GNU" a1.c

RCS file: a1.c, V

Done

vi a1.c,v

Head 1.1;

|

|

|

desc

@ GNU

@

-T: Preserves the modification time on the RCS file unless a revision is removed. This option can suppress extensive re-compilation caused by a make (1) dependency of some copy of the working file.

On the RCS file

-V: Prints RCS's version numbers

rcs –V a1.c

RCS version 5.7

-Vn : Emulate RCS version n.

- X suffixes : Use suffices to characterize RCS files.

-Z zone : Use zone as the default time zone. This option has no effect; it is present for compatibility with other RCS commands.

-K Subset: set the default key word substitution to subset. The affect of key substitution is described in co (1). Giving an explicit –k option to co, rcs diff and rcs merge overrides this default.

- u [rev] : Unlock the revision with number rev. If a branch is given, unlock the latest revision on that branch. If rev is omitted, remove the latest lock held by the caller. Normally only the locker of a revision can unlock it.

- L: Set locking to strict. Strict locking means that the owner of an RCS file is not exempt from locking for check in. * This option should be used for files that are shared.

- U: Set locking to non –strict. Non-strict locking means that the owner of a file need not lock a revision for check in. * This option should not be used for files that are shared.

- M: Do not send mail when breaking somebody else's lock. This options meant for programs that warn users by other uses.

- u [rev]:

touch gel..c

ci gel.c

RCS/gel.c,v gel.c

Enter description terminated with single '.' (or) end-of-file.

Note: This is not the log message !

> > this

> >

initial revision 1.1

done

initial revision 1.1

done

rcs -l1.1 gel.c

RCS file: RCS/gel.c,v

1. 1 (locked)

done

rcs – u1.1 gel.c

RCS file: gel. C, V

1.1 unlocked

done.

21.1.2 ci-Check in command

ci is one of the fundamental command used by the RCS. When a file is check in , RCS deletes source file and creates (or) modifies a file called source, v where source is the name of the original and, v is an extension that indicates an RCS file.

To do a simple check in, use the following command :

ci filename

This creates a new RCS version of your file. If he file is not currently managed by RCS, this command places the file under RCS management, gives it the version no. 1.1 , and prompt for a description of the file. If the file is already being managed by RCS, this command will assign the next higher version number in the sequence (1.2 follows 1.1) and will prompt for a description of the changes have made since the last check in.

The following example shows what happens when checking a version 1.4 of a file called my test.

ci mytest

Mytest, v ....► my test

New revision 1.4; previous revision : 1.3

Enter log message :

(terminate with ^D (or) single '.')

The prompt >> indicates that RCS is waiting for a line of text

RCS warns if a checking a file has not been modified since it was check out. We can force it to check the file in by typing y response to its warning message:

ci mytest

Mytest, v ····················▶ my test

New revision : 1.8; previous revision : 1.7

File mytest is unchanged with respect to revision 1.7

Checking anyway? [ny] (n) : y

Used by itself, the command ci deletes the working version of the file

If you want to retain a read-only version of the file,

Enter the command :

ci –u filename

in this case, a copy of filename for reference is retained .The ci command may refer to let check in a file, printing the message :

ci error ; no lock set by your name .

This can only occur under two circumstances :

1. If you did not lock the file upon checkout in the strict-access mode.
2. If someone locked the file after you checked it out in open-access mode.

If you want to do a checking, followed immediately by a checkout. You may want to install a version reflecting the current state of your program (possible as a back up), then continue editing immediately . other than using two operations, RCS lets you perform both with the command

ci – l filename

This updates the RCS file and gives a lock with a fresh copy of working file, allowing to edit continue immediately.

NAME

ci-checkin RCS revisions

SYNOPSIS

ci[options] file..........

DESCRIPTION

ci stores new revisions into RCS files. Each pathname matching an RCS suffix is taken to be RCS file. All others are assumed to be working files containing new revisions. Ci deposits the contents of each working file into the corresponding RCS file. For ci to work, the caller's login must be on the access list, except if the access list is empty (or) the caller is the super user (or) the owner of the file. To append a new revision to an existing branch, the top revision on that branch must be locked by the caller, otherwise, only a new branch can be created. This restriction is not enforced for the owner of the file if non-strict locking is used. A lock held by someone else can be broken with the RCS command.

Unless if option is given, ci checks whether the revision to be deposited differs from the preceding one. Ordinary ci removes the working file and nay lock ci - l keeps and ci -u removes any lock and then they both generate a new working file much as if co –l (or) co-u had been applied to the preceding revision.

When reverting, any –n and –s options apply to the preceding revision. For each revision deposited, ci prompts for a log message. The log message should summarize the change and must be terminated by end of the file (or) by a line containing by itself. If RCS file does not exist, ci creates it and deposits the contents of the working file as the initial revision (default number : 1.1). The access list is initialized to empty. Instead of the log message, ci requests descriptive text.

The number rev of the deposited revision can be given an of the options –f, -I, -I, -j, -k, -l, -m, -q, - r (or) –u. *rev can be symbolic, numeric (or) mixed. Symbols names in rev must already be defined. If rev is $, ci determines the revision no form keyboard values in the working file.

If rev begins with a period, then the default branch is prepended to it. If rev is a branch no. followed by a . Then the latest revision on that branch is used.

If rev is a revision no, it must be higher than the latest one on the branch to which rev belongs, (or) must start a new branch.

If rev is a branch rather than a revision no, the new revision is appended to that branch. The level number is obtained by incrementing the tip revision no. If the caller locked a non-tip revision, a new branch is started at that revision by incrementing the highest branch no. at that revision. The default initial branch and level no's are 1.

If rev is omitted and the caller has no lock, but owns the file and locking is not set to strict , then the revision is appended to the default branch.

Options

-mmsg : uses the string msg as the logmessage for all revisions checked in.

touch nw.c

ci new.c

    RCS/nw, c.v ············► nw.c
    :
    >> raja
    >>.
    Initial revision : 1.1
    done

co -l nw.c

    RCS / nw.c,v ············► nw.c
    Revision 1.1 (locked)
    done

vi nw.c

ci -mnaveen nw.c

    RCS/nw.c.v ············► nw.c
    new revision : 1.2; previous revision : 1.1
    done

vi nw.c.v

The log message is changed to Naveen

- name :assign the symbolic name to the number of the checked-in revision

co -l nw.c

RCS/nw.c,v ⟶ nw.c
new revision : 1.2 , previous revision :1.1
done

vi nw.c,v
The log message is changed to Naveen

- n name : assign the symbolic name to the number of the checked-in revision.

co -l nw.c

RCS / nw.c, v ⟶ nw.c
revision 1.2
done

vi nw.c
ci -nrp nw.c

vi nw.c,v
symbolic name is changed to rp.

- s state : set the state of checked-in revision to the identifier state. The default state is exp.

co -l nw.c

ci -sExp nw.c

vi nw.c, v
state is exp.

-t file : write descriptive text from the contents of the named file into the RC5 file, deleting the existing text.

co -l nw.c
co -t gel.c nw.c

vi nw.c,v

text is changed to raj.

-t -string:write descriptive text from the string into the RCS file

co -l nw.c
ci -t"raja" nw.c
vi nw.c,v

text is changed to raja.

-wlogin : uses login or the author field of the deposited revision.

-v : Print RCS'5 version number.

-x suffixes : specifies the suffices for RCS files. A non-empty suffix matches any pathname ending in the suffix.

-z zone : specifies the date output format in keyword substitution and specifies the default time zone for date in the –date option.

-q [rev] : quiet mode, diagnostic output is not printed.

-M [rev] : set the modification time on any new working file to be the date of the retrieved revision.

-d [date] : uses date for the checkin date and time

-I [rev] : interactive mode, the user is prompted and questioned even if the standard input is not a terminal.

-I [rev] : interactive mode, the user is prompted and questioned even if the standard input is not a terminal.

-f [rev] : forces a deposit; the new revision is deposited even it is not different from the preceding one.
touch s5.c
ci ss.c

```
RCS / ss.c, v  ----------->  ss.c
.
.
.
.
>> pittichi
>>.
initial revision : 1.1
done
```

co -l ss.c

vi ss.c

ci ss.c

RCS / ss.cn, ──────▶ ss.c

.

.

.

.

new revision ; 1.2; previous revision : 1.2; previous revision : 1.1

done

co -l ss.c

ci -f1.4 ss.c

RCS / ss.cn, ──────▶ ss.c,v

.

.

.

.

new revision 1.4; previous revision : 1.2;

.

.

.

done

-k [rev] : searches the working file for keyword values to determine its revision number , creation date, state and author, assign these values to the deposited revision , rather than computing them locally

-j [rev] : just checkin and do not initialise; report an error if the RCS file does not already exist .

-l [rev] : works like –r, except it performs an additional co –l for the deposited revision.

-u [rev] : works like –l, except that the deposited revision is not locked. The –l , bare – r and –u options are mutually exclusive and silently override each other for example, is –u -r is equipment to ci – r because –r overrides –u.

-rrev : checkin revision rev.

-r : with other RCS commands, a bare – r option specifies the most recent revision on the default branch, but with ci, a bare –r option re-established the default behaviour of releasing a lock and removing the working file.

21.1.3 CO-CHECK OUT COMMAND

Co-check out command can be used recover or restore file of any date or version.

Syntax of the co command.

co [options] file ...

co retrieves a revision from each RCS file and stores it into the corresponding working file. Revisions of an RCS file can be checked out locked or unlocked. Lock-ing a revision prevents overlapping updates. A revision checked out for reading or processing (e.g., compiling) need not be locked. A revision checked out for editing and later checkin must normally blocked. Checkout with locking fails if the revision to be checked out is currently locked by another user. (A lock can be broken with rcs(1).) Checkout with locking also requires the caller to be on the access list of the RCS file, unless he is the owner of the file or the super user, or the access list is empty. Checkout without locking is not subject to access list restrictions, and is not affected by the presence of locks.

A revision or branch number can be attached to any of the options -f, -I, -l, -M, -p, -q, -r, or -u. The options -d (date), -s (state), and -w (author) retrieve from a single branch, the selected branch, which is either specified by one of -f, ..., -u, or the default branch. A co command applied to an RCS file with no revisions creates a zero length working file.

OPTIONS

-r[rev]

retrieves the latest revision whose number is less than or equal to rev. If rev indicates a branch rather than a revision, the latest revision on that branch is retrieved. If rev is omitted, the latest revision on the default branch option of is retrieved. If rev is $, co determines the revision number from keyword values in the working file. Otherwise, a revision is composed of one or more numeric or symbolic fields separated by periods. If rev begins with a period, then the default branch (normally the trunk) is prepended to it. If rev is a branch number followed by a period, then the latest revision on that branch is used.

-l[rev]

same as -r, except that it also locks the retrieved revision for the caller.

-u[rev]

same as -r, except that it unlocks the retrieved revision if it was locked by the caller. If rev is omitted, -u retrieves the revision locked by the caller, if there is one; otherwise, it retrieves the latest revision on the default branch.

-f[rev]

forces the overwriting of the working file; useful in connection with -q. .

-kkv

Generate keyword strings using the default form, e.g. $Revision: 5.13 $ for the Revision keyword. A locker's name is inserted in the value of the Header, Id, and Locker keyword strings only as a file is being locked, i.e. by ci -l and co -l. This is the default.

-kkvl

Like -kkv, except that a locker's name is always inserted if the given revision is currently locked.

-kk

Generate only keyword names in keyword strings; omit their values. For example, for the revision keyword, generate the string $Revision$ instead of Revision: 5.13 $. This option is useful to ignore differences due to keyword substitution when comparing different revisions of a file. Log messages are inserted after Log keywords even f -kk is specified, since this tends to be more useful when merging changes.

-ko

Generate the old keyword string, present in the working file just before it was checked in. For example, for the Revision keyword, generate the string $Revision: 1.1 $ instead of $Revision: 5.13 $ if that is how the string appeared when the file was checked in. This can be useful for file formats that cannot tolerate any changes to substring's that happen to take the form of keyword strings.

-kb

Generate a binary image of the old keyword string. This acts like -ko, except it performs all working file input and output in binary mode. This makes little difference on POSIX and Unix hosts, but on DOS-like hosts one should use rcs -i -kb to initialize an RCS file intended to be used for binary files.

-kv

Generate only keyword values for keyword strings. For example, for the Revision keyword, generate the string 5.13 instead of $Revision: 5.13 $. This can help generate files in programming languages where it is hard to strip keyword delimiters like $Revision: $ from a string.

-p[rev]

prints the retrieved revision on the standard output rather than storing it in the working file. This option is useful when co is part of a pipe.

-q[rev]

quiet mode; diagnostics are not printed.

-I[rev]

interactive mode; the user is prompted and questioned even if the standard input is not a terminal.

-M[rev]

Set the modification time on the new working file to be the date of the retrieved revision.

-sstate

retrieves the latest revision on the selected branch whose state is set to state.

-T

Preserve the modification time on the RCS file even if the RCS file changes because a lock is added or removed. This option can suppress extensive recompilation caused by a make dependency of some other copy of the working file on the RCS file.

-w[login]

retrieves the latest revision on the selected branch which was checked in by the user with login name login. For each pair, co joins revisions rev1 and rev3 with respect torev2. This means that all changes that transform rev2 into rev1are applied to a copy of rev3. This is particularly useful ifrev1 and rev3 are the ends of two branches that have rev2 as a common ancestor. If rev1<rev2<rev3 on the same branch, joining generates a new revision which is like rev3, but with all changes that lead from rev1 to rev2 undone. If changes fromrev2 to rev1 overlap with changes from rev2 to rev3, For the initial pair, rev2 can be omitted.

-V Print RCS's version number.

-Vn Emulate RCS version n, where n can be 3, 4, or 5. This can be useful when interchanging RCS files with others who are running older versions of RCS.

-xsuffixes

Use suffixes to characterize RCS files.

21.2 Conclusions

SW management is explained and how RCS can be used under Linux to manage the code in a SW project. Few illustrative examples are included to let students to practice.

22 Lex and Yacc

22.1 Introduction

First phase in the compiler development is tokenization. That is, the input or source program is decomposed into tokens which are also known as lexeme's(thus this phase is also called as lexical analysis). Each language will be having its own lexical rules. Only after extracting the tokens, syntactical analysis is carried out to test the validity of the expression in terms of that language specific grammatical rules. After this, actual transformation to machine language (via assembly language in the case of C language) takes place.

Lex library is widely used for lexical analysis. However, in the recent years, under Free Software Foundation license, Flex (fast lexical analyzer) is distributed along with Gnu compiler package which can be effectively used for lexical analysis purpose. In compiler construction terminology these SW which are used for lexical analysis are called as scanners.

In addition to scanner development, Lex/Flex is also used for some other applications in system administration where text processing is needed.

22.2 Lex Specification File

In essence, while using lex or flex we have to first create a specification file (used to specify the tokenization rules, i.e. regular expressions to represent the tokens of the language and also C code, called as rules) and has to be presented to **lex** command which generates a C language file known as **lex.yy.c** (in which yylex() and other functions given in Table 22. 2 are defined) which when compiled with gcc (with -lfl option) we get an executable file which does the required tokenization.

The flex input or specification file consists of three sections namingly definitions, rules and user code.

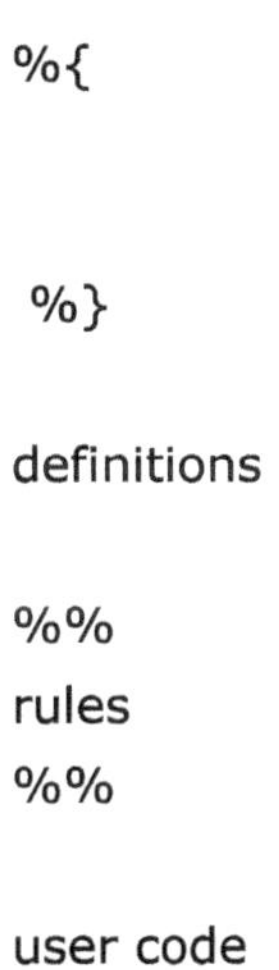

```
%{


 %}

definitions

%%
rules
%%

user code
```

22.2.1 The Definitions Section

The *definitions* section contains declarations of simple *name* definitions to simplify the scanner specification, and declarations of *start conditions*, which are explained in a later section.

Name definitions have the form:

Name definition

The "name" is a word beginning with a letter or an underscore ('_') followed by zero or more letters, digits, '_', or '-' (dash). The definition is taken to begin at the first non-white-space character following the name and continuing to the end of the line. The definition can subsequently be referred to using "{name}", which will expand to "(definition)". For example,

```
DIGIT   [0-9]
ID      [a-z][a-z0-9]*
```

defines "DIGIT" to be a regular expression which matches a single digit, and "ID" to be a regular expression which matches a letter followed by zero-or-more letters-or-digits. A subsequent reference to

```
{DIGIT}+"."{DIGIT}*
```

is identical to

```
([0-9])+"."([0-9])*
```

and matches one-or-more digits followed by a '.' followed by zero-or-more digits.

22.2.2 The Rules Section

The *rules* section of the flex input contains a series of rules of the form:

Pattern action

where the pattern must be unindented and the action must begin on the same line.

See below for a further description of patterns and actions.

22.2.3 The User Code Section

The user code section is simply copied to `lex.yy.c' verbatim. It is used for companion routines which call or are called by the scanner. The presence of this section is optional; if it is missing, the second `%%' in the input file may be skipped, too.

In the definitions and rules sections, any *indented* text or text enclosed in `%{' and `%}' is copied verbatim to the output (with the `%{' and '%}' removed). The `%{', and '%}'' must appear unindented on lines by themselves.

In the rules section, any indented or %{ } text appearing before the first rule may be used to declare variables which are local to the scanning routine and (after the declarations) code which is to be executed whenever the scanning routine is entered. Other indented or %{} text in the rule section is still copied to the output, but its meaning is not well-defined and it may well cause compile-time errors (this feature is present for POSIX compliance; see below for other such features).

In the definitions section (but not in the rules section), an unindented comment (i.e., a line beginning with "/*") is also copied verbatim to the output up to the next "*/".

22.2.4 Patterns

The patterns in the input are written using an extended set of regular expressions. These are:

`x'

match the character `x'

`.'

any character (byte) except new line

`[xyz]'

a "character class"; in this case, the pattern matches either an `x', a `y', or a `z'

`[abj-oZ]'

a "character class" with a range in it; matches an `a', a `b', any letter from `j' through `o', or a `Z'

`[^A-Z]'

a "negated character class", i.e., any character but those in the class. In this case, any character EXCEPT an uppercase letter.

`[^A-Z\n]'

any character EXCEPT an uppercase letter or a new line

`*r**'

zero or more *r*'s, where *r* is any regular expression

`*r*+'

one or more *r*'s

`*r*?'

zero or one *r*'s (that is, "an optional *r*")

`*r*{2,5}'

anywhere from two to five *r*'s

`*r*{2,}'

two or more *r*'s

`*r*{4}'

exactly 4 *r*'s

`{*name*}'

the expansion of the "*name*" definition (see above)

`"[xyz]\"foo"'

the literal string: `[xyz]"foo'

`*x*'

if *x* is an `a', `b', `f', `n', `r', `t', or `v', then the ANSI-C interpretation of \*x*. Otherwise, a literal `*x*' (used to escape operators such as `*')

`\0'

a NUL character (ASCII code 0)

`\123'

the character with octal value 123

`\x2a'

the character with hexadecimal value 2a

`(*r*)'

match an *r*; parentheses are used to override precedence (see below)

`*rs*'

the regular expression *r* followed by the regular expression *s*; called "concatenation"

`*r*|*s*'

either an *r* or an *s*

`*r*/*s*'

an *r* but only if it is followed by an *s*. The text matched by *s* is included when determining whether this rule is the *longest match*, but is then returned to the input before the action is executed. So the action only sees the text matched by *r*. This type of pattern is called *trailing context*. (There are some combinations of `*r*/*s*' that flex cannot match correctly; see notes in the Deficiencies / Bugs section below regarding "dangerous trailing context".)

`^*r*'

an *r*, but only at the beginning of a line (i.e., which just starting to scan, or right after a new line has been scanned).

`*r*$'

an *r*, but only at the end of a line (i.e., just before a new line). Equivalent to "*r*/\n". Note that flex's notion of "new line" is exactly whatever the C compiler used to compile flex interprets '\n' as; in particular, on some DOS systems you must either filter out \r's in the input yourself, or explicitly use *r*/\r\n for "r$".

`<*s*>*r*'

an *r*, but only in start condition *s* (see below for discussion of start conditions) <*s1*,*s2*,*s3*>*r* same, but in any of start conditions *s1*, *s2*, or *s3*

`<*>*r*'

an *r* in any start condition, even an exclusive one.

`<<EOF>>'

an end-of-file

`<*s1*,*s2*><<EOF>>'

an end-of-file when in start condition *s1* or *s2*

Note that inside of a character class, all regular expression operators lose their special meaning except escape ('\') and the character class operators, '-', ']', and, at the beginning of the class, '^'.

The regular expressions listed above are grouped according to precedence, from highest precedence at the top to lowest at the bottom. Those grouped together have equal precedence. For example,

```
foo|bar*
```

is the same as

```
(foo)|(ba(r*))
```

since the '*' operator has higher precedence than concatenation, and concatenation higher than alternation ('|'). This pattern therefore matches *either* the string "foo" *or* the string "ba" followed by zero-or-more r's. To match "foo" or zero-or-more "bar"'s, use:

```
foo|(bar)*
```

and to match zero-or-more "foo"'s-or-"bar"'s:

```
(foo|bar)*
```

In addition to characters and ranges of characters, character classes can also contain character class *expressions*. These are expressions enclosed inside `[': and `:'] delimiters (which themselves must appear between the '[' and ']' of the character class; other elements may occur inside the character class, too). The valid expressions are:

```
[:alnum:] [:alpha:] [:blank:]
[:cntrl:] [:digit:] [:graph:]
[:lower:] [:print:] [:punct:]
[:space:] [:upper:] [:xdigit:]
```

These expressions all designate a set of characters equivalent to the corresponding standard C `isXXX' function. For example, `[:alnum:]' designates those characters for which `isalnum()' returns true - i.e., any alphabetic or numeric. Some systems don't provide `isblank()', so flex defines `[:blank:]' as a blank or a tab.

For example, the following character classes are all equivalent:

```
[[:alnum:]]
[[:alpha:][:digit:]
[[:alpha:]0-9]
[a-zA-Z0-9]
```

If your scanner is case-insensitive (the `-i' flag), then `[:upper:]' and `[:lower:]' are equivalent to `[:alpha:]'.

Some notes on patterns :

- A negated character class such as the example "[^A-Z]" above *will match a new line* unless "\n" (or an equivalent escape sequence) is one of the characters explicitly present in the negated character class (e.g., "[^A-Z\n]"). This is unlike how many other regular expression tools treat negated character classes, but unfortunately the inconsistency is historically entrenched. Matching new lines means that a pattern like [^"]* can match the entire input unless there's another quote in the input.
- A rule can have at most one instance of trailing context (the '/' operator or the '$' operator). The start condition, '^', and "<<EOF>>" patterns can only occur at the beginning of a pattern, and, as well as with '/' and '$', cannot be grouped inside parentheses. A '^' which does not occur at the beginning of a rule or a '$' which does not occur at the end of a rule loses its special properties and is treated as a normal character. The following are illegal:

```
foo/bar$
<sc1>foo<sc2>bar
```

Note that the first of these, can be written "foo/bar\n". The following will result in '$' or '^' being treated as a normal character:

```
foo|(bar$)
foo|^bar
```

If what's wanted is a "foo" or a bar-followed-by-a-new line, the following could be used (the special '|' action is explained below):

```
foo     |
bar$    /* action goes here */
```

A similar trick will work for matching a foo or a bar-at-the-beginning-of-a-line.

22.2.5 How the input is matched

When the generated scanner is run, it analyzes its input looking for strings which match any of its patterns. If it finds more than one match, it takes the one matching the most text (for trailing context rules, this includes the length of the trailing part, even though it will then be returned to the input). If it finds two or more matches of the same length, the rule listed first in the flex input file is chosen.

Once the match is determined which satisfying one of the regular expression or rule, the text corresponding to the match (called the *token*) is made available in the global character pointer **yytext (see Table 22.1 for other lex specific variables)**, and its length in the global integer yyleng. The *action* corresponding to the matched pattern is then executed (a more detailed description of actions follows), and then the remaining input is scanned for another match.

If no match is found, then the *default rule* is executed: the next character in the input is considered matched and copied to the standard output. Thus, the simplest legal flex input is: (see Example 1).

```
%%
```

which generates a scanner that simply copies its input (one character at a time) to its output.

Note that yytext can be defined in two different ways: either as a character *pointer* or as a character *array*. You can control which definition flex uses by including one of the special directives `%pointer' or `%array' in the first (definitions) section of your flex input. The default is `%pointer', unless you use the `-l' lex compatibility option, in which case yytext will be an array. The advantage of using `%pointer' is substantially faster scanning and no buffer overflow when matching very large tokens (unless you run out of dynamic memory). The disadvantage is that you are restricted in how your actions can modify yytext (see the next section), and calls to the `unput()' function destroys the present contents of yytext, which can be a considerable porting headache when moving between different lex versions.

The advantage of `%array' is that you can then modify yytext to your heart's content, and calls to `unput()' do not destroy yytext (see below). Furthermore, existing lex programs sometimes access yytext externally using declarations of the form:

```
extern char yytext[];
```

This definition is erroneous when used with `%pointer', but correct for `%array'.

`%array' defines yytext to be an array of YYLMAX characters, which defaults to a fairly large value. You can change the size by simply #define'ing YYLMAX to a different value in the first section of your flex input. As mentioned above, with `%pointer' yytext grows dynamically to accommodate large tokens. While this means your `%pointer' scanner can accommodate very large tokens (such as matching entire blocks of comments), bear in mind that each time the scanner must resize yytext it also must rescan the entire token from the beginning, so matching such tokens can prove slow. yytext presently does *not* dynamically grow if a call to `unput()' results in too much text being pushed back; instead, a run-time error results.

Actions

Each pattern in a rule has a corresponding action, which can be any arbitrary C statement. The pattern ends at the first non-escaped white space character; the remainder of the line is its action. If the action is empty, then when the pattern is matched the input token is simply discarded.

Table 22.1 Lex variables.

yyin	Of the type FILE*. This points to the current file being parsed by the lexer.
Yyout	Of the type FILE*. This points to the location where the output of the lexer will be written. By default, both yyin and yyout point to standard input and output.
yytext	The text of the matched pattern is stored in this variable (char*).
yyleng	Gives the length of the matched pattern.
yylineno	Provides current line number information. (May or may not be supported by the lexer.)

Table 22.2 Lex Functions.

yylex()	The function that starts the analysis. It is automatically generated by Lex.
yywrap()	This function is called when end of file (or input) is encountered. If this function returns 1, the parsing stops. So, this can be used to parse multiple files. Code can be written in the third section, which will allow multiple files to be parsed. The strategy is to make yyin file pointer point to a different file until all the files are parsed. At the end, yywrap() can return 1 to indicate end of parsing.
yyless(int n)	This function can be used to push back all but first 'n' characters of the read token.
yymore()	This function tells the lexer to append the next token to the current token.

Example 1

This contains no patterns and no actions. Thus, any string matches and default action, i.e. printing takes place.

```
%{
%}
%%
%%
main()
{
yylex();
return 0;
}
```

Let the lex specification file as ex0.lex. Then, run the following sequence of commands.

```
lex   ex0.lex         (creates lex.yy.c)

gcc -o ex0  lex.yy.c  -lfl
```

To Use the generated program.

```
./ex0  < filename
```

This displays the content of the file "filename".

Even this ex0 program can take standard input. That is, we can simply type its name along the command line.

```
./ex0
dd
ds
dads
^d
```

We can also say from this program "ex0" from go on take input till we type a specified string with the help of "**Here the document (<<)**".

```
./ex0 <<END
dsdsa asdd
asdkads asdk
asdkd asd
asdsd
adsd sdd
END
```

This simply displays what ever we have typed on the screen again.

Example 2

A lex program which adds line numbers to the given file and displays the same onto the standard output

```
%{
/*

*/

int lineno=1;
%}

line        .*\n

%%
{line}      {       printf("%5d     %s",lineno++,yytext); }
%%
main()
{
yylex();
return 0;
}
```

If we assume this file name is "ex1.lex", at the command prompt we have to execute the following commands to use lex.

```
lex   ex1.lex        (creates lex.yy.c)

gcc -o ex1  lex.yy.c  -lfl
```

To use the program.

```
./ex1  < filename
```

This displays the content of the file "filename" along with line numbers.
This "ex1" program takes standard input also. Try at the command prompt.

```
./ex1
dd
ds
dads
^d
```

Also try at the command prompt the following.

```
./ex1 <<END
dsdsa asdd
asdkads asdk
asdkd asd
asdsd
adsd sdd
END
```

Example 3

This is also a lex specification program which adds line numbers to the given file and displays the same onto standard output Only difference is that main() is not included unlike previous example. However, automatically, main() is added by the lex.

```
%{
/*


*/

int lineno=1;
%}

line          .*\n

%%
{line}      {        printf("%5d     %s",lineno++,yytext); }
%%
```

Try at the command prompt the following commands.

```
lex   ex2.lex        (creates lex.yy.c)

gcc -o ex2  lex.yy.c  -lfl

./ex2  < filename
```

Example 4

This is a lex specification program which adds line numbers to the given file and displays the same onto standard output. However, it explains about the use of external variable yyin. The resultant program takes filename to be tokenized as command line argument unlike previous programs ex0, ex1 and ex2.

```
%{
/*

*/

int lineno=1;
%}

line        .*\n

%%
{line}      {       printf("%5d      %s",lineno++,yytext); }
%%
main(int argc, char*argv[])
{
extern FILE *yyin;
yyin=fopen(argv[1],"r");
yylex();
return 0;
}
```

If we assume this file name is "ex3.lex", at the command prompt we have to execute the following commands to use lex.

```
lex   ex3.lex        (creates lex.yy.c)

gcc -o ex3  lex.yy.c  -lfl
```

How to Use the program.

```
./ex3  filename
./ex3  < filename
```

Both the commands displays the file "filename" content on the screen along with the line numbers.

Also, try at the command prompt and note the difference.

```
./ex3
dd
ds
dads
^d

./ex3 <<END
dsdsa asdd
asdkads asdk
asdkd asd
asdsd
adsd sdd
END
```

Example 5

This specification program is an attempt to emulate od command.

```
%{


%}

character   .
new line            \n

%%
{character}         {       printf("%o ",yytext[0]); }
{new line} {        printf("%o ", '\n');}
%%
main(int argc, char*argv[])
{
extern FILE *yyin;
yyin=fopen(argv[1],"r");
yylex();
printf("\n");
return 0;
}
```

Let the specification file be "ex5.lex". Run the following commands.

```
lex ex5.lex
gcc –o ex5 lex.yy.c –lfl
./ex5 filename
```

Compare the result with the following command.

```
od -t oC filename
```

Example 6

This program is an attempt to extract only comments from a C program and display the same on standard output

```
%{

%}

comment        \/\*.*\*\/

%%
{comment}      ECHO;
%%
main(int argc, char*argv[])
{
extern FILE *yyin;
yyin=fopen(argv[1],"r");
yylex();
printf("\n");
return 0;
}
```

Let the above specification file be "ex6.lex". Run the following commands.

```
lex ex6.lex
gcc –o ex6 lex.yy.c –lfl
./ex6  filename.c
```

Example 7

This lex specification program is an attempt to replace all nonnull sequences of white spaces by a single blank character. Here, pattern 'ws" is specified as a series of spaces of tab characters and action is specified as return or print a single space. Any other string is returned as it is.

```
%{
%}
ws [ \t]

%%
{ws}+      {printf(" "); }
.   {printf("%s",yytext);}

%%
main(int argc, char*argv[])
{
extern FILE *yyin;
yyin=fopen(argv[1],"r");
yylex();
printf("\n");
return 0;
}
```

Let the above specification file be "ex7.lex". Run the following commands.

```
lex ex7.lex
gcc –o ex7 lex.yy.c –lfl
./ex7  filename
```

Example 8

This specification program replaces all the occurrences of "rama" with "RAMA" and "sita" with "SITA". This example is used from explain that we can use a string as a direct pattern in the specification file.

```
%{
%}

%%
"rama"      {printf("RAMA");}

"sita"      {printf("SITA"); }
%%
main(int argc, char*argv[])
{
extern FILE *yyin;
yyin=fopen(argv[1],"r");
yylex();
printf("\n");
return 0;
}
```

Let the above specification file be "ex8.lex". Run the following commands.

```
lex ex8.lex
gcc –o ex8 lex.yy.c –lfl
./ex8  filename
```

Example 9

This lex specification program is used to count all occurrences of "rama" and "sita" in a given file.

```
%{
int count=0;

%}



%%
"rama"      {count++;}

"sita"      {count++; }
.   ;
%%
main(int argc, char*argv[])
{
extern FILE *yyin;
yyin=fopen(argv[1],"r");
yylex();
printf("No of Occurrences=%d\n",count);
return 0;
}
```

Let the above specification file be "ex9.lex". Run the following commands.

```
lex ex9.lex
gcc –o ex9 lex.yy.c –lfl
./ex9  filename
```

Example 10

This lex specification program is used from generate a C program which removes all the occurrences of "sita" and "rama" in the given file.

```
%{
%}

%%
"rama"
"sita"
.   ECHO;

%%
```

Let the above specification file be "ex9a.lex". Run the following commands.

```
lex ex9a.lex
gcc -o ex9a lex.yy.c -lfl
./ex9a< filename
```

Example 11

This lex specification program is used to count and print the number of pages, lines, words and characters in a given file.

```
%{

int lines=0,words=0,characters=0,pages=0;

%}
%START   InWord
NewLine   [\n]
WhiteSpace         [\t ]
NewPage            [\f]

%%

{NewPage}          {BEGIN 0; characters++;pages++;}
{NewLine} {BEGIN 0; characters++;lines++;}
{WhiteSpace}       {BEGIN 0; characters++;}
<InWord>.characters++;
.             {BEGIN InWord; characters++; words++;}
%%
int main()
{
yylex();
printf("%d %d %d %d\n",lines,words,characters,pages);
}
```

Let the above specification file be "ex10.lex". Run the following commands.

```
lex ex10.lex
gcc -o ex10 lex.yy.c -lfl
./ex10  filename
```

Example 12

This lex specification program also can be used from find no of lines, words and characters in a given file. Here, yyleng indicates the length of the string yytext.

```
%{

int lines=0,words=0,characters=0;

%}
word        [^ \t\n]+
eol \n
%%
{word}      {words++;characters+=yyleng;}
{eol}       {characters++;lines++;}
.           { characters++; }
%%
int main()
{
yylex();
printf("%d %d %d \n",lines,words,characters);
}
```

Let the above specification file be "ex11.lex". Run the following commands.

```
lex ex11.lex
gcc -o ex11 lex.yy.c -lfl
./ex11  filename
```

Example 13

This lex specification program is to replace all the occurrences of the word "username" with users login name.

```
%{
%}

%%
username  printf("%s",getlogin() );
%%
main(int argc, char*argv[])
{
extern FILE *yyin;
yyin=fopen(argv[1],"r");
yylex();
printf("\n");
return 0;
}
```

Let the above specification file be "ex12.lex". Run the following commands.

```
lex ex12.lex
gcc –o ex12 lex.yy.c –lfl
./ex12  filename
```

Example 14

This lex specification program is to extract all html tags in the given file.

```
%{
%}

%%
"<"[^>]*>          {printf("%s\n", yytext); }
.   ;
%%
main(int argc, char*argv[])
{
extern FILE *yyin;
yyin=fopen(argv[1],"r");
yylex();
printf("\n");
return 0;
}
```

Let the above specification file be "ex13.lex". Run the following commands.

```
lex ex13.lex
gcc –o ex13 lex.yy.c –lfl
./ex13  filename.html
```

Example 15

This lex specification program is from generate a program which simulates cat command to create files. While giving input first "start" word has from be typed and at the end "end" word has from be typed.

```
%{
%}

%%
"start"        ;
"end"        exit(-1);
.   ECHO ;
%%
main(int argc, char*argv[])
{
extern FILE *yyin;
yyout=fopen(argv[1],"w");
yylex();
printf("\n");
return 0;
}
```

Let the above specification file be "ex14.lex". Run the following commands.

```
lex ex14.lex
gcc –o ex14 lex.yy.c –lfl
./ex14  filename
```

Example 16

This lex specification program is to eliminate multiple spaces and tabs and replace with a single space and remove empty lines. Here, yytext is processed in our actions.

```
%{

#include<stdlib.h>
#include<stdio.h>
```

```
int emptyline=0;
%}

SPACES    [ \t]
eol \n

%%
{SPACES}+  {printf(" "); }
\n|.             {
                char c=yytext[0];
               if(!isspace(c))  {
                                 emptyline=1;
                                 putchar(c);
                                 }
               if(c=='\n')
                      {
                      if(emptyline)putchar(c);
                      emptyline=0;
                      }
          }
%%
main(int argc, char*argv[])
{
extern FILE *yyin;
yyin=fopen(argv[1],"r");
yylex();
printf("\n");
return 0;
}
```

Example 17

This lex specification program is to display only C comments in a given C file. Here, whenever "/*" pattern is encountered in the input, we have written code to process next characters in the input till we encounter the pattern "*/". Whenever, "/*" pattern is encountered the C code will be executed. Here, we have used lex specific function (see Table 8.2)input() is used to read characters from the lex input buffer and print them till it encounters "*/" pattern.

```
%{
%}

%%
"/*"        {char c;
```

```
int done=0;
ECHO;
do
{
        while((c=input())!='*') putchar(c);
putchar(c);
while((c=input())=='*') putchar(c);
putchar(c);
if(c=='/') done=1;
}       while(!done);
}

.       ;
\n      ;
%%
main(int argc, char*argv[])
{
extern FILE *yyin;
yyin=fopen(argv[1],"r");
yylex();
printf("\n");
return 0;
}
```

Example 18

This lex specification file is to display a file's content by replacing ":" with \t

```
%{

%}

%%
":" {printf("\t");}

\n|.        ECHO ;
%%
main(int argc, char*argv[])
{
extern FILE *yyin;
yyin=fopen(argv[1],"r");
yylex();
```

```
printf("\n");
return 0;
}
```

Let the above specification file be "ex17.lex". Run the following commands.

```
lex ex17.lex
gcc –o ex17 lex.yy.c –lfl
./ex17  /etc/passwd
```

REJECT directs the scanner to proceed on to the "second best" rule which matched the input (or a prefix of the input). The rule is chosen as described above in "How the Input is Matched", and yytext and yyleng set up appropriately. It may either be one which matched as much text as the originally chosen rule but came later in the flex input file, or one which matched less text

Example 19

For example, to count all instance of she and he, including the instances of he that are included in she, use the following action:

```
%{
int s=0;
%}

%%
she            {s++; REJECT;}
he             {s++}
\n             |
.              ;

%%
main(int argc, char*argv[])
{
extern FILE *yyin;
yyin=fopen(argv[1],"r");
yylex();
printf("No of occurrences of he including in he in she=%d\n",s);
return 0;
}
```

After counting the occurrences of she, the **lex** command rejects the input string and then counts the occurrences of he. Because he does not include she, a **REJECT** action is not necessary on he.

Example 20

The following lex specification file is used to generate a C program which counts number of words in a file other than the word "incl".

```
%{
int nw=0;
%}
%%
incl                    nw--; REJECT;
[^ \t\n]+  nw++;
%%
main(int argc, char*argv[])
{
extern FILE *yyin;
yyin=fopen(argv[1],"r");
yylex();
printf("No of words other than the word incl=%d\n",nw);
return 0;
}
```

Example 21

The following lex specification program generates a C program which takes a string "abcd" and prints the following output. From terminate the program enter ^d.

```
abcd
abc
ab
a
%{
%}
%%
a|ab|abc|abcd      printf("%s\n",yytext);REJECT
.|\n

%%
main(int argc, char*argv[])
{
extern FILE *yyin;
yyin=fopen(argv[1],"r");
yylex();
return 0;
}
```

Example 22

The following lex specification file generates a C program which extract http, ftp or telnet tags from the given file.

```
%{
%}
%%
(ftp|http|telnet):\/\/[^ \n<>"]*
.|\n
%%
main(int argc, char*argv[])
{
extern FILE *yyin;
yyin=fopen(argv[1],"r");
yylex();
return 0;
}
```

The above program is supposed extract URL's with capitol letters such as HTTP, FTP or TELENT then we tell flex to build a case-insensitive lexer using the **"-i"** option.

Example 23

The following lex program generates a C program which takes standard input as output of Unix date and gives either of the following messages

Good Morning
Good Afternoon
Good Evening

```
        %{
        %}
%%
Morning       [ ](00|01|02|03|04|05|06|07|08|09|10|11)[:]
Afternoon     [ ](12|13|14|15|16|17)[:]
Evening       [ ](18|19|20|21|22|23)[:]

%%
{Morning}      printf("Good Morning ");
{Afternoon}    printf("Good Afternoon ");
{Evening}      printf("Good Evening ");
.              ;
```

If we assume that executable file name of the generated C program is "greet" then we can run the following command from see the output.

date | greet

BEGIN followed by the name of a start condition places the scanner in the corresponding start condition.

Example 24

The `yymore()' tells the scanner that the next time it matches a rule, the corresponding token should be *appended* onto the current value of yytext rather than replacing it. First, `yymore()' depends on the value of yyleng correctly reflecting the size of the current token, so you must not modify yyleng if you are using `yymore()'. Second, the presence of `yymore()' in the scanner's action entails a minor performance penalty in the scanner's matching speed.

Example 25

The yyless(n)' returns all but the first *n* characters of the current token back to the input stream, where they will be rescanned when the scanner looks for the next match. yytext and yyleng are adjusted appropriately (e.g., yyleng will now be equal to *n*). An argument of 0 to yyless will cause the entire current input string to be scanned again. Unless you've changed how the scanner will subsequently process its input (using BEGIN, for example), this will result in an endless loop. Note that yyless is a macro and can only be used in the flex input file, not from other source files.

Example 26

The following lex specification file is used to generate scanner program for a toy Pascal-like language which extracts integers type of numbers, float type of numbers, key words such as if, procedure etc.

```
%{
#include <math.h>
#include<stdlib.h>
%}

DIGIT   [0-9]
ID      [a-z][a-z0-9]*

%%

{DIGIT}+    {
            printf( "An integer: %s (%d)\n", yytext,
                    atoi( yytext ) );
            }

{DIGIT}+"."{DIGIT}*       {
            printf( "A float: %s (%g)\n", yytext,
                    atof( yytext ) );
            }

if|then|begin|end|procedure|function        {
            printf( "A keyword: %s\n", yytext );
            }
{ID}        printf( "An identifier: %s\n", yytext );
```

```
"+"|"-"|"*"|"/"   printf( "An operator: %s\n", yytext );

"{"[\^{$\;$}}\n]*"}"     /* eat up one-line comments */

[ \t\n]+          /* eat up whitespace */

.          printf( "Unrecognized character: %s\n", yytext );

%%

main( argc, argv )
int argc;
char **argv;
{
++argv, --argc;  /* skip over program name */
if ( argc > 0 )
        yyin = fopen( argv[0], "r" );
else
        yyin = stdin;

yylex();
}
```

Example 27

A lex input file that changes all numbers to hexadecimal in input file while ignoring all others.

```
%{

#include<stdlib.h>
 %}

digit  [0-9]
number {digit}+
%%
{number} { int n = atoi(yytext); printf("%x", n); }
. {;}
 %%
main(int argc, char*argv[])
{
extern FILE *yyin;
yyin=fopen(argv[1],"r");
yylex();
return 0;
}
```

Example 28

The lex specification file generates a C program which counts number of word with length 1 character, 2 characters vice versa in the given input.

```
%{
int leng[100];

%}
%%
[a-z]+      leng[yyleng]++;
.|\n        ;
%%
main(int argc, char*argv[])
{
extern FILE *yyin;
int i;
for(i=1;i<100;i++) leng[i]=0;
yyin=fopen(argv[1],"r");
yylex();
printf("Word Length Frequency\n");
for(i=1;i<100;i++)
printf("%11d %10d\n",i,leng[i]);
return 0;
}
```

Example 29

```
%{
int leng[100];

%}
%%
[a-z]+      leng[yyleng]++;
.|\n        ;
%%
int yywrap()
{
int i;
printf("Word Length   Frequency\n");

for(i=1;i<100;i++)
if(leng[i]) printf("%11d %10d\n",i,leng[i]);
return 1;
}
```

```
main(int argc, char*argv[])
{
extern FILE *yyin;
int i;
for(i=1;i<100;i++) leng[i]=0;
yyin=fopen(argv[1],"r");
yylex();
return 0;
}
```

Example 30

This lex specification file is used to generate a C program which counts how many times a given alphabet is next to another alphabet in the given input (This frequency table is called as diagram in natural language processing terminology and also in algorithms.

```
%{
#include<stdlib.h>
int F[26][26];

%}
%%
[A-Za-z][A-Za-z] {
    F[toupper(yytext[0])-65][toupper(yytext[1])-65]++;REJECT;
    }
.|\n          ;
%%
main(int argc, char*argv[])
{
extern FILE *yyin;
int i,j;
for(i=0;i<26;i++)
for(j=0;j<26;j++)F[i][j]=0;

yyin=fopen(argv[1],"r");
yylex();
for(i=0;i<26;i++){
for(j=0;j<26;j++) printf("%d", F[i][j]);
printf("\n");
}
return 0;
}
```

If we give the following input to the program which is created compiling lex.yy.c file generated from the above lex specification file.

ABCDEFGHIJKLMNOPQRSTUVWXYZabcdefghijklmnopqrstuvwxyz

Result is:

```
02000000000000000000000000
00200000000000000000000000
00020000000000000000000000
00002000000000000000000000
00000200000000000000000000
00000020000000000000000000
00000002000000000000000000
00000000200000000000000000
00000000020000000000000000
00000000002000000000000000
00000000000200000000000000
00000000000020000000000000
00000000000002000000000000
00000000000000200000000000
00000000000000020000000000
00000000000000002000000000
00000000000000000200000000
00000000000000000020000000
00000000000000000002000000
00000000000000000000200000
00000000000000000000020000
00000000000000000000002000
00000000000000000000000200
00000000000000000000000020
00000000000000000000000002
10000000000000000000000000
```

Example 31

In the C program generated by the lex specification file, when yylex() finished with the first file, it calls yywrap(), which opens the next file, and yylex() continues. When yywrap() has exhausted all the command line arguments, it returns 1, and yylex() returns with value 0 (but we don't use the return value).

Like previous examples, this also extracts URL's from the given files whose names are given along the command line to the above program.

```
%{
#include <stdio.h>
#include <errno.h>
int file_num;
int file_num_max;
char **files;
extern int errno;
%}
%%
(ftp|http):\/\/[^ \n<>"]*      printf("%s\n",yytext);
.|\n                           ;
%%
int main(int argc, char *argv[]) {
        file_num=1;
        file_num_max = argc;
        files = argv;
        if ( argc > 1 ) {
                if ( (yyin = fopen(argv[file_num],"r")) == 0 ) {
                        perror(argv[file_num]);
                        exit(1);
                }
        }
        while( yylex() )
                ;
        return 0;
}

int yywrap() {
        fclose(yyin);
        if ( ++file_num < file_num_max ) {
                if ( (yyin = fopen(files[file_num],"r")) == 0 ) {
                        perror(files[file_num]);
                        exit(1);
                }
                return 0;
        } else {
                return 1;
        }
}
```

Start Conditions

Also, flex provides a mechanism for conditionally activating rules. Any rule whose pattern is prefixed with "<sc>" will only be active when the scanner is in the start condition named "sc". For example,

```
<STRING>[^"]*      {                    }
```

will be active only match is found when the scanner is in the "STRING" start condition. Also, if we want same action to be done for a given regular expression under different states, we may have to enter all the states names like the following manner

```
<STRING, ERROR, WARNING>"\*";
```

where STRING, ERROR, and WARNING are different states.

Example 32

This example is used to remove C comments from the file. It uses states facility available in the lex. Initially, lex is assumed to be in INITIAL state and when "/*" pattern is found it will be changing to COMMENT state. When it is in COMMENT state then pattern "*/" puts the lex in again INITIAL state. When it is in COMMENT state, whatever it encounters it will be eaten whereas if it is in INITIAL state simply the same is displayed.

```
%{
%}


%s COMMENT

%%
<INITIAL>"//".*          ;
<INITIAL>"/*"            BEGIN COMMENT;
<INITIAL>.               ECHO;
<INITIAL>[\n]            ECHO;
<COMMENT>"*/"            BEGIN INITIAL;
<COMMENT>.               ;
<COMMENT>[\n]            ;
%%

main() {
  yylex();
}
```

Example 33

The following lex specification file is used to generate a C program which is used to generate a html file from a data file.

The input format is that of a textual spreadsheet. Each spreadsheet entry is numbered using an alphabetical character (indicating the row) and an integer (indicating the column).

To make the task easier, we can assume several things. First there will not be more than 26 columns. Second, that the entries will be ordered in the obvious way, i.e. A1, followed by B1, ... then A2, followed by B2, etc. Third, there will only be one entry per line and that all entries exist in the file. Finally, we are going to assume that there are no spreadsheet equations.

An example input might be

```
A0 = "Name"
B0 = "SSN"
C0 = "HW1"
D0 = "HW2"
A1 = "Scott Smith"
B1 = "123-44-5678"
C1 = 82
D1 = 44.2
A2 = "Sam Sneed"
B2 = "999-88-7777"
C2 = 92
D2 = 84
```

For output, we what to generate the appropriate HTML table. In html, tables are surrounded by <table> ... </table>. Each row of the table is surrounded by <tr> ... </tr> and each entry in a row by <td> ... </td>. For the above input we would want to output:

```
<table>
<tr>
<td> Name </td>
<td> SSN </td>
<td> HW1 </td>
<td> HW2 </td>
</tr>
<tr>
<td> Scott Smith </td>
<td> 123-44-5678 </td>
<td> 82 </td>
<td> 44.2 </td>
</tr>
<tr>
<td> Sam Sneed </td>
<td> 999-88-7777 </td>
<td> 92 </td>
<td> 84 </td>
</tr>
</table>
```

When viewed with a viewer, this looks like:

Name	SSN	HW1	HW2
Scott Smith	123-44-5678	82	44.2
Sam Sneed	999-88-7777	92	84

Lex specification for the conversion

```
%%
^A0              {printf("<table>\n<tr>\n");}
^A[0-9]*         {printf("</tr>\n<tr>\n");}
^[B-Z][0-9]*     ;
[0-9]*           {printf("<td> "); ECHO; printf(" </td>\n");}
[0-9]*"."[0-9]*  {printf("<td> "); ECHO; printf(" </td>\n");}
\"[^"]*\"  {printf("<td>   ");   yytext[yyleng-1]   =   '   ';   printf("%s
</td>\n",yytext+1);}
=          ;
[ \n]            ;
.          ECHO;
%%

main() {
  printf("<html>\n");
  yylex();
  printf("</tr>\n</table>\n</html>\n");
}
```

Example 34

The following specification file is for the opposite purpose. That is, given html languages <table> specification such the following it has to extract only field's information.

Sample Input :

```
<table>
<tr>
<td> Name </td>
<td> SSN </td>
<td> HW1 </td>
<td> HW2 </td>
</tr>
<tr>
<td> Scott Smith </td>
<td> 123-44-5678 </td>
```

```
<td> 82 </td>
<td> 44.2 </td>
</tr>
<tr>
<td> Sam Sneed </td>
<td> 999-88-7777 </td>
<td> 92 </td>
<td> 84 </td>
</tr>
</table>
```

Sample output:

Name SSN HW1 HW2 Scott Smith 123-44-5678 82 44.2 Sam Sneed 999-88-7777 92 84

Lex Specification File

```
%{
%}


%s  TABL REC DATA

%%
<INITIAL>"<table>"                    BEGIN TABL;
<TABL>"<\/table>"                     BEGIN INITIAL;
<TABL><tr>          BEGIN REC;
<REC><\/tr>         BEGIN TABL;
<REC><td>           BEGIN DATA;
<DATA><\/td>        BEGIN REC;
<DATA>.             ECHO;
<DATA>[ \t\n]                ;
<REC>[ \t\n]        ;
<TABL>[ \t\n]       ;
%%

main() {
  yylex();
}
```

Example 35

The above specification file can be also written as the following by combining last three state conditions.

```
%{
%}


%s  TABL REC DATA

%%
<INITIAL>"<table>"                BEGIN TABL;
<TABL>"<\/table>"                 BEGIN INITIAL;
<TABL><tr>        BEGIN REC;
<REC><\/tr>       BEGIN TABL;
<REC><td>         BEGIN DATA;
<DATA><\/td>      BEGIN REC;
<DATA>.           ECHO;
<DATA,REC,TABL>[ \t\n]                ;
%%

main() {
  yylex();
}
```

Example 36

This example is used to explain yymore() and other pattern usage. Run the program by giving input like BOMBAYB.

```
%{
  int flag=0;
%}

%%
B[^B]*      { if (flag == 0) {
               flag = 1;
               yymore();
             }
             else    {
               flag = 0;
              printf("%s", yytext);
               printf("%d\n",yyleng);
```

```
                }
            }
%%

int main()
{
yylex();
}
```

22.3 Yacc - A Parser Generator

Normally, syntax analysis is employed to validate or check the syntax of any program. SW systems which are used for this purpose is referred as parsers. It *is* also possible to create a simple parser using Lex alone by making extensive use of the user-defined states (i.e. start-conditions). However, such a parser quickly becomes un-maintainable, as the number of user-defined states tends to explode.

Once our input file syntax contains complex structures, such as "balanced" brackets, or contains elements which are context-sensitive, compiler-compilers such as **yacc (yet another compiler compiler)** is best available alternative. "Context-sensitive" in this case means that a word or symbol can have different interpretations, depending on *where* it appears in the input language. For example in C, the '*' character is used for both multiplication, and to specify indirection (i.e. to dereference a pointer to a piece of memory). That is, it's meaning is "context-sensitive".

Yacc provides a general tool for imposing structure on the input to a computer program. That is, yacc user prepares a specification of the input process (grammar rules) as explained in detail in the following sections. Then, when yacc command is used with this specification file as input, it generates a C language program which checks the grammar (specified in the **.y** file) in the given input file. This generated C language program in turn calls lexical analyzer, probably generated by using Lex command, to pick up the basic items (called tokens) and test their syntactical validity according to the specified grammatical rules. Thus, both lex and yacc commands are used while writing compilers. For detailed discussion on compilers one can refer [Aho, 1985].

To summarize, the steps in developing compilers (parsers) using Yacc and Lex are:

- Write the grammar in a .y file (also specify the actions here that are to be taken in C).
- Write a lexical analyzer to process input and pass tokens to the parser whenever it is needed. This can be done using Lex command as explained in previous section. That is, we may prepare Lex specification file also.
- Write error handling routines (like yyerror()).
- Run yacc command on .y file such that it gives **y.tab.c** file and **y.tab.h** file.
- Run lex command on lex specification file such that it gives **lex.yy.c** file.
- Compile code produced by Yacc and lex as well as any other relevant source files.
- Test the resulting executable file by giving input file.

22.3.1 The Yacc Specification Rules

Like lex, **yacc** has it's own specification language. A yacc specification is structured along the same lines as a Lex specification. By convention, a Yacc file has the suffix .y. The Yacc compiler is invoked from the compile line as **yacc -dv file.y**

```
%{
  /* C declarations and includes */
%}
  /* Yacc token and type declarations */
%%
  /* Yacc Specification
     in the form of grammar rules like this:
  */
  symbol    :    symbols tokens
                 { $$ = my_c_code($1); }
            ;
%%
  /* C language program (the rest) */
```

The Yacc Specification rules are the place where you "glue" the various tokens together that lex has conveniently provided to you.

Each grammar rule defines a symbol in terms of:

- other symbols
- tokens (or terminal symbols) which come from the lexer.

Each rule can have an associated action, which is executed *after* all the component symbols of the rule have been parsed. Actions are basically C-program statements surrounded by curly braces.

Terminal and non-terminal symbols

Terminal symbol: Represents a class of syntactically equivalent tokens. Terminal symbols are of three types:

Named token: These are defined via the %token identifier. By convention, these are all upper case.

Character token: A character constant written in the same format as in C. For example, + is a character token.

Literal string token: is written like a C string constant. For example, "<<" is a literal string token.

The lexer returns named tokens.

Non-terminal symbol: Is a symbol that is a group of non-terminal and terminal symbols. By convention, these are all lower case.

For example, in English one of the valid form of a sentence is the one having subject, verb and object.

Sentence : Subject Verb Object

Similarly, in US style, date is represented as:

Date: Month / Day / Year

Here, Date can be termed as Non-terminal and Month, '/', Day, and Year can be termed as terminals (i.e. they are not further decomposable). In Yacc specification, the same rule can be specified as:

Date: MONTH '/' DAY '/' YEAR { /*actions */}

Actual values for MONTH, DAY and YEAR are returned from the lexical analyzer by tokenizing the given input.

Similarly, Context-free grammar production such as:

p->AbC

will have equivalent Yacc Rule as:

p : A b C { /* actions */}

The general style for coding the rules is to have all Terminals in upper-case and all non-terminals in lower-case (Surprise!!. Exactly opposite to Automata Theory or compiler construction books notation's).

Also, we can use few Yacc specific declarations which begins with a %sign in yacc specification file such as:

1. **%union** It defines the Stack type for the Parser. It is a union of various datas/structures/ objects.
2. **%token** These are the terminals returned by the yylex function to the yacc. A token can also have type associated with it for good type checking and syntax directed translation. A type of a token can be specified as %token <stack member> tokenName.
3. **%type** The type of a non-terminal symbol in the Grammar rule can be specified with this.

   The format is %type <stack member> non-terminal.
4. **%noassoc** Specifies that there is no associativity of a terminal symbol.
5. **%left** Specifies the left associativity of a Terminal Symbol
6. **%right** Specifies the right assocoativity of a Terminal Symbol.
7. **%start** Specifies the L.H.S non-terminal symbol of a production rule which should be taken as the starting point of the grammar rules.
8. **%prec** Changes the precedence level associated with a particular rule to that of the following token name or literal.

Let us discuss about how to write a parser to recognize US style date.

File date.y

```
%token NUMBER SLASH NL
%%
date        :
    |NUMBER SLASH NUMBER SLASH NUMBER NL {printf("OK"); }
    ;
%%
void yyerror(char *s)
{
  printf("Error\n");
}
```

File date.lex

```
%{
#include"y.tab.h"
%}

%%
[0-9]+              return NUMBER;
"\/"                return SLASH;
'\n'        return NL;
```

Run the following command.

```
yacc -dv date.y
```

This command generates the files y.tab.c, y.tab.h and y.output.

File y.tab.h contains:

```
#ifndef YYERRCODE
#define YYERRCODE 256
#endif

#define NUMBER 257
#define SLASH 258
#define NL 259
```

The file y.tab.c contains the C code for the parser which recognizes the given grammatical rules (here it is date format) in a given input file.

Also, run the following commands to generate the final parser.

```
lex date.lex

gcc –o DATE y.tab.c lex.yy.c –ly –lfl
```

Run the program DATE and enter interactively a string other than of the format 12/31/1998 and observe the error message. Otherwise, it displays the message OK.

As mentioned earlier, Yacc uses symbolic tokens. In the above Yacc specification file we have declared symbolic Tokens such as NUMBER, NL, and SLASH using %token declaration. When we run Yacc command on this specification file it generates the file y.tab.h (an example is shown above) in which for all these token a number assigned starting from 257.

Also, observe that these symbolic tokens are used in lex specification file, in which when a regular expression match occurs, yylex() returns this symbolic token. That is, the lexical analyzer, yylex() generated by lex command takes responsibility of reading input stream and recognizing low level structures (regular expressions) historically called as terminal symbols and communicates these tokens to the parser which in turn recognizes the nonterminals, i.e. grammatical structures.

Tokens also will have assigned values during the scanning process and the same is assigned to variable yylval which is defined internally by Yacc.

Example 37

This example is to develop parser which recognizes strings of form $a^n b^n$, where n>=1.

Yacc Specification File (ab.y)

```
%token A B
%%
start: anbn '\n' {return 0;}
anbn :  A B
    | A anbn B
    ;
%%
#include"lex.yy.c"
```

Lex Specification File (ab.lex)

```
%%
a    return(A);
b    return(B);
.    return(yytext[0]);
\n   return('\n');
```

To create parser which recognizes strings of for a^nb^n, run the following commands

```
lex ab.lex
yacc –dv ab.y
gcc –o anbn y.tab.c lex.yy.c -ly –lfl
```

Run the resulting program (anbn) and check by giving pattern such as:

aabb or aaaabbbb.

If we do not give matching input it gives error message "Syntax Error". Otherwise it displays nothing.

Example 38

The following is a little modified version of the above program with error checking and better user interface when match occurs.

Yacc Specification File (ab1.y)

```
%token A B
%%
start: anbn '\n' { printf("  is in anbn\n");                return 0; }
anbn:  A B
    | A anbn B
    ;
%%
#include "lex.yy.c"

yyerror(s)
char *s;
{
  printf("%s, it is not in anbn\n", s);
}
```

Lex Specification File(ab1.lex)

```
%%
a    return(A);
b    return(B);
.    return(yytext[0]);
\n   return('\n');
```

To create parser, run the following commands

```
lex  ab1.lex
yacc –dv ab1.y
gcc –o anbn1 y.tab.c  lex.yy.c  -ly –lfl
```

Run the resulting program (anbn1) and check by giving pattern such as:

```
aabb   or aaaabbbb
```

Example 39

This example is also to explain simple yacc example.

Yacc Specification File(two.y)

```
%token DING DONG BELL
%%
rhyme      :     sound place
    ;
sound      :     DING DONG
    ;

place      :     BELL
    ;
%%
#include "lex.yy.c"
```

Lex Specification File (two.lex)

```
%%
"ding"     return (DING);
"dong"     return (DONG);
"bell"     return (BELL);
```

To create parser which accepts "ding dong bell", run the following commands

```
lex  two.lex
yacc –dv two.y
gcc –o two y.tab.c  lex.yy.c  -ly –lfl
```

After creating parser if we give input "ding dong bell" it accepts otherwise rejects, i.e. it gives an error message "Syntax Error".

Example 40

This Yacc specification and lex specification program's are for testing balanced parentheses.

Yacc Specification File (bp.y)

```
%{
#include <ctype.h>
#include <stdio.h>
#include "y.tab.h"
extern int yydebug;
%}
%token     OPEN   CLOSE
%%
lines         : s '\n' {printf("OK\n"); }
    ;
s   :
    | OPEN s CLOSE  s
       ;
%%

void yyerror(char * s)
{
  fprintf (stderr, "%s\n", s);
}

int yywrap(){return 1; }
int main(void) {
yydebug=1;
return yyparse();}
```

Lex Specification File (bp.lex)

```
%{
#include"y.tab.h"
%}

%%
[ \t]    { /* skip blanks and tabs */ }
"(" return OPEN;
")" return CLOSE;
\n|.     { return yytext[0]; }
```

To create parser which accepts strings having balanced parentheses, run the following commands

```
lex  bp.lex
yacc –dv bp.y
gcc –o bp y.tab.c  lex.yy.c  -ly –lfl
```

Test the generated parser (bp) by giving the following input.

```
(())   or (()(()()))
```

Example 41

The following Yacc and Lex specification files are used to generate parser which recognizes arithmetic expressions involving + and -.

Yacc Specification File (ath.y)

```
%{
%}

%token NAME NUMBER EQUL PLUS MINUS

%%

Stmt  :  NAME EQUL exp
      | exp
      ;

exp   :  NUMBER PLUS NUMBER
      | NUMBER MINUS NUMBER
      | NUMBER MINUS exp
      | NUMBER PLUS exp
      ;

%%

void yyerror(char * s)
{

  printf ( "%s\n", s);

}
```

```
int yywrap(){return 1;}

int main(void) {return yyparse();}
```

Lex Specification File (ath.lex)

```
%{
#include"y.tab.h"
%}

%%
[a-zA-Z\_][a-zA-Z\_0-9]*  return NAME;
[0-9]+      return NUMBER;
"+"         return PLUS;
"-" return MINUS;
"="         return EQUL;
```

To create parser which accepts arithmetic expressions with +, - operators, run the following commands

```
lex  ath.lex
yacc –dv ath.y
gcc –o ath y.tab.c  lex.yy.c  -ly –lfl
```

Run the command "ath" and enter the following expressions

```
1+2+3-2  or 1-2-3-5+4
```

Example 42

This Yacc and Lex specification files can be used to generate a tiny language which can be used (simulation only!!) to control a thermostat. It accepts commands such as "on", "off" etc.

Yacc Specification File (thermo.y)

```
%{
#include <stdio.h>
#include <string.h>
void yyerror(const char *str)
{
      fprintf(stderr,"error: %s\n",str);
}
```

```
int yywrap()
{
        return 1;
}

main()
{
        yyparse();
}

%}

%token NUMBER TOKHEAT STATE TOKTARGET TOKTEMPERATURE
%%
commands :
                | commands command
                ;

command:
        heat_switch
        |
        target_set
        ;

heat_switch:
        TOKHEAT STATE
        {
                printf("\tHeat turned on or off\n");
        }
        ;

target_set:
        TOKTARGET TOKTEMPERATURE NUMBER
        {
                printf("\tTemperature set\n");
        }
        ;
```

Lex Specification File (thermo.lex)

```
%{
#include <stdio.h>
```

```
#include "y.tab.h"
%}
%%
 [0-9]+                return NUMBER;
heat                  return TOKHEAT;
on|off                return STATE;
target                return TOKTARGET;
temperature             return TOKTEMPERATURE;
\n                   /* ignore end of line */;
[ \t]+                /* ignore whitespace */;
%%
```

To create parser which accepts the above language, run the following commands

```
lex  thermo.lex
yacc -dv thermo.y
gcc -o thermo y.tab.c  lex.yy.c  -ly -lfl
```

Example 43

The following Yacc and Lex specification files are used to recognize addresses which are in a specific format only.

Yacc Specification File (add.y)

```
%{
#include <stdio.h>
void yyerror(const char *str)
{

      fprintf(stderr,"error: %s\n",str);
}


int yywrap()
{
      return 1;
}

%}

%token CAPSTRING CAPLETTER NUMBER STATE ZIPPLUSFOUR COMMA HASH
DOT NEWLINE DOORNO

%%
```

```
sentence: firstline secondline thirdline { printf("Have a valid address.\n"); }
        ;

firstline: firstname surname NEWLINE
         | firstname middlename surname NEWLINE
         ;

secondline: DOORNO street NEWLINE
          | DOORNO street HASH NUMBER NEWLINE
          ;

thirdline: city STATE COMMA zip NEWLINE
         ;

firstname: CAPSTRING ;

middlename: CAPLETTER DOT ;

surname: CAPSTRING ;

street: CAPSTRING
      | CAPSTRING street
      ;

city: CAPSTRING
    | CAPSTRING city
    ;

zip: ZIPPLUSFOUR
   ;

%%


int main( void ) {

    yyparse();
return 0;
}
```

Lex Specification File (add.lex)

```
%{
#include "y.tab.h"
%}
%%
 [\t ]+              /* ignore whitespace */;
 [A-Z][a-z]+          { return CAPSTRING; };
 [A-Z][A-Z]          {return STATE; }
 [A-Z]               {return CAPLETTER; }
 [0-9]+              {return NUMBER; }
 [0-9]+-[0-9]+-[0-9]+      {return DOORNO; }
 PIN-[0-9][0-9][0-9][0-9][0-9][0-9]                 {return ZIPPLUSFOUR; }

\,          {return COMMA; }

#           {return HASH; }

\.          {return DOT; }

\n          {return NEWLINE; }

%%
```

To create parser which accepts addresses, run the following commands

```
lex  add.lex
yacc –dv add.y
gcc –o add y.tab.c  lex.yy.c  -ly –lfl
```

Sample input which is accepted by the parser developed is:

```
Ravi Teja
12-33-33 First Street
Visakhapatnam AP, PIN-121212
```

22.3.2 Use of Pseudovariables

While writing actions for each grammar rule, we can make use of pseudo variables supported by the Yacc. As mentioned earlier, when a grammar rule is matched, every symbol in the rule will have a value which is returned by yylex(). Usually, this is assumed to be integer unless redefined by the user. These values are maintained as a separate stack known as value stack in addition to parse stack which maintains the symbols.

The variable $$ represents the value of nonterminal and $1, $2, .. as the values of symbols on the right hand side of the nonterminal(rule). Thus, in the following example,

```
expr        : expr PLUS term        { $$ = $1 + $3; }
```

$$ refers to expression value and $1 and $3 refers to both the operands. That is sum of these operands are assigned to the expression.

In order to tell YACC about the new type of yylval, we add this line to the header of our YACC grammar:

```
#define YYSTYPE char *
extern YYSTYPE yylval;
```

Also, we can use the %union in yacc file such that we can declare that yylval to be a union of an integer, a string pointer, and a character.

```
%union { int integer_value; char *string_value; char op_value; }
```

Now, we can declare both terminals and nonterminals as either integer or char type using the following manner.

```
%token <int> OPRND1
%token<char> OPR1
%token<integer> exp
```

Run the Yacc command and check how the union is declared in the y.tab.h file.

Example 44

This Yacc specification file used to develop calculator which accepts single digit operands. Also, here we are not using any lexical specification file. The necessary lexical analysis program (yylex()) is written directly.

Yacc specification File (calc.y)

```
%{
#include<stdio.h>
#include<stdlib.h>
%}

%token PLUS MINUS MUL DIV NEWLINE RPAR LPAR
%token NUMBER

/* grammar rules & actions section */

%%
```

```
/* These two rules are for reading expressions from the keyboard */

lines       : lines line
    |
    ;
line        : expr NEWLINE                { printf("%d\n> ", $1); }
    | NEWLINE                 { printf ("> "); }
    ;

/* Grammar rules for integer expressions evaluation */

expr        : expr PLUS term        { $$ = $1 + $3; }
    | expr MINUS term       { $$ = $1 - $3; }
    | term                  { $$ = $1; } /* default action */
    ;
term        : term MUL factor       { $$ = $1 * $3; }
    | term DIV factor         { if ($3 == 0)
                            yyerror("divide by zero");
                                else
                                  $$ = $1 / $3;
                              }
    | factor            { $$ = $1; } /* default action */
    ;
factor      : LPAR expr RPAR        { $$ = $2; }
    | NUMBER                { $$ = $1; } /* default action */
    ;

%%


yylex() {
        /* My lexer */
    int c;
     do {
     c=getchar();
     switch (c) {
          case '0': case '1': case '2': case '3': case '4': case '5': case '6':
       case '7': case '8': case '9':
          yylval= c - '0';
          return NUMBER;
       case '+':  return PLUS;
```

```
          case '-':  return MINUS;
          case '*':  return MUL;
          case '/':  return DIV;
          case '(':  return LPAR;
          case ')':  return RPAR;
          case '\n':  return NEWLINE;
           }
      } while (c!= EOF);

    return(EOF);
}

main() {
    printf("> ");
    yyparse();
}
```

To generate the calculator program (executable file), run the following commands.

```
yacc –dv calc.y
gcc –o calc y.tab.c –ly
```

Example 45

This Yacc and Lex specification programs are used to generate a calculator which is flexible than the previous one. It accepts, integer and float type arguments.

Yacc Specification File (calculator.y)

```
%{
#include <stdio.h>
%}

%union{ double   real; /* real value */
      int   integer; /* integer value */
     }

%token <real> REAL
%token <integer> INTEGER
%token PLUS MINUS TIMES DIVIDE LP RP NL

%type <real> rexpr
```

```
%type <integer> iexpr

%left PLUS MINUS
%left TIMES DIVIDE
%left UMINUS

%%

lines: /* nothing */
    | lines line
    ;

line:  NL
    | iexpr NL
      { printf("%d) %d\n", lineno, $1);}
    | rexpr NL
      { printf("%d) %15.8lf\n", lineno, $1);}
    ;

iexpr: INTEGER
    | iexpr PLUS iexpr
      { $$ = $1 + $3;}
    | iexpr MINUS iexpr
      { $$ = $1 - $3;}
    | iexpr TIMES iexpr
      { $$ = $1 * $3;}
    | iexpr DIVIDE iexpr
      { if($3) $$ = $1 / $3;
        else { fprintf(stderr, "divide by zero\n");
             yyerror();
          }
      }
    | MINUS iexpr %prec UMINUS
      { $$ = - $2;}
    | LP iexpr RP
      { $$ = $2;}
    ;

rexpr: REAL
    | rexpr PLUS rexpr
      { $$ = $1 + $3;}
```

```
    | rexpr MINUS rexpr
     { $$ = $1 - $3;}
    | rexpr TIMES rexpr
     { $$ = $1 * $3;}
    | rexpr DIVIDE rexpr
     { if($3) $$ = $1 / $3;
       else { fprintf(stderr, "divide by zero\n");
              yyerror();
         }
     }
    | MINUS rexpr %prec UMINUS
     { $$ = - $2;}
    | LP rexpr RP
     { $$ = $2;}
    | iexpr PLUS rexpr
     { $$ = (double)$1 + $3;}
    | iexpr MINUS rexpr
     { $$ = (double)$1 - $3;}
    | iexpr TIMES rexpr
     { $$ = (double)$1 * $3;}
    | iexpr DIVIDE rexpr
     { if($3) $$ = (double)$1 / $3;
       else { fprintf(stderr, "divide by zero\n");
              yyerror();
         }
     }
    | rexpr PLUS iexpr
     { $$ = $1 + (double)$3;}
    | rexpr MINUS iexpr
     { $$ = $1 - (double)$3;}
    | rexpr TIMES iexpr
     { $$ = $1 * (double)$3;}
    | rexpr DIVIDE iexpr
     { if($3) $$ = $1 / (double)$3;
       else { fprintf(stderr, "divide by zero\n");
              yyerror();
         }
     }
    ;

%%
```

```
#include "lex.yy.c"
int lineno;
```

Lex Specification File (calculator.lex)

```
integer     [0-9]+
dreal       ([0-9]*\.[0-9]+)
ereal       ([0-9]*\.[0-9]+[Ee][+-]?[0-9]+)
real        {dreal}|{ereal}
nl          \n

%%
[ \t]       ;
{integer}   { sscanf(yytext, "%d", &yylval.integer);
             return INTEGER;
            }
{real}      { sscanf(yytext, "%lf", &yylval.real);
             return REAL;
            }
\+          { return PLUS;}
\-          { return MINUS;}
\*          { return TIMES;}
\/          { return DIVIDE;}
\(          { return LP;}
\)          { return RP;}

{nl}        { extern int lineno; lineno++;
             return NL;
            }
.           { return yytext[0]; }
```

To create parser which accepts arithmetic expressions with +, - operators, run the following commands

```
lex  calculator.lex
yacc –dv calculator.y
gcc –o calculator y.tab.c  lex.yy.c  -ly –lfl
```

Example 46

The following Yacc and Lex specification files are used to generate a program which identify the number of words in the given input file.

Yacc Specification File (words.y)

```
%{
#include<stdlib.h>
#include<string.h>
int yylex();
#include "words.h"
int nwords=0;
#define MAXWORDS 100
char * words[MAXWORDS];
%}

%token WORD
%%
text        : ;
    | text WORD; {
                    if($2<0) printf("New Word\n");
                    else  printf("Matched\n");
            }
%%

int find_word(char *x)
{
int i;

for(i=0;i<nwords;i++) if(strcmp(x,words[i])==0) return i;

words[nwords++]=strdup(x);
return -1;
}

int main()
{
yyparse();
printf("No of Words=%d\n", nwords);
}
```

```
void yyerror(char *a)
{
}

int yywrap()
{
return 1;
}
```

Lex Specification File (words.lex)

```
%{
#include "y.tab.h"
int find_word(char *);
extern int yylval;
%}

%%

[a-zA-Z]+  {yylval=find_word(yytext); return WORD;}
.|\n        ;
%%
```

To create parser which counts the number of words in a given file, run the following commands

```
lex  words.lex
yacc –dv words.y
gcc –o words y.tab.c  lex.yy.c  -ly –lfl
```

Tracing the execution of a Yacc generated parser can be done by including the following lines to the Yacc specification file and while compiling give –DYYDEBUG option.

```
extern in yydebug;
yydebug=1;
```

22.4 Conclusions

This chapter discusses about the use of Lex and Yacc libraries for developing lexical analysis programs (compilers), file processing utilities and parsers. Many practical and lucid examples are given to explain each concept of lex and yacc library.

23 A Brief Tour of Phython

23.1 Introduction

Python is an interpreted language, which can save you considerable time during program development because no compilation and linking is necessary unlike other programming languages such as C, C++, etc.,. The interpreter can be used interactively, which makes it easy to experiment with features of the language, to write throw-away programs, or to test functions during bottom-up program development. It is also a handy desk calculator.

It has high-level data types built in, such as flexible arrays and dictionaries that would cost you days to implement efficiently in C. Because of its more general data types Python is applicable to a much larger problem domain than Awk or even Perl, yet many things are at least as easy in Python as in those languages.

Python allows you to split up your program in modules that can be reused in other Python programs. It comes with a large collection of standard modules that you can use as the basis of your programs -- or as examples to start learning to program in Python. Some of these modules provide things like file I/O, system calls, sockets, and even interfaces to graphical user interface toolkits like Tk.

Python allows writing very compact and readable programs. Programs written in Python are typically much shorter than equivalent C or C++ programs, for several reasons:

- the high-level data types allow you to express complex operations in a single statement;
- statement grouping is done by indentation instead of beginning and ending brackets;
- no variable or argument declarations are necessary.

Python is extensible: if you know how to program in C it is easy to add a new built-in function or module to the interpreter, either to perform critical operations at maximum speed, or to link Python programs to libraries that may only be available in binary form (such as a vendor-specific graphics library). Once you are really hooked, you can link the Python interpreter into an application written in C and use it as an extension or command language for that application.

In summary, python has following characteristics.

1. Easy to learn and program and is object oriented.
2. Rapid application development
3. Readability is better
4. It can work with other languages such as C, C++ and Fortran.
5. Extensive modules support is available.
6. Powerful interpreter

Some of the success[1] stories are:

1. Zope: Commercial grade CMS
2. Redhat installation scripts
3. SciPy: A numerical Algorithms module
4. Envisage: Scientific Computing environment
5. MayaVi: A 3D data visualization system

---

[1] www.pythonology.com/success

23.2 Invoking Python

Python can be used either in interactive mode or in interpreted mode.

By typing the command "python" at the command prompt, we will see the following prompt. At this prompt, we can run python instruction; even we can use the same as desk calculator. Typing an end-of-file character (Control-D on Unix, Control-Z on Windows) at the primary prompt causes the interpreter to exit with a zero exit status. If that doesn't work, you can exit the interpreter by typing the following commands: "import sys; sys.exit()".

```
Python 2.3.4 (#1, Oct 26 2004, 16:42:40)
[GCC 3.4.2 20041017 (Red Hat 3.4.2-6.fc3)] on linux2
Type "help", "copyright", "credits" or "license" for more information.
>>> 2+3
5
>>> 3*3+4/2-3
8
>>> x=2
>>> y=3
>>> z=x+y
>>> print z
5
```

Python can allow us to use complex numbers also.

```
>>> x=complex(1,2)
>>> y=complex(2,3)
>>> x+y
(3+5j)
>>> z=x*y
>>> x.imag
2.0
>>> z.imag
7.0
>>> z.real
-4.0
>>> z
(-4+7j)
>>>
```

In interactive mode, the last printed expression is assigned to the variable _. This means that when you are using Python as a desk calculator, it is somewhat easier to continue calculations, for example :

```
 length=10
>>> height=20
>>> height * length
200
>>> print _
200
```

To exit from python we can use ^d or the following.

```
>>> import sys
>>> sys.exit(10)
```

You can check up the exit status by executing "echo $?" command at the shell prompt; note you will see 10.

We can also use python on python programs (such as ex.py) either of the following ways at the shell prompt.

```
python ex.py
python<ex.py
```

Also, python can be used as:

```
python  -c  "command" arguments.
```

For example the following command at the shell prompt displays 10.

```
python -c "print 10"
```

23.2.1 Data Types

Python supports variety of variables types such as integers, float, complex, strings, list, dictionary and classes.

For example the following example demonstrates the use of variable of numeric type at python prompt.

```
>>> x=int(12.12)
>>> x
12
>>> x=float(12)
```

```
>>> x
12.0
>>> x,y=1,30
>>> x,y
(1, 30)
>>> x,y=int(1.2),float(2)
>>> x,y
(1, 2.0)
>>> x=1.22121212112122121
>>> x
1.2212121211212212
>>> y=float(x)
>>> y
1.2212121211212212
>>> x=y=z=0
>>> x,y,z
(0, 0, 0)
>>>
```

Python assignment is done by reference. Also, variables are either mutable (lists, dictionaries) or immutable type (strings, numbers). Python supports strings equipped with variety of built in operations. It supports Unicode strings also.

Strings can be enclosed in single quotes or double quotes. Like Unix shell, we can use backslash character to escape from normal interpretation of the character.

String literals can span multiple lines in several ways. Continuation lines can be used, with a backslash as the last character (similar to definition of a C macro) on the line indicating that the next line is a logical continuation of the line.

```
hello = "Hello\n\
My Dear.\n\
   FOSS users."

print hello

Hello
My Dear
FOSS users.
```

Strings can be surrounded in a pair of matching triple-quotes: """ or ''' to print verbatim. End of lines do not need to be escaped when using triple-quotes, but they will be included in the string.

For example:

```
>>> print """ Hello
... How        are          you\n
... my dear"""
 Hello
How          are          you

my dear
```

Strings can be concatenated (glued together) with the + operator, and repeated with *:

```
>>> word = 'Hello'
>>> word
Hello
>>> '<' + word*5 + '>'
'<HelloHelloHelloHelloHello>'
```

The built-in function len() returns the length of a string:

```
>>> s = 'Hello'
>>> len(s)
5
```

Like C, strings can be subscripted, with the first character has subscript (index) 0. In reality, there is no separate character type; a character is simply a string of size one. Extra, in python substrings can be specified with the slice notation: two indices separated by a colon.

```
>>>word='Hello'
>>> word[4]
'o'
>>> word[0:2]
'He'
>>> word[2:4]
'll'
```

Slice indices have useful defaults; an omitted first index defaults to zero, an omitted second index defaults to the size of the string being sliced.

```
>>> word[:2]    # The first two characters
'He'
>>> word[2:]    # Everything except the first two characters
'llo'
```

Unlike a C string, Python strings cannot be changed, i.e. tiny attempt to change value at any indexed position in the string results in an error.

Here's a useful invariant of slice operations: s[:i] + s[i:] equals s.

```
>>> word[:2] + word[2:]
'Hello'
```

Degenerate slice indices are handled gracefully: an index that is too large is replaced by the string size, an upper bound smaller than the lower bound returns an empty string.

```
>>> word[1:100]
'ello'
>>> word[10:]
''
```

Indices may be negative numbers, to start counting from the right. For example:

```
>>> word[-1]     # The last character
'o'
>>> word[-2]     # The last-but-one character
'l'
>>> word[-2:]    # The last two characters
'lo'
>>> word[:-2]    # Everything except the last two characters
'Hel'
```

But note that -0 is really the same as 0, so it does not count from the right!

```
>>> word[-0]     # (since -0 equals 0)
'H'
```

23.2.2 Lists

Python supports another versatile unit called as lists. For a variable, we can assign a set of values as a comma separated list enclosed between [, and]. On this structure also, we can apply slicing, indexing. The elements of a list need not be of same type. We can join to lists and create another list. We can also apply len(), append(), function with it. More over, unlike strings, we can assign a value to an element of a list.

For example execute the following at python prompt.

```
>>> x=[1,2]
>>> y=[3,4]
>>> x
[1, 2]
>>> len(x)
2
>>> x[0]
1
>>> y[1]
4
>>> z=[x,y]
>>> z
[[1, 2], [3, 4]]
>>> z=[x[1:],y[1:]]
>>> z
[[2], [4]]
>>> z[1]
[4]
>>> z[1]=10
>>> z[1]
10
>>>
```

23.2.3 A Simple Program

In the following program (ex1.py), height and width of the triangle is read and area is printed.

```
H=float(raw_input("Enter Hieght of Right Angled Triangle\n"));
B=float(raw_input("Enter Breadth of Right Angled Triangle\n"));

area=B*H/2

print "Area=", area
```

The above program can be executed by typing the following command.

```
python ex1.py
```

The above program can also executed by replacing input() function instead of raw_input().

23.2.4 if condition

Python supports if condition in the same fashion as that of C language. It supports nested if also and the else part is optional like C language.

For example, consider the following program (ex2.py) which reads a student marks in a test and prints his class. The program has to be executed at the command prompt by typing "python ex2.py".

```
x = int(raw_input("Enter a student mark\n"))
if x>=60:
    print "First Class"
elif x>=50:
    print "Second Class"
elif x>=35:
    print "Third Class"
else:
    print "Failed"
```

23.2.5 for loop

The for loop in Python differs in some respects from C. However, it resembles a lot with for loop of shell. It takes a list as an argument and traverses the same element by element.

For example the following program (ex3.py) prints all the items in the list one by one.

```
a = ['cat', 'rat', 'mat']
for x in a:
print x
```

Where as the following program (ex4.py) prints only last two elements.

```
a = ['cat', 'rat', 'mat']
for x in a[1:]:
print x
```

The following program (ex4a.py) also prints elements of the lists along with the lists.

```
a = ['cat', 'mat', 'rat']
for x in range(len(a)):
   print x, a[x]
```

To iterate over a sequence of numbers, the built-in function range() comes handy. It generates lists containing arithmetic progressions.

```
>>> range(10)
    [0, 1, 2, 3, 4, 5, 6, 7, 8, 9]
```

The given end point is never part of the generated list; range(10) generates a list of 10 values, exactly the legal indices for items of a sequence of length 10. It is possible to let the range start at another number, or to specify a different increment (even negative; sometimes this is called the `step'):

```
>>> range(5, 10)
[5, 6, 7, 8, 9]
>>> range(0, 10, 3)
[0, 3, 6, 9]
>>> range(-10, -100, -30)
[-10, -40, -70]
```

The following program (ex5.py) calculates the average of given n students.

```
sum=0
n=input("Enter Number of Students\n");
for x in range(n):
   y=input("Enter A Student Marks\n");
   sum=sum+y

avg=sum/n
print "Average=", avg
```

The following program (ex6.py) prints the characters of the given string 'Rama' character by character.

```
Y='Rama'
for x in range(len(Y)):
      print Y[x]
```

If we want any string to be input, we can use raw_input() function.

while loop

Python also supports while loop and behaves similar to while loop of C language.

Moreover, both with for loop and while loop we can use break and continue statement which behaves similar to C language.

For example the following program (ex8.py) can be used to print the average of n students.

```
sum=0
n=input("Enter Number of Students\n");
i=0
while i<n:
   y=input("Enter A Student Marks\n");
   sum=sum+y
   i=i+1

avg=sum/n
print "Average=", avg
```

The following program (ex9.py) is used to print whether a given string is palindrome or not.

```
Y=raw_input("Enter a String\n")
i=0
j=len(Y)-1
while i<j:
      if Y[i]!=Y[j]:
       break
      i=i+1
      j=j-1

if i>=j:
      print "Palindrome"
else:
      print "Not a Palindrome"
```

Python loop statements may have an else clause; it is executed when the loop terminates through exhaustion of the list (with for) or when the condition becomes false (with while), but not when the loop is terminated by a break statement. This feature is not seen with any other languages such as C, C++, Java.

This is exemplified by the following example (ex9a.py), which searches for prime numbers:

```
for n in range(2, 10):
for x in range(2, n):
     if n % x == 0:
     print n, 'equals', x, '*', n/x
     break
else:
     print n, 'is a prime number'
```

The following program (ex10.py) reads a set of numbers and stores in a list and then add's one element after another and the calculates the average.

```
a=[]
n=input("Enter No of Students\n");
i=0
while i<n:
    x=input("Enter a number\n")
    a.insert(i,x)
    i=i+1

sum=0
i=0
while i<n:
    sum=sum+a[i]
    i=i+1

avg=sum/n

print "Average=", avg
```

Python supports the pass statement which does nothing and is similar to simple semicolon (;) statement in C. It can be used when a statement is required syntactically but the program requires no action.

23.2.6 Functions

Python supports functions also. The keyword def introduces a function definition. It must be followed by the function name and the parenthesized list of formal parameters. The statements that form the body of the function start at the next line, and must be indented. The first statement of the function body can optionally be a string literal; this string literal is the function's documentation string, or docstring.

There are tools which use docstrings to automatically produce online or printed documentation, or to let the user interactively browse through code; it's good practice to include docstrings in code that you write.

The execution of a function introduces a new symbol table used for the local variables of the function. More precisely, all variable assignments in a function store the value in the local symbol table; whereas variable references first look in the local symbol table, then in the global symbol table, and then in the table of built-in names. Thus, global variables cannot be directly assigned a value within a function (unless named in a global statement), although they may be referenced.

The actual parameters (arguments) to a function call are introduced in the local symbol table of the called function when it is called; thus, arguments are passed using call by value (where the value is always an object reference, not the value of the object). When a function calls another function, a new local symbol table is created for that call.

A function definition introduces the function name in the current symbol table. The value of the function name has a type that is recognized by the interpreter as a user-defined function. This value can be assigned to another name which can then also be used as a function.

For example consider the following program (ex11.py) which defines the function prime() and uses the same.

```
def  prime(n):
      i=1
      c=0
      while i<=n:
            if n%i==0:
                  c=c+1
            i=i+1

      if  c==2:
            return 1
      else:
            return 0

N=input("Enter a Integer\n")

if prime(N)==1:
      print "Prime Number"
else:
      print "Not a Prime Number"
```

The following program (ex12.py) defines a function which takes a list and return the average of the elements in it.

```
def  avg(a):
      i=1
      n=len(a)
      s=0
      while i<n:
            s=s+a[i]
            i=i+1

      avg=float(s/n)
      return avg


s=[12,22,33,33]

print "Average=", avg(s)
```

The following program (ex13.py) also defines a function which returns more than one value from the function. Here, we have appended whatever we wanted to return from the function to a list and that list is returned.

```
def  stat(a):
     i=1
     n=len(a)
     s=0
     max=0
     min=100
     while i<n:
          s=s+a[i]
          if a[i]>max:
               max=a[i]
          if a[i]<min:
               min=a[i]
          i=i+1

     avg=float(s/n)
     result=[]
     result.append(avg)
     result.append(max)
     result.append(min)
     return result


s=[12,22,33,33]

print stat(s)
```

Default Arguments

Like C++, Java and other languages, Python takes default arguments also. That is, we can assign a default value for the arguments and when function is called, fi we do not send actual arguments their default values will be taken.

Consider the following example (ex14.py) which calculates simple interest. You can observe the last but one function call in the following program. That is in Python, Functions can also be called using keyword arguments of the form "keyword = value". Is it possible in C++?

Also, an argument list may have any positional arguments followed by any keyword arguments, where the keywords must be chosen from the formal parameter names. It's not important whether a formal parameter has a default value or not. No argument may receive a value more than once.

```
def  interest(amount=100,rate=0.17, time=1.0):
     x=amount*rate*time
     return x

print interest()
print interest(1000)
print interest(1000,0.18)
print interest(1000,0.18,2)
print interest(time=2, amount=1000,rate=0.18)
print interest(1000,time=2, rate=0.18)
```

The lists supported in Python can be used as both stack and queue. The pop() function is called it removes the last element from the list, where as pop(0) removes the first element from the list. Thus, by using append() and pop() functions we can realize stack and with the help of append() and pop(0), we can implement queue.

Consider the following example ex15.py for explanation sake. This shows how to call reverse() and sort() functions also. In addition, by calling del command, we can delete item or items from a list.

```
a=[10,32,21,22,33,44,66]
print a
a.reverse()
print a
a.pop()
print a
a.append(20)
print a
a.sort()
print a
a.pop(0)
print a
del a[0]
print a
del a[2:3]
print a
```

23.2.7 Sets

Python also includes a data type for sets. A set is an unordered collection with no duplicate elements. Basic uses include membership testing and eliminating duplicate entries. Set objects also support mathematical operations like union, intersection, difference, and symmetric difference.

23.2.8 Dictionaries

Another useful data type built into Python is the dictionary, which is can be called as ``associative memories'' or ``associative arrays''. Unlike sequences, which are indexed by a range of numbers, dictionaries are indexed by keys, which can be any immutable type; strings and numbers can always be keys. Tuple's can be used as keys if they contain only strings, numbers, or tuple's; if a tuple contains any mutable object either directly or indirectly, it cannot be used as a key. You can't use lists as keys, since lists can be modified in place using their append() and extend() methods, as well as slice and indexed assignments.

It is best to think of a dictionary as an unordered set of key: value pairs, with the requirement that the keys are unique (within one dictionary). A pair of braces creates an empty dictionary: {}. Placing a comma-separated list of key:value pairs within the braces adds initial key:value pairs to the dictionary; this is also the way dictionaries are written on output.

The main operations on a dictionary are storing a value with some key and extracting the value given the key. It is also possible to delete a key:value pair with del. If you store using a key that is already in use, the old value associated with that key is forgotten. It is an error to extract a value using a non-existent key.

The keys() method of a dictionary object returns a list of all the keys used in the dictionary, in arbitrary order (if you want it sorted, just apply the sort() method to the list of keys). To check whether a single key is in the dictionary, use the has_key() method of the dictionary.

When looping through dictionaries, the key and corresponding value can be retrieved at the same time using the iteritems() method.

```
TNO={}
TNO['Rao']=200
TNO['Abhi']=300

print TNO
print TNO.keys()

TNO['Ram']=1212
print TNO

TNO.has_key('Raju')

for name,numb in TNO.iteritems():
    print name,numb
```

Also, When looping through a sequence, the position index and corresponding value can be retrieved at the same time using the enumerate() function.

For example, the following program ex17.py prints item number and item.

```
for i, v in enumerate(['tic', 'tac', 'toe']):
    print i, v
```

Sequence objects may be compared to other objects with the same sequence type. The comparison uses lexicographical ordering: first the first two items are compared, and if they differ this determines the outcome of the comparison; if they are equal, the next two items are compared, and so on, until either sequence is exhausted. If two items to be compared are themselves sequences of the same type, the lexicographical comparison is carried out recursively. If all items of two sequences compare equal, the sequences are considered equal. If one sequence is an initial sub-sequence of the other, the shorter sequence is the smaller (lesser) one. Lexicographical ordering for strings uses the ASCII ordering for individual characters. Some examples of comparisons between sequences with the same types:

For example the following gives true.

```
(1, 2, 3)          < (1, 2, 4)
```

23.2.9 Modules

A module is a file containing Python definitions and statements. The file name is the module name with the suffix .py appended. Within a module, the module's name (as a string) is available as the value of the global variable __name__. Definitions from a module can be imported into other modules or into the main module.

As our program gets longer, we may want to split it into several files for easier maintenance. We may also want to use a handy function that we have written in several programs without copying its definition into each program.

Python has a way to put definitions in a file and use them in a script and is called a module; definitions from a module can be imported into other modules or into the main module.

Each module has its own private symbol table, which is used as the global symbol table by all functions defined in the module. Thus, the author of a module can use global variables in the module without worrying about accidental clashes with a user's global variables. On the other hand, if you know what you are doing you can touch a module's global variables with the same notation used to refer to its functions, modname.itemname.

Modules can import other modules. normally, all import statements are kept at the beginning of a module though we can use them any where. The imported module names are placed in the importing module's global symbol table.

For instance, fibo.py is module having a function which prints n fibnocci numbers.

```
def fib(n):    # write Fibonacci series up to n
a, b = 0, 1
while b < n:
    print b,
    a, b = b, a+b
```

Let us consider another program ex19.py which imports fibo.py and calls the function fib(). We will get fibnocci numbers 1,1,2,3,5,8.

```
import fibo
fibo.fib(10)
```

Also, we can load a function from a module using from statement and call the same in our program. For example, ex19a.py also gives the same results.

```
from fibo import fib
fib(10)
```

Normally, whenever we import a module python interpreter searches in the current directory. This behavior can be changed by setting environment variable PYTHONPATH.

The built-in function dir() is used to find out which names a module defines. It returns a sorted list of strings i.e., names of the functions defined in the module. Test by executing dir(fibo) in the above program.

Like Java, python also supports packages. Packages are a way of structuring Python's module namespace by using ``dotted module names''. For example, the module name A.B designates a sub module named "B" in a package named "A". Just like the use of modules saves the authors of different modules from having to worry about each other's global variable names, the use of dotted module names saves the authors of multi-module packages like NumPy or the Python Imaging Library from having to worry about each other's module names.

Python also supports functions to open files and reading and writing into the file. For example, the following program ex20.py prints its content. The open() function returns, file object. With this we can use function such as read(), readline(), readlines() can be used.

```
f=open('ex20.py', 'r')
f.readlines()
```

Guess, what is going to happen if you replace 'r' with 'w' in the above program. You may loose the content of the file ex20.py!!!!!!!.

We can also use functions such as read(), write(), seek(), tell(), close() with opened files.

Also, in addition there is a special module known as pickle with which we can read and write at object level similar to ObjectInputReader() and ObjectOutputWriter() in Java. For example, the following program explains how the same can be used.

```
import pickle
x=30
y=1.222
f=open('ex21.dat', 'a+')
pickle.dump(x,f);
pickle.dump(y,f);
p=pickle.load(f)
print p
```

Classes

Like object oriented languages, python also supports classes. In fact, all the data members are consider as classes in python.

The simplest form of class definition looks like this:

```
class ClassName:
    <statement-1>
    .
    .
    .
    <statement-N>
```

We can define data members and member functions with def statement. Attribute references use the standard syntax used for all attribute references in Python: obj.name. Valid attribute names are all the names that were in the class's namespace when the class object was created.

The instantiation operation (``calling'' a class object) creates an empty object. Many classes like to create objects in a known initial state. Therefore a class may define a special method named __init__(), like the one in the following example. Also, we can create an object of the class and assign to a variable as shown below.

```
class Complex:
    def __init__(self, realpart, imagpart):
        self.r = realpart
        self.i = imagpart
    def retreal(self):
        return self.r
    def retimag(self):
        return self.i

x = Complex(3.0, -4.5)
print x.r, x.i
print x.retreal(), x.retimag()
```

Python supports inheritance and limited way multiple inheritance also.

Python also supports operating system related functions (system calls) such as getcwd(), getpid(), getppid(), etc. The command dir(os) displays all the function names, symbolic constants related to OS. Run the following program.

```
import os
import sys
print os.getcwd()
print os.getpid()
print os.getppid()
print dir(os)
help(os)
```

Python has extensive support for internet related services, compression, text utilities, video management utilities, data base utilities, system administration utilities. It can be used with XML, PHP, etc.

23.3 Conclusions

This chapter discusses about the Python scripting language. It explains the programming features available with Python with simple and lucid examples. However, as this book is aimed at giving initial boost or momentum to new Linux enthusiasts, we did expose only few features of the Python language.

Useful Websites

www.python.org
www.python.org/doc
www.python.org/tut/tut.html
www.byteofpython.info
www.diveintopython.org
www.pythonology.com/success

24 Introduction to Perl

24.1 Introduction

Perl is a language which was designed to retain the immediateness of shell languages, but at the same time capture some of the flexibility of C. Perl is a good alternative to the shell which has much of the power of C and is therefore ideal for simple and more complex system programming tasks. If you intend to be a system administrator for UNIX systems, you could do much worse than to read the Perl book and learn Perl inside out.

Perl is an acronym for *Practical extraction and report language*. In this chapter, we shall not aim to teach Perl from scratch -- the best way to learn it is to use it! Rather we shall concentrate on demonstrating some principles.

One of the reasons for using Perl is that it is extremely good at textfile handling--one of the most important things for UNIX users, and particularly useful in connection with CGI script processing on the World Wide Web. It has simple built-in constructs for searching and replacing text, storing information in arrays and retrieving them in sorted form. We did do all of the these things previously using the UNIX shell commands such as Sed, awk, cut, paste etc.,. Perl unifies all of these operations and more. It also makes them much simpler.

24.1.1 Program structure

Perl's strength is not as a general programming language but as a specialized language for textfile handling. The syntax of Perl is in many ways like the C programming language, but there are important differences. Recent versions of perl supports object oriented features in addition to normal loops, arrays, etc.,.

- Variables do not have *types*. They are interpreted in a context sensitive way. The operators which acts upon variables determine whether a variable is to be considered a string or as an integer etc.
- Although there are no types, Perl defines *arrays* of different kinds. There are three different kinds of array, labeled by the symbols `$', `@' and `%'.
- Perl keeps a number of standard variables with special names e.g. `$_ @ARGV' and `%ENV'. Special attention should be paid to these. They are very important!
- The shell reverse apostrophe notation `command` can be used to execute UNIX programs and get the result into a Perl variable.

Example 1

Here is a simple perl program which reads a number and prints the same.

```
#!/usr/bin/perl -w

print 'Enter a number';
$N=<STDIN>;
print $N;
```

Like shell programs, here also we may specify that the program has to be interpreted through interpreter in /usr/bin directory. The –w option is used to specify that the perl can enable all the useful warnings while running the perl script. Here, we are asking to take a number from standard input and then the same to be printed.

Let the above program is enter'd in a file say **a.pl**. To execute the same, we have to run the following commands at shell prompt.

```
chmod u+x  a.pl
./a.pl
or
a.pl
```

Example 2

Here is another example which demonstrates the use of length function which takes a string and returns its length. Also it demonstrates the use of shell commands in perl script. Like shell, **any command enclosed in between back quotes is executed**. This, we can observe in this program. **The chop function removes the last character, i.e. new line.**

```
#!/usr/bin/perl -w
print("length: " ,length("hello world"));
print "\n";

print `date`;
$date=`date`;
chop($date);
print $date;
```

24.1.2 Perl variables

Perl supports variety of variables namingly scalar, array and associated array.

Scalar variables

In Perl, variables need not be declared before they are used. Whenever you use a new symbol, Perl automatically adds the symbol to its symbol table and initializes the variable to the empty string. It is important to understand that there is no practical difference between zero and the empty string in perl -- except in the way that you, the user, choose to use it. Perl makes no distinction between strings and integers or any other types of data -- except when it wants to interpret them. For instance, to compare two variables as strings is not the same as comparing them as integers, even if the string contains a textual representation of an integer. Perl assume any string prepended with `$' symbol as scalar variable.

The default scalar variable.

The special variable `$_' is used for many purposes in Perl. It is used as a buffer to contain the result of the last operation, the last line read in from a file etc. It is so general that many functions which act on scalar variables work by default on `$_' if no other argument is specified. For example,

```
print;
is the same as
print $_;
```

Array (vector) variables

An array, in Perl is identified by the `@' symbol and, like scalar variables, space is allocated and initialized dynamically.

```
@array[0] = "This little piggy went to market";
@array[2] = "This little piggy stayed at home";

print "@array[0] @array[1] @array[2]";
```

The index of an array is always understood to be a number, not a string, so if you use a non-numerical string to refer to an array element, you will always get the zero'th element, since a non-numerical string has an integer value of zero.

An important array which every program defines is @ARGV. This is the argument vector array, and contains the command line arguments similar to the shell's positional variables $0, $1, $2, etc.,.

Given an array, we can find the last element by using the `$#' operator. For example, $last_element = $ARGV[$#ARGV];

Notice that each element in an array is a scalar variable. The `$#' cannot be interpreted directly as the number of elements in the array, as it can in the C-shell.

Special array commands

The `shift' command acts on arrays and returns and removes the first element of the array. Afterwards, all of the elements are shifted down one place. So one way to read the elements of an array in order is to repeatedly call `shift'.

```
$next_element=shift(@myarray);
```

Note that, if the array argument is omitted, then `shift' works on `@ARGV' by default. Another useful function is `split', which takes a string and turns it into an array of strings. `split' works by choosing a character (usually a space) to delimit the array elements, so a string containing a sentence separated by spaces would be turned into an array of words.

The syntax is

```
@array = split;                        # works with spaces on $_
@array = split(pattern,string);        # Breaks on pattern
($v1,$v2...) = split(pattern,string);  # Name array elements with scalars
```

In the first of these cases, it is assumed that the variable `$_' is to be split on whitespace characters. In the second case, we decide on what character the split is to take place and on what string the function is to act. For instance

```
@new_array = split(":","name:passwd:uid:gid:gcos:home:shell");
```

The result is a seven element array called `@new_array', where `$new_array[0]' is `name' etc.

In the final example, the left hand side shows that we wish to capture elements of the array in a named set of scalar variables. If the number of variables on the left-hand side is fewer than the number of strings which are generated on the right hand side, they are discarded. If the number on the left hand side is greater, then the remainder variables are empty.

Associated arrays

One of the very nice features of Perl is the ability to use one string as an index to another string in an array and this type of arrays are called associative arrays. For example, we can make a short encyclopedia of zoo animals by constructing an associative array in which the keys (or indices) of the array are the names of animals, and the contents of the array are the information about them.

```
$animals{"Penguin"} = "Lives in Antarctica.";
$animals{"dog"} = "senses smells";

if ($index eq "fish")
  {
  $animals{$index} = "Often comes in square boxes. Very cold.";
  }
```

An entire associated array is written `%array', while the elements are `$array{$key}'. Perl provides a special associative array for every program called `%ENV'. This contains the *environment variables* defined in the parent shell which is running the Perl program.

For example

```
print "Username = $ENV{"USER"}\n";

$ld = "LD_LIBRARY_PATH";
print "The link editor path is $ENV{$ld}\n";
```

To get the current path into an ordinary array, one could write,

```
@path_array= split(":",$ENV{"PATH"});
```

24.1.3 Loops and conditionals

Here are some of the most commonly used decision-making constructions and loops in Perl.

if (*expression*)

```
  {
  block;
  }
else
  {
  block;
```

```
  }

command if (expression);

unless (expression)
  {
  block;
  }
else
  {
  block;
  }

while (expression)
  {
  block;
  }

do
  {
  block;
  }
while (expression);

for (initializer; expression; statement)
  {
  block;
  }

foreach variable(array)
  {
  block;
  }
```

The for loop

The for loop is exactly like that in C or C++ and is used to iterate over a numerical index, like this:

```
for ($i = 0; $i < 10; $i++)
  {
  print $i, "\n";
  }
```

The foreach loop

The foreach loop is like its counterpart in the C shell. It is used for reading elements one by one from a regular array. For example,

```
foreach $i ( @array )
  {
  print $i, "\n";
  }
```

In all cases, the `else' clauses may be omitted.

Be careful to distinguish between the comparison operator for integers `==' and the corresponding operator for strings `eq'. These do not work in each other's places so if you get the wrong comparison operator your program might not work and it is quite difficult to find the error.

Strangely, perl does not have a `switch' statement, but the Perl book describes how to make one using the features provided.

Example 3

The following program prints either good morning, good evening, good after noon or good night depending on the current time which is calculated by running 'date' command of Unix.

```
#!/usr/bin/perl -w

$date=`date`;
@par=split(" ", $date);


@hours=split(":", $par[3]);

$hr=$hours[0];
if ($hr <11)
{
 print("Good Morning\n");
}
elsif ($hr < 16)
{
 print("Good After Noon\n");
}
elsif ($hr < 20)
{
 print("Good Evening\n");
}
else
{
 print("Good Night\n");
}
```

Example 4

This perl program takes a name along the command line and prints the message "Hello " with the entered name. If no command line argument is given it displays "Hello World".

```
#!/usr/bin/perl -w
    if ($#ARGV >= 0) { $who = join(' ', @ARGV); }
    else { $who = 'World'; }
    print "Hello, $who!\n";
```

Example 5

This program takes a student marks in a test and prints his class.

```
#!/usr/bin/perl -w

print("Enter a student Marks\t");
$INP=<STDIN>;
if ($INP >=60)
{
 print("First Class\n");
}
elsif ($INP >=50)
{
 print("Second Class\n");
}
elsif ($INP >=35)
{
 print("Third Class\n");
}
else
{
 print("Failed\n");
}
```

Example 6

This program takes a date and then prints whether it is valid or not.

```
#!/usr/bin/perl -w
print "Enter numeric:  day month  year\n";
$_ = <STDIN>;
print ;
($day ,$month,$year) = split(" ",$_);
```

```
if ( $month > 12 || $month <1 )
{
 print "Invalid Month",$month;
exit;
}

@days={31,28,31,30,31,30,31,31,30,31,31,31};
if($days[$month] != $day )
{
print "Invalid Date\n";
exit;
}
```

Example 7

This example is to explain how variables can be used in perl.

```
#!/usr/bin/perl -w
$ABC="3";
$AB=3;
print "$ABC + $AB ";
$A=$ABC <=> $AB;
print "\n$A";
$Q =<STDIN>;
chomp $Q;
print "$Q";
$XX=<STDIN>;
$YY=<STDIN>;
chomp $XX, $YY;
print "$XX   $YY";
for($x=0; $x<3; $x++)
{
if ( $XX > $YY )
{
print "YES";
chomp $YY;
}
else
{
print "NO";
chomp $YY;
}
}
```

Iterating over elements in arrays

One of the main uses for `for' type loops is to iterate over successive values in an array. This can be done in two ways which show the essential difference between for and foreach.

If we want to fetch each value in an array in turn, without caring about numerical indices, the it is simplest to use the foreach loop.

```
@array = split(" ","a b c d e f g");

foreach $var ( @array )
  {
  print $var, "\n";
  }
```

This example prints each letter on a separate line. If, on the other hand, we are interested in the index, for the purposes of some calculation, then the for loop is preferable.

```
@array = split(" ","a b c d e f g");

for ($i = 0; $i <= $#array; $i++)
  {
  print $array[$i], "\n";
  }
```

Notice that, unlike the for-loop idiom in C/C++, the limit is `$i <= $#array', i.e. `less than or equal to' rather than `less than'. This is because the `$#' operator does not return the number of elements in the array but rather the last element.

Associated arrays are slightly different, since they do not use numerical keys. Instead they use a set of strings, like in a database, so that you can use one string to look up another. In order to iterate over the values in the array we need to get a list of these strings. The keys command is used for this.

```
$assoc{"mark"} = "cool";
$assoc{"GNU"} = "brave";
$assoc{"zebra"} = "stripy";

foreach $var ( keys %assoc )
  {
  print "$var , $assoc{$var} \n";
  }
```

The order of the keys is not defined in the above example, but you can choose to sort them alphabetically by writing

```
foreach $var ( sort keys %assoc )
```

instead.

Example 8

This program prints numbers from 1 to 10. Here, the statement last is used to come out from the loop.

```
#!/usr/bin/perl -w

$number = 0;
while(1) {
$number++;
print $number, "\n";
if ($number >= 10 ) {
	last;
}
}
```

Example 9

This program prints digits from 1 to 10 in words.

```
#!/usr/bin/perl -w
@digt=("zero", "one", "two", "Three", "Four", "Five", "Six", "seven", "Eight",
"Nine");

$number = 0;
while(1) {
print $digt[$number],"\n";
$number++;
if ($number >= 10 ) {
	last;
}
}
```

Example 10

This program prints digits from 1 to 10 in words. Here, foreach loop is used.

```
#!/usr/bin/perl -w
foreach $digt("zero", "one", "two", "Three", "Four", "Five", "Six", "seven",
"Eight", "Nine"){

print $digt,"\n";
}
```

Example 11

This program takes lines and prints them till we enter ^d.

```
#!/usr/bin/perl -w

while(<STDIN>)
{
print();
}
```

Example 12

This is another example to explain the use of for loop in perl.

```
#!/usr/bin/perl -w

@arr=(1..5);

for($i=0;$i<$#arr;$i++)
{
print $arr[$i],"\n";
}

for($i=$#arr;$i>=0;$i--)
{
print $arr[$i],"\n";
}
```

Example 13

This program prints the output of date command in word by word. First date command is executed and each word of its output is stored as element in the array.

```
#!/usr/bin/perl -w

@arr=split(" ",`date`);

for($i=0;$i<$#arr;$i++)
{
print $arr[$i],"\n";
}

for($i=$#arr;$i>=0;$i--)
{
print $arr[$i],"\n";
}
```

Example 14

This program also takes strings and prints them till we enter ^d.

```
#!/usr/bin/perl -w
print STDOUT "Enter a string: ";
   $input = <STDIN>;
   while ($input ne '') {
   print $input, "\n";
         chop $input;
   }
```

Example 15

This example is used to demonstrate the use of command line argument with perl script. In addition, how they can be used with for loop, foreach loop is also emphasized.

```
#!/usr/bin/perl -w
 print "$#ARGV is the subscript of the ",
      "last command argument.\n";

   # Iterate on numeric subscript 0 to $#ARGV:

   for ($i=0; $i <= $#ARGV; $i++) {
      print "Argument $i is $ARGV[$i].\n";
   }

   #print "A variation on the preceding loop\n";
   foreach $item (@ARGV) {
      print "The word is:  $item.\n";
   }

print " A similar variation, using the Default Scalar Variable\$_\n" ;

   foreach (@ARGV) {
      print "Say:  $_.\n";
   }
```

Example 16

This program also takes input from the key board and prints the same till we enter ^d.

```
#!/usr/bin/perl -w

while($INP=<STDIN>)
{
print($INP);
}
```

Example 17

This program reads number of students and their marks and prints their average.

```
#!/usr/bin/perl -w

print("No of Students\t");
$N=<STDIN>;
$sum=0;
$I=0;
while($I < $N)
{
print("Enter a student Marks\t");
$INP=<STDIN>;
$sum = $sum + $INP;

$I++;
}
$avg=$sum/$N;
print("Average=\t", $avg, "\n");
```

Example 18

This example is used explain the use of associative arrays.

```
#!/usr/bin/perl -w
%states=('AP','Hyderabad','UP','Lucknow','MP','Bhopal','HP','XYZ','TN','Chennai')
;

print keys %states;
print "\n";
print values %states;
print "\n";

foreach (keys %states) {
      print "The key $_ contains $states{$_}\n";
}

printf "\n\n";
foreach (sort keys %states) {
      print "The key $_ contains $states{$_}\n";
}
```

```
printf "\n\n";
foreach (reverse sort keys %states) {
      print "The key $_ contains $states{$_}\n";
}
```

Example 19

This program sorts the elements of the array using bubble sorting principle.

```
#!/usr/bin/perl -w

@a=(2,2,3,12,12,12,12,12,33,31);

for my $i (0..$#a-1) {
   for (0..$#a-1-$i) {
      ($a[$_],$a[$_+1]) = ($a[$_+1],$a[$_])
         if ($a[$_+1] < $a[$_]);
  }
}


for($i=0; $i<$#a; $i++)
{
print $a[$i], "\n";
}
```

Example 20

Here is an example which prints out a list of files in a specified directory, in order of their UNIX protection bits. The *least* protected file files come first. For each file and directory given along the command line first mode bits are calculated using stat() system call. By using this mode or permissions as key the file/directory is stored in an associative array and then all the files are printed.

```
#!/usr/bin/perl

print "You typed in ",$#ARGV+1," arguments to command\n";

if ($#ARGV < 1)
  {
  print "That's not enough to do anything with!\n";
  }
```

```
while ($next_arg = shift(@ARGV))
  {
  if ( ! ( -f $next_arg || -d $next_arg))
    {
    print "No such file: $next_arg\n";
    next;
    }

  ($dev,$ino,$mode,$nlink,$uid,$gid,$rdev,$size) = stat($next_arg);
  $octalmode = sprintf("%o",$mode & 0777);

  $assoc_array{$octalmode} .= $next_arg.
        " : size (".$size."), mode (".$octalmode.")\n";
  }

print "In order: LEAST secure first!\n\n";

foreach $i (reverse sort keys(%assoc_array))
  {
  print $assoc_array{$i};
  }
```

Example 21

This program takes a set integers along the command line and prints their average.

```
#!/usr/bin/perl –w

$s=0

for($i=0; $i<=$#ARGV;$i++)

{
$s =$s + $ARGV[$i];
}

print "Average=", $s/$#ARGV, "\n";
```

Example 22

This program takes a set names along the command line and prints whether they are regular files or special files..

```
#!/usr/bin/perl –w

foreach(@ARGV)
{
  next  unless –f;
```

```
print();
print("\t");
print ( (-f)? "Regular\n":"Special\n");
}
```

Example 23

This program takes a set names along the command line and prints their sizes.

```
#!/usr/bin/perl -w

foreach(@ARGV)
{
  next unless -f;
$SZ= -s $_;
print ("$_ \t $SZ \n");

}
```

Example 24

Perl has another facility known as with which we can insert elements into an array. Also, we can remove elements from an array using pop. This example is given to explain about push and pop and how they can be used.

```
#!/usr/bin/perl -w
@arr=();
push (@arr, "Hello");
push (@arr, "How" );
push(@arr, "are");
push(@arr, "you");
for ($x=0;  $x<=$#arr; $x++)
{
print " $arr[ $x ] ";
}
print "\n";
while ( $#arr >= 0 )
{
 $X=pop(@arr);
print "$X";
}
```

Example 25

This example is to explain how arrays can be used and joined.

```
#!/usr/bin/perl -w

@arr = ( JUNK , Tue, Wed );
@arr2 = ( JUNK , Tue, Wed );
@arr3 = ( @arr, @arr2 );
print  @arr;
print "\n";
$N=@arr;
print "SIZE= $N \n";

print  @arr2;
print "\n";
$N=@arr2;
print "SIZE= $N \n";

print  @arr3;
print "\n";
$N=@arr3;
print "SIZE= $N \n";

@arr1=@arr[2, 3];

print @arr1;
print "\n";

$aa=$arr[1];
print $aa;
print "\n";

($a1, $a2)=@arr[0,2];
print $a1 ;
print $a2;

@abb=("Ram", "June", "Ravi", "May");
$abb{"Sita"}="Dec";

print $abb{"Ram"};
```

Iterating over lines in a file

Perl file handling is very interesting unlike C and C++; perl reads files line by line. The angle brackets are used for this. Assuming that we have some file handle `<file>', for instance `<STDIN>', we can always read the file line by line with a while-loop like this.

```
while ($line = <file>)
  {
  print $line;
  }
```

Note that $line includes the end of line character on the end of each line. If you want to remove it, you should add a `chop' command:

```
while ($line = <file>)
  {
  chop $line;
  print "line = ($line)\n";
  }
```

24. 1.5 Files in perl

Opening files is straightforward in Perl. Files must be opened and closed using -- wait for it -- the commands `open' and `close'. You should be careful to close files after you have finished with them -- especially if you are writing *to* a file. Files are buffered and often large parts of a file are not actually written until the `close' command is received.

Three files are, of course, always open for every program, namely `STDIN', `STDOUT'and `STDERR'.

Formally, to open a file, we must obtain a file descriptor or file handle. This is done using `open';

```
open (file_descrip,"Filename");
```

The angular brackets `<..>' are used to read from the file. For example,

```
$line = <file_descrip>;
```

reads one line from the file associated with `file_descrip'.

Example 26

In this example, a file is opened and read line by line and from each line second word is printed; thus cut command of Unix can be emulated.

```
#!/usr/bin/perl
# to cut the second column

open (file1,"@ARGV[0]") || die "Can't open @ARGV[0]\n";
```

```
while (<file1>)
  {
  @cut_array = split;

  print "@cut_array[1]\n";
  }
```

Example 27

This program is to explain how perl can be used to simulate `paste' command of Unix. Here, first two files whose names are given along the command line are opened and from both the files one line is read till both the files are not having any more lines. Both the lines are printed at once.

```
#!/usr/bin/perl


open (file1,"@ARGV[0]") || die "Can't open @ARGV[0]\n";
open (file2,"@ARGV[1]") || die "Can't open @ARGV[1]\n";

while (($line1 = <file1>) || ($line2 = <file2>))
  {
  chop $line1;
  chop $line2;

  print "$line1      $line2\n";    # tab character between
  }
```

Here we see more formally how to read from two separate files at the same time. Notice that, by putting the read commands into the test-expression for the `while' loop, we are using the fact that `<..>' returns a non-zero (true) value unless we have reached the end of the file.

To write and append to files, we use the shell redirection symbols inside the `open' command.

```
open(fd,"> filename");    # open file for writing
open(fd,">> filename");   # open file for appending
```

We can also open a pipe from an arbitrary UNIX command and receive the output of that command as our input:

```
open (fd,"/bin/ps aux | ");
```

Example 28

A simple perl program

Let us now write the simplest perl program which illustrates the way in which perl can save time. We shall write it in three different ways to show what the short cuts mean. Let us implement the `cat' command, which copies files to the standard output. The simplest way to write this is perl is the following:

```
#!/local/bin/perl

while (<>)
  {
   print;
  }
```

Here we have made heavy use of the many default assumptions which perl makes. The program is simple, but difficult to understand for novices. First of all we use the default file handle <> which means, take one line of input from a default file. This object returns true as long as it has not reached the end of the file, so this loop continues to read lines until it reaches the end of file. The default file is standard input, unless this script is invoked with a command line argument, in which case the argument is treated as a filename and perl attempts to open the argument-filename for reading. The print statement has no argument telling it what to print, but perl takes this to mean: print the default variable `$_'.

We can therefore write this more explicitly as follows:

```
#!/usr/bin/perl

open (HANDLE,"$ARGV[1]");

while (<HANDLE>)
  {
   print $_;
  }
```

Example 29

Here we have simply filled in the assumptions explicitly. The command `<HANDLE>' now reads a single line from the named file-handle into the default variable `$_'. To make this program more general, we can eliminate the defaults entirely.

```
#!/usr/bin/perl

open (HANDLE,"$ARGV[1]");

while ($line=<HANDLE>)
  {
   print $line;
  }
```

Example 30

This program reads students data and prints whether they are passed or failed. The data file is assumed to be as shown below.

```
#!/usr/bin/perl -w

  $stufile='stud';

  # If file opens successfully, this evaluates as "true", and Perl
  # does not evaluate rest of the "or" "||" like C language
  open (NAMES,"<$stufile")
    || die "Can't open $stufile $!";


  while (<NAMES>) {
       ($stuid,$name,$math,$phy,$chem,$engl,$tel) = split('\|',$_);
    if($math >=35 && $phy >=35 && $chem >=35 && $engl >=35 &&
$tel>=35)
        {
         print $stuid, $name, "Passed\n";
        }
       else
        {
        print $stuid, $name, "Failed\n";
       }

        }
  close NAMES;
```

The date file "stud" contains the data like the following.

```
111|P.N.Rao|70|77|36|46|89
121|P.K.Rao|80|47|86|44|39
122|K.Reddy|00|37|56|94|79
```

Example 31

This program opens file "aaa" and copies its content to the file "sss".

```
#!/usr/bin/perl -w
$INP="aaa";
```

```
$OUT="sss";
open(INPUT,"<$INP");
open(OUTPUT,">$OUT");
@arr=<INPUT>;
foreach(@arr)
{
print OUTPUT;
}
close OUTPUT;
close(INPUT);
```

Example 32

This program is same as above except that it writes on the screen.

```
#!/usr/bin/perl -w
$INP="aaa";

open(INP);
@arr=<INP>;
close(INP);
foreach(@arr)
{
print ();
}
```

Example 33

This program opens a file and reads its lines then print them after converting into lower case. Here, lc function is used for this purpose.

```
#!/usr/bin/perl -w

   if ($#ARGV !=1) {
      die "Usage:  $0 inputfile outputfile\n";
   }
   ($infile,$outfile) = @ARGV;
   if (! -r $infile) {
      die "Can't read input $infile\n";
   }
   if (! -f $infile) {
      die "Input $infile is not a plain file\n";
```

```
}

open(INPUT,"<$infile") ||
   die "Can't input $infile $!";
if ( -e $outfile) {
   print STDERR "Output file $outfile exists!\n";
   until ($ans eq 'r' || $ans eq 'a' || $ans eq 'e' ) {
      print STDERR "replace, append, or exit? ";
      $ans = getc(STDIN);
   }
   if ($ans eq 'e') {exit}
}
if ($ans eq 'a') {$mode='>>'}
else {$mode='>'}
open(OUTPUT,"$mode$outfile") ||
   die "Can't output $outfile $!";

while (<INPUT>) {
   chop $_;

   $_ = lc  $_;
   print OUTPUT $_,"\n";
}

close INPUT,OUTPUT;
exit;
```

Example 34

This program opens a file (standard input) and reads and prints. This example is used to explain that perl can allow us to use Unix system calls read(), open() etc.,.

```
#!/usr/bin/perl -w
$buffer="";
open(INP,"xx");
read(INP,$buffer,20,0);
close(INP);
foreach (split(//,$buffer))
{
printf ( "%02x", ord($_) );
print "\n",  if $_ eq "\n";
}
```

24.1.6 Perl subroutines

Here is another simple `structured hello world' program in Perl. Notice that subroutines are called using the `&' symbol. There is no special way of marking the main program -- it is simply that part of the program which starts at line 1.

Example 35

```
#!/usr/bin/perl

&Hello();
&World;

# end of main

sub Hello
  {
  print "Hello";
  }

sub World
  {
  print "World\n";
  }
```

The parentheses on subroutines are optional, if there are no parameters passed. Notice that each line must end in a semi-colon.

When parameters are passed to a Perl subroutine, they are handed over as an array called `@_'. Which is analogous to the `$_' variable. Here is a simple example:

Example 36

```
#!/usr/bin/perl

$a="silver";
$b="gold";

&PrintArgs($a,$b);

# end of main

sub PrintArgs

  {
```

```
($local_a,$local_b) = @_;

print "$local_a, $local_b\n";
}
```

Example 37

This program reads a number from key board and prints its factorial value by calling the function.

```
#!/usr/bin/perl -w

print "Enter a number:";
$N=<STDIN>;
$ff=fact($N);
print "Factorial Value of=\t", $ff,"\n";

sub fact{
$i=1;
$f=1;
$M=$_[0];
print $N;
while($i<=$M)
{
$f =$f*$i;
$i++;
}
return $f;
}
```

Example 38

This example is to explain how to write functions in perl.

```
#!/usr/bin/perl -w
sub cube { return $_[0] ** 3; }

print "5 cube is ", &cube(5);

$i=1;
while ($i <= 10 )
{
```

```
print "Cube of\t", $i, "\tis\t", &cube($i),"\n";

$i++;
}
```

Example 39

This is also another example to explain about the use of perl functions. We can see that the function is called with out parenthesis.

```
#!/usr/bin/perl -w
$num=10;        # sets $num to 10
&print_results;     # prints variable $num

$num++;
&print_results;

$num*=3;
&print_results;

$num/=3;
&print_results;

sub print_results {
      print "\$num is $num\n";
}
```

Example 40

This example is to explain recursive functions in perl. The famous towers of honoi is simulated with this program.

```
#!/usr/bin/perl -w

use warnings;
use strict;


my $numdisks = 0;

print "Number of disks? ";
chomp( $numdisks = <STDIN> );
```

```
print "The moves are:\n\n";
movedisks( $numdisks, 'A', 'B', 'C' );

sub movedisks {

  my( $num, $from, $to, $aux ) = @_;

  if( $num == 1 ) {
    print "Move disk $num from $from to $to\n";
  }

  else {
    movedisks( $num-1, $from, $aux, $to );
    print "Move disk $num from $from to $to\n";
    movedisks( $num-1, $aux, $to, $from );
  }
}
```

24.1.7 die - exit on error

When a program has to quit and give a message, the `die' command is normally used. If called without an argument, Perl generates its own message including a line number at which the error occurred. To include your own message, you write

```
die "My message....";
```

If the string is terminated with a `\n' new line character, the line number of the error is not printed, otherwise Perl appends the line number to your string.

When opening files, it is common to see the syntax:

```
open (filehandle,"Filename") || die "Can't open...";
```

The logical `OR' symbol is used, because `open' returns true if all goes well, in which case the right hand side is never evaluated. If `open' is false, then die is executed. You can decide for yourself whether or not you think this is good programming style -- we mention it here because it is common practice.

The stat() idiom

The UNIX library function stat() is used to find out information about a given file. This function is available both in C and in Perl. In perl, it returns an array of values. Usually we are interested in knowing the access permissions of a file. stat() is called using the syntax

```
@array = stat ("filename");
```

or alternatively, using a named array

```
($device,$inode,$mode) = stat("filename");
```

The value returned in the *mode* variable is a bit-pattern, See section Protection bits. The most useful way of treating these bit patterns is to use octal numbers to interpret their meaning.

To find out whether a file is readable or writable to a group of users, we use a programming idiom which is very common for dealing with bit patterns: first we define a mask which zeroes out all of the bits in the mode string except those which we are specifically interested in. This is done by defining a mask value in which the bits we want are set to 1 and all others are set to zero. Then we AND the mask with the mode string. If the result is different from zero then we know that all of the bits were also set in the mode string. As in C, the bitwise AND operator in perl is called `&'.

For example, to test whether a file is writable to other users in the same group as the file, we would write the following.

```
$mask = 020;   # Leading 0 means octal number

($device,$inode,$mode) = stat("file");

if ($mode & $mask)
  {
  print "File is writable by the group\n";
  }
```

Here the 2 in the second octal number means "write", the fact that it is the second octal number from the right means that it refers to "group". Thus the result of the if-test is only true if that particular bit is true. We shall see this idiom in action below.

Example 41

Here is a simple implementation of the UNIX `passwd' program in Perl.

```
#!/usr/bin/perl
#
# A perl version of the passwd program.
#
# Note - the real passwd program needs to be much more
# secure than this one. This is just to demonstrate the
# use of the crypt() function.
#
##################################################
###########

print "Changing passwd for $ENV{'USER'} on $ENV{'HOST'}\n";

system 'stty','-echo';
print "Old passwd: ";

$oldpwd = <STDIN>;
chop $oldpwd;
```

```
($name,$coded_pwd,$uid,$gid,$x,$y,$z,$gcos,$home,$shell)
                              = getpwnam($ENV{"USER"});

if (crypt($oldpwd,$coded_pwd) ne $coded_pwd)
  {
  print "\nPasswd incorrect\n";
  exit (1);
  }

$oldpwd = "";                    # Destroy the evidence!

print "\nNew passwd: ";

$newpwd = <STDIN>;

print "\nRepeat new passwd: ";

$rnewpwd = <STDIN>;

chop $newpwd;
chop $rnewpwd;

if ($newpwd ne $rnewpwd)
  {
  print "\n Incorrectly typed. Password unchanged.\n";
  exit (1);
  }

$salt = rand();
$new_coded_pwd = crypt($newpwd,$salt);

print "\n\n$name:$new_coded_pwd:$uid:$gid:$gcos:$home:$shell\n";
```

Example 41

This example is used to explain how Unix system calls such as opendir(), readdir(), closedir(), etc., can be used in perl.

```
#!/usr/bin/perl -w
use Env;
use strict;

my(@files);
```

```
opendir(DIR, $main::TMP);
@files=readdir(DIR);
closedir(DIR);

print "$main::TMP\n";

foreach (@files)
{
print("\t$_\n") if /\.c/i;
}
```

Example 42

Example with `fork()'

The following example uses the `fork' function to start a daemon which goes into the background and watches the system to which process is using the greatest amount of CPU time each minute. A pipe is opened from the BSD `ps' command.

```
#!/usr/bin/perl
#
# A fork() demo. This program will sit in the background and
# make a list of the process which uses the maximum CPU average
# at 1 minute intervals. On a quiet BSD like system this will
# normally be the swapper (long term scheduler).
#

$true = 1;
$logfile="perl.cpu.logfile";

print "Max CPU logfile, forking daemon...\n";

if (fork())
  {
  exit(0);
  }

while ($true)
  {
  open (logfile,">> $logfile") || die "Can't open $logfile\n";
  open (ps,"/bin/ps aux |") || die "Couldn't open a pipe from ps !!\n";

  $skip_first_line = <ps>;
```

```
$max_process = <ps>;
close(ps);

print logfile $max_process;
close(logfile);
sleep 60;

($a,$b,$c,$d,$e,$f,$g,$size) = stat($logfile);

if ($size > 500)
  {
  print STDERR "Log file getting big, better quit!\n";
  exit(0);
  }
}
```

Example 43

Example reading databases

Here is an example program with several of the above features demonstrated simultaneously. This following program lists all users who have home directories on the current host. If the home area has sub-directories, corresponding to groups, then this is specified on the command line. The word `home' causes the program to print out the home directories of the users.

```
#!/usr/bin/perl
##################################################
################
#
# allusers - list all users on named host, i.e. all
#            users who can log into this machine.
#
# Syntax: allusers group
#         allusers mygroup home
#         allusers myhost group home
#
# NOTE : This command returns only users who are registered on
#        the current host. It will not find users which cannot
#        be validated in the passwd file, or in the named groups
#        in NIS. It assumes that the users belonging to
#        different groups are saved in subdirectories of
#        /home/hostname.
#
```

```
####################################################
################

&arguments();

die "\n" if ( ! -d "/home/$server" );

$disks = `/bin/ls -d /home/$server/$group`;

foreach $home (split(/\s/,$disks))
  {
  open (LS,"cd $home; /bin/ls $home |") || die "allusers: Pipe didn't open";

  while (<LS>)
    {
    $exists = "";
    ($user) = split;
    ($exists,$pw,$uid,$gid,$qu,$cm,$gcos,$dir)=getpwnam($user);

    if ($exists)
      {
      if ($printhomes)
        {
        print "$dir\n";
        }
      else
        {
        print "$user\n";
        }
      }
    }
  close(LS);
  }

####################################################
######

sub arguments
  {
  $printhomes = 0;
  $group = "*";
  $server = `/bin/hostname`;
  chop $server;

  foreach $arg (@ARGV)
```

```
          {
          if (substr($arg,0,1) eq "u")
            {
            $group = $arg;
            next;
            }

          if ($arg eq "home")
            {
            $printhomes = 1;
            next;
            }

          $server= $arg;     #default is to interpret as a server.
          }
        }
```

Example 44

This example is to explain how to connect to a MySQl database table.

```
#!/usr/bin/perl -w -T
use DBI;
{
my $dbh;
my $sth;
my $cmd;

my $restype;
my $ret_val;

my $data;
my @rawResults;

$dbh=DBI->connect('dbi:mysql:STUD', 'root', 'ritchvenkat');

if( !defined($dbh)) { print "cannot connect\n";  exit 1; }
else
{
print "Success\n";
 }


exit 0;
}
```

Example 45

This example explains how to connect to a MySQL table, preparing a statement, executing the statement and displaying the results.

```
#!/usr/bin/perl -w -T
use DBI;
{
my $dbh;
my $sth;
my $cmd;

my $restype;
my $ret_val;

my $data;
my @rawResults;

$dbh=DBI->connect('dbi:mysql:STUD', 'rao', 'ritchvenkat');

if( !defined($dbh)) { print "cannot connect\n";  exit 1; }
else
{
print "Success\n";
 }


$sth=$dbh->prepare('SELECT NAME FROM STUDENT');

if( !defined($sth))
{
print "Prepartion fialed\n";
$dbh->disconnect();
exit 0;
}
else
{
print "Statment Preparation Success";
}

$ret_val=$sth->execute;
if(!defined($ret_val))
```

```
{
print "Execution fiailed\n";
$dbh->disconnect();
exit 0;
}
print"\nQuery Results are\n";
$sth->dump_results();

$dbh->disconnect();
exit 0;
}
```

Example 46

This example explains how to connect to a MySQL table and inserts .into the table.

```
#!/usr/bin/perl -w -T
use DBI;
{
my $dbh;
my $sth;
my $cmd;

my $restype;
my $ret_val;

my $data;
my @rawResults;

$dbh=DBI->connect('dbi:mysql:STUD', 'rao', 'ritchvenkat');

if( !defined($dbh)) { print "cannot connect\n";  exit 1; }
else
{
print "Success\n";
 }

$ret_val=$dbh->do("INSERT INTO STUDENT (SNO, NAME) VALUES('121',
'Rao')" );
if(!defined($ret_val))
{
```

```
print "Execution fiailed\n";
$dbh->disconnect();
exit 0;
}
else
{
print "\nQuery success\n";
}

$dbh->disconnect();
exit 0;
}
```

Example 47

This example explains how to connect to a MySQL table, preparing a statement, executing the statement and displaying the results.

```
#!/usr/bin/perl -w -T
use DBI;
{
my $dbh;
my $sth;
my $cmd;

my $restype;
my $ret_val;

my $data;
my @rawResults;

$dbh=DBI->connect('dbi:mysql:STUD', 'rao', 'ritchvenkat');

if( !defined($dbh)) { print "cannot connect\n";  exit 1; }
else
{
print "Success\n";
 }

$sth=$dbh->prepare('SELECT NAME FROM STUDENT');

if( !defined($sth))
```

```
{
print "Prepartion fialed\n";
$dbh->disconnect();
exit 0;
}
else
{
print "Statment Preparation Success";
}

$ret_val=$sth->execute;
if(!defined($ret_val))
{
print "Execution fiailed\n";
$dbh->disconnect();
exit 0;
}

print"\nQuery Results are\n";
my $data;
while($data=$sth->fetchrow_arrayref())
{
 print "@$data\n";
}

$dbh->disconnect();
exit 0;
}
```

Example 48

This example explains how to connect to a MySQL table, preparing a statement, executing the statement and displaying the results.

```
#!/usr/bin/perl -w -T
use DBI;
{
my $dbh;
my $sth;
my $cmd;

my $restype;
```

```
my $ret_val;

my @rawResults;

$dbh=DBI->connect('dbi:mysql:STUD', 'rao', 'ritchvenkat');

if( !defined($dbh)) { print "cannot connect\n";  exit 1; }
else
{
print "Success\n";
 }

$sth=$dbh->prepare('SELECT NAME FROM STUDENT WHERE NAME = ?');

if( !defined($sth))
{
print "Prepartion fialed\n";
$dbh->disconnect();
exit 0;
}
else
{
print "Statment Preparation Success";
}

$NN;
$sth->bind_param(1,$NN);
print "Enter search Name";
$NN=<STDIN>;
chomp ($NN);

$ret_val=$sth->execute;
if(!defined($ret_val))
{
print "Execution fiailed\n";
$dbh->disconnect();
exit 0;
}

print"\nQuery Results are\n";
my $data;
```

```
while($data=$sth->fetchrow_arrayref())
{
 print "@$data\n";
}

$dbh->disconnect();
exit 0;
}
```

Example 49

This example explains how to connect to a MySQL database and display the details of the tables.

```
#!/usr/bin/perl -w -T
use DBI;
{
my $dbh;
my $sth;
my $cmd;

my $restype;
my $ret_val;

my @rawResults;

$dbh=DBI->connect('dbi:mysql:STUD', 'rao', 'ritchvenkat');

if( !defined($dbh)) { print "cannot connect\n";  exit 1; }
else
{
print "Success\n";
 }


@tables=$dbh->tables();
print "\n Tables Available Are\n";

foreach (@tables)
{
```

```
print "$_\n";
}

$sth=$dbh->table_info();
$sth->dump_results();

$dbh->disconnect();
exit 0;
}
```

24.1.8 Pattern matching and extraction

Perl has regular expression operators for identifying patterns. The operator

/regular expression/

returns true of false depending on whether the regular expression matches the contents of $_. For example

```
if (/perl/)
  {
  print "String contains perl as a substring";
  }

if (/(Sat|Sun)day/)
  {
  print "Weekend day....";
  }
```

The effect is rather like the grep command. To use this operator on other variables you would write:

$variable =~ */regexp/*

Regular expression can contain parenthetic sub-expressions, e.g.

```
        if (/(Sat|Sun)day (..)th (.*)/)
  {
  $first = $1;
  $second = $2;
  $third = $3;
  }
```

in which case perl places the objects matched by such sub-expressions in the variables $1, $2 etc.

Searching and replacing text

The `sed'-like function for replacing all occurrences of a string is easily implemented in Perl using

```
while (<input>)
  {
  s/$search/$replace/g;
  print output;
  }
```

This example replaces the string inside the default variable. To replace in a general variable we use the operator `=~', with syntax:

$variable =~ s/*search*/*replace*/

Example 50

Here is an example of some of this operator in use. The following is a program which searches and replaces a string in several files. This is useful program indeed for making a change globally in a group of files! The program is called `file-replace'.

```
#!/usr/bin/perl
##################################################
############
#
# Look through files for find string and change to new string
# in all files.
#
##################################################
############

#
# Define a temporary file and check it doesn't exist
#

$outputfile = "tmpmarkfind";
unlink $outputfile;

#
# Check command line for list of files
#

if ($#ARGV < 0)
  {
  die "Syntax: file-replace [file list]\n";
  }
```

```
print "Enter the string you want to find (Don't use quotes):\n\n:";
$findstring=<STDIN>;
chop $findstring;

print "Enter the string you want to replace with (Don't use quotes):\n\n:";
$replacestring=<STDIN>;
chop $replacestring;

#

print "\nFind: $findstring\n";
print "Replace: $replacestring\n";
print "\nConfirm (y/n)  ";
$y = <STDIN>;
chop $y;

if ( $y ne "y")
  {
  die "Aborted -- nothing done.\n";
  }
else
  {
  print "Use CTRL-C to interrupt...\n";
  }

#
# Now shift default array @ARGV to get arguments 1 by 1
#

while ($file = shift)
  {
  if ($file eq "file-replace")
    {
    print "Findmark will not operate on itself!";
    next;
    }

  #
  # Save existing mode of file for later
  #

  ($dev,$ino,$mode)=stat($file);
```

```
open (INPUT,$file) || warn "Couldn't open $file\n";
open (OUTPUT,"> $outputfile") || warn "Can't open tmp";

$notify = 1;

while (<INPUT>)
  {
  if (/$findstring/ && $notify)
    {
    print "Fixing $file...\n";
    $notify = 0;
    }
  s/$findstring/$replacestring/g;
  print OUTPUT;
  }

close (OUTPUT);

#
# If nothing went wrong (if outfile not empty)
# move temp file to original and reset the
# file mode saved above
#

if (! -z $outputfile)
  {
  rename ($outputfile,$file);
  chmod ($mode,$file);
  }
else
  {
  print "Warning: file empty!\n.";
  }
}
```

Example 51

Similarly we can search for lines containing a string. Here is the grep program written in perl

```
#!/usr/bin/perl

while (<>)
  {
  print if (/$ARGV[1]/);
  }
```

The operator `*/search-string/*' returns true if the search string is a substring of the default variable $_. To search an arbitrary string, we write

.... if (*teststring* =~ */search-string/*);

Here *teststring* is searched for occurrences of *search-string* and the result is true if one is found.

In perl you can use regular expressions to search for text patterns. Note however that, like all regular expression dialects, perl has its own conventions. For example the dollar sign does not mean "match the end of line" in perl, instead one uses the `\n' symbol. Here is an example program which illustrates the use of regular expressions in perl:

```
#!/usr/bin/perl
#
# Test regular expressions in perl
#
# NB - careful with \ $ * symbols etc. Use '' quotes since
#      the shell interprets these!
#

open (FILE,"regex_test");

$regex = $ARGV[$#ARGV];

print "Looking for $ARGV[$#ARGV] in file...\n";

while (<FILE>)
  {
  if (/$regex/)
    {
    print;
    }
  }

#
# Test like this:
#
#  regex '.*'      - prints every line (matches everything)
#  regex '.'       - all lines except those containing only blanks
#                  (. doesn't match ws/white-space)
#  regex '[a-z]'   - matches any line containing lowercase
#  regex '[^a-z]'  - matches any line contain something which is
```

```
# not lowercase a-z
# regex '[A-Za-z]' - matches any line containing letters of any kind
# regex '[0-9]'   - match any line containing numbers
# regex '#.*'     - line containing a hash symbol followed by anything
# regex '^#.*'    - line starting with hash symbol (first char)
# regex ';\n'     - match line ending in a semi-colon
#
```

Try running this program with the test data on the following file which is called `regex_test' in the example program.

```
# A line beginning with a hash symbol
JUST UPPERCASE LETTERS
just lowercase letters
Letters and numbers 123456
123456
A line ending with a semi-colon;
Line with a comment # COMMENT...
```

Example 52

Here is an example program which you could use to automatically turn a mail message of the form

```
From    : Newswire
To      : Mail2html
Subject : Nothing happened
On the 13th February at kl. 09:30 nothing happened. No footprints
were found leading to the scene of a terrible murder, no evidence
of a struggle .... etc etc
```

into an html-file for the world wide web. The program works by extracting the message body and subject from the mail and writing html-commands around these to make a web page. The subject field of the mail becomes the title. The other headers get skipped, since the script searches for lines containing the sequence "colon-space" or `: '. A regular expression is used for this.

```
#!/usr/bin/perl
#
# Make HTML from mail
#

&BeginWebPage();
&ReadNewMail();
&EndWebPage();
```

```
##################################################
########

sub BeginWebPage

{
   print "<HTML>\n";
   print "<BODY>\n";
}

##################################################
########

sub EndWebPage

{
   print "</BODY>\n";
   print "</HTML>\n";
}

##################################################
########

sub ReadNewMail

{
while (<>)
  {
  if (/Subject:/)   # Search for subject line
     {
     # Extract subject text...

     chop;
     ($left,$right) = split(":",$_);
     print "<H1> $right </H1>\n";
     next;
     }
  elsif (/.*: .*/)  # Search for - anything: anything
     {
     next;          # skip other headers
     }

  print;
  }
}
```

Example 53

Generate WWW pages automatically

The following program scans through the password database and build a standardized html-page for each user it finds there. It fills in the name of the user in each case. Note the use of the `<<' operator for extended input, already used in the context of the shell, See section Pipes and redirection in csh. This allows us to format a whole passage of text, inserting variables at strategic places, and avoid having to the print over many lines.

```
#!/usr/bin/perl
#
# Build a default home page for each user in /etc/passwd
#
#

############################################################
##################
# Level 0 (main)
############################################################
##################

$true = 1;
$false = 0;

# First build an associated array of users and full names

setpwent();

while ($true)
  {
  ($name,$passwd,$uid,$gid,$quota,$comment,$fullname) = getpwent;
  $FullName{$name} = $fullname;
  print "$name - $FullName{$name}\n";
  last if ($name eq "");
  }

print "\n";

# Now make a unique filename for each page and open a file

foreach $user (sort keys(%FullName))
  {
  next if ($user eq "");
```

```
  print "Making page for $user\n";
  $outputfile = "$user.html";

  open (OUT,"> $outputfile") || die "Can't open $outputfile\n";

  &MakePage;

  close (OUT);
  }

##############################################################
##################
# Level 1
##############################################################
##################

sub MakePage

{
print OUT <<ENDMARKER;

<HTML>
<BODY>
<HEAD><TITLE>$FullName{$user}'s Home Page</TITLE></HEAD>
<H1>$FullName{$user}'s Home Page</H1>

Hi welcome to my home page. In case you hadn't
got it yet my name is: $FullName{$user}...

I study at <a href=http://www.heaven.com>venkat</a>.

</BODY>
</HTML>

ENDMARKER
}
```

Example 54

This example is to explain about how perl can be used for grep style of operations on the file(s).

```
#!/usr/bin/perl -w
$original="gopher";
$replacement="World Wide Web";
$nchanges=0;
```

```
undef $/;
foreach $file (@ARGV) {
    if (! open(INPUT,"<$file") ) {
        print STDERR "Can't open input file $bakfile\n";
        next;
    }

# Read input file as one long record.
$data=<INPUT>;
close INPUT;

if ($data =~ s/$original/$replacement/gi) {
        $bakfile = "$file.bak";
# Abort if can't backup original or output.
        if (! rename($file,$bakfile)) {
            die "Can't rename $file $!";
        }
        if (! open(OUTPUT,">$file") ) {
            die "Can't open output file $file\n";
        }
        print OUTPUT $data;
        close OUTPUT;
        print STDERR "$file changed\n";
        $nchanges++;
    }

    else {  print STDERR "$file not changed\n"; }
  }
print STDERR "$nchanges files changed.\n";
  exit(0);
```

Other supported functions

Perl has very many functions which come directly from the C library such as *sockets which* for network socket communication.

Example 55

This program is to explain how perl can be used for network related applications such as creating sockets, connecting(), accepting connection requests etc.,.

```
#!/usr/bin/perl -w
use Socket;
use strict;

my($remoteserver)='localhost';
```

```
my($secsIn70years)=220899900;
my($buffer)='';
my($socketStructure);
my($serverTime);

my($proto)=getprotobyname('tcp')||6;
my($port)=getservbyname('time','tcp')||37;

my($packFormat)='S n a4 x8';
connect(SOCKET,pack($packFormat, AF_INET(), $port, $remoteserver)) or
die("connect: $1");

read(SOCKET,$buffer,4);
close(SOCKET);

$serverTime=unpack("N", $buffer);
$serverTime -=$secsIn70years;
print ("$serverTime\n");
```

24.2 Conclusions

The Practical Extraction and Report Language is a powerful tool which goes beyond the shell programming, but which retains much of the immediateness of shell programming in a more formal programming environment. The success of Perl has led many programmers to use it exclusively. This chapter dealt with perl programming with lucid examples which are of practical in nature. Examples related to Web Page handling, database operations using perl are included.

25 A peep into Ruby

25.1 Introduction

In the recent years Ruby is becoming popular. Ruby is also "an interpreted scripting language for quick and easy object-oriented programming".

It is interpreted scripting language and thus:

- ability to make operating system calls directly
- powerful string operations and regular expressions
- immediate feedback during development

quick and easy:

- variable declarations are unnecessary
- variables are not typed
- syntax is simple and consistent
- memory management is automatic

object oriented programming:

- everything is an object
- classes, inheritance, methods, etc.
- singleton methods
- mixin by module
- iterators and closures

also:

- multiple precision integers
- exception processing model
- dynamic loading
- threads

Ruby can be used to execute instructions from the command line itself. For example,

```
ruby   -e 'print "Hello Dear User. You will enjoy me"'
```

Command at the dollar prompt gives you the message between double quotes.

Also, we can enter ruby program in a file (say ex.rb) and then its name can be given as command line argument to ruby command like

```
ruby  ex.rb
```

In addition, if we simply type **ruby** command at the shell prompt ruby interpreter will be started and we will see the prompt ruby>. At this prompt also we can execute ruby commands or programs. We can have interactive ruby running by executing **irb** command or **irb –simple-prompt** at the shell prompt.

At the Ruby prompt we can do calculations interactively like calculator. Interestingly, we can work with large numbers also.

25.1.1 Variables

Ruby supports variety of variables such as int, float, strings, arrays, associative arrays etc. Normal variables including strings can be simply used without declaring them. In fact there is no type associated with variables. However, variables whose names starts with uppercase character is considered as constant. Other conventions are given below. With the help of gets, puts functions we can do I/O operations. For example the following program (a.rb) takes a string and prints the same.

```
puts "Enter Name"
name =gets
puts name
```

Ruby supports almost all the operators which are available in C. In addition it supports exponentiation operator (**) in the lines of FORTRAN. The following example is used to explain the same. We can observe that ruby handling the big number unlike other languages.

```
a=10**100
b=a**a
print a,"\n", b
```

In Ruby, the first character of an identifier categorizes it at a glance:

$	global variable
@	instance variable
[a-z] or _	local variable
[A-Z]	constant

The only exceptions to the above are ruby's pseudo-variables: self, which always refers to the currently executing object, and nil, which is the meaningless value assigned to uninitialized variables. Both are named as if they are local variables, but self is a global variable maintained by the interpreter, and nil is really a constant. As these are the only two exceptions, they don't confuse things too much

There is a collection of special variables whose names consist of a dollar sign ($) followed by a single character which you can recollect similar to shell's positional variables.

$!	latest error message
$@	location of error
$_	string last read by gets
$.	line number last read by interpreter
$&	string last matched by regexp
$~	the last regexp match, as an array of sub expressions
$n	the nth sub expression in the last match (same as $~[n])
$=	case-insensitivity flag
$/	input record separator
$\	output record separator
$0	the name of the ruby script file
$*	the command line arguments
$$	interpreter's process ID
$?	exit status of last executed child process

In the above, $_ and $~ have local scope.

25.1.2 Strings

Ruby has excellent means for management of strings. Similar to Java, it gives freedom to add two strings with +, a string and number, etc.,. If we multiply a string with an integer (say n) then the result is a string which contains the string n times. In the following example, various operations on the springs are emphasized. Readers has to remember that all the variables in Ruby are assumed as objects. Thus, the functions are invoked with **.** delimiter.

Example 1

```
puts "Enter a string"
name= gets
puts "You have entered", name
name=name.swapcase
puts "After swapping upper cases to lower case and vice versa", name
name=name.downcase;
puts "After Converting into lower case", name
name=name.upcase;
puts "After Converting into Upper case", name
name=name.capitalize;
puts "After Converting into Upper case", name
name=name.next;
puts "Next string in the alphabetical sequence", name
name=name.reverse;
puts "After reversing", name
```

25.1.3 if condition

The syntax of the if condition in Ruby can be as follows.

```
if condition
statements
end

if  condition
statements
else
statements
end

if condition
statements
elsif condition
```

```
statements
elsif condition
statements
else
statements
end
```

Always a if condition should terminate with end statement.

Example 2

The following example takes two strings and prints them in accordance with their length.

```
puts "Enter two strings"
str1 =gets
str2 =gets
l=str1.length
k=str2.length

if ( l > k)
print str1, str2
else
print str2, str1
end
```

Example 3

The following program reads a students marks and prints their class. The chomp is used to remove last character, i.e., new line. The functions or methods such as to_i, to_f etc., (see Table 25. 1) are used to convert the string into integer, float respectively.

```
puts "Enter Marks"
mark = gets.chomp.to_i
if (mark >=60 )
puts "First Class"
elsif (mark >=50)
puts "Second Class"
elsif (mark >=35 )
puts "Third Class"
else
puts "Failed"
end
```

Table 25.1 Functions to convert one type to another type.

Method	Converts	
	From	To
String#to_i	string	integer
String#to_f	string	float
Float#to_i	float	integer
Float#to_s	float	string
Integer#to_f	integer	float
Integer#to_s	integer	string

Like C language, Ruby also supports implicit assignment statements. That is, a statement such as var = var + identifier can be written as var += identifier. This is meaningful for other operators such as -,*,/,%, and ** also. However, note that unary increment/decrement operators can not be applicable here.

You can make lines "wrap around" by putting a backslash - \ - at the very end of the line.

Example 4

This is another example to explain how to read numeric data and manipulate. Here, principal amount, rate and time is read and the interest is printed.

```
puts "Enter Principal Amount"
p=gets.chomp.to_f
puts "Enter Rate"
r=gets.chomp.to_f
puts "Enter Time"
t=gets.chomp.to_f

s_interest=p*r*t/100
print " Simple Interest=", s_interest, "\n"
c_interest=p*(1 + r/100)**t -p
print " Compound Interest=", c_interest, "\n"
```

25.1.4 case construct

Ruby also supports case construct like C and Java. However, it gives freedom to have variety of situations to be represented. Unlike C, where integer or character constants are used as cases, here we can use strings, regular expressions (like shell) and range expressions.

Example 5

The following example takes a student marks and prints his class. We can see how a range expression can be used in case.

```
puts "Enter Marks"
mark = gets.chomp.to_i
case mark
when 1..34
puts "Failed"
when 35..49
puts "Third Class"
when 50..59
puts "Second Class"
when 60..100
puts "First Class"
end
```

25.1.5 Arrays

The class **Array** is used to represent a *collection* of items. Unlike other languages, Ruby supports arrays with different type of elements. For example:

```
Arr=[12,34,33,12]
Arr1=["ram", "rao", "abhi"]
```

We can use functions such as reverse, sort, length, to_s etc,. in addition to operations such as +, - etc,.

Ruby also supports a special arrays like perl known as associative arrays or hash's. Hashes are a generalization of arrays. Instead of only permitting integer indices, as in array[3], hashes allow any object to be used as an "index". So, you can write hash["name"]

Example 6

For example, the following program displays all states and capitols. Also, all the state names and capitals names.

```
States["AP"]="Hyderabad"
States["UP"]="Lucknow"
States["MP"]="Bhopal"

States.each  do |key,value|
puts  key + value
end
```

```
States.each_key  do |key|
puts  key
end

States.each_value  do |value|
puts  value
end
```

25.1.6 while loop

Ruby supports while loop also whose behavior is same as while of C language. There are four ways to interrupt the progress of a loop from inside. First, break means, as in C, to escape from the loop entirely. Second, next skips to the beginning of the next iteration of the loop (corresponding to C's continue). Third, ruby has redo, which restarts the current iteration. The fourth way to get out of a loop from the inside is return. An evaluation of return causes escape not only from a loop but from the method that contains the loop. If an argument is given, it will be returned from the method call, otherwise nil is returned

Example 7

The following example is used to explain the use of while loop. Here, a string is read from the key board then it is palindrome or not is tested. Two approaches are used a) comparing first and last character, second and last but one character et.,. b) calculating reverse of the given string and comparing it with the original one.

```
puts "Enter a String"
str1=gets.chomp

l=str1.length;
i=0
j=l-1
while i<j
if ( str1[i] != str1[j] )
 break;
end
i=i+1
j=j-1
end

if ( i >=j )
puts "Palindrome"
else
puts "Not a Palindrome"
end
```

```
if ( str1 == str1.reverse )
puts "Palindrome"
else
puts "Not a Palindrome"
end
```

Example 8

This program reads a set of students marks and then calculates their average.

```
puts "Enter Number of Students"
N=gets.chomp.to_i;
i=0
s=0
while i < N
puts "Enter a marks"
s=s+gets.chomp.to_i
i=i+1
end

average=s/N
print average
```

Example 9

This program reads a number and calculates the factorial value of it and prints the same.

```
puts "Enter a number "
N=gets.chomp.to_i;
i=1
s=1
while i <= N
s=s*i
i=i+1
end

print "Factorial=", s
```

Example 10

This example takes a integer and prints whether it is prime number or not.

```
puts "Enter a number "
N=gets.chomp.to_i;
i=1
c=0
while i <= N
```

```
if N%i == 0
  c+=1
end
i=i+1
end

if( c==2 )
print "Prime\n"
else
print "Not a Prime\n"
end
```

Example 11

This is simple program to explain how rand function can be used to develop computer aided testing program to test multiplication abilities of small kids. Here, we are generating two random numbers whose values of are less than 10 and then asking the user (kid) to enter the product of them. He will be given ten chances and if he guesses correctly within that he will be praised else he will be informed 'next time better luck'. The first two while loops are two generate random numbers other than zero.

```
while ( x=rand(10)) ==0
end
while (y=rand(10)) == 0
end

print "Enter the Product of\n", x, "\tand\t", y, "\n"

i=0
while i<10
ans =gets.chomp.to_i

if(ans == x*y )
print "You won\n"
break
else
print "Try Again\n"
end
i=i+1
end

if ( i==10)
print "Next Time better luck"
end
```

Example 12

This another example to explain the use of random numbers. A set of state's names and their capitols are remembered in arrays, then randomly some state name is displayed and the user required to enter its capitol. Depending on his response the answer is verified.

```
states =[ "AP", "HP", "UP", "TN", "MP", "WB"]
capitols =["Hyderabad", "Itanagar", "Lucknow", "Chennai", "Bhopal", "Calcutta"]

points=0
j=0
while j<10
i=rand(6)
puts "Enter Capitol of", states[i]
x=gets.chomp

if  x.downcase == capitols[i].downcase
points +=1
end

j =j+1
end

puts "Your Score is=", points, "\n"
```

Example 13

The following program is explain how regular expressions can be used in Ruby. This program reads standard input till we enter ^d and counts in how many lines string Ruby is found. Here also, like perl $_ refers to the current line which is now read from key board.

```
n=0
while gets          # assigns line to $_
  if /Ruby/         # matches against $_
    print           # prints $_
  n=n+1
 end
end
print n
```

Example 14

The following example prints "Hello" message 5 times.

```
5.times do
print "Hello\n"
end
```

25.1.7 for loop

Ruby's for is a little more interesting than C's for loop. For example, the loop below runs once for each element in the collection (Hope you remember for loop of shell).

```
for var in collection

        ....
        end
```

Example 15

The collection can be a range of values (this is what most people mean when they talk about a for loop). The following program prints numbers from 2 to 5.

```
for x in (2..5)
print x, "\n"
end
```

Example 16

The collection can be an array. For example the following program prints Hello and "How are you" messages in one line.

```
for x in ["Hello", "How are you"]
#single quotes also works in the same fashion
print x, "\n"
end
```

Example 17

The following program also uses an array is collection in the for loop. Note that ruby can support arrays with different type of elements.

```
for x in ["Hello", 14, 13.44]
print x, "\n"

end
```

Like perl, output of a shell command can be used in ruby. For example, output of date command is used and each word of it is printed.

```
for i in `date`
print  i, "\n"
end
```

25.1.8 Iterators

Iterators can often be substituted for conventional loops, and once you get used to them, they are generally easier to deal with. For example, in the following program string length is calculated with each iterator.

Example 18

```
str=gets
i=0
str.chop.each_byte { i=i+1 }

j=0
k=i-1

while j<k
if ( str[j] != str [k] )
print " Not Palindrome\n"
break
end
j=j+1
k=k-1
end

print "Palindrome"
```

Example 19

The following program uses iterator to find out the length of a string.

```
str=gets
i=0
str.chop.each_byte { i=i+1 }
print "Length of the string=",  i, "\n"
```

Example 20

The following example is used explain the iterators. With the help of each iterator each element is printed. Array is sorted with sort function and then it will be printed.

```
arr=[1,81,21,22,22,12,13,31]
print "Before Sorting the elements :\t"
arr.each {|i| print i, "\t" }
print "\n"
```

```
arr.sort

print "AfterSorting the elements :\t"
arr.each {|i| print i, "\t" }
print "\n"
```

Iterators are not an original concept with ruby. They are in common use in object-oriented languages. They are also used in Lisp, though there they are not called iterators. However the concept of iterator is an unfamiliar one for many so it should be explained in more detail.

The verb *iterate* means to do the same thing many times, you know, so an *iterator* is something that does the same thing many times.

Ruby's String type has some useful iterators:

```
"rama".each_byte{|c| printf "%c", c}; print "\n"
```

each_byte is an iterator for each character in the string. Each character is substituted into the local variable c.

Another iterator of String is each_line.

25.1.8 Functions/subroutines

Ruby also supports functions like C and other languages. For example the following example prints whether a given number is prime or not.

Example 21

```
$c=0
def DIV(n,i)

 if n%i ==0
 $c=$c+1
end
end

n=gets.chop.to_i
2.upto(n-1) {|i|  DIV(n,i) }

if ( $c ==0 )
print "Prime\n"
else
print "Not Prime\n"
end
```

Example 22

The following program defines a function to calculate factorial value and is used.

```
def fact(n)
 if n == 0
  1
 else
  n * fact(n-1)
 end
end

print fact(ARGV[0].to_i), "\n"
```

25.1.9 Modules

Ruby has excellent set of loadable modules such as mathematical related, windows related etc.,. The module can be loaded with the help of include statement.

Modules in ruby are similar to classes, except:

- A module can have no instances.
- A module can have no subclasses.
- A module is defined by module ... end.

There are two typical uses of modules. One is to collect related methods and constants in a central location. The Math module in ruby's standard library plays such a role

Example 23

For example, in the following example math module is loaded and the constant PI is used. Note the scope result ion operator while doing so.

```
include Math
print "Enter Radius\n"
r=gets.chop.to_f
area=Math::PI*r*r

print "Area=", area, "\n"
```

Remember that modules cannot be instantiated or subclassed; but if we include a module in a class definition, its methods are effectively appended, or "mixed in", to the class. Ruby purposely does not implement true multiple inheritance, but the *mixin* technique is used for whatever particular properties we want to have. For example, if a class has a working each method, mixing in the standard library's Enumerable module gives us sort and find methods for free.

This use of modules gives us the basic functionality of multiple inheritance but allows us to represent class relationships with a simple tree structure, and so simplifies the language implementation considerably (a similar choice was made by the designers of Java).

Example 24

This example show how 'tk' library can be used from ruby.

```
require 'tk'
root = TkRoot.new { title "Ex1" }
TkLabel.new(root) {
  text  'Hello, World!'
  pack  { padx 15 ; pady 15; side 'left' }
}
Tk.mainloop
```

25.1.10 Files

Example 25

The following program opens a file and reads the data from it and prints on the screen. If the specified file is not available it reads from key board.

```
begin
  file = open("AAA")
rescue
  file = STDIN
end

while data=file.gets
print data
end
```

25.1.11 Exceptions

Ruby allow us to handle exceptions for blocks of code in a compartmentalized way. The block of code marked with begin executes until there is an exception (like try block in C++, Java), which causes control to be transferred to a block of error handling code, which is marked with rescue. If no exception occurs, the rescue code is not used. See the above program the method returns the first line of a text file, or nil if there is an exception:

25.2 Object oriented Programming through Ruby

Ruby is fully object oriented language. Like any OO languages, we can define classes and use them.

Example 26

```
class Simham
  def speak
      print "Gow Gow"
  end
end
sarada=Simham.new
sarada.speak
```

Example 27

The following program defines complex class.

```
class Complex
@real
@imag

  def Read()
  @real=gets.chop.to_f
  @imag=gets.chop.to_f
  end

  def Print()
  print @real, "\t", @imag, "\n"
  end

end
sarada=Complex.new
sarada.Read
sarada.Print
```

Example 28

This example is used to explain the functions initialize (such as constructor), dump, load.

```
class Klass
  def initialize(str)
    @str = str
  end
  def sayHello
    @str
  end
end

o = Klass.new("hello\n")
data = Marshal.dump(o)
print data
obj = Marshal.load(data)
obj.sayHello
```

25.3 Profiling

By loading profile module, we an profile a ruby program. For example, we can run the sorting problem as discussed above. We have asked to load 'profile' module to profile this program.

Example 29

```
require 'profile'
arr=[1,81,21,22,22,12,13,31]
print "Before Sorting the elements :\t"
arr.each {|i| print i, "\t" }
print "\n"

arr.sort

print "AfterSorting the elements :\t"
arr.each {|i| print i, "\t" }
print "\n"
```

25.4 Calling Unix System Calls

Ruby gives freedom to call Unix system calls directly. For example, the following program calls fork() system call which creates new process which behaves similar to this process. Statement after fork() are executed in both the process. Thus, we will see Hello message two times.

Example 30

```
fork()
print "Hello\n"
```

25.5 Conclusions

This chapter explains a new object oriented language namingly RUBY. It explores about Ruby's object oriented behavior and how it makes programming easy. Also, how system calls can be called from Ruby program is emphasized. In addition, how GUI programming can be done is explained with simple examples.

26 X Window System Architecture and GUI Programming

26.1 Introduction

Nowadays, any operating system in hopes of being competitive needs to have an excellent GUI subsystem. GUIs are supposed to be easier to use. Microsoft became so popular in home market because of its user friendly GUI. X windows is the GUI used widely in Unix.

X was developed by the Athena project at MIT, and released in 1984. In 1988 an entity called the "X Consortium" took over X, and to this day handles its development and distribution. The X specification is freely available, this was a smart move as it has made X almost ubiquitous. This is how XFree86 came to be. XFree86 is the implementation of X we use on our Linux computers. XFree86 also works on other operating systems, like the BSD lineage, OS/2 and maybe others. Also, despite its name, XFree86 is also available for other CPU architectures.

Main advantages of X windows

- **Separation of computing and Graphics**
- **Different systems under X**
- **Only Mechanism, No policy**
- **Network Transparency**
- **Room for future Extensions**
- **Load Sharing**
- **Resource Sharing**

The X Window System Architecture: overview

X was designed with a client-server architecture. The applications themselves are the clients; they communicate with the server and issue requests, also receives information from the server (see Figure 26.1).

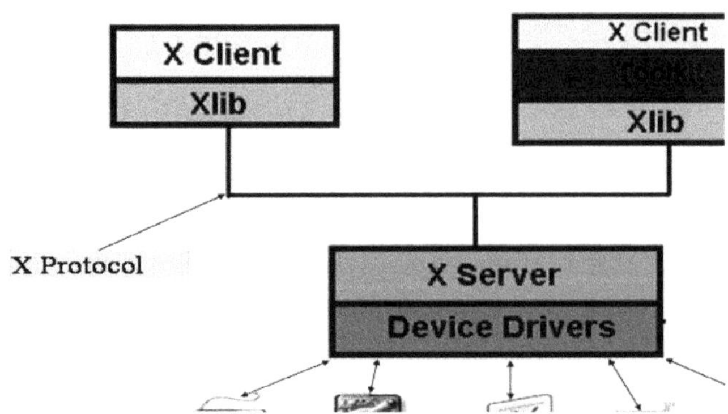

Figure 26.1 X Widows Architecture.

The X server maintains exclusive control of the display and services requests from the clients. At this point, the advantages of using this model are pretty clear. Applications (clients) only need to know how to communicate with the server, and need not be concerned with the details of talking to the actual graphics display device. At the most basic level, a client tells the server stuff like "draw a line from here to here", or "render this string of text, using this font, at this position on-screen".

This would be no different from just using a graphics library to write our application. However the X model goes a step further. It doesn't constrain the client being in the same computer as the server. The protocol used to communicate between clients and server can work over a network, or actually, any "inter-process communication mechanism that provides a reliable octet stream". Of course, the preferred way to do this is by using the TCP/IP protocols. As we can see, the X model (X protocol) is really powerful; the classical example of this is running a processor-intensive application on a Cray computer, a database monitor on a Solaris server, an e-mail application on a small BSD mail server, and a visualization program on an SGI server, and then displaying all those on my Linux workstation's screen.

Some facts about the X protocol are:

- **Introduced around mid 1980**
- **Network transparent GUI**
- **Distribute (Client & Server)**
- **Machine Code of X**
- **Asynchrnous/Synchrnous**
- **Same Look and Feel**
- **Highly Portable (OS/Language/Hardware)**
- **Better Performance**

We have seen that the X server is the one handling the actual graphics display. Also, since it's the X server which runs on the physical, actual computer the user is working on, it's the X server's responsibility to perform all actual interactions with the user. This includes reading the mouse and keyboard. All this information is relayed to the client, which of course will have to react to it.

X provides a library, aptly called Xlib, which handles all low-level client-server communication tasks. It sounds obvious that, then, the client has to invoke functions contained within Xlib to get work done.

Some facts about Xlib are:

- **Uses ASM language of X**
- **Contains Set of C Library functions**
- **Functions are used to create the X Protocol**
- **Basic text and graphics handlings capabilities**
- **Very tedious**
- **Huge**

In a nutshell, we have a server in charge of visual output and data input, client applications, and a way for them to communicate between each other. In picturing a hypothetical interaction between a client and a server, the client could ask the server to assign a rectangular area on the screen. Client is not concerned with where ii is being displayed on the screen. Client just tell the server "give me an area X by Y pixels in size", and then call functions to perform actions like "draw a line from here to there", "tell me whether the user is moving the mouse in my screen area" and so on.

Window Managers

However, we never mentioned how the X server handles manipulation of the clients' on-screen display areas (called windows). It's obvious, to anyone who's ever used a GUI, that you need to have control over the "client windows". Typically you can move and arrange them; change size, maximize or minimize windows. How, then, does the X server handle these tasks? The answer is: it doesn't.

One of X's fundamental tenets is "we provide mechanism, but not policy". So, while the X server provides a way (mechanism) for window manipulation, it doesn't actually say how this manipulation behaves (policy).

All that mechanism/policy weird stuff basically boils down to this: it's another program's responsibility to manage the on-screen space. This program decides where to place windows, gives mechanisms for users to control the windows' appearance, position and size, and usually provides "decorations" like window titles, frames and buttons, that give us control over the windows themselves. This program, which manages windows, is called (guess!) a "**window manager**".

"The window manager in X is just another client -- it is not part of the X window system, although it enjoys special privileges -- and so there is no single window manager; instead, there are many, which support different ways for the user to interact with windows and different styles of window layout, decoration, and keyboard and color map focus."

The X architecture provides ways for a window manager to perform all those actions on the windows; but it doesn't actually provide a window manager.

There are, of course, a lot of window managers, because since the window manager is an external component, it's (relatively) easy to write one according to your preferences, how you want windows to look, how you want them to behave, where do you want them to be, and so on. Some window managers are simplistic and ugly (twm); some are flashy and include everything but the kitchen sink (enlightenment); and everything in between; fvwm, amiwm, icewm, windowmaker, afterstep, sawfish, kwm, and countless others. There's a window manager for every taste.

A window manager is a "meta-client", whose most basic mission is to manage other clients. Most window managers provide a few additional facilities (and some provide a lot of them). However one piece of functionality that seems to be present in most window managers is a way to launch applications. Some of them provide a command box where you can type standard commands (which can then be used to launch client applications). Others have a nice application launching menu of some sort. This is not standardized, however; again, as X dictates no policy on how a client application should be launched, this functionality is to be implemented in client programs. While, typically, a window manager takes on this task (and each one does it differently), it's conceivable to have client applications whose sole mission is to launch other client applications; think a program launching pad. And of course, people have written large amounts of "program launching" applications.

Client Applications

Let's focus on the client programs for a moment. Imagine we want to write a client program from scratch, using only the facilities provided by X. We would quickly find that Xlib is pretty spartan, and that doing things like putting buttons on screen, text, or nice controls (scrollbars, radio boxes) for the users, is terribly complicated.

Luckily, someone else went to the trouble of programming these controls and giving them to us in a usable form; a library. These controls are usually known as "widgets" and of course, the library is a "widget library". Then we just have to call a function from this library with some parameters and have a button on-screen. Examples of widgets include menus, buttons, radio buttons, scrollbars, and canvases.

A "canvas" is an interesting kind of widget, because it's basically a sub-area within the client where i can draw stuff. Understandably, since we shouldn't use Xlib directly, because that would interfere with the widget library, the library itself gives a way to draw arbitrary graphics within the canvas widget.

Since the widget library is the one actually drawing the elements on-screen, as well as interpreting user's actions into input, the library used is largely responsible for each client's aspect and behavior. From a developer's point of view, a widget library also has a certain API (set of functions), and that might define which widget library we want to use.

Widget Libraries or toolkits

The original widget library, developed for the Athena Project, is of course the Athena widget library, also known as Athena Widgets. It's very basic, very ugly, and the usage is not intuitive by today's standards (for instance, to move a scrollbar or slider control, we don't drag it; instead, we click the right button to scroll up and the left button to scroll down). As such, it's pretty much not used a lot these days.

Just as it happens with window managers, there are a lot of toolkits, with different design goals in mind. One of the earliest toolkits is the well-known Motif, which was part of the Open Software Foundation's Motif graphical environment, consisting of a window manager and a matching toolkit is identified to be superior to Athena. In the recent times, Gtk, Qt, LessTif are in predominant use.

The widely known and used Gtk, was specifically created to replace Motif in the GIMP project (one possible meaning of Gtk is "GIMP ToolKit, although, with its widespread use, it could be interpreted as the GNU ToolKit). Gtk is now very popular because it's relatively lightweight, feature-rich, extensible and totally free.

Another very popular toolkit these days is Qt. It was not too well-known until the advent of the KDE project, which utilizes Qt for all its GUI elements.

Finally, another alternative worth mentioning is LessTif. The name is a pun on Motif, and LessTif aims to be a free, API-compatible replacement for Motif.

We may have several possible window managers, which manage our screen real estate; we also have our client applications, which are where we actually get our work done, and clients can be programmed using several possible different toolkits.

Desktop environments

The concept of a desktop environment is something new to people coming for the first time to Linux because it's something that other operating systems (like Windows and the Mac OS) intrinsically have. Main objective of desktop environment is to provide consistent look-and-feel during the computing session. The operating system provides a default file manager (the finder), a system wide control panel, and single toolkit that all applications have to use (so they all look the same), a window manager to manage all application windows and a set of guidelines that tell developers how their applications should behave, recommend control looks and placement, and suggest behaviors according to those of other applications on the system.

For example, KDE includes a single window manager (kwm), which manages and controls the behavior of our windows. It recommends using a certain graphic toolkit (Qt), so that all KDE applications look the same, as far as their on-screen controls go. KDE further extends Qt by providing a set of environment-specific libraries (kdelibs) for performing common tasks like creating menus, "about" boxes, program toolbars, communicating between programs, printing, selecting files, and other things. These make the programmer's work easier and standardize the way these special features behave. KDE also provides a set of design and behavior guidelines to programmers, with the idea that, if everybody follows them, programs running under KDE will both look and behave very similarly. Finally, KDE provides, as part of the environment, a launcher panel (kpanel), a standard file manager (which is, at the time being, Konqueror), and a configuration utility (control panel) from which we can control many aspects of our computing environment, from settings like the desktop's background and the windows' title bar color to hardware configurations.

The KDE panel is an equivalent to the MS Windows taskbar. It provides a central point from which to launch applications, and it also provides for small applications, called "applets", to be displayed within it. This gives functionality like the small, live clock most users can't live without.

GNOME is another popular desktop environment. The most obvious difference is that GNOME doesn't mandate a particular window manager (the way KDE has kwm). Originally GNOME favored the Enlightenment window manager, and currently their preferred window manager is Sawfish, but the GNOME control panel has always had a window manager selector box.

Other than this, GNOME uses the Gtk toolkit, and provides a set of higher-level functions and facilities through the gnome-libs set of libraries. GNOME has its own set of programming guidelines in order to guarantee a consistent behavior between compliant applications; it provides a panel (called just "panel"), a file manager (gmc, altough it's probably going to be superseded by Nautilus), and a control panel (the gnome control center).

A quick internet search will reveal about half a dozen desktop environments: GNUStep, ROX, GTK+XFce, UDE, to name a few. They all provide the basic facilities we mentioned earlier. GNOME and KDE have had the most support, both from the community and the industry, so they're the most advanced ones, providing a large amount of services to users and applications.

After that, I go back to my spreadsheet, now that I'm finished I want to print my document. Gnumeric is a GNOME application, so it can use the facilities provided by the GNOME environment. When I print, Gnumeric calls the gnome-print library, which actually communicates with the printer and produces the hard copy I need.

Example 1

The following example discusses about how we can create a simple window with the help of Xlib.

```
/*
 * simple-window.c - demonstrate creation of a simple window.
 */

#include <X11/Xlib.h>

#include <stdio.h>
#include <stdlib.h>      /* getenv(), etc. */
#include <unistd.h>      /* sleep(), etc.  */

int
main(int argc, char* argv[])
{
Display* display;       /* pointer to X Display structure.           */
  int screen_num;       /* number of screen to place the window on.  */
  Window win;           /* pointer to the newly created window.      */
  unsigned int display_width,
              display_height;
```

```
/* height and width of the X display.        */
 unsigned int width, height;

/* height and width for the new window.      */
 unsigned int win_x, win_y;

/* location of the window's top-left corner. */
 unsigned int win_border_width;
/* width of window's border.                 */
 char *display_name = getenv("DISPLAY");
/* address of the X display.       */

 display = XOpenDisplay(display_name);
 if (display == NULL) {
   fprintf(stderr, "%s: cannot connect to X server '%s'\n",
           argv[0], display_name);
   exit(1);
 }

 /* get the geometry of the default screen for our display. */
 screen_num = DefaultScreen(display);
 display_width = DisplayWidth(display, screen_num);
 display_height = DisplayHeight(display, screen_num);

 /* make the new window occupy 1/9 of the screen's size. */
 width = (display_width / 3);
 height = (display_height / 3);

 /* the window should be placed at the top-left corner of the screen. */

 win_x = 0;
 win_y = 0;

 /* the window's border shall be 2 pixels wide. */

  win_border_width = 2;

 /* create a simple window, as a direct child of the screen's   */
 /* root window. Use the screen's white color as the background */
 /* color of the window. Place the new window's top-left corner */
 /* at the given 'x,y' coordinates.                             */
```

```
win = XCreateSimpleWindow(display, RootWindow(display, screen_num),
                          win_x, win_y, width, height, win_border_width,
                          BlackPixel(display, screen_num),
                          WhitePixel(display, screen_num));

/* make the window actually appear on the screen. */

XMapWindow(display, win);

/* flush all pending requests to the X server, and wait until */
/* they are processed by the X server.                        */

XSync(display, False);

/* make a delay for a short period. */

sleep(4);

/* close the connection to the X server. */
XCloseDisplay(display);

exit(1);
}
```

To compile (assuming program name is sample-window.c)

```
gcc simple-window.c -o simple-window -L/usr/X11R6/lib -lX11
```

To run

```
./sample-window
```

26.2 GTK Programming

GTK (GIMP Toolkit) is a library for creating graphical user interfaces and is called the GIMP toolkit because it was originally written for developing the GNU Image Manipulation Program (GIMP), but GTK has now been used in a large number of software projects, including the GNU Network Object Model Environment (GNOME) project. GTK is built on top of GDK (GIMP Drawing Kit) which is basically a wrapper around the low-level functions for accessing the underlying windowing functions (Xlib in the case of the X windows system), and gdk-pixbuf, a library for client-side image manipulation.

GTK is essentially an object oriented application programmers interface (API) although written completely in C and implemented using the idea of classes and callback functions (pointers to functions).

In addition, GLib is used with GTK which contains a few replacements for some standard calls to increase portability; additional functions for handling linked lists, etc.

Also, GTK uses the Pango library for internationalized text output.

All GTK programs has to include gtk/gtk.h which declares the variables, functions, structures, etc. that will be used in your GTK application.

While writing GTK programs, we use gint, gchar, etc., types of variable which are typedefs to int and char, respectively, that are part of the GLib system. This is done to get around that nasty dependency on the size of simple data types when doing calculations. A good example is "gint32" which will be typedef'd to a 32 bit integer for any given platform, whether it be the 64 bit alpha, or the 32 bit i386. The typedefs are very straightforward and intuitive. They are all defined in glib/glib.h (which gets included from gtk.h).

All GTK programs has to first call the following function.

```
gtk_init (&argc, &argv);
```

This further calls function gtk_init(gint *argc, gchar ***argv) which will be called in all GTK applications; This function initializes such as the default visual and color map and then calls gdk_init(gint *argc, gchar ***argv)which initializes the library for use, sets up default signal handlers, and checks the arguments passed to your application on the command line. This creates a set of standard arguments accepted by all GTK applications.

Then, we have to write code to create and display a window. For this, the following function calls are used.

```
window = gtk_window_new (GTK_WINDOW_TOPLEVEL);
gtk_widget_show (window);
```

The GTK_WINDOW_TOPLEVEL argument specifies that we want the window to undergo window manager decoration and placement.

The gtk_widget_show() function lets GTK know that we are done setting the attributes of this widget, and that it can display it.

After this, we have to call GTK main processing loop,

```
gtk_main ();
```

This, gtk_main() call seen in every GTK application. When control reaches this point, GTK will sleep waiting for X events (such as button or key presses), timeouts, or file IO notifications to occur.

GTK is an event driven toolkit and an event occurs then the control is passed to the appropriate function. This passing of control is done using the idea of "signals". (Note that these signals are not the same as the Unix system signals, and are not implemented using them, although the terminology is almost identical.) When an event occurs, such as the press of a mouse button, the appropriate signal will be "emitted" by the widget that was pressed. This is how GTK does most of its useful work. There are signals that all widgets inherit, such as "destroy", and there are signals that are widget specific, such as "toggled" on a toggle button.

To make a button perform an action, we set up a signal handler to catch these signals and call the appropriate function. This is done by using a function such as:

```
gulong g_signal_connect( gpointer   *object,
                         const gchar *name,
                         GCallback   func,
                         gpointer    func_data );
```

where the first argument is the widget which will be emitting the signal, and the second the name of the signal you wish to catch. The third is the function you wish to be called when it is caught, and the fourth, the data you wish to have passed to this function.

The function specified in the third argument is called a "callback function", and should generally be of the form

```
void callback_func( GtkWidget *widget,
                    gpointer  callback_data );
```

where the first argument will be a pointer to the widget that emitted the signal, and the second a pointer to the data given as the last argument to the g_signal_connect() function as shown above.

Note that the above form for a signal callback function declaration is only a general guide, as some widget specific signals generate different calling parameters.

Another call which can be used to connect function to signal is:

```
gulong g_signal_connect_swapped( gpointer   *object,
                                 const gchar *name,
                                 GCallback   func,
                                 gpointer    *slot_object );
```

g_signal_connect_swapped() is the same as g_signal_connect() except that the callback function only uses one argument, a pointer to a GTK object. So when using this function to connect signals, the callback should be of the form

```
void callback_func( GtkObject *object );
```

where the object is usually a widget. We usually don't setup callbacks for g_signal_connect_swapped() however. They are usually used to call a GTK function that accepts a single widget or object as an argument.

The purpose of having two functions to connect signals is simply to allow the callbacks to have a different number of arguments. Many functions in the GTK library accept only a single GtkWidget pointer as an argument, so you want to use the g_signal_connect_swapped() for these, whereas for your functions, you may need to have additional data supplied to the callbacks.

To begin our introduction to GTK, we'll start with the simplest program possible. This program will create a 200x200 pixel window and has no way of exiting except to be killed by using the shell.

Example 2

This program (first.c)just creates a widget and calls show() function to show the widget.

```
#include <gtk/gtk.h>

int main( int   argc,
       char *argv[] )
{
   GtkWidget *window;

   gtk_init (&argc, &argv);

   window = gtk_window_new (GTK_WINDOW_TOPLEVEL);
   gtk_widget_show  (window);

   gtk_main ();

   return 0;
}
```

We can compile the above program with gcc using:

```
gcc first.c -o first `pkg-config --cflags --libs gtk+-2.0`
```

pkg-config --cflags --libs gtk+-2.0 will output a list of include directories for the compiler to look in, and list of libraries for the compiler to link with and the directories to find them in.

If we want to know what directories and libraries are used by gcc, we can run gcc command with -v option such as the following.

```
gcc -v  -o first frist.c `pkg-config --cflags --libs gtk+-2.0`
```

Example 3

Little more practical program which contains a button and when we press the same it displays "Hello World".

```
#include <gtk/gtk.h>

/* This is a callback function.
```

```
*/

void hello( GtkWidget *widget,
        gpointer   data )
{
   g_print ("Hello World\n");
}

gint delete_event( GtkWidget *widget,
            GdkEvent  *event,
     gpointer   data )
{

   /* If you return FALSE in the "delete_event" signal handler,
    * GTK will emit the "destroy" signal. Returning TRUE means
    * you don't want the window to be destroyed.
    * This is useful for popping up 'are you sure you want to quit?'
    * type dialogs.
   */

   g_print ("delete event occurred\n");

   return TRUE;
}

/* Another callback which will be called when we press close */

void destroy( GtkWidget *widget,
         gpointer   data )
{
   gtk_main_quit ();
}

int main( int   argc,
       char *argv[] )
{
   GtkWidget *window;
   GtkWidget *button;

   gtk_init (&argc, &argv);
```

```
/* create a new window */

window = gtk_window_new (GTK_WINDOW_TOPLEVEL);

/* When the window is given the "delete_event" signal (this is given
 * by the window manager, usually by the "close" option, or on the
 * titlebar), we ask it to call the delete_event () function
 * as defined above. The data passed to the callback
 * function is NULL and is ignored in the callback function. */

g_signal_connect (G_OBJECT (window), "delete_event",
     G_CALLBACK (delete_event), NULL);

/* Here we connect the "destroy" event to a signal handler.
 * This event occurs when we call gtk_widget_destroy() on the window,
 * or if we return FALSE in the "delete_event" callback. */

g_signal_connect (G_OBJECT (window), "destroy",
     G_CALLBACK (destroy), NULL);

/* Sets the border width of the window. */

gtk_container_set_border_width (GTK_CONTAINER (window), 10);

/* Creates a new button with the label "Hello World". */

button = gtk_button_new_with_label ("Hello World");

/* When the button receives the "clicked" signal, it will call the
 * function hello() passing it NULL as its argument.  The hello()
 * function is defined above. */

g_signal_connect (G_OBJECT (button), "clicked",
     G_CALLBACK (hello), NULL);

/* This will cause the window to be destroyed by calling
 * gtk_widget_destroy(window) when "clicked".  Again, the destroy
 * signal could come from here, or the window manager. */

g_signal_connect_swapped (G_OBJECT (button), "clicked",
         G_CALLBACK (gtk_widget_destroy),
                  G_OBJECT (window));

/* This packs the button into the window (a gtk container). */
```

```
  gtk_container_add (GTK_CONTAINER (window), button);

  /* The final step is to display this newly created widget. */

  gtk_widget_show (button);

  /* show the window */

  gtk_widget_show (window);

  /* as mentioned earlier all GTK applications must have a gtk_main() */

  gtk_main ();

  return 0;
}
```

GTK also supports many means such as boxes, tables to place visual elements such as Labels, buttons, text boxes, sliders, etc.

Example 4

The following program adds three text fields and a button to a window. When a user enters integers in first two text fields and enters enter key the values are stored in global variable x,y. When user presses close button or simply enters enter key in third text area then the product of x and y is displayed in third text field.

```
#include <stdio.h>
#include <stdlib.h>
#include <gtk/gtk.h>

GtkWidget *entry2;
int x,y,prod;

void enter_callback( GtkWidget *widget,
                GtkWidget *entry )
{
  const gchar *entry_text;
  entry_text = gtk_entry_get_text (GTK_ENTRY (entry));
x=atoi(entry_text);
}

void enter_callback1( GtkWidget *widget,
                GtkWidget *entry )
```

```
{
  const gchar *entry_text;
  entry_text = gtk_entry_get_text (GTK_ENTRY (entry));
y=atoi(entry_text);
}

void enter_callback2( GtkWidget *widget,
              GtkWidget *entry )
{
prod=x*y;

char *str = g_strdup_printf ("%d", prod);
  gtk_entry_set_text(GTK_ENTRY(entry2),str);
g_free(str);
}


int main( int   argc,
       char *argv[] )
{

   GtkWidget *window;
   GtkWidget *vbox;
   GtkWidget *entry,*entry1;
   GtkWidget *button;
   GtkWidget *check;
   gint tmp_pos;

   gtk_init (&argc, &argv);

   /* create a new window */
   window = gtk_window_new (GTK_WINDOW_TOPLEVEL);
   gtk_widget_set_size_request (GTK_WIDGET (window), 200, 100);
   gtk_window_set_title (GTK_WINDOW (window), "GTK Entry");
   g_signal_connect (G_OBJECT (window), "destroy",
              G_CALLBACK (gtk_main_quit), NULL);
   g_signal_connect_swapped (G_OBJECT (window), "delete_event",
                     G_CALLBACK (gtk_widget_destroy),
                     G_OBJECT (window));

   vbox = gtk_vbox_new (FALSE, 0);
```

```
    gtk_container_add (GTK_CONTAINER (window), vbox);
    gtk_widget_show (vbox);

    entry = gtk_entry_new ();
    entry1 = gtk_entry_new ();
    entry2 = gtk_entry_new ();

    gtk_entry_set_max_length (GTK_ENTRY (entry), 50);
    gtk_entry_set_max_length (GTK_ENTRY (entry1), 50);
    gtk_entry_set_max_length (GTK_ENTRY (entry2), 50);

    g_signal_connect (G_OBJECT (entry), "activate",
        G_CALLBACK (enter_callback),
        (gpointer) entry);
    g_signal_connect (G_OBJECT (entry1), "activate",
        G_CALLBACK (enter_callback1),
        (gpointer) entry1);
    g_signal_connect (G_OBJECT (entry2), "activate",
        G_CALLBACK (enter_callback2),
        (gpointer) entry2);

    gtk_box_pack_start (GTK_BOX (vbox), entry, TRUE, TRUE, 0);
    gtk_box_pack_start (GTK_BOX (vbox), entry1, TRUE, TRUE, 0);
    gtk_box_pack_start (GTK_BOX (vbox), entry2, TRUE, TRUE, 0);
    gtk_widget_show (entry);
    gtk_widget_show (entry1);
    gtk_widget_show (entry2);

    button = gtk_button_new_from_stock (GTK_STOCK_CLOSE);
    g_signal_connect_swapped (G_OBJECT (button), "clicked",
            G_CALLBACK (enter_callback2),
            G_OBJECT (window));
    gtk_box_pack_start (GTK_BOX (vbox), button, TRUE, TRUE, 0);
    GTK_WIDGET_SET_FLAGS (button, GTK_CAN_DEFAULT);
    gtk_widget_grab_default (button);
    gtk_widget_show (button);

    gtk_widget_show (window);

    gtk_main();

    return 0;
}
```

Example 5

The following example demonstrates what color will be displayed for a given values of R,G and B. R,G, and B values can be adjusted through scrollbars or directly entering them.

```
#include <glib.h>
#include <gdk/gdk.h>
#include <gtk/gtk.h>

GtkWidget *colorseldlg = NULL;
GtkWidget *drawingarea = NULL;
GdkColor color;

/* Color changed handler */

void color_changed_cb( GtkWidget         *widget,
                       GtkColorSelection *colorsel )
{
  GdkColor ncolor;

  gtk_color_selection_get_current_color (colorsel, &ncolor);
  gtk_widget_modify_bg (drawingarea, GTK_STATE_NORMAL, &ncolor);
}

/* Drawingarea event handler */

gint area_event( GtkWidget *widget,
                 GdkEvent  *event,
                 gpointer   client_data )
{
  gint handled = FALSE;
  gint response;
  GtkColorSelection *colorsel;

  /* Check if we've received a button pressed event */

  if (event->type == GDK_BUTTON_PRESS)
    {
     handled = TRUE;

      /* Create color selection dialog */
     if (colorseldlg == NULL)
```

```
      colorseldlg = gtk_color_selection_dialog_new ("Select background color");

      /* Get the ColorSelection widget */
      colorsel  =  GTK_COLOR_SELECTION  (GTK_COLOR_SELECTION_DIALOG
(colorseldlg)->colorsel);

      gtk_color_selection_set_previous_color (colorsel, &color);

      gtk_color_selection_set_current_color (colorsel, &color);

      gtk_color_selection_set_has_palette (colorsel, TRUE);

      /* Connect to the "color_changed" signal, set the client-data
       * to the colorsel widget */
      g_signal_connect (G_OBJECT (colorsel), "color_changed",
                 G_CALLBACK (color_changed_cb), (gpointer) colorsel);

      /* Show the dialog */
      response = gtk_dialog_run (GTK_DIALOG (colorseldlg));

      if (response == GTK_RESPONSE_OK)
        gtk_color_selection_get_current_color (colorsel, &color);
      else
        gtk_widget_modify_bg (drawingarea, GTK_STATE_NORMAL, &color);

      gtk_widget_hide (colorseldlg);
    }

  return handled;
}

/* Close down and exit handler */

gint destroy_window( GtkWidget *widget,
                 GdkEvent  *event,
                 gpointer   client_data )
{
  gtk_main_quit ();
  return TRUE;
}
```

```
/* Main */

gint main( gint   argc,
        gchar *argv[] )
{
 GtkWidget *window;

 /* Initialize the toolkit, remove gtk-related command line stuff */

 gtk_init (&argc, &argv);

 /* Create top-level window, set title and policies */

 window = gtk_window_new (GTK_WINDOW_TOPLEVEL);
 gtk_window_set_title (GTK_WINDOW (window), "Color selection test");
 gtk_window_set_policy (GTK_WINDOW (window), TRUE, TRUE, TRUE);

 /* Attach to the "delete" and "destroy" events so we can exit */

 g_signal_connect (GTK_OBJECT (window), "delete_event",
             GTK_SIGNAL_FUNC (destroy_window), (gpointer) window);

 /* Create drawingarea, set size and catch button events */

 drawingarea = gtk_drawing_area_new ();

 color.red = 0;
 color.blue = 65535;
 color.green = 0;
 gtk_widget_modify_bg (drawingarea, GTK_STATE_NORMAL, &color);

 gtk_widget_set_size_request (GTK_WIDGET (drawingarea), 200, 200);

 gtk_widget_set_events (drawingarea, GDK_BUTTON_PRESS_MASK);

 g_signal_connect (GTK_OBJECT (drawingarea), "event",
        GTK_SIGNAL_FUNC (area_event), (gpointer) drawingarea);

 /* Add drawingarea to window, then show them both */

 gtk_container_add (GTK_CONTAINER (window), drawingarea);
 gtk_widget_show (drawingarea);
 gtk_widget_show (window);
```

```
    /* Enter the gtk main loop (this never returns) */

    gtk_main ();

    /* Satisfy grumpy compilers */

    return 0;
}
```

26.3 Qt Programming

Qt is a multiplatform C++ GUI application framework. It provides application developers with all the functionality needed to build applications with state-of-the-art graphical user interfaces. Qt is fully object-oriented, easily extensible, and allows true component programming.

Since its commercial introduction in early 1996, Qt has formed the basis of many thousands of successful applications worldwide. Qt is also the basis of the popular KDE Linux desktop environment, a standard component of all major Linux distributions.

For a tutorial on Qt programming, refer to:
http://doc.trolltech.com/3.3/tutorial.html

26.4 Glade: A Visual Designer Tool for GTK, GNOME

Glade enables the developer to quickly and efficiently design an application visually and then move on to concentrate on actual program implementation instead of being bogged down with user interface issues.

1. Start up glade. Usually, we may find in programs option in our start toolbar. We will see the following three windows (see Figure 26.2)

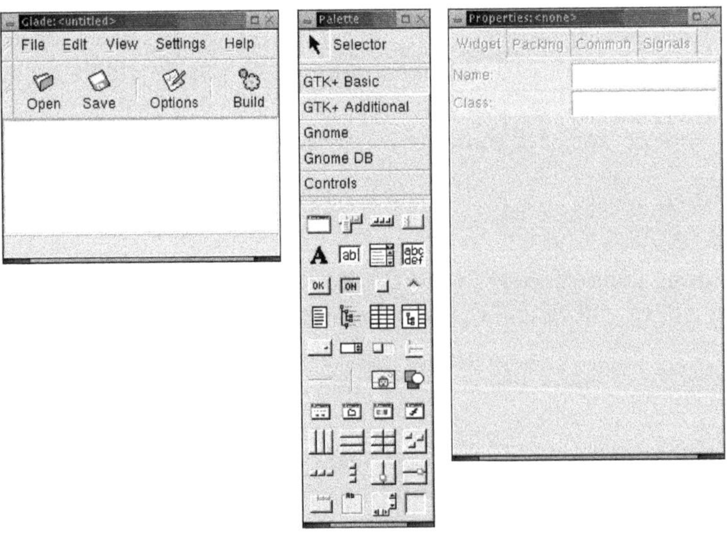

Figure 26.2 A sample Glade window.

2. Opt for New Project. We can specify either GTK or GNOME. Now you may find Palette window becomes active.
3. Now click "Window" icon palette window. We will see a popup window with name window1. At the same time we will see in properties window to become active. Now, we can change the properties of the window from the properties window.
4. Now, if we wanted to use more than one visual element (such as buttons, labels etc.,) and want some organization of them on the screen, we can do so with the help of vertical and horizontal boxes from palette window. Simply, we can click any item on the palette window and then click on the new window (the user's window or canvas).
5. With the help of properties window we can change the look, feel of buttons. Also, we can connect the events on them to some functions. For example, click on a button in our window and then go to properties window and select Signals option (see Figure 26. 3). Then, we can select which events to be added to this button.

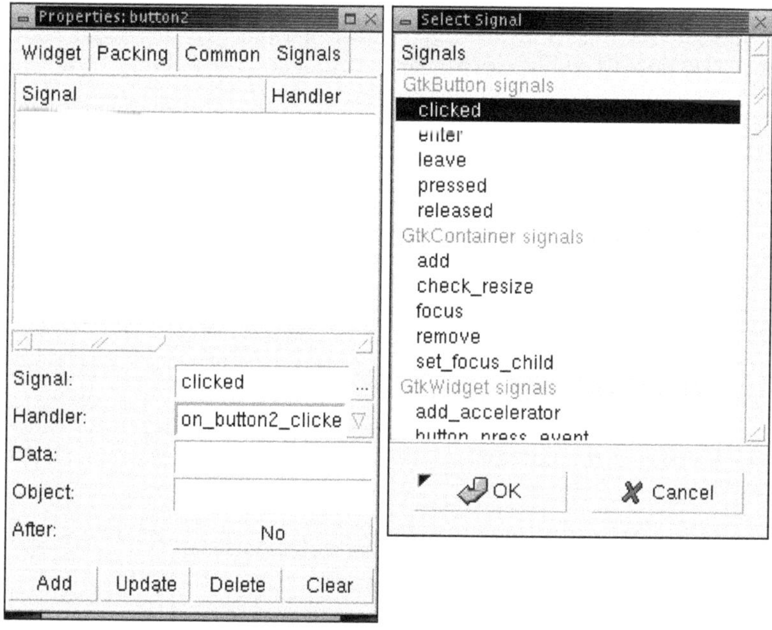

Figure 26.3 Handling Signals.

6. Once we are satisfied with our main widget's layout we can select Build option to generate the code.

   If we now look in our Project directory (remember we saved it in /home/[your username]/Projects/hello) we will see all the files Glade has created. The actual source code resides in the "src" subdirectory. Some files such as README, ChangeLog and such you'll probably modify yourself when you actually develop an application. For now though we can let them be.
7. Build the Makefiles by executing **./autogen.sh** from this directory in your favorite terminal. A bunch of messages will scroll by as it checks your particular environment and creates appropriate Makefiles.
8. Now go to src directory and edit callbacks.c according to our requirement. That is, we can write the code in the callback functions whose skeletons are generated by Glade.

For example if we want some message to be displayed when button2 is clicked, we can add a line g_printf("Hello\n")to on_button2_clicked() function.

```
void on_button2_clicked (GtkButton *button, gpointer user_data)
{
g_printf("Hello\n");

}
```

9. We can actually build our application by simply executing **make**.
10. The final binary will be available in src directory.

26.5 Conclusions

This chapter explores GUI programming under Linux. It explains about X windows architecture, Xlib, GTK and Qt toolkit programming. Also, it explains how Glade can be used for designing GUI using either GTK or GNOME.

References

1. Matt Welsh, Matthias Kalle Dalheimer, Terry Dawson, and Lar Kaufman, Running Linux, Fourth Edition, O'Reilly Publishers, December 2002, ISBN: 0-596-00272-6.
2. Carla Schroder, Linux Cookbook, First Edition, O'Reilly Cookbooks Series, November 2004, ISBN: 0-596-00640-3.
3. Venkateshwarlu N.B, Advanced Unix Programming, BS Publishers, Hyderabad, 2005.
4. Venkateshwarlu N.B, Unix and Windows NT, BS Publishers, Hyderabad, 2005.
5. Gary Nutt, *Operating Systems: A Modern Perspective*, First Edition, Addison-Wesley, Reading, MA, 1997.
6. B.W. Kernigham and R. Pike, The Unix Programming Environment, Prentice Hall India, New Delhi, 1994.
7. S. Prata, Advanced Unix-A programmer's Guide, SAMS, New Delhi, 1986.
8. G.Nutt, Operating Systems Projects Using Windows NT, Pergamon, 1999.
9. Aho, Sethi and Ullman, Compilers: Principles, Techniques and Tools, Addison-Wesley Pub. Co., Nov, 1985
10. Chris Drake and K. Brown, Panic! Unix System Crash Dump Analysis handbook, PH,2003.
11. Richard L. Petersen, LINUX fifth edition, The Complete Reference, TMH .
12. Shelley Powers, Jerry Peek, Timo Reilly, Mike loukides, UNIX power tools. BP Publishers, New Delhi, Hyderabad, 2002.
13. Michael K. Johnson, Erik W. Troan, Linux Application DevelopmentAddison-Wesley, Hardcover, 2nd edition, Published November 2004, 702 pages, ISBN 0321219147.
14. Phillip G. Ezolt, Optimizing Linux Performance: A Hands-on Guide to Linux(R) Performance, Prentice Hall, March 2005.
15. Davide Evans and David Larochelle, Improoving Security Using Extensible lightweight static analysis, IEEE Software, Jan/Feb, 2002.
16. Robert Mecklenburg, Managing Projects with GNU Make, 3E; Addison-Wesley, 2003.
17. Robert Love, Linux Kernel Development, Addison Wesley, 2005.
18. Chris Drake, Kimberley Brown, PANIC! UNIX System Crash Dump Analysis Handbook , www.amazon.com.
19. Ronald F. Guilmette, Compiling and Linking Under the Hood, February 2002, Linux Magazine.
20. Jeffrey Stedfast, Alleyoop:A GUI front end for Valgrind, <fejj@ximian.com>.
21. Patrick Alken, ald:a The Assembly Language Debugger, http://ald.sourceforge.net
22. Richard Stevens, Advanced Unix Programming, Addison Wesley, Singapore,2002,

On-line material

1. Open Sources: Voices from the Open Source Revolution, First Edition, January 1999, ISBN: 1-56592-582-3. URL: http://www.oreilly.com/catalog/opensources/book/toc.html
2. Michael Stutz, The Linux Cookbook: Tips and Techniques for Everyday Use, First Edition, 2001. URL: http://dsl.org/cookbook/cookbook_toc.html
3. Lars Wirzenius, Joanna Oja, Stephen Stafford, and Alex Weeks, The Linux System Administrators' Guide, December 2003. URL: http://www.tldp.org/guides.html
4. Richard Stallman et al., Using GCC, URL: http://www.gnu.org/doc/using.html
5. Brian Gough, An Introduction to GCC, URL: http://www.network-theory.co.uk/docs/gccintro/
6. Gary V. Vaughan, Ben Elliston, Tom Tromey and Ian Lance Taylor, GNU Autoconf, Automake and Libtool, URL: http://sources.redhat.com/autobook/
7. Karl Fogel and Moshe Bar, Open Source Development with CVS, Third Edition, URL: http://cvsbook.red-bean.com/
8. Mendel Cooper, Advanced Bash Scripting Guide, June 2005. URL: http://www.tldp.org/guides.html
9. Havoc Pennington, GTK+/GNOME Application Development, URL: http://developer.gnome.org/doc/GGAD/
10. Guido van Rossum, Fred L. Drake, Jr., Editor, Python Tutorial, URL: http://www.python.org/doc/current/tut/tut.html
11. Mike Heffner, BFBtester: Brute Force Binary Tester, mheffner@vt.edu http://bfbtester.sourceforge.net
12. Data Display Debugger http://www.gnu.org/software/ddd/
13. The GNU Debugger http://sources.redhat.com/gdb/
14. Electric Fence ftp://ftp.perens.com/pub/ElectricFence/
15. Steve Best, Mastering Linux debugging techniques, IBM devloperWorks Journal, Aug, 2002.
16. Filip Rooms, Some Advanced Debuuging techniques in C Under Linux, filip_rooms@hotmail.com.
17. Steve Best, Debugging Memory Problems May 2003, Linux Magazine. Benjamin Chelf, Dynamic MemoryAllocation -- Part II July 2001, Linux Magazine.
18. Benjamin Chelf, Dynamic MemoryAllocation -- Part I June 2001, Linux Magazine.
19. Finding memory Leaks and invalid memory use using Valgrind, Cprogramming.com.

Index

D

E

F

G

H

I

J

K

www.ingramcontent.com/pod-product-compliance
Ingram Content Group UK Ltd.
Pitfield, Milton Keynes, MK11 3LW, UK
UKHW061535190726
13845UKWH00005B/106

9 789352 300174